An Introduction to Poetry

An Introduction to Poetry

THIRD EDITION

X. J. KENNEDY

Tufts University

LITTLE, BROWN AND COMPANY

Boston • Toronto

Library of Congress Catalog Card No. 73-21450

SIXTH PRINTING

Published simultaneously in Canada
by Little, Brown & Company (Canada) Limited

Printed in the United States of America

Acknowledgments

Edward Allen. "The Best Line Yet," © 1972 by Edward H. Allen. First appeared in Counter/Measures.

A. R. Ammons. "Auto Mobile" and "Spring Coming" from *Collected Poems, 1951–1971* by A. R. Ammons. Copyright © 1972 by A. R. Ammons. Reprinted by permission of W. W. Norton & Company, Inc.

W. H. Auden. "As I Walked Out One Evening," "Musée des Beaux Arts," and "The Unknown Citizen" from *Collected Shorter Poems, 1927–1957*. Copyright 1940, renewed 1968 by W. H. Auden. Reprinted by permission of Random House, Inc., and Faber and Faber Ltd. "James Watt" from "Academic Graffiti" from *Homage to Clio* by W. H. Auden. Copyright © 1960 by W. H. Auden. Reprinted by permission of Random House, Inc.

Max Beerbohm. "On the imprint of the first English edition of *The Works of Max Beerbohm*," reprinted by permission of Sir Geoffrey Keynes.

Hilaire Belloc. "The Hippopotamus" from *Cautionary Verses* by Hilaire Belloc. Published in 1941 by Alfred A. Knopf, Inc. Reprinted by permission of Alfred A. Knopf, Inc., and Gerald Duckworth & Co. Ltd.

Edmund Clerihew Bentley. "Sir Christopher Wren" from *Clerihews Complete* by E. C. Bentley. Reprinted by permission of the Estate of E. C. Bentley.

John Berryman. "Life, friends, is boring. We must not say so" from *77 Dream Songs* by John Berryman. Reprinted by permission of Farrar, Straus & Giroux, Inc.

John Betjeman. "In Westminster Abbey" from *Collected Poems* by John Betjeman (Houghton Mifflin Company, 1959). Reprinted by permission of John Murray Publishers Ltd.

Elizabeth Bishop. "The Fish" from *The Complete Poems* by Elizabeth Bishop. Copyright © 1940, 1946, 1947, 1948, 1949, 1951, 1952, 1955 by Elizabeth Bishop. Reprinted by permission of Farrar, Straus & Giroux, Inc.

Robert Bly. "Driving to Town Late to Mail a Letter" and "Inward Conversation," reprinted by permission of the poet.

Richard Brautigan. "Haiku Ambulance" from *The Pill Versus the Springhill Mine Disaster* by Richard Brautigan. Copyright © 1968 by Richard Brautigan. First published by Four Seasons Foundation in its writing series, ed. Donald Allen. "Have You Ever Had a Witch Bloom like a Highway" from *Rommel Drives on Deep into Egypt* by Richard Brautigan. Copyright © 1970 by Richard Brautigan. Both poems reprinted by permission of Seymour Lawrence/Delacorte Press.

Gwendolyn Brooks. "First fight. Then fiddle. Ply the slipping string" (copyright © 1949 by Gwendolyn Brooks Blakely) and "We Real Cool" (copyright © 1959 by Gwendolyn Brooks) from *The World of Gwendolyn Brooks* by Gwendolyn Brooks. Both poems reprinted by permission of Harper & Row, Publishers, Inc.

Taniguchi Buson. "The piercing chill I feel" from *An Introduction to Haiku* by Harold G. Henderson. Copyright © 1958 by Harold G. Henderson. Reprinted by permission of Doubleday & Company, Inc.

Roy Campbell. "On Some South African Novelists" from *Adamaster* by Roy Campbell. Reprinted by permission of Curtis Brown Ltd.

Geoffrey Chaucer. "The Complaint of Chaucer to His Purse" from *The Poetical Works of Chaucer*, ed. F. N. Robinson. Reprinted by permission of Houghton Mifflin Company.

John Ciardi. "Credibility" from *In Fact* by John Ciardi. Reprinted by permission of the poet.

Lucille Clifton. "the lost baby poem" from *Good News about the Earth* by Lucille Clifton. Copyright © 1970, 1971, 1972 by Lucille Clifton. Reprinted by permission of Random House, Inc.

Cid Corman. "The Tortoise" from *Words for Each Other* by Cid Corman. Reprinted by permission of Rapp & Carroll. First appeared in *In Good Time* by Cid Corman.

Frances Cornford. "The Watch" from *Collected Poems* by Frances Cornford. Reprinted by permission of Barrie & Jenkins Ltd.

Hart Crane. "Black Tambourine" from *The Collected Poems and Selected Letters and Prose of Hart Crane*. Copyright 1933, 1958, 1966 by the Liveright Publishing Corporation. Reprinted by permission of Liveright Publishers, New York.

Robert Creeley. "I Know a Man," "Kore," and "Oh No" from *For Love* by Robert Creeley. Copyright © 1962 by Robert Creeley. Reprinted by permission of Charles Scribner's Sons.

Countee Cullen. "For a Lady I Know" and "Saturday's Child" from *On These I Stand* by Countee Cullen. Copyright 1925 by Harper & Row, Publishers, Inc., renewed 1953 by Ida M. Cullen. Reprinted by permission of Harper & Row, Publishers, Inc.

E. E. Cummings. These poems from *Complete Poems 1913–1962*: "anyone lived in a pretty how town" (copyright 1940 by E. E. Cummings, copyright 1968 by Marion Morehouse Cummings); "All in green went my love riding," "Buffalo Bill's," "the Cambridge ladies," and "in Just-" (all copyright 1923, 1951 by E. E. Cummings); "next to of course god america i" (copyright 1926 by Horace Liveright, copyright 1954 by E. E. Cummings); "a politician is an arse upon" (copyright 1944 by E. E. Cummings); "r-p-o-p-h-e-s-s-a-g-r" (copyright 1935 by E. E. Cummings, copyright 1963 by Marion Morehouse Cummings); "when serpents bargain for the right to squirm" (copyright 1950 by E. E. Cummings). Reprinted by permission of Harcourt Brace Jovanovich, Inc.

J. V. Cunningham. "Epitaph," "Friend, on this scaffold Thomas More lies dead," "Motto for a Sun Dial," and "You serve the best wines always, my dear sir" from *The Exclusions of a Rhyme* by J. V. Cunningham. Copyright 1960 by J. V. Cunningham. Reprinted by permission of The Swallow Press, Chicago.

H. D. "Heat" from *Selected Poems* by H. D. Copyright © 1957 by Norman Holmes Pearson. Reprinted by permission of Grove Press, Inc., and Norman Holmes Pearson.

Peter Davison. "The Last Word" (Part IV of "Four Love Poems") from *Pretending to Be Asleep* by Peter Davison. Copyright © 1970 by Peter Davison. Reprinted by permission of Atheneum Publishers.

Walter de la Mare. "The Listeners," reprinted by permission of the Literary Trustees of Walter de la Mare and The Society of Authors as their representative.

James Dickey. "Cherrylog Road" from *Poems 1957–1967* by James Dickey. Copyright © 1963 by James Dickey. Reprinted by permission of Wesleyan University Press. First appeared in *The New Yorker*.

Emily Dickinson. "Because I could not stop for Death," "I heard a Fly buzz – when I died," "I like to see it lap the Miles," "I started Early – Took my Dog," "It dropped so low – in my Regard," "It was not Death, for I stood up," "The Lightning is a yellow Fork," "The Soul selects her own Society," and "Victory comes late" from *The Poems of Emily Dickinson*, ed. Thomas H. Johnson (Cambridge, Mass.: The Belknap Press of Harvard University Press). Copyright 1951, 1955 by the President and Fellows of Harvard College. Reprinted by permission of the publishers and the Trustees of Amherst College.

Isak Dinesen. Selection from "Natives and Verse," chapter 4 of *Out of Africa* by Isak Dinesen. Reprinted by permission of Random House, Inc., and Putnam & Co. Ltd., London.

Emanuel diPasquale. "Rain," reprinted by permission of the poet.

Alan Dugan. "Love Song: I and Thou" from *Poems* by Alan Dugan. Copyright © 1961 by Alan Dugan. Reprinted by permission of Yale University Press.

Richard Eberhart. "The Fury of Aerial Bombardment" from *Collected Poems 1930–1960* by Richard Eberhart. Copyright © 1960 by Richard Eberhart. Reprinted by permission of Oxford University Press, Inc., and Chatto and Windus, Ltd.

T. S. Eliot. "The *Boston Evening Transcript*," lines from "Little Gidding," "The Love Song of J. Alfred Prufrock," lines from "Mr. Eliot's Sunday Morning Service," and "Sweeney Among the Nightingales" from *Collected Poems 1909–1962* by T. S. Eliot. Copyright 1936 by Harcourt Brace Jovanovich, Inc., copyright © 1963, 1964 by T. S. Eliot. Reprinted by permission of Harcourt Brace Jovanovich, Inc., and Faber and Faber Ltd. Lines from "A Lyric" and "Song" from *Poems Written in Early Youth* by T. S. Eliot. Copyright © 1967 by Valerie Eliot. Reprinted by permission of Farrar, Straus & Giroux, Inc., and Faber and Faber Ltd.

William Empson. "Legal Fiction" from *Collected Poems of William Empson*. Copyright 1949 by William Empson. Reprinted by permission of Harcourt Brace Jovanovich, Inc., and Chatto and Windus Ltd.

Kenneth Fearing. "Dirge" from *New and Selected Poems* by Kenneth Fearing. Reprinted by permission of Indiana University Press.

Donald Finkel. "Gesture" from *The Garbage Wars* by Donald Finkel. Copyright © 1969, 1970 by Donald Finkel. Reprinted by permission of Atheneum Publishers.

Ian Hamilton Finlay. "The Horizon of Holland," reprinted by permission of the poet.

Dudley Fitts. "Elegy on Herakleitos," a translation of the poem by Kallimachos, from *Poems from the Greek Anthology* by Dudley Fitts. Copyright 1938, 1941, © 1956 by New Directions Publishing Corporation. Reprinted by permission of New Directions Publishing Corporation.

Robert Francis. "Catch" from *The Orb Weaver* by Robert Francis. Copyright © 1950 by Robert Francis. Reprinted by permission of Wesleyan University Press.

Robert Frost. "Departmental," "Design," "Fire and Ice," "Never Again Would Birds' Song Be the Same," "Provide, Provide," "The Silken Tent," "Stopping by Woods on a Snowy Evening," and "Tree at My Window" from *The Poetry of Robert Frost*, ed. Edward Connery Lathem. Copyright 1923, 1928, © 1969 by Holt, Rinehart and Winston, Inc.; copyright 1936, 1942, 1951, © 1956 by Robert Frost; copyright © 1964, 1970 by Lesley Frost Ballantine. Reprinted by permission of Holt, Rinehart and Winston, Inc.

Frederico García Lorca. "La guitarra" from *Obras Completas* by Frederico García Lorca. Copyright © Aguilar, S.A. de Ediciones. All rights reserved. Permission to publish in original Spanish and in English translation by New Directions Publishing Corporation.

Gary Gildner. "First Practice" from *First Practice* by Gary Gildner. © 1969 by The University of Pittsburgh Press. Reprinted by permission of The University of Pittsburgh Press.

Allen Ginsberg. "In back of the real" from *Howl and Other Poems* by Allen Ginsberg. Copyright © 1956, 1959 by Allen Ginsberg. Reprinted by permission of City Lights Books.

Nikki Giovanni. "Kidnap Poem" from *Re: Creation* by Nikki Giovanni. Copyright © 1970 by Nikki Giovanni. Reprinted by permission of the poet.

Robert Graves. "A Civil Servant" from *Collected Poems 1959* by Robert Graves. Reprinted by permission of Robert Graves.

Ronald Gross. "Yield" from *Pop Poems* by Ronald Gross. Copyright © 1967 by Ronald Gross. Reprinted by permission of Simon & Schuster, Inc.

Arthur Guiterman. "On the Vanity of Earthly Greatness" from *Gaily the Troubadour* by Arthur Guiterman. Reprinted by permission of Vida Lindo Guiterman, copyright owner.

John Haines. "The Cauliflower" from *The Stone Harp* by John Haines. Copyright © 1968 by John Haines. Reprinted by permission of Wesleyan University Press.

Donald Hall. "My Son, My Executioner" from *The Alligator Bride: Poems New and Selected*. Copyright 1954 by Donald Hall. Reprinted by permission of Harper & Row, Publishers, Inc. First appeared in *The New Yorker* as "First Child."

Thomas Hardy. "Channel Firing," "The Convergence of the Twain," "During Wind and Rain," "Neutral Tones," "The Oxen," "The Ruined Maid," and "The Workbox" from *Collected Poems* by Thomas Hardy. Copyright 1925 by Macmillan Publishing Co., Inc. Reprinted by permission of Macmillan Publishing Co., Inc., the Trustees of the Hardy Estate, Macmillan London & Basingstoke, and the Macmillan Co. of Canada Ltd.

John Heath-Stubbs. "A Charm Against the Toothache," reprinted by permission of David Higham Associates Ltd.

Anthony Hecht. "Japan" from *The Hard Hours* by Anthony Hecht. Copyright © 1954, 1967 by Anthony Hecht. Reprinted by permission of Atheneum Publishers.

John Hollander. "Skeleton key" from *Types of Shape* by John Hollander. Copyright © 1969 by John Hollander. Reproduced by permission of Atheneum Publishers.

A. D. Hope. "The Brides" from *Poems* by A. D. Hope. Copyright © 1961 by A. D. Hope. Reprinted by permission of Hamish Hamilton Ltd.

Gerard Manley Hopkins. "Carrion Comfort," "From Horace," "God's Grandeur," "Inversnaid," "Pied Beauty," "Spring and Fall," and "The Windhover" from *Poems of Gerard Manley Hopkins*, 4th ed., eds. W. H. Gardner and N. H. MacKenzie. © 1967 by The Society of Jesus. Reprinted by permission of Oxford University Press, Inc.

A. E. Housman. "Loveliest of trees, the cherry now," "Terence, this is stupid stuff," "To an Athlete Dying Young," and "With rue my heart is laden" from *A Shropshire Lad*, authorized edition from *The Collected Poems of A. E. Housman*. Copyright 1939, 1940, © 1965 by Holt, Rinehart and Winston, Inc., copyright © 1967, 1968 by Robert E. Symons. "Eight O' Clock," "From the wash the laundress sends," and "In the morning, in the morning" from *The Collected Poems of A. E. Housman*. Copyright 1922 by Holt, Rinehart and Winston, Inc., copyright 1936, 1950 by Barclays Bank Ltd., copyright © 1964 by Robert E. Symons. All poems reprinted by permission of Holt, Rinehart and Winston, Inc., The Society of Authors as the literary representative of the Estate of A. E. Housman, and Jonathan Cape Ltd., British publishers of A. E. Housman's *Collected Poems*.

Langston Hughes. "Dream Deferred" from *The Panther and the Lash* by Langston Hughes. Copyright 1951 by Langston

Hughes. "The Weary Blues" from *Selected Poems* by Langston Hughes. Copyright 1926 by Alfred A. Knopf, Inc., re-newed 1954 by Langston Hughes. Both poems reprinted by permission of Alfred A. Knopf, Inc.

Ted Hughes. "Secretary" from *The Hawk in the Rain* by Ted Hughes. Copyright © 1957 by Ted Hughes. Reprinted by permission of Harper & Row, Publishers, Inc.

T. E. Hulme. "Image" from *The Life and Opinions of T. E. Hulme* by Alun R. Jones. Copyright © 1960 by Alun R. Jones. Reprinted by permission of Beacon Press and Victor Gollancz Ltd.

David Ignatow. "Get the Gasworks" from *Figures of the Human* by David Ignatow. Copyright © 1948 by David Ignatow. Reprinted by permission of Wesleyan University Press.

Imamu Amiri Baraka. "Preface to a Twenty Volume Suicide Note" from *Preface to a Twenty Volume Suicide Note*. Copy-right © 1961 by LeRoi Jones. Reprinted by permission of Corinth Books.

Randall Jarrell. "The Death of the Ball Turret Gunner" from *The Complete Poems* by Randall Jarrell. Copyright © 1945, 1969 by Mrs. Randall Jarrell. Reprinted by permission of Farrar, Straus & Giroux, Inc. "The Old and the New Masters" from *The Lost World* by Randall Jarrell. Copyright © 1965 by Randall Jarrell. Reprinted by permission of Macmillan Publishing Co., Inc.

Elizabeth Jennings. "Delay" from *Collected Poems* by Elizabeth Jennings. Reprinted by permission of Macmillan London & Basingstoke.

James Joyce. "I hear an army charging upon the land" from *Collected Poems* by James Joyce. Copyright 1918 by B. W. Huebsch, Inc., renewed 1946 by Nora Joyce. Reprinted by permission of the Viking Press, Inc.

Donald Justice. "In Bertram's Garden" from *The Summer Anniversaries* by Donald Justice. Copyright © 1954 by Donald Justice. Reprinted by permission of Wesleyan University Press.

James C. Kilgore. "The White Man Pressed the Locks" from *A Time of Black Devotion* by James C. Kilgore. Copyright © 1970 by James C. Kilgore. Reprinted by permission of the poet and The Ashland Poetry Press. First appeared in *Poets on the Platform*.

Hugh Kingsmill. "What, still alive at twenty-two," reprinted by permission of Victor Gollancz Ltd.

Galway Kinnell. "To Christ Our Lord" from *What a Kingdom It Was* by Galway Kinnell. Copyright © 1960 by Galway Kinnell. Reprinted by permission of Houghton Mifflin Company.

Kenneth Koch. "Mending Sump" from *The New American Poetry* ed. Donald M. Allen. Copyright 1960 by Kenneth Koch. Reprinted by permission of International Famous Agency and the poet.

Greg Kuzma. "Peace, so that" from *What Friends Are For* by Greg Kuzma. Copyright by Greg Kuzma. Reprinted by permission.

Philip Larkin. "As Bad as a Mile" from *The Whitsun Weddings* by Philip Larkin. Copyright © 1960 by Philip Larkin. Reprinted by permission of Faber and Faber Ltd. "Church Going" from *The Less Deceived* by Philip Larkin. Copyright © 1955, 1971 by The Marvell Press. Reprinted by permission of The Marvell Press, England.

Richmond Lattimore. Lines from *The Iliad of Homer* (1951), Book 14, translated by Richmond Lattimore. Reprinted by permission of Richmond Lattimore and The University of Chicago Press.

D. H. Lawrence. "Bavarian Gentians," "The Elephant Is Slow to Mate," and "Piano" from *The Complete Poems of D. H. Lawrence*, eds. Vivian de Sola Pinto and F. Warren Roberts. Copyright © 1964, 1971 by Angelo Ravagli and C. M. Weekley, Executors of the Estate of Frieda Lawrence Ravagli. Quotation from *Studies in Classic American Literature* by D. H. Lawrence. Copyright 1923, renewed 1951 by Frieda Lawrence. All material reprinted by permission of The Viking Press, Inc. All rights reserved.

Irving Layton. "The Bull Calf" from *A Red Carpet for the Sun* by Irving Layton. Reprinted by permission of the Cana-dian publishers McClelland and Stewart Ltd., Toronto.

Denise Levertov. "Come into Animal Presence" and "Six Variations (part iii)" from *The Jacob's Ladder* by Denise Levertov. Copyright © 1960, 1961 by Denise Levertov Goodman. Reprinted by permission of New Directions Publish-ing Corporation. "Six Variations" first appeared in *Poetry*.

Philip Levine. "To a Child Trapped in a Barber Shop" from *Not This Pig* by Philip Levine. Copyright © 1966 by Philip Levine. Reprinted by permission of Wesleyan University Press.

J. A. Lindon. "My Garden," reprinted by permission of the poet.

Robert Lowell. "At the Altar" from *Lord Weary's Castle* by Robert Lowell. Copyright 1946 by Robert Lowell. Reprinted by permission of Harcourt Brace Jovanovich, Inc. "Meditation" from *Imitations* by Robert Lowell. Copyright © 1958, 1959, 1960, 1961 by Robert Lowell. Reprinted by permission of Farrar, Straus & Giroux, Inc. "Skunk Hour" from *Life Studies* by Robert Lowell. Copyright © 1956, 1959 by Robert Lowell. Reprinted by permission of Farrar, Straus & Giroux, Inc.

Mina Loy. "Omen of Victory," reprinted by permission of *The Jargon Society*.

Hugh MacDiarmid. "Wheesht, Wheesht" from *Collected Poems* by Hugh MacDiarmid. © 1948, 1962 by Christopher Murray Grieve. Reprinted by permission of The Macmillan Company.

Rod McKuen. "Thoughts on Capital Punishment" from *Stanyan Street and Other Sorrows* by Rod McKuen. Copyright 1954, © 1960–1966 by Rod McKuen. Reprinted by permission of Random House, Inc.

Archibald MacLeish. "Ars Poetica" and "The End of the World" from *Collected Poems 1917–1952* by Archibald MacLeish. Reprinted by permission of Houghton Mifflin Company.

Edgar Lee Masters. "Petit, the Poet" from *Spoon River Anthology* by Edgar Lee Masters. Reprinted by permission of Weissberger & Frosch.

James Merrill. "Laboratory Poem" from *The Country of a Thousand Years of Peace* by James Merrill. Copyright © 1958 by James Merrill. Reprinted by permission of Atheneum Publishers. First appeared in *Poetry*.

W. S. Merwin. "Dead Hand" from *The Moving Target* by W. S. Merwin. Copyright © 1963 by W. S. Merwin. "For the Anniversary of My Death" from *The Lice* by W. S. Merwin. Copyright © 1967 by W. S. Merwin. First appeared in *The Southern Review*. Both poems reprinted by permission of Atheneum Publishers.

Josephine Miles. "Reason" from *Poems 1930–1960* by Josephine Miles. Reprinted by permission of Indiana University Press.

A. A. Milne. Lines from "Disobedience" from *When We Were Very Young* by A. A. Milne. Reprinted by permission of the publishers, E. P. Dutton & Co., Inc.

Marianne Moore. "A Grave" from *Collected Poems* by Marianne Moore. Copyright 1935 by Marianne Moore, renewed 1963 by Marianne Moore and T. S. Eliot. Reprinted by permission of Macmillan Publishing Co., Inc.

Edwin Morgan. "Siesta of a Hungarian Snake" from *The Second Life* by Edwin Morgan. Copyright © 1968 by Edwin Morgan and Edinburgh University Press. Reprinted by permission of the poet and Aldine Publishing Company.

Emanuel Morgan. "Opus 6," reprinted by permission of the poet.

Ogden Nash. "Very Like a Whale" from *Verses from 1929 On* by Ogden Nash. Copyright 1934 by The Curtis Publish-ing Company. Reprinted by permission of Little, Brown and Company, Inc.

Howard Nemerov. "The Goose Fish" from *The Salt Garden* by Howard Nemerov. Copyright © 1950, 1951, 1952, 1953, 1954, 1955 by Howard Nemerov; later published in *New and Selected Poems*, copyright 1960 by The University of Chi-cago. Reprinted by permission of the Margot Johnson Agency.

John Frederick Nims. "Visiting Poet" from *Of Flesh and Bone* by John Frederick Nims. Reprinted by permission of Rutgers University Press. "Love Poem" from *The Iron Pastoral* by John Frederick Nims. Copyright 1947 by John Fred-erick Nims. Reprinted by permission of William Morrow & Company, Inc.

Charles Olson. "La Chute," copyright by Charles Olson. Reprinted by permission of the Estate of Charles Olson.

Guy Owen. "The White Stallion" from *The White Stallion* by Guy Owen. Published in 1969 by John Blair, publishers. Reprinted by permission of the author.

Wilfred Owen. "Dulce et Decorum Est" from *The Collected Poems of Wilfred Owen*. Copyright 1946, © 1963 by Chatto and Windus Ltd. Reprinted by permission of New Directions Publishing Corporation and Chatto and Windus Ltd.

Acknowledgments vii

TOPICAL CONTENTS

TO THE MUSE   xxix

TO THE STUDENT   xxx

TO THE INSTRUCTOR   xxxiii

1   **Entrances**   1

2   **The Person in the Poem**   8

     THE POET'S "I"   8
     SUBJECT, THEME, AND TONE   13
     LYRIC AND DIDACTIC   20
     MASK AND IRONY   23
     FOR REVIEW AND FURTHER STUDY   28

3   **Words and Their Order**   34

     THE RIGHT WORD   34
     SPEECH AND POETIC DICTION   40
     WORD ORDER   46
     FOR REVIEW AND FURTHER STUDY   50

4   **Saying and Suggesting**   56

     DENOTATION AND CONNOTATION   56
     ALLUSION   62
     FOR REVIEW AND FURTHER STUDY   64

5   **Imagery**   67

     FOR REVIEW AND FURTHER STUDY   74

6   Figures of Speech   79

    WHY SPEAK FIGURATIVELY?   79
    METAPHOR AND SIMILE   80
    OTHER FIGURES   88
    FOR REVIEW AND FURTHER STUDY   94

7   Song   100

    SINGING AND SAYING   100
    BALLADS AND OTHER POEMS TO SING   107
    FOR REVIEW AND FURTHER STUDY   120

8   Sound   125

    SOUND AS MEANING   125
    ALLITERATION AND ASSONANCE   129
    RIME   133
    READING POEMS ALOUD   138
    FOR REVIEW AND FURTHER STUDY   139

9   Rhythm   142

    STRESSES AND PAUSES   142
    METER   150
    FOR REVIEW AND FURTHER STUDY   157

10   Closed Form, Open Form   161

    CLOSED FORM   161
    THE SONNET AND OTHERS   170
    OPEN FORM   178
    FOR REVIEW AND FURTHER STUDY   186

11   Poems for the Eye   193

    WORD SHAPES   193
    CONCRETE POETRY   198

12   Symbol and Allegory   203

    SYMBOL   203
    ALLEGORY   208
    FOR REVIEW AND FURTHER STUDY   212

13 Myth   215

TRADITIONAL MYTH   215
PERSONAL MYTH   219
ARCHETYPES   223
FOR REVIEW AND FURTHER STUDY   229

14 Telling Good from Bad   237

IMPRECISIONS   237
SENTIMENTALITY   242
PARODY   247
FOR REVIEW AND FURTHER STUDY   249

15 Knowing Excellence   253

FOR REVIEW AND FURTHER STUDY   263

16 Alternatives   269

THE POET'S REVISIONS   269
TRANSLATIONS   274

17 Writing about Poems   280

18 What Is Poetry?   302

ANTHOLOGY   307

INDEX OF FIRST LINES   423
INDEX OF AUTHORS AND TITLES   429
INDEX OF TERMS   *inside back cover*

CONTENTS

TO THE MUSE   xxix

TO THE STUDENT   xxx

TO THE INSTRUCTOR   xxxiii

1   Entrances   1

A. E. HOUSMAN, *Loveliest of trees, the cherry now*   3
ROBERT FRANCIS, *Catch*   5
A. E. HOUSMAN, *In the morning, in the morning*   5
EMILY DICKINSON, *It was not Death, for I stood up*   6
RICHARD BRAUTIGAN, *Have You Ever Had a Witch Bloom like a Highway*   7
WILLIAM SHAKESPEARE, *Not marble nor the gilded monuments*   7

2   The Person in the Poem   8

THE POET'S "I"   8

ARCHIBALD MACLEISH, *The End of the World*   8
TRUMBULL STICKNEY, *Sir, say no more*   9
WILLIAM WORDSWORTH, *I Wandered Lonely as a Cloud*   10
W. H. AUDEN, *The Unknown Citizen*   12
THOMAS LOVELL BEDDOES, *Resurrection Song*   13
WILLIAM CARLOS WILLIAMS, *The Red Wheelbarrow*   13

SUBJECT, THEME, AND TONE   13

THEODORE ROETHKE, *My Papa's Waltz*   14
ANNE BRADSTREET, *The Author to Her Book*   16
WALT WHITMAN, *To a Locomotive in Winter*   17
EMILY DICKINSON, *I like to see it lap the Miles*   17
REED WHITTEMORE, *The Fall of the House of Usher*   18
RICHARD LOVELACE, *To Lucasta*   19

WILFRED OWEN, *Dulce et Decorum Est*   19

JAMES SIMMONS, *Cavalier Lyric*   20

LYRIC AND DIDACTIC   20

COUNTEE CULLEN, *For a Lady I Know*   22

AMBROSE BIERCE, *Art*   22

MASK AND IRONY   23

ROBERT HERRICK, *Another Grace for a Child*   23

ROBERT CREELEY, *Oh No*   24

THOMAS HARDY, *The Workbox*   26

JOHN BETJEMAN, *In Westminster Abbey*   27

FOR REVIEW AND FURTHER STUDY   28

ANONYMOUS, *Johnny, I Hardly Knew Ye*   28

BARRY SPACKS, *Malediction*   29

TED HUGHES, *Secretary*   30

JOHN BERRYMAN, *Life, friends, is boring. We must not say so*   30

WILLIAM BLAKE, *The Chimney Sweeper*   32

JOHN MILTON, *On the Late Massacre in Piemont*   32

JONATHAN SWIFT, *On Stella's Birthday*   33

3   Words and Their Order   34

THE RIGHT WORD   34

WALTER SAVAGE LANDOR, *Mother, I Cannot Mind My Wheel*   35

RICHARD WILBUR, *In the Elegy Season*   38

JOHN CLARE, *Mouse's Nest*   38

KNUTE SKINNER, *The Cold Irish Earth*   39

PETER DAVISON, *The Last Word*   39

SPEECH AND POETIC DICTION   40

JOSEPHINE MILES, *Reason*   43

HUGH MACDIARMID, *Wheesht, Wheesht*   44

THOMAS HARDY, *The Ruined Maid*   44

RICHARD EBERHART, *The Fury of Aerial Bombardment*   45

WORD ORDER   46

E. E. CUMMINGS, *anyone lived in a pretty how town*   48

GERARD MANLEY HOPKINS, *Carrion Comfort*   49

WALTER SAVAGE LANDOR, *Age*   50

FOR REVIEW AND FURTHER STUDY   50

LEWIS CARROLL, *Jabberwocky*   50
WALLACE STEVENS, *Metamorphosis*   51
ANONYMOUS, *As I was laying on the green*   53
A. R. AMMONS, *Spring Coming*   53
WILLIAM WORDSWORTH, *My heart leaps up when I behold*   54
WILLIAM WORDSWORTH, *Mutability*   54
ANONYMOUS, *Scottsboro*   54

4   Saying and Suggesting 56

DENOTATION AND CONNOTATION   56

WILLIAM BLAKE, *London*   57
SAMUEL JOHNSON, *A Short Song of Congratulation*   59
WALLACE STEVENS, *Disillusionment of Ten O'Clock*   60
ROBERT HERRICK, *Upon Julia's Voice*   61
GUY OWEN, *The White Stallion*   61
J. V. CUNNINGHAM, *Motto for a Sun Dial*   61
W. S. MERWIN, *Dead Hand*   62
EZRA POUND, *The Jewel Stairs' Grievance*   62

ALLUSION   62

CID CORMAN, *The Tortoise*   63
JOHN KEATS, *On First Looking into Chapman's Homer*   63
JOHN DRYDEN, *Lines Printed Under the Engraved Portrait of Milton*   64
J. V. CUNNINGHAM, *Friend, on this scaffold Thomas More lies dead*   64

FOR REVIEW AND FURTHER STUDY   64

PHILIP LARKIN, *As Bad as a Mile*   64
ROBERT HERRICK, *To Daisies, Not to Shut So Soon*   65
TIMOTHY STEELE, *Epitaph*   65
ROBERT FROST, *Fire and Ice*   65
E. E. CUMMINGS, *the Cambridge ladies who live in furnished souls*   66

5   Imagery 67

EZRA POUND, *In a Station of the Metro*   67
WILLIAM CARLOS WILLIAMS, *This Is Just to Say*   67
TANIGUCHI BUSON, *The piercing chill I feel*   68
WALLACE STEVENS, *Study of Two Pears*   69

John Keats, *Ode to a Nightingale*   70
Elizabeth Bishop, *The Fish*   72

FOR REVIEW AND FURTHER STUDY   74

William Carlos Williams, *Poem ("As the cat")*   74
T. E. Hulme, *Image*   75
Gary Snyder, From *Hitch Haiku*   75
Richard Brautigan, *Haiku Ambulance*   75
Robert Bly, *Driving to Town Late to Mail a Letter*   76
Sylvia Plath, *Cut*   76
Jean Toomer, *Reapers*   77
Walt Whitman, *The Dalliance of the Eagles*   77
H. D., *Heat*   78

6   Figures of Speech 79

WHY SPEAK FIGURATIVELY?   79

Alfred, Lord Tennyson, *The Eagle*   80

METAPHOR AND SIMILE   80

Richard Wilbur, *A Simile for Her Smile*   82
Alfred, Lord Tennyson, *Flower in the Crannied Wall*   82
William Blake, *To see a world in a grain of sand*   83
Sylvia Plath, *Metaphors*   83
Emily Dickinson, *It dropped so low – in my Regard*   84
Anonymous, *There was a man of double deed*   84
Ruth Whitman, *Castoff Skin*   85
Robert Graves, *A Civil Servant*   85
Ogden Nash, *Very Like a Whale*   86
Langston Hughes, *Dream Deferred*   87

OTHER FIGURES   88

James Stephens, *The Wind*   88
Chidiock Tichborne, *Elegy, Written with His Own Hand in the
    Tower Before His Execution*   90
George Herbert, *The Pulley*   91
Robert Frost, *Tree at My Window*   92
Edmund Waller, *On a Girdle*   93
John Donne, *A Hymn to God the Father*   93

FOR REVIEW AND FURTHER STUDY   94

Anne Sexton, *You All Know the Story of the Other Woman*   94
Elizabeth Jennings, *Delay*   95
Andrew Marvell, *The Definition of Love*   95

ANONYMOUS, *The fortunes of war, I tell you plain*   96
A. R. AMMONS, *Auto Mobile*   97
THEODORE ROETHKE, *I Knew a Woman*   97
ISHMAEL REED, *.05*   98
A. E. HOUSMAN, *From the wash the laundress sends*   98
JOHN CIARDI, *Credibility*   98
JAMES KILGORE, *The White Man Pressed the Locks*   99
ANONYMOUS, *I sing of a maiden that is makeless*   99
WILLIAM SHAKESPEARE, *Shall I compare thee to a summer's day?*   99

7   Song   100

SINGING AND SAYING   100

BEN JONSON, *To Celia*   101
ANONYMOUS, *The Cruel Mother*   102
ANONYMOUS, *Lady, when I behold the roses sprouting*   103
EDWIN ARLINGTON ROBINSON, *Richard Cory*   105
PAUL SIMON, *Richard Cory*   105
ANONYMOUS, *On Top of Old Smoky*   106

BALLADS AND OTHER POEMS TO SING   107

ANONYMOUS, *Bonny Barbara Allan*   107
ANONYMOUS, *Still Growing*   110
ANONYMOUS, *Squire and Milkmaid, or, Blackberry Fold*   111
WOODY GUTHRIE, *Plane Wreck at Los Gatos (Deportee)*   113
WILLIAM SHAKESPEARE, *Fear no more the heat o' th' sun*   115
ROBERT BROWNING, *The year's at the spring*   116
ANONYMOUS, *The Unquiet Grave*   116
ANONYMOUS, *Frankie and Johnny*   117

FOR REVIEW AND FURTHER STUDY   120

ANONYMOUS, *Fa, mi, fa, re, la, mi*   120
ANONYMOUS, *The silver swan, who living had no note*   120
THOMAS CAMPION, *Rose-cheeked Laura, come*   120
ANONYMOUS, *Good Mornin', Blues*   121
ERN ALPAUGH AND DEWEY G. PELL, *Swinging Chick*   121
JOHN LENNON AND PAUL MCCARTNEY, *Eleanor Rigby*   122
LEONARD COHEN, *Suzanne*   123

8   Sound   125

SOUND AS MEANING   125

WILLIAM BUTLER YEATS, *Who Goes with Fergus?*   127

JOHN UPDIKE, *Winter Ocean*   128
FRANCES CORNFORD, *The Watch*   128
WILLIAM WORDSWORTH, *A Slumber Did My Spirit Seal*   129
GERARD MANLEY HOPKINS, *Pied Beauty*   129

ALLITERATION AND ASSONANCE   129

ALFRED, LORD TENNYSON, *The splendor falls on castle walls*   131
A. E. HOUSMAN, *Eight O'Clock*   132
ALEXANDER POPE, *Intended for Sir Isaac Newton in Westminster
    Abbey*   132
J. C. SQUIRE, *It Did Not Last*   132

RIME   133

ANONYMOUS, *Julius Caesar*   133
WILLIAM BLAKE, *The Angel that presided o'er my birth*   134
HILAIRE BELLOC, *The Hippopotamus*   136
GERARD MANLEY HOPKINS, *God's Grandeur*   137
EMANUEL MORGAN, *Opus 6*   137

READING POEMS ALOUD   138

FOR REVIEW AND FURTHER STUDY   139

WILLIAM SHAKESPEARE, *It was a lover and his lass*   139
ROBERT HERRICK, *Delight in Disorder*   140
JOHN MILTON, *Rivers arise; whether thou be the son*   140
LEIGH HUNT, *Rondeau ("Jenny kissed me")*   141
EMANUEL diPASQUALE, *Rain*   141
CHARLES REZNIKOFF, *How shall we mourn you who are killed and
    wasted*   141
A. E. HOUSMAN, *With rue my heart is laden*   141

9   **Rhythm**   142

STRESSES AND PAUSES   142

GWENDOLYN BROOKS, *We Real Cool*   147
ROBERT FROST, *Never Again Would Birds' Song Be
    the Same*   147
BEN JONSON, *Slow, slow, fresh fount, keep time with my salt
    tears*   148
ROBERT LOWELL, *At the Altar*   148
SIR THOMAS WYATT, *With serving still*   149
DOROTHY PARKER, *Résumé*   150

METER   150

    MAX BEERBOHM, *On the imprint of the first English edition of* The
       Works of Max Beerbohm   151

    WALTER SAVAGE LANDOR, *On Seeing a Hair of Lucretia*
       Borgia   155

    PERCY BYSSHE SHELLEY, *A Dirge*   156

FOR REVIEW AND FURTHER STUDY   157

    SIR THOMAS WYATT, *They flee from me that sometime did me*
       sekë   157

    GERARD MANLEY HOPKINS, *Inversnaid*   158

    ALFRED, LORD TENNYSON, *Dark house, by which once more*
       I stand   158

    WILLIAM CARLOS WILLIAMS, *The Descent of Winter (section*
       10/30)   159

    WALT WHITMAN, *Beat! Beat! Drums!*   159

10 Closed Form, Open Form   161

CLOSED FORM   161

    STEVIE SMITH, *I Remember*   163

    ROY CAMPBELL, *On Some South African Novelists*   164

    JOHN KEATS, *This living hand, now warm and capable*   164

    JOHN DONNE, *Song ("Go and catch a falling star")*   166

    DYLAN THOMAS, *Fern Hill*   167

    SIR WALTER SCOTT, *Proud Maisie*   169

    RONALD GROSS, *Yield*   169

THE SONNET AND OTHERS   170

    WILLIAM SHAKESPEARE, *My mistress' eyes are nothing like*
       the sun   171

    MICHAEL DRAYTON, *Since there's no help come let us kiss*
       and part   172

    ELIZABETH BARRETT BROWNING, *Grief*   173

    JOHN DONNE, *Antiquary*   174

    MARTIAL, *You serve the best wines always, my dear sir*   174

    SIR JOHN HARRINGTON, *Of Treason*   174

    JOHN WILMOT, EARL OF ROCHESTER, *Impromptu on*
       Charles II   174

    WILLIAM BLAKE, *Her whole life is an epigram*   175

    E. E. CUMMINGS, *a politician*   175

    JOHN FREDERICK NIMS, *Visiting Poet*   175

    DYLAN THOMAS, *Do Not Go Gentle into That Good Night*   176

    EDGAR LEE MASTERS, *Petit, the Poet*   177

OPEN FORM   178

DENISE LEVERTOV, *Six Variations (part iii)*   178
E. E. CUMMINGS, *Buffalo Bill's*   181
EMILY DICKINSON, *Victory comes late*   182
WILLIAM CARLOS WILLIAMS, *The Dance*   183
ROBERT HERRICK, *Upon a Child That Died*   183
SAINT GERAUD, *Poem ("The only response")*   184
STEPHEN CRANE, *The Heart*   184
WALT WHITMAN, *Cavalry Crossing a Ford*   184
GARY GILDNER, *First Practice*   185

FOR REVIEW AND FURTHER STUDY   186

WALLACE STEVENS, *Thirteen Ways of Looking at a Blackbird*   186
ALEXANDER POPE, *Atticus*   188
HENRY TAYLOR, *Remembering Kevan MacKenzie*   189
E. E. CUMMINGS, *in Just-*   190
DONALD FINKEL, *Gesture*   191
JOHN HAINES, *The Cauliflower*   191
CHARLES OLSON, *La Chute*   192

11   Poems for the Eye   193

WORD SHAPES   193

GEORGE HERBERT, *Easter Wings*   193
JOHN HOLLANDER, *Skeleton key*   195
E. E. CUMMINGS, *r-p-o-p-h-e-s-s-a-g-r*   196
MAY SWENSON, *Stone Gullets*   197
ROBERT HERRICK, *Upon Prew His Maid*   198

CONCRETE POETRY   198

WANG WEI, *Bird-Singing Stream*   198
IAN HAMILTON FINLAY, *The Horizon of Holland*   200
EDWIN MORGAN, *Siesta of a Hungarian Snake*   201
DORTHI CHARLES, *Concrete Cat*   201

12   Symbol and Allegory   203

SYMBOL   203

T. S. ELIOT, *The* Boston Evening Transcript   204
EMILY DICKINSON, *The Lightning is a yellow Fork*   205
EMILY DICKINSON, *I heard a Fly buzz – when I died*   207
THOMAS HARDY, *Neutral Tones*   208

ALLEGORY   208

   MATTHEW 13:24–30, *The Parable of the Good Seed*   209
   SIR WALTER RALEIGH, *What is our life? A play of passion*   209
   SIR PHILIP SIDNEY, *You that with allegory's curious frame*   210
   ROBERT FROST, *Departmental*   211

   FOR REVIEW AND FURTHER STUDY   212

   WALLACE STEVENS, *Anecdote of the Jar*   212
   WILLIAM SHAKESPEARE, *Lo, as a careful housewife runs
      to catch*   212
   MINA LOY, *Omen of Victory*   213
   THEODORE ROETHKE, *Night Crow*   213
   JOHN DONNE, *A Burnt Ship*   213
   ROBERT FROST, *The Silken Tent*   213
   WALT WHITMAN, *A Noiseless Patient Spider*   214

13 Myth   215

TRADITIONAL MYTH   215

   D. H. LAWRENCE, *Bavarian Gentians*   217
   THOMAS HARDY, *The Oxen*   218
   WILLIAM WORDSWORTH, *The World Is Too Much with Us*   219

PERSONAL MYTH   219

   WILLIAM BUTLER YEATS, *The Second Coming*   220
   JOHN HEATH-STUBBS, *A Charm Against the Toothache*   221
   EDWARD ALLEN, *The Best Line Yet*   222
   WILLIAM BUTLER YEATS, *Leda and the Swan*   223

ARCHETYPES   223

   ANONYMOUS, *Thomas the Rimer*   225
   JOHN KEATS, *La Belle Dame sans Merci*   228

FOR REVIEW AND FURTHER STUDY   229

   JOHN MILTON, *Lycidas*   229
   ISHMAEL REED, *I Am a Cowboy in the Boat of Ra*   235

14 Telling Good from Bad   237

IMPRECISIONS   237

   ANONYMOUS, *O Moon, when I gaze on thy beautiful face*   240
   GRACE TREASONE, *Life*   240
   WILLIAM ERNEST HENLEY, *Madam Life's a piece in bloom*   240
   STEPHEN TROPP, *My Wife Is My Shirt*   241

SENTIMENTALITY 242

ROBERT BURNS, *John Anderson my jo, John* 244
Exercise
    The Bull Calf 244
    The Old Arm-Chair 245
    Piano 246
    Tears, idle tears, I know not what they mean 246

PARODY 247

T. E. BROWN, *My Garden* 247
J. A. LINDON, *My Garden* 247
HUGH KINGSMILL, *What, still alive at twenty-two* 248
KENNETH KOCH, *Mending Sump* 248

FOR REVIEW AND FURTHER STUDY 249

ROD McKUEN, *Thoughts on Capital Punishment* 249
WILLIAM STAFFORD, *Traveling Through the Dark* 250
Exercise
    Janet Waking 250
    Mary and Her Dead Canary 251
    Spring and Fall 252

15 Knowing Excellence 253

WILLIAM BUTLER YEATS, *Sailing to Byzantium* 254
ARTHUR GUITERMAN, *On the Vanity of Earthly Greatness* 256
PERCY BYSSHE SHELLEY, *Ozymandias* 257
WALT WHITMAN, *O Captain! My Captain!* 260
WILLIAM BLAKE, *The Little Black Boy* 261
JOHN KEATS, *Bright star! would I were steadfast as thou art* 262
CARL SANDBURG, *Fog* 263

FOR REVIEW AND FURTHER STUDY 263

JOSEPH SKIPSEY, *Get Up!* 263
MARK ALEXANDER BOYD, *Fra bank to bank, fra wood to wood
    I rin* 264
J. V. CUNNINGHAM, *Epitaph* 264
FRED EMERSON BROOKS, *Pat's Opinion of Flags* 265
ANTHONY HECHT, *Japan* 266

16 Alternatives 269

THE POET'S REVISIONS 269

WILLIAM BUTLER YEATS, *The Old Pensioner* 270

WILLIAM BUTLER YEATS, *The Lamentation of the Old Pensioner* 270

DONALD HALL, *My Son, My Executioner* 273

TRANSLATIONS 274

WILLIAM CORY, *Heraclitus* 275

DUDLEY FITTS, *Elegy on Herakleitos* 275

FEDERICO GARCÍA LORCA, *La guitarra (Guitar)* 275

RAINER MARIA RILKE, *Vorgefühl (Foreboding)* 276

HORACE, *Odes I (38)* 277

CHARLES BAUDELAIRE, *Recueillement (Meditation)* 278

17 Writing about Poems 280

EDGAR ALLAN POE, *Sonnet — To Science* 281

RICHARD WILBUR, Commentary 282

ROBERT FROST, *Design* 283

RANDALL JARRELL, Commentary 284

GWENDOLYN BROOKS, *First fight. Then fiddle. Ply the slipping string* 285

JAMES A. EMANUEL, Commentary 286

MATTHEW ARNOLD, *Dover Beach* 287

JAMES DICKEY, Commentary 288

A. ALVAREZ, Sylvia Plath (Commentary) 290

SYLVIA PLATH, *Ariel* 293

SYLVIA PLATH, *Daddy* 296

18 What Is Poetry? 302

ARCHIBALD MACLEISH, *Ars Poetica* 302

ANTHOLOGY 307

ANONYMOUS, *Western Wind* 309

ANONYMOUS, *Edward* 309

ANONYMOUS, *Sir Patrick Spence* 310

ANONYMOUS, *The Three Ravens* 311

ANONYMOUS, *The Twa Corbies* 312

GEOFFREY CHAUCER, *The Complaint of Chaucer to His Purse* 313

SIR THOMAS WYATT, *Whoso list to hunt, I know where is an hind* 314

SIR PHILIP SIDNEY, *With how sad steps, O moon, thou climb'st the skies* 314

CHRISTOPHER MARLOWE, *The Passionate Shepherd to His Love* 314

WILLIAM SHAKESPEARE, *When daisies pied and violets blue* 315

WILLIAM SHAKESPEARE, *When icicles hang by the wall* 316

WILLIAM SHAKESPEARE, *Let me not to the marriage of true minds* 316

WILLIAM SHAKESPEARE, *Full fathom five thy father lies* 317

WILLIAM SHAKESPEARE, *Poor soul, the center of my sinful earth* 317

WILLIAM SHAKESPEARE, *That time of year thou mayst in me behold* 318

THOMAS CAMPION, *There is a garden in her face* 318

JOHN DONNE, *A Lecture upon the Shadow* 319

JOHN DONNE, *A Valediction: Forbidding Mourning* 319

JOHN DONNE, *Batter my heart, three-personed God, for you* 320

JOHN DONNE, *The Bait* 321

ROBERT HERRICK, *To the Virgins, to Make Much of Time* 322

GEORGE HERBERT, *Love* 322

EDMUND WALLER, *Go, lovely rose* 323

JOHN MILTON, *When I consider how my light is spent* 323

ANDREW MARVELL, *To His Coy Mistress* 324

JOHN DRYDEN, *To the Memory of Mr. Oldham* 325

JONATHAN SWIFT, *The Day of Judgment* 326

ALEXANDER POPE, *Epigram Engraved on the Collar of a Dog Which I Gave to His Royal Highness* 326

THOMAS GRAY, *Elegy Written in a Country Churchyard* 326

CHRISTOPHER SMART, *For I will consider my Cat Jeoffry* 330

WILLIAM BLAKE, *Long John Brown and Little Mary Bell* 332

WILLIAM BLAKE, *The Sick Rose* 332

WILLIAM BLAKE, *The Tyger* 332

WILLIAM WORDSWORTH, *Composed upon Westminster Bridge* 333

WILLIAM WORDSWORTH, *To Toussaint L'Ouverture* 333

SAMUEL TAYLOR COLERIDGE, *Kubla Khan* 334

GEORGE GORDON, LORD BYRON, *Lines Inscribed upon a Cup Formed from a Skull* 335

JOHN KEATS, *Ode on a Grecian Urn* 336

JOHN KEATS, *When I have fears that I may cease to be* 337

ALFRED, LORD TENNYSON, *Crossing the Bar* 338

ALFRED, LORD TENNYSON, *Ulysses* 338

ROBERT BROWNING, *Soliloquy of the Spanish Cloister* 340

HERMAN MELVILLE, *The Berg* 341

WALT WHITMAN, *I Saw in Louisiana a Live-Oak Growing* 343

WALT WHITMAN, *The City Dead-House*   343

GEORGE MEREDITH, *Lucifer in Starlight*   344

DANTE GABRIEL ROSSETTI, *The Woodspurge*   344

EMILY DICKINSON, *Because I could not stop for Death*   344

EMILY DICKINSON, *I started Early–Took my Dog*   345

EMILY DICKINSON, *The Soul selects her own Society*   346

THOMAS HARDY, *Channel Firing*   346

THOMAS HARDY, *The Convergence of the Twain*   347

THOMAS HARDY, *During Wind and Rain*   349

GERARD MANLEY HOPKINS, *The Windhover*   349

KATIE V. HALL, *The Old, Filthy Beer Pail*   350

OSCAR WILDE, *The Harlot's House*   351

A. E. HOUSMAN, *Terence, this is stupid stuff*   352

A. E. HOUSMAN, *To an Athlete Dying Young*   354

WILLIAM BUTLER YEATS, *Crazy Jane Talks with the Bishop*   355

WILLIAM BUTLER YEATS, *For Anne Gregory*   355

WILLIAM BUTLER YEATS, *Lapis Lazuli*   356

WILLIAM BUTLER YEATS, *Long-Legged Fly*   356

WILLIAM BUTLER YEATS, *The Magi*   358

EDWIN ARLINGTON ROBINSON, *Mr. Flood's Party*   358

WALTER DE LA MARE, *The Listeners*   360

ROBERT FROST, *Provide, Provide*   361

ROBERT FROST, *Stopping by Woods on a Snowy Evening*   361

WALLACE STEVENS, *The Emperor of Ice-Cream*   362

WALLACE STEVENS, *Peter Quince at the Clavier*   362

WALLACE STEVENS, *The Snow Man*   364

JAMES JOYCE, *I hear an army charging upon the land*   365

WILLIAM CARLOS WILLIAMS, *Danse Russe*   365

WILLIAM CARLOS WILLIAMS, *To Waken an Old Lady*   366

EZRA POUND, *The River-Merchant's Wife: a Letter*   366

D. H. LAWRENCE, *The Elephant Is Slow to Mate*   367

MARIANNE MOORE, *A Grave*   368

T. S. ELIOT, *The Love Song of J. Alfred Prufrock*   368

T. S. ELIOT, *Sweeney among the Nightingales*   372

JOHN CROWE RANSOM, *Bells for John Whiteside's Daughter*   373

E. E. CUMMINGS, *All in green went my love riding*   374

E. E. CUMMINGS, *when serpents bargain for the right to squirm*   375

E. E. CUMMINGS, *next to of course god america i*   375

HART CRANE, *Black Tambourine*   375

YVOR WINTERS, *At the San Francisco Airport*   376

KENNETH FEARING, *Dirge*   377

LANGSTON HUGHES, *The Weary Blues*   378

COUNTEE CULLEN, *Saturday's Child*   379

WILLIAM EMPSON, *Legal Fiction*   379

W. H. AUDEN, *As I Walked Out One Evening*   380

W. H. AUDEN, *Musée des Beaux Arts*   381

A. D. HOPE, *The Brides*   382

THEODORE ROETHKE, *Dolor*   383

THEODORE ROETHKE, *Elegy for Jane*   383

THEODORE ROETHKE, *Frau Bauman, Frau Schmidt, and Frau
    Schwartze*   384

THEODORE ROETHKE, *The Meadow Mouse*   385

MURIEL RUKEYSER, *Boy with His Hair Cut Short*   385

KARL SHAPIRO, *The Dirty Word*   386

DAVID IGNATOW, *Get the Gasworks*   387

RANDALL JARRELL, *The Death of the Ball Turret Gunner*   387

RANDALL JARRELL, *The Old and the New Masters*   388

JOHN FREDERICK NIMS, *Love Poem*   389

HENRY REED, *Naming of Parts*   390

WILLIAM STAFFORD, *Written on the Stub of the First
    Paycheck*   391

DYLAN THOMAS, *After the Funeral*   391

DUDLEY RANDALL, *Ballad of Birmingham*   392

ROBERT LOWELL, *Skunk Hour*   393

WILLIAM JAY SMITH, *American Primitive*   394

HOWARD NEMEROV, *The Goose Fish*   395

RICHARD WILBUR, *Junk*   396

PHILIP LARKIN, *Church Going*   397

JAMES DICKEY, *Cherrylog Road*   399

DENISE LEVERTOV, *Come into Animal Presence*   401

ALAN DUGAN, *Love Song: I and Thou*   402

DONALD JUSTICE, *In Bertram's Garden*   403

ROBERT CREELEY, *Kore*   403

ROBERT CREELEY, *I Know a Man*   404

ALLEN GINSBERG, *In back of the real*   404

JAMES MERRILL, *Laboratory Poem*   405

W. D. SNODGRASS, *The Operation*   405

GALWAY KINNELL, *To Christ Our Lord*   406

W. S. MERWIN, *For the Anniversary of My Death*   407

JAMES WRIGHT, *A Blessing*   407

JAMES WRIGHT, *Trouble*   408

PHILIP LEVINE, *To a Child Trapped in a Barber Shop*   409

ANNE SEXTON, *For Eleanor Boylan Talking with God*   410

ADRIENNE RICH, *The Insusceptibles*   410

GARY SNYDER, *Milton by Firelight*   411

SYLVIA PLATH, *Face Lift*   412

SYLVIA PLATH, *Lady Lazarus*   412

SYLVIA PLATH, *Morning Song*   415

KEITH WALDROP, *Before Bed*   415

IMAMU AMIRI BARAKA (LEROI JONES), *Preface to a Twenty Volume Suicide Note*   416

MARGE PIERCY, *Different persuasions*   416

LUCILLE CLIFTON, *the lost baby poem*   417

C. K. WILLIAMS, *Hood*   418

BOB DYLAN, *Subterranean Homesick Blues*   418

NIKKI GIOVANNI, *Kidnap Poem*   420

MICK JAGGER AND KEITH RICHARD, *Live with me*   420

JAMES TATE, *Flight*   421

GREG KUZMA, *Peace, so that*   422

INDEX OF FIRST LINES   423

INDEX OF AUTHORS AND TITLES   429

INDEX OF TERMS   *inside back cover*

TO THE MUSE

Give me leave, Muse, in plain view to array
Your shift and bodice by the light of day.
I would have brought an epic. Be not vexed
Instead to grace a niggling schoolroom text;
Let down your sanction, help me to oblige
Him who would lead fresh devots to your liege,
And at your altar, grant that in a flash
They, he and I know incense from dead ash.

X. J. K.

TO THE STUDENT

I do not say these things for a dollar or to fill up the time while I wait for
    a boat,
(It is you talking just as much as myself, I act as the tongue of you,
Tied in your mouth, in mine it begins to be loosen'd.)
    — Walt Whitman, "Song of Myself"

What is poetry? Pressed for an answer, Robert Frost made a classic reply: "Poetry is the kind of thing poets write." In all likelihood, Frost was not trying merely to evade the question but to chide his questioner into thinking for himself. A trouble with definitions is that they may stop thought. If Frost had said, "Poetry is a rhythmical composition of words expressing an attitude, designed to surprise and delight, and to arouse an emotional response," the questioner might have settled back in his chair, content to have learned the truth about poetry. He would have learned nothing, or not so much as he might learn by continuing to wonder. And Frost knew — for he says so in a poem — that there can be truth that sets the logical mind going vainly in circles:

Robert Frost (1874–1963)

THE SECRET SITS

We dance round in a ring and suppose,
But the Secret sits in the middle and knows.

Though not wholly a Secret, the nature of poetry does elude simple definitions. (In this respect it is rather like jazz. Asked after one of his concerts, "What is jazz?" Louis Armstrong replied, "Man, if you gotta ask, you'll never know.") Definitions will be of little help at first, if we are to know poetry and respond to it. We have to go to it willing to see and hear. For this reason, you are asked in reading this book not to be in any hurry to decide what poetry is, but instead to study poems and to let them grow in your mind. At the end of the book, the problem of definition will be taken up again (for those who may wish to pursue it).

Confronted with *An Introduction to Poetry*, you may be wondering "Who needs it?" and you may well be right. You hardly can have avoided meeting poetry before; and perhaps you already have a friendship, or at least a fair acquaintance, with some of the great English-speaking poets of all time. What this book provides is an introduction to the *study* of poetry. It tries to help you look at a poem closely, to offer you a wider and more accurate vocabulary with which to express what poems say to you. It will suggest ways to judge for yourself the poems you read. It may set forth some poems new to you.

A frequent objection to a book such as this is that poetry ought not to be studied at all. In this view, a poem is either a series of gorgeous noises to be funneled through one ear and out the other without being allowed to trouble the mind or an experience so holy that to analyze it in a classroom is as cruel and mechanical as dissecting a hummingbird. To the first view, it might be countered that a good poem has something to say that perhaps is worth listening to. To the second view, it might be argued that poems are much less perishable than hummingbirds, and luckily, we can study them in flight. The risk of a poem's dying from observation is not nearly so great as the risk of not really seeing it at all. It is doubtful that any excellent poem has ever vanished from human memory because people have read it too closely. More likely, poems that vanish are poems that no one reads closely, for no one cares.

Good poetry is something to care about. In fact, an ancient persuasion of mankind is that the hearing of a poem, as well as the making of a poem, can be a religious act. Poetry, in speech and song, was part of classic Greek drama, which for playwright, actor, and spectator alike was a holy-day ceremony. The Greeks' belief that a poet writes a poem only by supernatural assistance is clear from the invocations to the Muse that begin the *Iliad* and the *Odyssey* and from the opinion of Socrates (in Plato's *Ion*) that a poet has no powers of invention until divinely inspired. Among the ancient Celts, poets were regarded as magicians and priests, and whoever insulted one of them might expect to receive a curse in rime potent enough to afflict him with boils and to curdle the milk of his cows. Such identifications between the poet and the magician are less common these days, although we know that poetry is involved in the primitive white-magic of children, who bring themselves good luck in a game with the charm "Roll, roll, Tootsie-roll! / Roll the marble in the hole!" and who warn against a hex while jumping a sidewalk: "Step on a crack, / Break your mother's back." But in this age when men pride themselves that a computer may solve the riddle of all creation as soon as it is programmed, magic seems to some people of small importance and so does poetry. It is dangerous, however, to dismiss what we do not logically understand.

To read a poem at all, we have to be willing to offer it responses *besides* a logical understanding. Whether we attribute the effect of a poem to a divine spirit or to the reactions of our glands and cortexes, we have to take the reading of poetry seriously (not solemnly), if only because — as some of the poems in this book may demonstrate — few other efforts can repay us so generously, both in wisdom and in joy.

If, as I hope you will do, you sometimes browse in the book for fun, you may be annoyed to see so many questions following the poems. Should you feel this way, try reading with a slip of paper to cover up the questions. You will then — if the Muse should inspire you — have paper in hand to write a poem.

TO THE INSTRUCTOR

Renovations

After the extensive alterations made in the second edition, I had hoped that all the third would need would be a dab of fresh paint and a little reshuffling of the furniture. But new requests have had to be met, new changes called for. Instructors who know the previous edition will find that the largest addition is a new chapter, "Writing About Poems." It offers a few brief models of criticism, a few discussions of poems that students may use as a guide in writing their own papers. Many instructors have asked for a higher proportion of contemporary poems; and so most of the fifty poems new to this edition are recent ones. Sylvia Plath and Theodore Roethke have joined the core of poets (now nineteen strong) represented by seven or more poems apiece. Besides, there are added poems by James Wright, Robert Creeley, Richard Wilbur, Randall Jarrell, Wallace Stevens, Anne Sexton, Langston Hughes, W. S. Merwin, Gwendolyn Brooks, and others; and among the poets now first included are Philip Levine, A. R. Ammons, Alan Dugan, Galway Kinnell, Muriel Rukeyser, Jean Toomer, and such relative newcomers to American poetry as Marge Piercy, Nikki Giovanni, Lucille Clifton, and Greg Kuzma.

In Chapter Ten, I have been wrestling again with the problem of how best to deal with the formal differences between a sonnet and an Allen Ginsberg sutra. It now seems that the most useful distinction is that between *closed form* and *open form*; and so it has replaced the old distinction between such inadequate terms as "patterned poem" (suggesting something cut out with a scissors) and "free verse" (suggesting poetry in which "anything goes").

New also to this edition is the system of cross-references in the anthology. Brief notes following some poems direct the student to other poems similar in subject, theme, or technique. I hope it will now be easier to notice such similarities, for writing assignments and for class discussion.

Assumptions

I assume that appreciation of poetry cannot be created but may be increased. I would not usurp the instructor's right to teach poetry after his own fashion, but I do offer short discussions of the elements of poetry, which (if he agrees with me) students may read for themselves, freeing class time for the study of poems.

Plan of the Book

There is one, but I have tried to oblige no one to follow it. Chapters may be taken up in any order. If the student meets terms unknown to him, he can find them defined and their use illustrated by referring to the index of terms. The sections "For Review and Further Study" at the ends of most chapters are intended not to review the entire book but mainly to go back over points introduced in each chapter. These sections contain additional poems for optional use, some of them of greater complexity than those poems in the main body of the chapter. The sections called "Exercises" offer problems for class solution or discussion; those called "Experiment" suggest investigations for the student to make on his own, outside of class.

Selection of Poems

Nineteen poets are represented with seven or more poems each — Shakespeare, Donne, Herrick, Blake, Wordsworth, Keats, Emily Dickinson, Whitman, Tennyson, Housman, Hopkins, Yeats, Hardy, Frost, Cummings, William Carlos Williams, Wallace Stevens, Sylvia Plath, and Theodore Roethke — for those who may wish to study a poet's work in more depth than isolated poems allow. Otherwise, the only criteria of selection have been excellence (or illustrative inferiority), usefulness for teaching, and a wish to offer variety and some historical distribution. In general, complicated poems have been chosen over very simple ones; there are few "hey-nonny-nonny" songs and only a sampling of light verse. The assumption was that difficult poems are frequently easier and more rewarding to teach than poems about which one has little to say but "Look at this."

Anthology

With limited space, it seemed impracticable to offer a full history of English poetry. All I can claim for this anthology is that it has an additional 140 poems, for those who wish more poems to teach, unencumbered by apparatus. The anthology has been arranged in a rough chronological order, by birth dates of poets and by approximate ages of certain anonymous poems.

Texts

Spelling has been modernized (*rose-lipped* for *ros-lip'd*) and made American, unless the sound of a word would be changed. But I have left the *y* in Blake's strange "Tyger" and let Whitman keep his *bloom'd* on the conviction that *bloomed* would no more resemble Whitman than a portrait of him in a starched collar would. Untitled poems, except for those that have titles assigned by custom ("The Twa Corbies," "Carrion Comfort"), are identified by their first lines. Chaucer's "Complaint" is given as edited by F. N. Robinson; the poems of Emily Dickinson, as edited by Thomas H. Johnson.

Glosses

It would have been simpler to gloss no word a student could find in a desk dictionary, on the grounds that the rummaging of dictionaries is good moral discipline; but it seemed best not to require the student to exchange text for dictionary as many as ten times in reading a single poem. Glosses have been provided for whatever seemed likely to interfere with pleasure and understanding.

Line Numbers

Wherever the structure of a poem has made it meaningful to do so, line numbers indicate rime schemes and stanza patterns. An English sonnet, for instance, instead of having numbers opposite lines 5 and 10, has them opposite lines 4, 8, 12, and 14.

Orthography

The spelling *rime* is used instead of *rhyme*, on the theory that *rime* is easier to distinguish from *rhythm*.

Acknowledgments

Again, my debts have multiplied, and besides those owed to friends in the past I must now also thank LeRoy Badger, Elizabeth Bates, Jerene Cline, Kathleen Field, Ian Hamilton Finlay, Dale Helgeson, Lee Hotz, Thomas M. Johnson (again), Marjorie Kaiser, Richard L. Loughlin, G. B. Montague, Maurice Naughton, Allen Neff, Gibbons Ruark, James Quivey, and Richard Schramm. Sylvan Barnet has continued to lend his valuable hand. I am still grateful to my students at Tufts, Wellesley, Michigan, North Carolina (Greensboro), and California (Irvine) for explaining some of the poems to me. And most of all, I thank Dorothy M. Kennedy.

An Introduction to Poetry

1 Entrances

How do we read a poem? A literal-minded answer might be, "Just let your eye light on it," but there is more to poetry than meets the eye. What Shakespeare called "the mind's eye" also plays a part. Many a reader who has no trouble understanding and enjoying prose finds poetry difficult. This is to be expected. At first glance, a poem usually will make some sense and give some pleasure, but it may not yield everything at once. Sometimes it only hints at meaning still to come if we will keep after it. Poetry is not to be galloped over like the daily news: a poem differs from most prose in that it is to be read slowly, carefully, and attentively. Not all poems are difficult, of course, and some can be understood and enjoyed on first seeing. But good poems yield more if read twice; and the best poems — after ten, twenty, or a hundred readings — can still go on yielding.

Approaching a thing written in lines and surrounded with white space, we need not expect it to be a poem just because it is **verse** (any composition in lines of more or less regular rhythm, usually ending in rimes). Here, for instance, is a specimen of verse that few will call poetry:

Thirty days hath September,
April, June, and November;
All the rest have thirty-one
Excepting February alone,
To which we twenty-eight assign
Till leap year makes it twenty-nine.

To a higher degree than that classic memory-tickler, poetry appeals to the mind and arouses feelings. Poetry may state facts, but, more important, it makes imaginative statements that we may value even if its facts are incorrect. Coleridge's error in placing a star within the horns of the crescent moon in "The Rime of the Ancient Mariner" does not stop the passage from being good poetry, though it is faulty astronomy. According to one poet, Gerard Manley Hopkins, poetry is "to be heard for its own sake and interest even over and above its interest of meaning." There are other elements in a poem besides plain prose sense: sounds, images, patterns, rhythms, figures of speech. These may strike us and please us even before we ask ourselves, "But what does it all mean?"

This is a truth not readily grasped by anyone who regards a poem as a kind of puzzle written in secret code with a message slyly concealed. The **effect** of a poem (one's whole mental and emotional response to it) consists in much more than simply a message or the dictionary definitions of its words. By its musical qualities, by its suggestions, it can work upon the reader's unconscious. T. S. Eliot put it well when he said in *The Use of Poetry and the Use of Criticism* that the prose sense of a poem is chiefly useful in keeping the reader's mind "diverted and quiet, while the poem does its work upon him." Eliot went on to liken the meaning of a poem to the bit of meat a burglar brings along to throw to the family dog. What is the work of a poem? To touch us, to stir us, to make us glad, and possibly even to tell us something.

How, then, does one set about reading an unfamiliar poem, especially a poem with apparent difficulties? Here are some suggestions.

On first look, try reading the poem once straight through, pushing on despite all obstacles. Don't dwell on a troublesome word, at least not until you have read the poem as a whole, for as you read the poem for a second time some of its difficulties may resolve themselves when seen as parts of a larger design.

On second reading, pick out for special attention whatever words, phrases, lines, or passages are not yet clear. Look up unfamiliar words. In a dictionary or encyclopedia, look up names of persons and places, foreign words, references to mythology.

Read the poem silently to yourself, sounding its words in your mind. (This is a technique that will get you nowhere in a speed reading course, but it may help the poem to do its work on you.)

Better still, read the poem aloud, or hear someone else read it. Further meaning may be discovered. Even if you are no actor, to decide how to speak a poem can be an excellent method of understanding. Some poems, like bells, seem heavy till heard. Listen while reading the following lines from Alexander Pope's *Dunciad*. Attacking the minor poet James Ralph, who had sung the praises of a mistress named Cynthia, Pope makes the goddess of Dullness exclaim:

> "Silence, ye wolves! while Ralph to Cynthia howls,
> And makes night hideous — answer him, ye owls!"

When *ye owls* slide together and become *yowls,* poor Ralph's serenade is turned into the nightly outcry of a cat.

Try to **paraphrase** the poem as a whole, or perhaps just the more difficult lines. In paraphrasing, we put into our own words what we understand the poem to say, restating ideas that seem essential, coming out and stating what the poem may only suggest. This may sound like a heartless thing to do to a poem, but good poems can stand it. In fact, to compare a poem to its paraphrase is an excellent way to see the distance between poetry and prose.

A. E. Housman (1859–1936)
LOVELIEST OF TREES, THE CHERRY NOW

Loveliest of trees, the cherry now
Is hung with bloom along the bough,
And stands about the woodland ride
Wearing white for Eastertide. 4

Now, of my threescore years and ten,
Twenty will not come again,
And take from seventy springs a score,
It only leaves me fifty more. 8

And since to look at things in bloom
Fifty springs are little room,
About the woodlands I will go
To see the cherry hung with snow. 12

Though simple, Housman's poem is far from simple-minded, and it contains at least one possible problem: what, in this instance, is a *ride?* If we guess, we won't be far wrong; but a dictionary helps: "a road or path through the woods, especially for horseback riding." A paraphrase of the poem might say something like this (in language easier to forget than the original): "Now it is Easter time, and the cherry tree in the woods is in blossom. I'm twenty, my life is passing. I expect to live the average life-span of seventy. That means I'm going to see only fifty more springs, so I had better go out into the woods and start looking." And the paraphrase might add, to catch the deeper implication, "Life is brief and fleeting: I must enjoy beauty while I may."

These dull remarks, roughly faithful to what Housman is saying, are clearly as far from being poetry as a cherry pit is far from being a cherry. Nevertheless, they have the value of helping whoever makes the paraphrase see the argument of Housman's poem and its attitude. To make a fair paraphrase, weigh each word of the original. A classic failure is that of the boy (quoted by Matthew Arnold) who took the line in *Macbeth,* "Can'st thou not minister to a mind diseased?" and paraphrased it, "Can you not wait upon the lunatic?"

A paraphrase, of course, never tells *all* that a poem contains, nor will every reader agree that it is accurate. We all make our own interpretations, and even to the poet himself the total meaning of a poem may be inexplicable. Asked to explain his difficult *Sordello*, Robert Browning replied that when he had written the poem only God and he knew what it meant; but "Now, only God knows." Still, to analyze a poem *as if* we could be certain of its meaning is, in general, more fruitful than to proceed as if no certainty could ever be had. The latter approach is likely to end in complete subjectivity: the attitude of the reader who says, "Housman's 'Loveliest of trees' is really about a walk in the snow; it is, because I think it is. How can you prove me wrong?"

All of us bring to our readings of poems certain personal associations, as Housman's "Loveliest of trees" might convey a particular pleasure to a reader who had climbed cherry trees when he was small. To some extent, these associations are inevitable, even to be welcomed. But we need to distinguish between irrelevant, tangential responses and those the poem calls for. The reader who can't stand "Loveliest of trees" because cherries remind him of blood, is reading a poem of his own, not Housman's.

One warning: occasionally we meet a poem, perhaps startling and memorable, into which the method of paraphrase will not take us far. Some portion of any good poem resists explanation, but certain poems resist it almost entirely. Now and then the poems of religious mystics, poems that record hallucinations or drug experiences — as Coleridge's "Kubla Khan" — poems that embody private knowledge — as William Blake's "The Sick Rose" or the same poet's lines from *Jerusalem,*

> For a Tear is an Intellectual thing,
> And a Sigh is the Sword of an Angel King,

nonsense poems, translations of primitive folk poetry, and surreal[1] poems (to mention only a few to watch out for) may seem closer to dream than to waking and may tease the conscious mind that would unravel them. Sometimes they move us and so give pleasure (though not the pleasure of mental understanding). We do them no harm by trying to paraphrase them, even though we may fail. Good poems, whether logically clear or strangely opaque, appeal to the intelligence and do not shrink from it. To search them for meanings we can put in our own words is only a way to behold them, that they may act on us.

We have taken it for granted, so far, that poetry differs from prose; yet all these strategies — reading straight through and then going back, isolating difficulties, trying to paraphrase, reading aloud, using a dictionary — are no different from those we might employ in unraveling a complicated piece of prose. Poetry, after all, is similar to prose in most respects; at the very least, it is written in the same language. And like

---

[1] The French poet André Breton, founder of **Surrealism,** a movement in art and writing, declared that a higher reality exists, which to mortal eyes looks absurd. To mirror that reality, Surrealist poets are fond of bizarre and dreamlike objects such as soluble fish and white-haired revolvers.

prose, poetry imparts knowledge. It tells us, for instance, something about the season and habitat of cherry trees and how one can feel toward them. But the knowledge to be gained from Housman's poem is knowledge of a different order from that in a textbook of botany. Maybe a poet knows no more of cherry trees than a writer of seed-catalog descriptions, if as much. And yet Housman's perception of cherry blossoms as snow, with the implication that they too will soon melt and disappear, indicates a kind of knowledge that seed catalogs do not ordinarily reveal.

Robert Francis (b. 1901)
CATCH

Two boys uncoached are tossing a poem together,
Overhand, underhand, backhand, sleight of hand, every hand,
Teasing with attitudes, latitudes, interludes, altitudes,
High, make him fly off the ground for it, low, make him stoop,
Make him scoop it up, make him as-almost-as-possible miss it,   5
Fast, let him sting from it, now, now fool him slowly,
Anything, everything tricky, risky, nonchalant,
Anything under the sun to outwit the prosy,
Over the tree and the long sweet cadence down,
Over his head, make him scramble to pick up the meaning,   10
And now, like a posy, a pretty one plump in his hands.

A. E. Housman (1859–1936)
IN THE MORNING, IN THE MORNING

In the morning, in the morning,
  In the happy field of hay,
Oh they looked at one another
  By the light of day.   4

In the blue and silver morning
  On the haycock as they lay,
Oh they looked at one another
  And they looked away.   8

QUESTIONS

1. Who are *they?* How do you know?
2. Sum up their story.
3. In your summary, what did you find necessary to say that Housman leaves unsaid?
4. From your answer to question 3, what inferences can be drawn about the nature of certain poetry?
5. Read the poem aloud. In what respects is its sound more memorable than that of the same story told in prose?

Emily Dickinson (1830–1886)

IT WAS NOT DEATH, FOR I STOOD UP

It was not Death, for I stood up,   *a*
And all the Dead, lie down –
It was not Night, for all the Bells
Put out their Tongues, for Noon.

It was not Frost, for on my Flesh   *b*
I felt Siroccos – crawl –
Nor Fire – for just my Marble feet
Could keep a Chancel, cool –

And yet, it tasted, like them all,   *c*
The Figures I have seen
Set orderly, for Burial,
Reminded me, of mine –

As if my life were shaven,   *d*
And fitted to a frame,
And could not breathe without a key,
And 'twas like Midnight, some –

When everything that ticked – has stopped –   *e*
And Space stares all around –
Or Grisly frosts – first Autumn morns,
Repeal the Beating Ground –

But, most, like Chaos – Stopless – cool –   *f*
Without a Chance, or Spar –
Or even a Report of Land –
To justify – Despair.

QUESTIONS

1. Here, in paraphrase, are the first three stanzas of this poem:

   a. I was sure I wasn't dead, as I might have thought I was. I knew I was alive from the fact that I found myself standing up, and I know that the dead always lie down. It wasn't night; instead, all the bells were ringing the noon hour.

   b. I didn't feel cold, for I felt warm winds blowing across my skin. I didn't feel hot, for my feet were like marble, so cold that all by themselves they could have cooled the space in back of a church altar.

   c. And yet somehow I felt as if I really were dead, and in the dark, and simultaneously hot and cold. I have seen corpses laid out for burial, and the sight of my own body made me think of them.

   So far, how faithful to the meaning of the poem do you find this paraphrase? What, besides coldness, do the words *Frost* and *Marble* (stanza *b*) also suggest? What other interpretations might be given to any of these lines, or indeed to the speaker's situation?

2. In other respects besides meaning, how do paraphrase and poem compare?

3. Paraphrase the rest of the poem.

4. In this book, those poems by Emily Dickinson for which the poet's own manuscripts survive are capitalized and punctuated as she wrote them. Can you see any good reasons for her practice?

Richard Brautigan (b. 1935)
HAVE YOU EVER HAD A WITCH BLOOM LIKE A HIGHWAY

Have you ever had a witch bloom like a highway
on your mouth? and turn your breathing to her
fancy? like a little car with blue headlights
    passing forever in a dream?

QUESTION

Can you paraphrase this poem? What other ways of reading it can you suggest?

EXPERIMENT: *Paraphrase*

Write a paraphrase of the following poem or of a poem from the anthology at the back of this book. If possible, compare your paraphrase with paraphrases written by other students.

William Shakespeare (1564–1616)
NOT MARBLE NOR THE GILDED MONUMENTS

Not marble nor the gilded monuments
Of princes shall outlive this pow'rful rime;
But you shall shine more bright in these contènts
Than unswept stone, besmeared with sluttish time.   4
When wasteful war shall statues overturn,
And broils° root out the work of masonry,   *brawls, battles*
Nor Mars his sword nor war's quick fire shall burn
The living record of your memory.   8
'Gainst death and all oblivious enmity
Shall you pace forth; your praise shall still find room
Even in the eyes of all posterity
That wear this world out to the ending doom.   12
    So, till the Judgment that° yourself arise,   *when*
    You live in this, and dwell in lovers' eyes.   14

2 The Person in the Poem

THE POET'S "I"

"I wandered lonely as a cloud," said William Wordsworth in the open-ing line of a famous poem. Most of us probably will accept this state-ment at face value. Evidently it is the poet's way of telling us that he, William Wordsworth, British subject, age thirty-seven, of Dove Cottage, Grasmere, took a walk by himself. And yet, despite the first-person pronoun, a moment's thought will reveal that, for all we know, the truth may be otherwise. For a poem is not *necessarily* autobiographical, and the fact that a poet says "I" gives us no guarantee that he is not creating a fictitious person to speak through, as Samuel L. Clemens in a familiar novel puts words into the mouth of a first-person speaker named Huckleberry Finn. In poetry some distinction needs to be made be-tween the living writer and his words on the printed page.

Most of us find it easy to tell the difference between an experience in life and an experience conveyed to us in a work of art — unlike that man in the Philippines who, watching a movie of a villain sneaking up on a cowboy hero, pulled out a revolver and peppered the screen. Read-ing a poem or story about the death of someone, our emotions are different from those we might feel if we were actually present to wit-ness the final agonies. It is even possible to derive a kind of pleasure from such a poem, not because we are hardhearted or sadistic, but because "pleasure is inherent even in the act of understanding."[1] The following poem is not grim, though it speaks of the most horrific event imaginable.

Archibald MacLeish (b. 1892)
THE END OF THE WORLD

Quite unexpectedly as Vasserot
The armless ambidextrian was lighting
A match between his great and second toe,
And Ralph the lion was engaged in biting   4

[1] Karl Shapiro and Robert Beum, *A Prosody Handbook* (New York, 1965), p. 100.

The neck of Madame Sossman while the drum
Pointed, and Teeny was about to cough
In waltz-time swinging Jocko by the thumb —
Quite unexpectedly the top blew off: 8

And there, there overhead, there, there hung over
Those thousands of white faces, those dazed eyes,
There in the starless dark the poise, the hover,
There with vast wings across the canceled skies,   12
There in the sudden blackness the black pall
Of nothing, nothing, nothing — nothing at all.   14

We can take pleasure from this poem not because of the nature of its
subject but because of other elements: its sound, its portrait of a circus
frozen in a split-second, and the colossal pun in "the top blew off" (*top*
being also the "big top" or circus tent and perhaps the lid of the enormous pot of all creation). The fact that MacLeish's poem employs rime
and lines of uniform length sets it apart from prose and indicates that
it is something other than description of experience. Such artifice, as
Richard Wilbur has suggested, serves to declare that the poem "is not
the world, but a pattern imposed upon the world or found in it."

Some poets, of course, speak directly of their personal experiences.
They do not insist that, in order to read their poems, we study their
biographies. Yet there are some poems whose effect depends in part
upon our being aware of the poet himself:

Trumbull Stickney (1874–1904)

Sir, say no more

Sir, say no more,
Within me 'tis as if
The green and climbing eyesight of a cat
Crawled near my mind's poor birds.

The subject of Stickney's poem is not some nightmare or hallucination.
The poem may mean more to you if you know that Stickney, who wrote
it shortly before his death, had been afflicted by cancer of the brain.
But the poem is not a prosaic entry in the diary of a dying man, nor is
it a good poem because a dying man wrote it. Not only does it tell truth
from experience, it speaks in memorable words.

Recent years have seen much poetry written in the first person,
apparently speaking of the poet's own torments, sorrows, and difficulties. Robert Lowell, Anne Sexton, Sylvia Plath, W. D. Snodgrass,
and Allen Ginsberg have given us such **confessional poetry.** Like all
good poems, confessional poems that succeed do so by doing more

than confessing: they arrange language (as well as experience) into works of art.

This point is crucial: let us not *expect* the person in a poem to be the poet speaking for himself. Nor is he necessarily speaking at the time of the experience his poem relates, nor even recently afterward. In a famous definition, Wordsworth called poetry "the spontaneous overflow of powerful feelings . . . recollected in tranquility." In writing this poem, however, Wordsworth's moment of tranquility had to go on for years.

William Wordsworth (1770–1850)

I WANDERED LONELY AS A CLOUD

I wandered lonely as a cloud
    That floats on high o'er vales and hills,
When all at once I saw a crowd,
    A host, of golden daffodils,   4
Beside the lake, beneath the trees,
Fluttering and dancing in the breeze.   6

Continuous as the stars that shine
    And twinkle on the milky way,
They stretched in never-ending line
    Along the margin of a bay: 10
Ten thousand saw I at a glance,
Tossing their heads in sprightly dance.   12

The waves beside them danced; but they
    Out-did the sparkling waves in glee;
A poet could not but be gay,
    In such a jocund company;   16
I gazed — and gazed — but little thought
What wealth the show to me had brought: 18

For oft, when on my couch I lie
    In vacant or in pensive mood,
They flash upon that inward eye
    Which is the bliss of solitude;   22
And then my heart with pleasure fills,
And dances with the daffodils.   24

Between the first printing of the poem in 1807 and the version of 1815 given here, Wordsworth made several deliberate improvements. He changed *dancing* to *golden* in line 4, *Along* to *Beside* in line 5, *Ten thousand* to *Fluttering and* in line 6, *laughing* to *jocund* in line 16, and he added a whole stanza (the second). In fact, the writing of the poem was unspontaneous enough for Wordsworth, at a loss for lines 21–22, to take them from his wife Mary. It is likely that the experience of daffodil-watching was not entirely his to begin with but was derived in part from the recollections his sister Dorothy Wordsworth had set down in her journal of April 15, 1802, two years before he first drafted his poem:

> It was a threatening, misty morning, but mild. We set off after dinner from Eusemere. Mrs. Clarkson went a short way with us, but turned back. The wind was furious, and we thought we must have returned. We first rested in the large boat-house, then under a furze bush opposite Mr. Clarkson's. Saw the plough going in the field. The wind seized our breath. The Lake was rough. . . . When we were in the woods beyond Gowbarrow Park we saw a few daffodils close to the water-side. We fancied that the lake had floated the seeds ashore, and that the little colony had so sprung up. But as we went along there were more and yet more; and at last, under the boughs of the trees, we saw that there was a long belt of them along the shore, about the breadth of a country turnpike road. I never saw daffodils so beautiful. They grew among the mossy stones about and about them; some rested their heads upon these stones as on a pillow for weariness; and the rest tossed and reeled and danced, and seemed as if they verily laughed with the wind, that flew upon them over the Lake; they looked so gay, ever glancing, ever changing. This wind blew directly over the Lake to them. There was here and there a little knot, and a few stragglers a few yards higher up; but they were so few as not to disturb the simplicity, unity, and life of that one busy highway.

Notice that Wordsworth's poem echoes a few of his sister's words. Weaving poetry out of their mutual memories, Wordsworth has offered the experience as if altogether his own, made himself lonely, and left Dorothy out. The point is not that Wordsworth is a liar or a plagiarist but that, like any other good poet, he has transformed ordinary life into art. A necessary process of interpreting, shaping, and ordering had to intervene between the experience of looking at daffodils and the finished poem.

We need not deny that a poet's experience can contribute to his poem nor that the emotion in the poem can belong to him. Still, to write a good poem one has to do more than live and feel. It seems a pity that, as Randall Jarrell has said of bad poets in *Poetry and the Age*, a cardinal should write verses worse than his youngest choirboy's. But writing poetry, more than keeping a diary, requires skill and imagination — qualities that travel and breadth of experience do not necessarily give. For much of her mature life, Emily Dickinson seldom strayed far from her father's house and grounds in Amherst, Massachusetts; yet her rimed lifestudies of a snake, a bee, and a hummingbird contain more poetry than there is in any firsthand description (so far) of the surface of the moon.

W. H. Auden (1907–1973)

THE UNKNOWN CITIZEN

(To JS/07/M/378
This Marble Monument
Is Erected by the State)

He was found by the Bureau of Statistics to be
One against whom there was no official complaint,
And all the reports on his conduct agree
That, in the modern sense of an old-fashioned word, he was a saint,
For in everything he did he served the Greater Community.   5
Except for the War till the day he retired
He worked in a factory and never got fired,
But satisfied his employers, Fudge Motors Inc.
Yet he wasn't a scab or odd in his views,
For his Union reports that he paid his dues,   10
(Our report on his Union shows it was sound)
And our Social Psychology workers found
That he was popular with his mates and liked a drink.
The Press are convinced that he bought a paper every day
And that his reactions to advertisements were normal in every way.   15
Policies taken out in his name prove that he was fully insured,
And his Health-card shows he was once in hospital but left it cured.
Both Producers Research and High-Grade Living declare
He was fully sensible to the advantages of the Installment Plan
And had everything necessary to the Modern Man,   20
A phonograph, a radio, a car and a frigidaire.
Our researchers into Public Opinion are content
That he held the proper opinions for the time of year;
When there was peace, he was for peace; when there was war, he went.
He was married and added five children to the population,   25
Which our Eugenist says was the right number for a parent of his
      generation,
And our teachers report that he never interfered with their education.
Was he free? Was he happy? The question is absurd:
Had anything been wrong, we should certainly have heard.

QUESTIONS

1. Read the three-line epitaph at the beginning of the poem as carefully as you read what follows. How does the epitaph help establish the voice by which the rest of the poem is spoken?
2. Who is speaking?
3. What discrepancies do you find between the speaker's attitude toward his subject and that of the poet himself? By what is the poet's attitude made clear?
4. What does the word *unknown* mean in the name Auden echoes? The Unknown Soldier? What does it mean in the title of this poem?

5. What tendencies in our civilization does Auden satirize?
6. How would you expect the speaker to define a Modern Man, if to such a man, a phonograph, a radio, a car, and a refrigerator are "everything necessary"?

Thomas Lovell Beddoes (1803–1849)
RESURRECTION SONG

Thread the nerves through the right holes,
Get out of my bones, you wormy souls,   2
Shut up my stomach, the ribs are full:
Muscles be steady and ready to pull.   4
Heart and artery merrily shake
And eyelid go up, for we're ready to wake. —   6
His eye must be brighter — one more rub!
And pull up the nostrils! his nose was snub.   8

QUESTION
Who or what is the speaker in this poem? Try to account for the way the pronouns keep changing in person and number (from *my* to *we* to *his*).

EXPERIMENT: *Reading with and without Biography*
Read the following poem and state what you understand from it. Then consider the circumstances in which it probably came to be written. (Some information is offered in a note at the end of this chapter.) Does the meaning of the poem change? To what extent does an appreciation of the poem need the support of biography?

William Carlos Williams (1883–1963)
THE RED WHEELBARROW

so much depends
upon

a red wheel
barrow

glazed with rain   5
water

beside the white
chickens.

SUBJECT, THEME, AND TONE

Poems, like Wordsworth's on daffodils, make statements. But because these are not the direct statements we expect from letters and diary entries, often what a poet *states* tells us less about his attitudes than does whatever he *implies*. Like any other work of art, a poem is likely to reflect the moral and political views of its craftsman, but it does not have to be a declaration of personal belief. To read poetry, we do not have to know the poet's personal creed. That Andrew Marvell belonged to the religious and political party of the Puritans is a fact that few readers have found necessary to recall in reading "To His Coy Mistress."

In looking for the attitude expressed in a poem, it may be helpful to try to state the **theme:** the central thought the poem as a whole conveys. Theme is not the same as "subject matter." For instance:

Theodore Roethke (1908–1963)
My Papa's Waltz

The whiskey on your breath
Could make a small boy dizzy;
But I hung on like death:
Such waltzing was not easy.   4

We romped until the pans
Slid from the kitchen shelf;
My mother's countenance
Could not unfrown itself.   8

The hand that held my wrist
Was battered on one knuckle;
At every step you missed
My right ear scraped a buckle.   12

You beat time on my head
With a palm caked hard by dirt,
Then waltzed me off to bed
Still clinging to your shirt.   16

In this short poem the **subject** — the topic dealt with — is summed up in the title "My Papa's Waltz." The *theme* might be stated: "What fun it was to have my old man romp with me when I was a kid!" Or perhaps: "I really loved my father, I didn't mind his being a rough and dirty drunk."

To state a poet's theme is useful mainly as a way to help oneself understand a poem. The strategy will work more successfully on some poems than on others, with best results to be had from poems that assert some proposition. Some poems declare their themes in their opening lines, as does Wordsworth's "The World Is Too Much With Us" and Herrick's "To the Virgins, to Make Much of Time" ("Gather ye rose-buds while ye may, / Old Time is still a-flying"). The theme of the latter, in fact is so well known that it has a name: **carpe diem** (seize the day), a favorite argument of poets from Catullus to A. E. Housman. Recall Housman's "Loveliest of trees": the subject is cherry blossoms, or the need to look at them; but the theme is "Time flies. Enjoy beauty now!" Theme may be central to a poem by Robert Frost, who prided himself on saying something. "Theme alone can steady us down," wrote Frost of himself and his fellow poets: it can prevent poets from "giving way to undirected associations and kicking ourselves from one chance suggestion to another in all directions as of a hot afternoon in the life of a grasshopper."[2]

EXPERIMENT: *Subject and Theme*

Read a few poems in the anthology at the back of this book and try to state their subjects and their themes. It may help you see the difference between subject and theme if you express each theme in a complete sentence of your own.

In late-show Westerns, when one hombre taunts another, it is customary for the second to drawl, "Smile when you say that, pardner" or "Mister, I don't like your tone of voice." In reading a poem, because we can neither see the poet's face nor hear his voice, we have to infer his attitude from other evidence.

Like tone of voice, **tone** in literature is whatever conveys an attitude toward the person being addressed. Like the manner of a person, the manner of a poem may be friendly or belligerent toward its reader, condescending or respectful. And again, like tone of voice, tone in a poem may tell us how the speaker feels about *himself*; for example, his manner may be cocksure or humble. But most of the time when we ask, "What is the tone of a poem?" we mean, "What attitude does the poet take toward his theme or subject?" Is he affectionate, hostile, earnest, playful, sentimental, sarcastic, or what? We may never be able to know, of course, the poet's true feelings. All we need know are the feelings we are supposed to share while reading the poem on the page. Tone, strictly speaking, is not an attitude but whatever in the poem makes an attitude clear.

In some poems the poet's attitude toward theme and subject, reader and himself may be plain enough to sum up in a word. But in other poems his attitudes may be so mingled that it becomes impossible to describe them tersely without doing his poem an injustice. In "To His Coy Mistress" (p. 324), for instance, does Marvell take a serious or a playful attitude toward the fact that he and his lady are destined to be food for worms? There is no one-word answer. And what of T. S. Eliot's "Love Song of J. Alfred Prufrock" (p. 368)? In his attitude to-

[2] "The Figure a Poem Makes," Frost's preface to *Complete Poems* (New York, 1949).

ward his redemption-seeking hero who wades with trousers rolled, Eliot is seriously funny. Such a mingled tone may be seen in the following poem by the wife of a governor of the Massachusetts Bay Colony and the earliest American poet of note. Anne Bradstreet's first book, *The Tenth Muse Lately Sprung Up in America* (1650), had been published in England without her consent. She wrote these lines to preface a second edition:

Anne Bradstreet (1612?–1672)

THE AUTHOR TO HER BOOK

Thou ill-formed offspring of my feeble brain,
Who after birth did'st by my side remain,   2
Till snatched from thence by friends, less wise than true,
Who thee abroad exposed to public view;   4
Made thee in rags, halting, to the press to trudge,
Where errors were not lessened, all may judge.   6
At thy return my blushing was not small,
My rambling brat (in print) should mother call;   8
I cast thee by as one unfit for light,
Thy visage was so irksome in my sight;   10
Yet being mine own, at length affection would
Thy blemishes amend, if so I could: 12
I washed thy face, but more defects I saw,
And rubbing off a spot, still made a flaw.   14
I stretched thy joints to make thee even feet,
Yet still thou run'st more hobbling than is meet;   16
In better dress to trim thee was my mind,
But nought save homespun cloth in the house I find.   18
In this array, 'mongst vulgars may'st thou roam;
In critics' hands beware thou dost not come;   20
And take thy way where yet thou are not known.
If for thy Father asked, say thou had'st none;   22
And for thy Mother, she alas is poor,
Which caused her thus to send thee out of door.   24

In the author's comparison of her book to an illegitimate ragamuffin, we may be struck by the details of scrubbing and dressing a child: real details that might well occur to a mother who had scrubbed and dressed many. As she might feel toward such a child, so she feels toward her book. She starts by deploring it but, as the poem goes on, cannot deny it her affection. Humor enters (as in the pun in line 15). She must dress the creature in *homespun cloth*, something both crude and serviceable. By the end of her poem, Mrs. Bradstreet seems to regard her book-child with tenderness, amusement, and a certain indulgent awareness of all its faults. To read this poem is to sense its mingling of several attitudes. Simultaneously, a poet can be merry and in earnest.

Walt Whitman (1819–1892)

To a Locomotive in Winter

Thee for my recitative,
Thee in the driving storm even as now, the snow, the winter-day
    declining,
Thee in thy panoply°, thy measur'd dual throbbing and thy   *suit of*
    beat convulsive,   *armor*
Thy black cylindric body, golden brass and silvery steel,
Thy ponderous side-bars, parallel and connecting rods, gyrating,
    shuttling at thy sides,   5
Thy metrical, now swelling pant and roar, now tapering in the distance,
Thy great protruding head-light fix'd in front,
Thy long, pale, floating vapor-pennants, tinged with delicate purple,
The dense and murky clouds out-belching from thy smoke-stack,
Thy knitted frame, thy springs and valves, the tremulous twinkle of
    thy wheels,   10
Thy train of cars behind, obedient, merrily following,
Through gale or calm, now swift, now slack, yet steadily careering;
Type of the modern — emblem of motion and power — pulse of the
    continent,
For once come serve the Muse and merge in verse, even as here I
    see thee,
With storm and buffeting gusts of wind and falling snow,   15
By day thy warning ringing bell to sound its notes,
By night thy silent signal lamps to swing.

Fierce-throated beauty!
Roll through my chant with all thy lawless music, thy swinging lamps
    at night,
Thy madly-whistled laughter, echoing, rumbling like an earthquake,
    rousing all,   20
Law of thyself complete, thine own track firmly holding,
(No sweetness debonair of tearful harp or glib piano thine,)
Thy trills of shrieks by rocks and hills return'd,
Launch'd o'er the prairies wide, across the lakes,
To the free skies unpent and glad and strong.   25

Emily Dickinson (1830–1886)

I like to see it lap the Miles

I like to see it lap the Miles –
And lick the Valleys up –
And stop to feed itself at Tanks –
And then – prodigious step   4

Around a Pile of Mountains —
And supercilious peer

In Shanties – by the sides of Roads –
And then a Quarry pare 8

To fit its Ribs
And crawl between
Complaining all the while
In horrid – hooting stanza –
Then chase itself down Hill – 13

And neigh like Boanerges –
Then – punctual as a Star
Stop – docile and omnipotent
At its own stable door – 17

QUESTIONS

1. What differences in tone do you find between Whitman's and Emily Dickinson's two poems? Point out in each poem whatever contributes to these differences.
2. *Boanerges* in Emily Dickinson's last stanza means "sons of thunder," a name given by Christ to the disciples John and James (see Mark 3:17). How far should the reader work out the particulars of this comparison? Does it make the tone of the poem serious?
3. In Whitman's opening line, what is a *recitative?* What other specialized terms from the vocabulary of music and poetry does each poem contain? How do they help underscore Whitman's theme?
4. Poets and song-writers probably have regarded the locomotive with more affection than they have shown most other machines. Why do you suppose this to be? Can you think of any other poems or songs for example?
5. What do these two poems tell you about locomotives that you would not be likely to find in a technical book on railroading?
6. Are the subjects of both poems identical? Discuss.

Reed Whittemore (b. 1919)

THE FALL OF THE HOUSE OF USHER

It was a big boxy wreck of a house
Owned by a classmate of mine named Rod Usher,
Who lived in the thing with his twin sister.
He was a louse and she was a souse. 4

While I was visiting them one wet summer, she died.
We buried her,
Or rather we stuck her in a back room for a bit, meaning to bury her
When the graveyard dried. 8

But the weather got wetter.
One night we were both waked by a twister,
Plus a screeching and howling outside that turned out to be sister
Up and dying again, making it hard for Rod to forget her. 12

He didn't. He and she died in a heap, and I left quick,
Which was lucky since the house fell in right after,
            Like a ton of brick. 15

QUESTIONS

1. See, if you do not already know it, Edgar Allan Poe's tale of this same name. What differences of tone do you find between Poe's version of the Usher tragedy and Whittemore's?
2. By what means does each writer express his attitude?

EXERCISE: *Telling Subject from Theme*

Here are two radically different poems on a similar subject. Try stating the theme of each poem in your own words. How is tone (the speaker's attitude) also different in each poem? It may not be enough to state a poem's subject. Important, too, are what the poet says and feels about it.

Richard Lovelace (1618–1658)

To Lucasta

On Going to the Wars

Tell me not, Sweet, I am unkind
  That from the nunnery
Of thy chaste breast and quiet mind,
  To war and arms I fly.   4

True, a new mistress now I chase,
  The first foe in the field;
And with a stronger faith embrace
  A sword, a horse, a shield.   8

Yet this inconstancy is such
  As you too shall adore;
I could not love thee, Dear, so much,
  Loved I not Honor more.   12

Wilfred Owen (1893–1918)

Dulce et Decorum Est

Bent double, like old beggars under sacks,
Knock-kneed, coughing like hags, we cursed through sludge,
Till on the haunting flares we turned our backs
And towards our distant rest began to trudge.   4
Men marched asleep. Many had lost their boots
But limped on, blood-shod. All went lame; all blind;
Drunk with fatigue; deaf even to the hoots
Of tired, outstripped Five-Nines° that dropped behind.   *gas-shells* 8

Gas! Gas! Quick, boys! — An ecstasy of fumbling,
Fitting the clumsy helmets just in time;
But someone still was yelling out and stumbling
And flound'ring like a man in fire or lime . . .   12
Dim, through the misty panes and thick green light,
As under a green sea, I saw him drowning.

In all my dreams, before my helpless sight,
He plunges at me, guttering, choking, drowning.   16

If in some smothering dreams you too could pace
Behind the wagon that we flung him in,
And watch the white eyes writhing in his face,
His hanging face, like a devil's sick of sin;   20
If you could hear, at every jolt, the blood
Come gargling from the froth-corrupted lungs,
Obscene as cancer, bitter as the cud
Of vile, incurable sores on innocent tongues, —   24
My friend, you would not tell with such high zest
To children ardent for some desperate glory,
The old Lie: Dulce et decorum est
Pro patria mori.   28

DULCE ET DECORUM EST. A British infantry officer in World War I, Owen was killed in action. 17. *you too:* Some manuscript versions of this poem carry the dedication "To Jessie Pope" (a writer of patriotic verse) or "To a certain Poetess." 27–28. *Dulce et . . . mori:* A quotation from the Latin poet Horace, "It is sweet and fitting to die for one's country."

James Simmons (b. 1933)

CAVALIER LYRIC

I sometimes sleep with other girls
in boudoir or cheap joint,
with energy and tenderness
trying not to disappoint.   4
So do not think of helpful whores
as aberrational blots;
I could not love you half so well
without my practice shots.   8

QUESTIONS

1. What does Simmons owe to Richard Lovelace's "To Lucasta"?
2. To what do you attribute the difference in tone between the two poems?

LYRIC AND DIDACTIC

A lyric, as its Greek name suggests, was a poem sung to the music of a lyre. Today, **lyric** denotes a short poem expressing the thoughts and feelings of a single speaker: "I like to see it lap the Miles." Lyrics at present are more plentiful than any other kind of poem in English (short stories and novels having virtually replaced long narrative poems formerly popular, such as Browning's *The Ring and the Book* and Tennyson's *Idylls of the King*).

A lyric is often written in the first person ("I wandered lonely as a cloud"), but not always. It may be a description of, say, a landscape, in which the poet does not mention himself at all; for instance, Hopkins's "Inversnaid" (p. 158). Though a lyric may relate an incident or episode, we tend to think of it as a reflective poem in which little physical action takes place. Lyric poetry includes such varieties as the **ode**, usually longer than other lyrics and characterized by a tone of seriousness and elevation (Wordsworth's "Ode: Intimations of Immortality," Shelley's "Ode to the West Wind," Keats's "Ode to a Nightingale" and "Ode on a Grecian Urn"); and the **elegy**, whose tone is melancholy or sadly contemplative, often on the subject of a death (Milton's "Lycidas" and Whitman's "When Lilacs Last in the Dooryard Bloom'd").

In **didactic poetry** — poetry apparently written to teach or convey a message — themes are more evident. In a lyric, the speaker may express sadness; in a didactic poem, he may explain that sadness is inherent in life. Usually a didactic poem clearly states or implies a moral or sets forth a critical comment on society. The name can also refer to a long poem that imparts a body of knowledge: Lucretius's *On the Nature of Things*, Ovid's *Art of Love*, Karl Shapiro's *Essay on Rime*. Such poetry was favored especially by classical Latin poets and by English poets of the eighteenth century. In *The Fleece* (1757), John Dyer celebrated the British woolen industry and included practical advice on raising sheep:

> In cold stiff soils the bleaters oft complain
> Of gouty ails, by shepherds termed the halt:
> Those let the neighboring fold or ready crook
> Detain, and pour into their cloven feet
> Corrosive drugs, deep-searching arsenic,
> Dry alum, verdegris, or vitriol keen.
> But if the doubtful mischief scare appears,
> 'Twill serve to shift them to a dryer turf,
> And salt again: the utility of salt
> Teach thy slow swains; redundant humors cold
> Are the diseases of the bleating kind.

One might agree with Dr. Johnson's comment on Dyer's effort: "The subject, Sir, cannot be made poetical." But it may be argued that didactic poetry — to quote a recent view — "is not intrinsically any less poetic because of its subject matter than lines about a rose fluttering in the breeze are intrinsically more poetic because of their subject-matter."[3] John Milton also described sick sheep in "Lycidas," a poem few readers have thought unpoetic:

> The hungry sheep look up, and are not fed,
> But, swoll'n with wind and the rank mist they draw,
> Rot inwardly, and foul contagion spread . . .

[3] Sylvan Barnet, Morton Berman, and William Burto, *A Dictionary of Literary Terms* (Boston, 1960).

What makes Milton's lines better poetry than Dyer's is, among other things, a difference in tone. Sick sheep to Dyer mean the loss of a few shillings and pence; to Milton, whose sheep stand for English Christendom, they mean a moral catastrophe.

A tone of detached amusement, withering contempt, and implied superiority is characteristic of **satiric poetry,** a kind of didactic poetry. In a satiric poem, the poet ridicules some person or persons, or some aspect of human behavior, examining his victim by the light of his own principles and implying that the reader ought to share his view.

Countee Cullen (1903–1946)

FOR A LADY I KNOW

She even thinks that up in heaven
   Her class lies late and snores,
While poor black cherubs rise at seven
   To do celestial chores.

QUESTIONS

1. What is Cullen's message?
2. How would you characterize the tone of this poem? Wrathful? Amused?

Ambrose Bierce (1842–1914?)

ART

One day a wag — what would the wretch be at? —	
Shifted a letter of the cipher RAT,	2
And said it was a god's name! Straight arose	
Fantastic priests and postulants (with shows,	4
And mysteries, and mummeries, and hymns,	
And disputations dire that lamed their limbs)	6
To serve his temple and maintain the fires,	
Expound the law, manipulate the wires.	8
Amazed, the populace the rites attend,	
Believe whate'er they cannot comprehend,	10
And, inly edified to learn that two	
Half-hairs joined so and so (as Art can do)	12
Have sweeter values and a grace more fit	
Than Nature's hairs that never have been split,	14
Bring cates° and wines for sacrificial feasts,	*delicacies*
And sell their garments to support the priests.	16

QUESTIONS

1. What is the tone of this poem? By what various means is it communicated?
2. What is Bierce against? Is it art?

MASK AND IRONY

In classic Greek drama, actors wore *personae:* the Latin term for megaphone-like masks through which sound came. From this term is derived our word *person.* In the works of great playwrights, whether classical or modern, those speaking masks we call the persons of a drama are such persuasive imitations of life that we may forget we are watching a performance in a theater. We do not think, when Romeo plights his tragic love or when King Oedipus at last perceives the trick of the Fates against him, that what we hear is the voice of one man representing a fictive man, speaking words that still another man wrote.

And so, reading many a poem, we overhear words spoken to us through a **mask** (or fictitious person); and if the poem succeeds, we accept a convincing imitation of life. The mask and the poet's face may not be similar: a young male poet may write a lyric spoken by an elderly female. William Blake was white, but he wrote a poem uttered by a black child; he was an eighteenth-century engraver, but he wrote a poem spoken by the ancient magician Merlin. The speaker in a poem need not even be human: there are good poems spoken by clouds, pebbles, and cats. An evident mask-making occurs in a **dramatic monologue:** a poem cast as a speech by a single person, made at a decisive or revealing moment, addressed to some other character, who does not speak. Robert Browning, who perfected the form, was fond of putting words into the mouths of characters only remotely like himself. (See "Soliloquy of the Spanish Cloister," p. 340. Browning, from most reports, was likable.)

To notice a distance between the poet and his mask is to be aware of **irony:** a manner of speaking that implies a discrepancy. If the mask says one thing and we sense that the writer is in fact saying something else, the writer is using an **ironic point of view.** No finer illustration exists in English than Jonathan Swift's "A Modest Proposal," an essay in which Swift speaks as an earnest, humorless citizen who sets forth his reasonable plan to aid the Irish poor. The plan is so monstrous no sane reader can assent to it: the poor are to sell their children as meat for the tables of their landlords. From behind his falseface, Swift recommends not cannibalism but love and Christian charity. An ironic point of view need not imply bitter humor, as it does in Swift's essay. Here is a poem in which an innocent child speaks. Behind the mask of the child, though, we sense a compassionate and knowing poet.

Robert Herrick (1591–1674)
ANOTHER GRACE FOR A CHILD

Here a little child I stand,
Heaving up my either hand;

Cold as paddocks° though they be,   *toads*
Here I lift them up to Thee
For a benison° to fall   *benediction*
On our meat, and on us all. *Amen.*

A poem is often made complicated and more interesting by another kind of irony. **Verbal irony** occurs whenever words say one thing
but mean something else, usually the opposite. The word *love* means
hate here: "I just *love* to stay home and do my hair on a Saturday
night!" **Sarcasm,** a kind of verbal irony, occurs in heavy-handed, bitter, and mocking statements designed to hurt someone: "Oh, he's
the biggest spender in the world, all right!" (The irony, if that statement
were spoken, would be underscored by the speaker's tone of voice.) A
famous instance of sarcasm is Mark Antony's line in his oration over
the body of slain Julius Caesar: "Brutus is an honorable man." Antony
repeats this line until the enraged populace begins shouting exactly
what he means to call Brutus and the other conspirators: traitors, vil-
lains, murderers. We had best be alert for irony on the printed page,
for if we miss it, our interpretations of a poem may go wild.

Robert Creeley (b. 1926)
Oh No

If you wander far enough
you will come to it
and when you get there
they will give you a place to sit   4

for yourself only, in a nice chair,
and all your friends will be there
with smiles on their faces
and they will likewise all have places.   8

This poem is rich in verbal irony. The title helps point out that between
the speaker's words and his attitude lie deep differences. In line 2,
what is *it*? Old age? The wandering suggests a conventional metaphor:
the journey of life. Is *it* literally a rest home for "senior citizens," or
perhaps some naïve popular concept of heaven (such as we meet in
comic strips: harps, angels with hoops for haloes) in which the saved
all sit around in a ring, smugly congratulating one another? We cannot be sure, but the speaker's attitude toward this final sitting-place
is definite. It is a place for the selfish, as we infer from the phrase
for yourself only. And *smiles on their faces* may hint that the smiles are
unchanging and forced. There is a difference between saying "They

had smiles on their faces" and "They smiled": the latter suggests that the smiles came from within. The word *nice* is to be regarded with distrust. If we see through this speaker, as Creeley implies we can do, we realize that, while pretending to be sweet-talking us into a seat, actually he is revealing the horror of a little hell. And the title is the poet's reaction to it (or the speaker's unironic, straightforward one): "Oh no! Not *that!*"

Dramatic irony usually refers to a situation in a play wherein a character, whose knowledge is limited, says, does, or encounters something of greater significance than he knows. We, the spectators, realize the meaning of this speech or action, for the playwright has afforded us superior knowledge. In Sophocles' *King Oedipus*, when Oedipus vows to punish whoever has brought down a plague upon the city of Thebes, we know — as he does not — that the man he would punish is himself. (Referring to such a situation that precedes the downfall of a hero in a tragedy, some critics speak of **tragic irony** instead of dramatic irony.) Superior knowledge can be enjoyed not only by spectators in a theater but by readers of poetry as well. In *Paradise Lost*, we know in advance that Adam will fall into temptation, and we recognize his overconfidence when he neglects a warning. The situation of Oedipus contains also **cosmic irony,** or **irony of fate:** some Fate with a grim sense of humor seems cruelly to trick a man. Cosmic irony clearly exists in poems in which fate or the Fates are personified and seen as hostile, as in Thomas Hardy's "The Convergence of the Twain" (p. 347); and it may be said to occur too in a poem such as Robinson's "Richard Cory" (p. 105) and in MacLeish's "The End of the World" (p. 8). Evidently it is a twist of fate for the most envied man in town to kill himself and another twist of fate for spectators at a circus to find themselves suddenly beholding a greater and more horrific show than they had paid for.

To sum up: the effect of irony depends upon the reader's noticing some incongruity or discrepancy between two things. In *verbal irony*, there is a contrast between the speaker's words and his meaning; in an *ironic point of view*, between the writer's attitude and those spoken by a fictitious character; in *dramatic irony*, between the limited knowledge of a character and the fuller knowledge of the reader or spectator; in *cosmic irony*, between a character's aspirations and the treatment he receives at the hands of Fate. Although in the work of an inept poet, irony can be crude and obvious sarcasm, it is invaluable to a poet of more complicated mind, who imagines more than one perspective.

EXERCISE: *Detecting Irony*
Point out the kinds of irony that occur in the following poem.

Thomas Hardy (1840–1928)

THE WORKBOX

"See, here's the workbox, little wife,
  That I made of polished oak."
He was a joiner°, of village life;   *carpenter*
  She came of borough folk.   4

He holds the present up to her
  As with a smile she nears
And answers to the profferer,
  " 'Twill last all my sewing years!"   8

"I warrant it will. And longer too.
  'Tis a scantling that I got
Off poor John Wayward's coffin, who
  Died of they knew not what.   12

"The shingled pattern that seems to cease
  Against your box's rim
Continues right on in the piece
  That's underground with him.   16

"And while I worked it made me think
  Of timber's varied doom:
One inch where people eat and drink,
  The next inch in a tomb.   20

"But why do you look so white, my dear,
  And turn aside your face?
You knew not that good lad, I fear,
  Though he came from your native place?"   24

"How could I know that good young man,
  Though he came from my native town,
When he must have left far earlier than
  I was a woman grown?"   28

"Ah, no. I should have understood!
  It shocked you that I gave
To you one end of a piece of wood
  Whose other is in a grave?"   32

"Don't, dear, despise my intellect,
  Mere accidental things
Of that sort never have effect
  On my imaginings."   36

Yet still her lips were limp and wan,
  Her face still held aside,
As if she had known not only John,
  But known of what he died.   40

John Betjeman (b. 1906)

In Westminster Abbey

Let me take this other glove off
  As the *vox humana* swells,
And the beauteous fields of Eden
  Bask beneath the Abbey bells.
Here, where England's statesmen lie,
Listen to a lady's cry.   6

Gracious Lord, oh bomb the Germans.
  Spare their women for Thy Sake,
And if that is not too easy
  We will pardon Thy Mistake.   10
But, gracious Lord, whate'er shall be,
Don't let anyone bomb me.   12

Keep our Empire undismembered,
  Guide our Forces by Thy Hand,
Gallant blacks from far Jamaica,
  Honduras and Togoland;   16
Protect them Lord in all their fights,
And, even more, protect the whites.   18

Think of what our Nation stands for:
  Books from Boots' and country lanes,
Free speech, free passes, class distinction,
  Democracy and proper drains.   22
Lord, put beneath Thy special care
One-eighty-nine Cadogan Square.   24

Although dear Lord I am a sinner,
  I have done no major crime;
Now I'll come to Evening Service
  Whensoever I have the time.   28
So, Lord, reserve for me a crown,
And do not let my shares go down.   30

I will labor for Thy Kingdom,
  Help our lads to win the war,
Send white feathers to the cowards,
  Join the Women's Army Corps,   34
Then wash the Steps around Thy Throne
In the Eternal Safety Zone.   36

Now I feel a little better,
  What a treat to hear Thy Word,
Where the bones of leading statesmen,
  Have so often been interred.   40
And now, dear Lord, I cannot wait
Because I have a luncheon date.   42

IN WESTMINSTER ABBEY. Published during World War II. 2. *vox humana:* An organ stop that makes tones similar to those of the human voice. 20. *Boots':* A cut-rate pharmacy.

QUESTIONS

1. Who is the speaker? What do we know about her life style? About her prejudices?
2. Point out some of the places in which she contradicts herself.
3. How would you describe the speaker's attitude toward religion?
4. Through the medium of irony, what positive points do you believe Betjeman makes?

FOR REVIEW AND FURTHER STUDY

Anonymous (Irish ballad; eighteenth century)
JOHNNY, I HARDLY KNEW YE

While going the road to sweet Athy,
  Hurroo! Hurroo!
While going the road to sweet Athy,
  Hurroo! Hurroo!
While going the road to sweet Athy,   5
A stick in my hand and a drop in my eye,
A doleful damsel I heard cry:
  "Och, Johnny, I hardly knew ye!

Chorus:

"With drums and guns, and guns and drums
  The enemy near slew ye;   10
My darling dear, you look so queer,
  Och, Johnny, I hardly knew ye!

"Where are your eyes that looked so mild?
  Hurroo! Hurroo!
Where are your eyes that looked so mild   15
When my poor heart you first beguiled?
Why did you run from me and the child?
  Och, Johnny, I hardly knew ye!

"Where are the legs with which you run?
  Hurroo! Hurroo!   20
Where are the legs with which you run
When you went off to carry a gun? —
Indeed your dancing days are done!
  Och, Johnny, I hardly knew ye!

"It grieved my heart to see you sail,   25
  Hurroo! Hurroo!
It grieved my heart to see you sail
Though from my heart you took leg bail°   *escaped from custody*

Like a cod you're doubled up head and tail,
   Och, Johnny, I hardly knew ye!   30

"You haven't an arm and you haven't a leg,
   Hurroo! Hurroo!
You haven't an arm and you haven't a leg,
You're an eyeless, noseless, chickenless egg,
You'll have to be put in a bowl to beg,   35
   Och, Johnny, I hardly knew ye!

"It's happy I am for to see you home,
   Hurroo! Hurroo!
It's happy I am for to see you home,
All from the island of Sulloon,   40
So low in flesh, so high in bone,
   Och, Johnny, I hardly knew ye!

"But sad as it is to see you so,
   Hurroo! Hurroo!
But sad as it is to see you so,   45
And to think of you now as an object of woe,
Your Peggy'll still keep ye on as her beau —
   Och, Johnny, I hardly knew ye!"

JOHNNY, I HARDLY KNEW YE. A forerunner of the song "When Johnny Comes Marching Home Again (Hurrah! Hurrah!)." Each stanza, like the first, repeats the opening two lines and concludes with the chorus. 40. *Sulloon:* Ceylon. In the eighteenth century, Irish troops fought in the British colonization of Ceylon and India.

QUESTIONS

1. What attitude or attitudes does Peggy take toward Johnny?
2. What does the poem lead us to feel toward her?
3. What does the poet gain by placing Peggy's words within a dramatic frame (by having her lament overheard by another speaker)?
4. Taking the poem as a whole, how would you describe its tone?

Barry Spacks (b. 1931)

MALEDICTION

You who dump the beer cans in the lake;
who in the strict woods sow
the bulbous polyethylene retorts;
who from your farting car
with spiffy rear-suspension toss   5
your tissues, mustard-streaked, upon
the generating moss; who drop
the squamules° of your reckless play,   *small scales (of a fish or snake)*
grease-wrappers, unspare parts, lie-labeled
cultures even flies would scorn   10
to spawn on — total Zed, my kinsman

ass-on-wheels, my blare-bred bray
and burden, may the nice crabs thread
your private wilds with turnpikes; weasels'
condoms squish between your toes   15
and plastic-coated toads squat *plop*
upon your morning egg — may gars
come nudge you from your inner-tube,
perch hiss you to the bottom, junked,
a discard, your dense self your last   20
enormity.

QUESTIONS

1. What is the subject of this poem? Its theme? Its tone?
2. What kinds of irony does the poet employ?

Ted Hughes (b. 1930)

SECRETARY

If I should touch her she would shriek and weeping
Crawl off to nurse the terrible wound: all
Day like a starling under the bellies of bulls
She hurries among men, ducking, peeping,   4

Off in a whirl at the first move of a horn.
At dusk she scuttles down the gauntlet of lust
Like a clockwork mouse. Safe home at last
She mends her socks with holes, shirts that are torn   8

For father and brother, and a delicate supper cooks:
Goes to bed early, shuts out with the light
Her thirty years, and lies with buttocks tight,
Hiding her lovely eyes until day break.   12

QUESTIONS

1. Comment on the phrase in line 2, *the terrible wound*. Would the speaker
   himself regard the offense as "terrible"?
2. What traits has the secretary in common with *a starling* (line 3) and *a clockwork mouse* (line 7)?
3. Does the poet express one attitude toward his subject or is the tone of his
   poem a mingling of more than one? Explain, referring to particulars in the
   poem.

John Berryman (1914–1972)

LIFE, FRIENDS, IS BORING. WE MUST NOT SAY SO

Life, friends, is boring. We must not say so.
After all, the sky flashes, the great sea yearns,
we ourselves flash and yearn,

and moreover my mother told me as a boy
(repeatedly) "Ever to confess you're bored
means you have no   6

Inner Resources." I conclude now I have no
inner resources, because I am heavy bored.
Peoples bore me,
literature bores me, especially great literature,
Henry bores me, with his plights & gripes
as bad as achilles,

who loves people and valiant art, which bores me.
And the tranquil hills, & gin, look like a drag
and somehow a dog
has taken itself & its tail considerably away
into mountains or sea or sky, leaving
behind: me, wag.   18

QUESTIONS

1. Henry (line 11) is the central figure of Berryman's *77 Dream Songs*. Achilles
   (line 12), Greek hero of the Trojan war, was portrayed by Shakespeare as a
   sulking malcontent. Is a comparison of Henry, a rather ordinary American
   citizen, to Achilles likely to result in a heightening of Henry's importance
   or in a sense of ironic discrepancy? Discuss.
2. What is confused or self-contradictory in the precept "Ever to confess you're
   bored means you have no Inner Resources"?
3. What could the poet be trying to indicate by capitalizing *Inner Resources* in
   line 7 but not in line 8? By writing *achilles* with a small letter?
4. In line 14, what discrepancy do you find between the phrases *the tranquil
   hills* and *a drag*?
5. In the last line, what double meaning is there in the word *wag*?
6. True or false? "In comparing 'ourselves' to the sky and to the 'great sea,'
   the speaker takes the attitude that he and his readers have dignity and
   grandeur, their emotions being as powerful as lightningbolts and tides."
   Do you find this paraphrase consistent or inconsistent with the tone of the
   poem? Why?

EXERCISE: *Persons in Poems*

For each of the following poems, consider these questions:

1. What is the poet's subject?
2. What is his theme?
3. Does he speak as himself, or through the mask of any particular character?
4. What is the speaker's attitude toward his subject?
5. Whom does the speaker address? What attitude does he take toward this
   hearer?
6. Is there any ironic discrepancy between attitudes expressed by the speaker
   and those we are supposed to feel?
7. Is this poem a lyric? A didactic poem? Or does neither label apply?

William Blake (1757–1827)

THE CHIMNEY SWEEPER

When my mother died I was very young,
And my father sold me while yet my tongue
Could scarcely cry " 'weep! 'weep! 'weep! 'weep!"
So your chimneys I sweep, and in soot I sleep.   4

There's little Tom Dacre, who cried when his head,
That curled like a lamb's back, was shaved: so I said
"Hush, Tom! never mind it, for when your head's bare
You know that the soot cannot spoil your white hair."   8

And so he was quiet, and that very night,
As Tom was a-sleeping, he had such a sight!
That thousands of sweepers, Dick, Joe, Ned, and Jack,
Were all of them locked up in coffins of black.   12

And by came an Angel who had a bright key,
And he opened the coffins and set them all free;
Then down a green plain leaping, laughing, they run,
And wash in a river, and shine in the sun.   16

Then naked and white, all their bags left behind,
They rise upon clouds and sport in the wind;
And the Angel told Tom, if he'd be a good boy,
He'd have God for his father, and never want joy.   20

And so Tom awoke; and we rose in the dark,
And got with our bags and our brushes to work.
Though the morning was cold, Tom was happy and warm;
So if all do their duty they need not fear harm.   24

John Milton (1608–1674)

ON THE LATE MASSACRE IN PIEMONT

Avenge, O Lord, thy slaughtered saints, whose bones
  Lie scattered on the Alpine mountains cold;
  Even them who kept thy truth so pure of old,
  When all our fathers worshiped stocks and stones,   4
Forget not: in thy book record their groans
  Who were thy sheep, and in their ancient fold
  Slain by the bloody Piemontese, that rolled
  Mother with infant down the rocks. Their moans   8
The vales redoubled to the hills, and they
  To heaven. Their martyred blood and ashes sow
  O'er all the Italian fields, where still doth sway
The triple Tyrant; that from these may grow
  A hundredfold, who, having learnt thy way,
  Early may fly the Babylonian woe.   14

On the Late Massacre in Piemont. Despite hostility between Catholics and Protestants, the Waldenses, members of a Puritan sect, had been living in the Piemont, that region in northwest Italy bounded by the crests of the Alps. In 1655, ignoring a promise to observe religious liberty, troops of the Roman Catholic ruler of the Piemont put to death several members of the sect. 4. *When . . . stones:* Englishmen had been Catholics, worshiping stone and wooden statues (so Milton charges) when the Waldensian sect was founded in the twelfth century. 12. *The triple Tyrant:* The Pope, to whom is attributed authority over earth, heaven, and hell. 14. *Babylonian woe:* Destruction expected to befall the city of Babylon at the world's end as punishment for its luxury and other wickedness (see Revelation 18:1–24). Protestants took Babylon to mean the Church of Rome.

Jonathan Swift (1667–1745)

On Stella's Birthday

Stella this day is thirty-four
(We shan't dispute a year or more) —   2
However, Stella, be not troubled,
Although thy size and years are doubled,   4
Since first I saw thee at sixteen,
The brightest virgin on the green,   6
So little is thy form declined,
Made up so largely in thy mind.   8
   Oh, would it please the gods, to split
Thy beauty, size, and years, and wit,   10
No age could furnish out a pair
Of nymphs so graceful, wise, and fair,   12
With half the luster of your eyes,
With half your wit, your years, and size.   14
And then, before it grew too late,
How should I beg of gentle Fate   16
(That either nymph might have her swain)
To split my worship too in twain.   18

On Stella's Birthday. 18. *my worship:* As Dean of St. Patrick's in Dublin, Swift was addressed as "Your Worship."

Information for Experiment: *Reading with and without Biography*

The Red Wheelbarrow (p. 13). Dr. Williams's poem reportedly contains a personal experience: he was gazing from the window of the house where one of his patients, a small girl, lay suspended between life and death. (This account, from the director of the public library in Williams's native Rutherford, N.J., is given by Geri M. Rhodes in "The Paterson Metaphor in William Carlos Williams' *Paterson*," master's essay, Tufts University, June 1965.)

3 Words and Their Order

Whether the poet wears a mask or speaks to us person-to-person, a poem confronts us with some kind of face. We have now to consider what comes through this face: words.

THE RIGHT WORD

Unable to fill a two-syllable gap in an unfinished line that went "The seal's wide — — gaze toward Paradise," the American poet Hart Crane began paging through an unabridged dictionary. When he had reached *S*, he found the object of his quest in *spindrift:* sea spray driven by a strong wind. The word is exact and memorable. A word, however, does not have to be so unusual to be *le mot juste.* Any word can be the right word, if used in the right place. It may be a word as ordinary and everyday as *from.* Consider the difference between "The sedge is withered *on* the lake" (a misquotation of a line by Keats) and "The sedge is withered *from* the lake" (what Keats in fact wrote). Keats's line suggests, as the altered line does not, that, because the sedge (a growth of grasslike plants) has withered *from* the lake, it seems to have withdrawn mysteriously.

It is a temptation for some poets, especially novices, to invent new words, ignoring the existing resources of the English language. Such a poet will never say "Her eyes shine like a chipmunk's" or "Her chipmunk eyes shine" if he can say "Her chipmunkeyeshine" or "Her chipmunkily-shiny eyes." But a master poet — even experiment-loving E. E. Cummings — seems to regard an invented word as a thing for special occasions. When Gerard Manley Hopkins calls a falcon "dapple-dawn-drawn," the coined word startles, but startles us into the realization that the poet really *is* looking at bird and dawn through fresh eyes, seeing qualities that could hardly be expressed in language more conventional. Memorable, too, is the coined word in the opening of a poem by Emily Dickinson: "The overtakelessness of those/ Who have accomplished Death. . . ." Most words in poetry, however, are the common property of all of us, and often *le mot juste* is what novelist Joseph Conrad called "the fresh usual word." Each word is both fresh and usual in the following poem:

Walter Savage Landor (1775–1864)
MOTHER, I CANNOT MIND MY WHEEL

Mother, I cannot mind my wheel;
   My fingers ache, my lips are dry:
Oh! if you felt the pain I feel!
   But oh, who ever felt as I!   4

No longer could I doubt him true,
   All other men may use deceit;
He always said my eyes were blue,
   And often swore my lips were sweet.   8

The words are those we might expect to break from the lips of an actual girl expressing grief. How well Landor has chosen them and set them in place may be seen by rewriting the poem, substituting a few different words:

> Mom, I can't tend my spinningwheel;
>   I have chapped lips, my fingers hurt:
> Ouch! you should feel the pain I feel!
>   No girl was ever done such dirt!

The superiority of Landor's version should be evident. It inheres not in unusual words, but in his ability to persuade us that his words correspond to the girl's feelings.

If a poet troubles to seek out the best words available, the least we can do is to find out what his words mean. This is to suggest that the dictionary is a firm ally in reading poems and, if the poems are more than a century old, is indispensable. Meanings change. As T. S. Eliot reminds us in "Burnt Norton,"

>   Words strain,
> Crack and sometimes break, under the burden,
> Under the tension, slip, slide, perish,
> Decay with imprecision, will not stay in place,
> Will not stay still.

When the Elizabethan poet George Gascoigne wrote, "O Abraham's brats, O brood of blessed seed," the word *brats* implied neither irritation nor contempt. When in the seventeenth century Andrew Marvell imagined two lovers' "vegetable love," he referred to a vegetative or growing love, not one resembling a lettuce. And when King George III called a building an "awful artificial spectacle," he was not condemning it but praising it as an awe-inspiring work of art.

In reading poetry, there is nothing to be done about this inevitable tendency of language except to watch out for it. If you suspect that a word has shifted in meaning over the years, most standard desk dictionaries will be helpful, an unabridged dictionary more helpful yet, and most helpful of all the *Oxford English Dictionary* (*OED*), which gives, for each definition, successive examples of the word's written use down through the past thousand years. (No reader need feel a grim obligation to keep interrupting a poem in order to rummage his dictionary; but if the poem is worth reading very closely, he may wish any aid he can find.)

When is a word the right word? No ironclad rules can decide. And yet, because precise observation — whether of something real or something imaginary — is a quality we expect of good poetry, we do find a poet often striving for words that point to physical details and solid objects. He may do so even when his subject is an abstract idea:

> Beauty is but a flower
> Which wrinkles will devour;
> Brightness falls from the air,
> Queens have died young and fair,
> Dust hath closed Helen's eye.
> I am sick, I must die:
>   Lord, have mercy on us!

In these lines by Thomas Nashe, the abstraction *beauty* has grown petals that shrivel. Brightness may be a general name for light, but Nashe succeeds in giving it the weight of a falling body. By the way, some editors believe that *air* in the third line is a printer's error for "hair." Which version makes for a better poem?

If a poem reads *daffodils* instead of *vegetation, diaper years* instead of *infancy*, and *eighty-four* instead of *numerous*, we may call its **diction** — its choice of words — particular and concrete, rather than general and abstract. In an apt criticism, William Butler Yeats once took to task the poems of W. E. Henley for lacking particularity and concreteness. Henley's poetry (said Yeats) is "abstract, as even an actor's movement can be when the thought of doing is plainer to his mind than the doing itself: the straight line from cup to lip, let us say, more plain than the hand's own sensation weighed down by that heavy spillable cup."[1] To find words to convey the sense of that heavy spillable cup was to Yeats a goal, one that surely he attained in "Among School Children" by describing a woman's stark face: "Hollow of cheek as though it drank the wind / And took a mess of shadows for its meat." A more abstract-minded poet might have written "Her hollow cheek and wasted, hungry look." Ezra Pound gave a famous piece of advice to

---

[1] *The Trembling of the Veil* (1922), reprinted in *The Autobiography of William Butler Yeats* (New York, 1953), p. 177.

his fellow poets: "Go in fear of abstractions." This is *not* to say that a poet cannot employ abstract words, nor that all poems have to be about physical things. The abstractness of much of T. S. Eliot's *Four Quartets* — a poem concerned with time, eternity, history, language, reality, and other things that cannot be handled — is evidence to the contrary.

One of the valuable services of poetry is to recall for us the concrete, physical sense that certain words once had but have lost. "Every word which is used to express a moral or intellectual fact," said Emerson in *The Conduct of Life,* "if traced to its root, is found to be borrowed from some material appearance. Right means straight; wrong means twisted. Spirit primarily means wind; transgression, the crossing of a line; supercilious, the raising of an eyebrow." Browse among the derivations of English words given in a dictionary, and you will discover such concretenesses (*squirrel,* for one more instance, comes from two Greek words meaning *shadow-tail*). We tend to forget that words depend on what is tangible. As the English critic H. Coombes has remarked in *Literature and Criticism,*

> We use a word like *powerful* without feeling that it is really "power-full." We do not seem today to taste the full flavor of words as we feel that Falstaff (and Shakespeare, and probably his audience) tasted them when he was applauding the virtues of "good sherris-sack," which makes the brain "apprehensive, quick, forgetive, full of nimble, fiery, and delectable shapes." And being less aware of the life and substantiality of words, we are probably less aware of the things . . . that these words stand for.

A good writer, said Thomas Carlyle, makes us aware of things: "Wonderful it is with what cutting words, now and then, he severs asunder the confusion; shears it down, were it furlongs deep, into the true center of the matter; and there not only hits the nail on the head, but with crushing force smites it home, and buries it." Like other good writers, good poets remind us of that smitten nail and that spillable cup. "Perhaps indeed," wrote Walt Whitman in *Specimen Days,* "the efforts of the true poets, founders, religions, literatures, all ages, have been, and ever will be, our time and times to come, essentially the same — to bring people back from their persistent strayings and sickly abstractions, to the costless, average, divine, original concrete."

EXPERIMENT: *Seeing Words' Origins*

Much of the effect of the following poem depends upon our awareness of the precision with which the poet selects his words. We can better see this by knowing their derivations. For instance, *potpourri* comes from French: *pot* plus *pourri.* What do these words mean? (If you do not know French, look up the etymology of the word in a dictionary.) Look up the definitions and etymologies of *revenance, circumstance, inspiration, conceptual, commotion, cordial,* and *azure;* and try to state the meanings these words have in Wilbur's poem.

Richard Wilbur (b. 1921)

In the Elegy Season

Haze, char, and the weather of All Souls':
A giant absence mopes upon the trees:
Leaves cast in casual potpourris
Whisper their scents from pits and cellar-holes.   4

Or brewed in gulleys, steeped in wells, they spend
In chilly steam their last aromas, yield
From shallow hells a revenance of field
And orchard air. And now the envious mind   8

Which could not hold the summer in my head
While bounded by that blazing circumstance
Parades these barrens in a golden trance,
Remembering the wealthy season dead,   12

And by an autumn inspiration makes
A summer all its own. Green boughs arise
Through all the boundless backward of the eyes,
And the soul bathes in warm conceptual lakes.   16

Less proud than this, my body leans an ear
Past cold and colder weather after wings'
Soft commotion, the sudden race of springs,
The goddess' tread heard on the dayward stair,   20

Longs for the brush of the freighted air, for smells
Of grass and cordial lilac, for the sight
Of green leaves building into the light
And azure water hoisting out of wells.   24

John Clare (1793–1864)

Mouse's Nest

I found a ball of grass among the hay
And progged it as I passed and went away;   2
And when I looked I fancied something stirred,
And turned again and hoped to catch the bird —   4
When out an old mouse bolted in the wheats
With all her young ones hanging at her teats;   6
She looked so odd and so grotesque to me,
I ran and wondered what the thing could be,   8
And pushed the knapweed bunches where I stood;
Then the mouse hurried from the craking° brood.   *crying*   10
The young ones squeaked, and as I went away
She found her nest again among the hay.   12
The water o'er the pebbles scarce could run
And broad old cesspools glittered in the sun.   14

1. "To prog" (line 2) means "to poke about for food, to forage." In what ways does this word fit more exactly here than *prodded, touched,* or *searched?*
2. Is *craking* (line 10) better than *crying?* Which word better fits the poem? Why?
3. What connections do you find between the last two lines and the rest of the poem? To what are water that *scarce could run* and *broad old cesspools* (lines 13, 14) likened?

Knute Skinner (b. 1929)

THE COLD IRISH EARTH

I shudder thinking
of the cold Irish earth.
The firelighter flares
in the kitchen range,
but a cold rain falls   5
all around Liscannor.
It scours the Hag's face
on the Cliffs of Moher.
It runs through the bog
and seeps up into mounds   10
of abandoned turf.
My neighbor's fields are chopped
by the feet of cattle
sinking down to the roots
of winter grass.   15
That coat hangs drying now
by the kitchen range,
but down at Healy's cross
the Killaspuglonane graveyard
is wet to the bone.   20

QUESTIONS

1. To what familiar phrase does Skinner's poem lend fresh meaning? What is its usual meaning?
2. What details in the poem show us that, in using the old phrase, Skinner literally means what he says?

Peter Davison (b. 1928)

THE LAST WORD

When I saw your head bow, I knew I had beaten you.
You shed no tears — not near me — but held your neck
Bare for the blow I had been too frightened
Ever to deliver, even in words. And now,
In spite of me, plummeting it came.   5
Frozen we both waited for its fall.

Most of what you gave me I have forgotten
With my mind but taken into my body,
But this I remember well: the bones of your neck
And the strain in my shoulders as I heaved up that huge   10
Double blade and snapped my wrists to swing
The handle down and hear the axe's edge
Nick through your flesh and creak into the block.

QUESTIONS

1. "The Last Word" stands fourth in a series titled "Four Love Poems." Sum up what happens in this poem. Do you take this to be a literal account of an execution?
2. Which words embody concrete things and show us physical actions? Which words have sounds that especially contribute to the poem's effectiveness?

SPEECH AND POETIC DICTION

Even if Samuel Johnson's famous *Dictionary* of 1755 had been as thick as Webster's unabridged, an eighteenth-century poet searching through it for words to use would have had a narrower choice. For in English literature of the **neoclassical period** or **Augustan age** — that period from about 1660 into the late eighteenth century — many poets subscribed to a belief in **poetic diction:** "A system of words," said Dr. Johnson, "refined from the grossness of domestic use." The system admitted into a serious poem only certain words and subjects, excluding others as violations of **decorum** (propriety). Accordingly such common words as *rat, cheese, big, sneeze,* and *elbow,* although admissible to satire, were thought inconsistent with the loftiness of tragedy, epic, ode, and elegy. Dr. Johnson's biographer, James Boswell, tells how a poet writing an epic on the sugar industry in the British West Indies reconsidered the word "rats" and instead wrote that "the whiskered vermin race, / A countless clan, despoil the lowland cane." Johnson himself objected to Lady Macbeth's allusion to her "keen knife," saying that "we do not immediately conceive that any crime of importance is to be committed with a knife; or who does not, at last, from the long habit of connecting a knife with sordid offices, feel aversion rather than terror?" Probably Johnson was here the victim of his age, and Shakespeare was right, but Johnson in one of his assumptions was right too: there are inappropriate words as well as appropriate ones.

Neoclassical poets chose their classical models more often from Roman writers than from Greek, as their diction suggests by the frequency of Latin derivatives. For example, a *net,* according to Dr. Johnson's dictionary, is "any thing reticulated or decussated, at equal distances, with interstices between the intersections." In company with Latinate words often appeared fixed combinations of adjective and noun ("finny prey" for "fish"), poetic names (a song to a lady named Molly might rechristen her Parthenia), and allusions to classical mythology.

Neoclassical poetic diction was evidently being abused when, instead of saying "uncork the bottle," a poet could write,

Apply thine engine to the spongy door,
Set *Bacchus* from his glassy prison free,

in some bad lines ridiculed by Alexander Pope in *Peri Bathous, or, Of the Art of Sinking in Poetry.* Too strictly applied, standards of decorum can lead a poet into such circumlocution and absurdity. An American neo-neoclassicist, E. J. Runk, in his *Washington: A National Epic* (1897), struggled manfully to preserve epic decorum though obliged to mention such New York place-names as Anthony's Nose:

Where Bear Hill rears its gloomy flank,
Confronting the Antonian Nose . . .

Not all poetic diction is excess baggage. To a reader who knew at firsthand both living sheep and the pastoral poems of Virgil — as most readers nowadays do not — such a fixed phrase as "the fleecy care," which seems stilted to us, conveyed pleasurable associations. But "fleecy care" was more than a hifalutin way of saying "sheep"; as one scholar has pointed out, "when they wished, our poets could say 'sheep' as clearly and as often as anybody else. In the first place, 'fleecy' drew attention to wool, and demanded the appropriate visual image of sheep; for aural imagery the poets would refer to 'the bleating kind'; it all depended upon what was happening in the poem."[2]

Other poets have found some special kind of poetic language valuable: Anglo-Saxon poets, with their standard figures of speech, or **kennings** ("whale-road" for the sea, "ring-giver" for a ruler); authors of folk ballads who, no less than neoclassicists, love fixed epithet-noun combinations ("milk-white steed," "blood-red wine," "steel-driving man"); and Edmund Spenser, whose example made popular the adjective ending in -y (*fleecy, grassy, milky*).

In a sense, every poet employs poetic diction in that he selects certain words for a poem and excludes others. When Wordsworth, in his Preface to *Lyrical Ballads,* asserted that "the language really spoken by men," especially by humble rustics, is plainer, more emphatic, and conveys "elementary feelings . . . in a state of greater simplicity," he was, in effect, advocating a new poetic diction. Wordsworth's ideas invited freshness into English poetry and, by admitting words that neoclassical poets would have called "low" ("His poor old *ankles*

---

[2] Bonamy Dobrée, *English Literature in the Early Eighteenth Century, 1700–1740* (New York, 1959), p. 161.

swell"), helped rid poets of the fear of being thought foolish for mentioning a commonplace.

This theory of the superiority of rural diction was, as Coleridge pointed out, hard to adhere to, and, in practice, Wordsworth was occasionally to write a language as Latinate and citified as these lines on yew trees:

> Huge trunks! — and each particular trunk a growth
> Of intertwisted fibers serpentine
> Up-coiling, and inveterately convolved . . .

Language so Latinate sounds pedantic to us, especially the phrase *inveterately convolved.* In fact, some poets, notably Gerard Manley Hopkins, have subscribed to the view that English words derived from Anglo-Saxon (Old English) have more force and flavor than their Latin equivalents. *Kingly,* one may feel, has more power than *regal.* One argument for this view is that so many words of Old English origin — *man, wife, child, house, eat, drink, sleep* — are basic to our living speech. It may be true that a language closer to Old English is particularly fit for rendering abstract notions concretely — as does the memorable title of a medieval work of piety, the *Ayenbite of Inwit* ("again-bite of inner wit" or "remorse of conscience"). And yet this view, if accepted at all, must be accepted with reservations. Some words of Latin origin carry meanings both precise and physical. In the King James Bible men are told, "See then that ye walk circumspectly, not as fools, but as wise" (Ephesians 5:15). To be *circumspect* (a word from two Latin roots meaning "to look" and "around") is to be watchful on all sides — a meaning altogether lost in a modernized wording of the passage once printed on a subway poster for a Bible society: "Be careful how you live, not thoughtlessly but thoughtfully."

When E. E. Cummings begins a poem, "mr youse needn't be so spry / concernin questions arty," we recognize another kind of diction available to poetry: **vulgate** (speech not much affected by schooling). Handbooks of grammar sometimes distinguish various **levels of usage.** A sort of ladder is imagined, on whose rungs words, phrases, and sentences may be ranked in an ascending order of formality, from the curses of an illiterate thug to the commencement-day address of a doctor of divinity. These levels range from vulgate through **colloquial** (the casual conversation or informal writing of literate people) and **general English** (most literate speech and writing, more studied than colloquial but not pretentious), up to **formal English** (the impersonal language of educated persons, usually only written, possibly spoken on dignified occasions). Recently, however, lexicographers have been shunning such labels. The designation "colloquial" has been expelled (*bounced* would be colloquial; *trun out,* vulgate) from *Webster's Third New International Dictionary* on the grounds that "it is impossible to know whether a word out of context is colloquial or not" and that the diction of Americans nowadays is more fluid than the labels suggest. Aware that we are being unscientific, we may find the labels useful. They may help roughly to describe what happens when, as in the following poem, a poet shifts from one level of usage to another. This poem employs, incidentally, a colloquial device throughout: omitting the subjects of sentences. In keeping the characters straight, it may be helpful to fill in the speaker for each *said* and for the verbs *saw* and *ducked* (lines 9 and 10).

Josephine Miles (b. 1911)
REASON

Said, Pull her up a bit will you, Mac, I want to unload there.
Said, Pull her up my rear end, first come first serve.
Said, Give her the gun, Bud, he needs a taste of his own bumper.

Then the usher came out and got into the act:
Said, Pull her up, pull her up a bit, we need this space, sir.   5
Said, For God's sake, is this still a free country or what?
You go back and take care of Gary Cooper's horse
And leave me handle my own car.

Saw them unloading the lame old lady,
Ducked out under the wheel and gave her an elbow,   10
Said, All you needed to do was just explain;
Reason, Reason is my middle name.

Language on more than one level enlivens this miniature comedy: the vulgate of the resentful driver ("Pull her up my rear end," "leave me handle my own car") and the colloquial of the bystander ("Give her the gun"). There is also a contrast in formality between the old lady's driver, who says "Mac," and the usher, who says "sir." These varied levels of language distinguish the speakers in the poem from one another.

The diction of "Reason" is that of speech; that of Coleridge's "Kubla Khan" (p. 334) is more bookish. Coleridge is not at fault, however: the language of Josephine Miles's reasonable driver might not have contained Kubla Khan's stately pleasure dome. At present, most poetry in English appears to be shunning expressions such as "fleecy care" in favor of general English and the colloquial. In Scotland, there has been an interesting development: the formation of an active group of poets who write in Scots, a **dialect** (variety of a language spoken by a social group or spoken in a certain locality). Perhaps, whether a poet writes in language close to speech or in language of greater formality, his poem will ring true if he chooses appropriate words.

Reword the following poem from Scots dialect into general English, using the closest possible equivalents. Then try to assess what the poem has gained or lost. (In line 4, a "ploy," as defined by *Webster's Third New International Dictionary*, is a pursuit or activity, "especially one that requires eagerness or finesse.")

Hugh MacDiarmid
[Christopher Murray Grieve] (b. 1892)
WHEESHT, WHEESHT

Wheesht°, wheesht, my foolish hert,	*hush*
For weel ye ken°	*know*
I widna ha'e ye stert	
Auld ploys again.	4
It's guid to see her lie	
Sae snod° an' cool,	*smooth*
A' lust o' lovin' by —	
Wheesht, wheesht, ye fule!	8

Thomas Hardy (1840–1928)
THE RUINED MAID

"O 'Melia, my dear, this does everything crown!	
Who could have supposed I should meet you in Town?	
And whence such fair garments, such prosperi-ty?" —	
"O didn't you know I'd been ruined?" said she.	4
— "You left us in tatters, without shoes or socks,	
Tired of digging potatoes, and spudding up docks°;	*spading up dockweed*
And now you've gay bracelets and bright feathers three!" —	
"Yes: that's how we dress when we're ruined," said she.	8
— "At home in the barton° you said 'thee' and 'thou,'	*farmyard*
And 'thik oon,' and 'theäs oon,' and 't'other'; but now	
Your talking quite fits 'ee for high compa-ny!" —	
"Some polish is gained with one's ruin," said she.	12
— "Your hands were like paws then, your face blue and bleak	
But now I'm bewitched by your delicate cheek,	
And your little gloves fit as on any la-dy!" —	
"We never do work when we're ruined," said she.	16
— "You used to call home-life a hag-ridden dream,	
And you'd sigh, and you'd sock°; but at present you seem	*groan*
To know not of megrims° or melancho-ly!" —	*blues*
"True. One's pretty lively when ruined," said she.	20

— "I wish I had feathers, a fine sweeping gown,
And a delicate face, and could strut about Town!" —
"My dear — a raw country girl, such as you be,
Cannot quite expect that. You ain't ruined," said she.   24

QUESTIONS

1. Where does this dialogue take place? Who are the two speakers?
2. Comment on Hardy's use of the word *ruined*. What is the conventional meaning of the word when applied to a girl? As 'Melia applies it to herself what is its meaning?
3. Sum up the attitude of each speaker toward the other. What details of the new 'Melia does the first speaker most dwell upon? Would you expect Hardy to be so impressed by all these details, or is there, between his view of the characters and their view of themselves, any hint of an ironic discrepancy?
4. In losing her country dialect (*thik oon* and *theäs oon* for *this one* and *that one*), 'Melia is presumed to have gained in sophistication. What does Hardy suggest by her *ain't* in the last line?

Richard Eberhart (b. 1904)

THE FURY OF AERIAL BOMBARDMENT

You would think the fury of aerial bombardment
Would rouse God to relent; the infinite spaces
Are still silent. He looks on shock-pried faces.
History, even, does not know what is meant.   4

You would feel that after so many centuries
God would give man to repent; yet he can kill
As Cain could, but with multitudinous will,
No farther advanced than in his ancient furies.   8

Was man made stupid to see his own stupidity?
Is God by definition indifferent, beyond us all?
Is the eternal truth man's fighting soul
Wherein the Beast ravens in its own avidity?   12

Of Van Wettering I speak, and Averill,
Names on a list, whose faces I do not recall
But they are gone to early death, who late in school
Distinguished the belt feed lever from the belt holding pawl.   16

QUESTIONS

1. As a naval officer during World War II, Richard Eberhart was assigned for a time as an instructor in a gunnery school. How has this experience apparently contributed to the diction of his poem?
2. In his *Life of John Dryden,* complaining about a description of a sea fight Dryden had filled with nautical language, Samuel Johnson argued that technical terms should be excluded from poetry. Is this criticism applicable to Eberhart's last line? Can a word succeed for us in a poem, even though

we may not be able to define it? (For more evidence, see also the technical terms in Henry Reed's "Naming of Parts," p. 390).

3. Critics have found a contrast in tone between the first three stanzas of this poem and the last stanza. How would you describe this contrast? What does diction contribute to it?

WORD ORDER

Not only the poet's choice of words makes his poem seem more formal, or less, but also the way he arranges them into sentences. Compare these lines,

> Jack and Jill went up the hill
> To fetch a pail of water.
> Jack fell down and broke his crown
> And Jill came tumbling after.

with Milton's account of a more significant downfall:

> Earth trembled from her entrails, as again
> In pangs, and Nature gave a second groan;
> Sky loured, and, muttering thunder, some sad drops
> Wept at completing of the mortal sin
> Original; while Adam took no thought
> Eating his fill, nor Eve to iterate
> Her former trespass feared, the more to soothe
> Him with her loved society, that now
> As with new wine intoxicated both
> They swim in mirth, and fancy that they feel
> Divinity within them breeding wings
> Wherewith to scorn the Earth.

Not all the words in Milton's lines are bookish: indeed, many of them can be found in nursery rimes. What helps, besides diction, to distinguish this account of the fall of man from "Jack and Jill" is that Milton's nonstop sentence seems farther removed from usual speech in its length (83 words), in its complexity (subordinate clauses), and in its word order ("with new wine intoxicated both" rather than "both intoxicated with new wine"). Should we think less (or more highly) of Milton for choosing a style so elaborate and formal? No judgment need be passed: both Mother Goose and the author of *Paradise Lost* use language appropriate to their purposes.

Among the languages of mankind, English is by no means the most flexible. English words must be used in fairly definite and inviolable patterns, and whoever departs too far from them will not be understood. In the sentence "Cain slew Abel," if you change the word order, you change the meaning: "Abel slew Cain." Such inflexibility was not true of Latin, in which a poet could lay down his words in almost whatever sequence he liked and, because their endings (inflections) showed what parts of speech they were, could trust that no reader would mistake a noun for an adjective. (E. E. Cummings has striven, in certain poems, for the freedom of Latin. One such poem will be found on page 48.)

One advantage of English word order is that it gives a word greater or lesser prominence. One place of emphasis is the beginning of a sentence. Yeats, for instance, opens "The Scholars" with a direct look at his subject: "*Bald heads,* forgetful of their sins, / Old, learned, respectable bald heads . . ."; and Poe starts "To Helen" with direct address: "*Helen,* thy beauty is to me / Like those Nicéan barks of yore. . . ." In a sentence, even greater emphasis falls on words placed last. And when the last word or words also carries the impact of a rime, emphasis is greater yet. Notice how much weight there is on the end of this sentence, from blind Milton's dream of his dead wife:

> Her face was veiled, yet to my fancied sight
> Love, sweetness, goodness in her person shined
> So clear, as in no face with more delight;
> But oh, as to embrace me she inclined,
> I walked, she fled, and day brought back my night.

The rigidity of English word order challenges the poet to defy it and to achieve unusual effects by **inverted word order.** It is customary in English to place adjective in front of noun (*a blue mantle, new pastures*). But an unusual emphasis is achieved when Milton ends "Lycidas" by reversing the pattern:

> At last he rose, and twitched his mantle blue:
> Tomorrow to fresh woods, and pastures new.

Perhaps the inversion in *mantle blue* gives more prominence to the color associated with heaven (and in "Lycidas," heaven is of prime importance). Perhaps the inversion in *pastures new*, stressing the *new*, heightens the sense of a rebirth.

If a poet's switching-about of words is too far out of the ordinary, however, the result may be ludicrous. In "Rabbi Ben Ezra," Robert Browning has a sage ask, "Irks care the crop-full bird? Frets doubt the maw-crammed beast?" Turned around and slightly rewritten into a more readily understandable order, the line might read: "Does care irk the bird whose crop is full? Does doubt fret the beast whose maw is crammed?" Unintentional humor may result when an incompetent poet inverts words to get his rime to come out right:

> He took her hand, and held it for a few
> Moments or so, his courage up to screw.

But there is nothing ludicrous in Milton's description of God's casting Satan out of heaven — "Him the Almighty Power / Hurled headlong flaming from th' ethereal sky." The out-of-the-ordinary syntax (object then subject, instead of the usual subject then object) seems fitting to the extraordinary nature of the event and perhaps even imitates Satan's upside-down departure.

Coleridge offered two "homely definitions of prose and poetry; that is, *prose*: words in their best order; *poetry*: the best words in the best order." If all goes well, a poet may fasten the right word into the right place, and the result may be — as T. S. Eliot said in "Little Gidding" — a poem

> where every word is at home,
> Taking its place to support the others,
> The word neither diffident nor ostentatious,
> An easy commerce of the old and the new,
> The common word exact without vulgarity,
> The formal word precise but not pedantic,
> The complete consort dancing together . . .

E. E. Cummings (1894–1962)

ANYONE LIVED IN A PRETTY HOW TOWN

anyone lived in a pretty how town
(with up so floating many bells down)
spring summer autumn winter
he sang his didn't he danced his did.   4

Women and men(both little and small)
cared for anyone not at all
they sowed their isn't they reaped their same
sun moon stars rain   8

children guessed(but only a few
and down they forgot as up they grew
autumn winter spring summer)
that noone loved him more by more   12
when by now and tree by leaf
she laughed his joy she cried his grief
bird by snow and stir by still
anyone's any was all to her   16

someones married their everyones
laughed their cryings and did their dance
(sleep wake hope and then)they
said their nevers they slept their dream   20

stars rain sun moon
(and only the snow can begin to explain
how children are apt to forget to remember
with up so floating many bells down)   24

one day anyone died i guess
(and noone stooped to kiss his face)
busy folk buried them side by side
little by little and was by was   28

all by all and deep by deep   *they get worse & worse as they*
and more by more they dream their sleep   *get older:*
noone and anyone earth by april
wish by spirit and if by yes.   32

Women and men(both dong and ding)
summer autumn winter spring
reaped their sowing and went their came
sun moon stars rain   36

QUESTIONS

1. Summarize the story told in this poem. Who are the main characters?
2. Rearrange the words in the two opening lines into the order you would expect them usually to follow. What effect does Cummings obtain by his unconventional syntax?
3. Another of Cummings's strategies is to use one part of speech as if it were another; for instance, in line 4, *didn't* and *did* ordinarily are verbs, but here they
   are used as nouns. What other words in the poem perform functions other
   than their expected ones?

Gerard Manley Hopkins (1844–1889) *has wrestling with*
CARRION COMFORT   *his sense of inadequacy*

Not, I'll not, carrion comfort, Despair, not feast on thee;
Not untwist — slack they may be — these last strands of man
In me ór, most weary, cry *I can no more.* I can;
Can something, hope, wish day come, not choose not to be.   4
But ah, but O thou terrible, why wouldst thou rude on me
Thy wring-world right foot rock? lay a lionlimb against me? scan
With darksome devouring eyes my bruisèd bones? and fan,
O in turns of tempest, me heaped there; me frantic to avoid thee and
      flee?   8

   Why? That my chaff might fly; my grain lie, sheer and clear.
Nay in all that toil, that coil, since (seems) I kissed the rod,
Hand rather, my heart lo! lapped strength, stole joy, would laugh,
      chéer.
Cheer whom though? the hero° whose heaven-handling flung   *Christ*
      me, fóot tród
Me? or me that fought him? O which one? is it each one? That night,
      that year
Of now done darkness I wretch lay wrestling with (my God!) my God. 14

QUESTIONS

1. Robert Bridges, Hopkins's first editor, gave this poem its title. What does it mean?
2. In what places is the word order difficult to follow? Try to paraphrase, adding any words that Hopkins has left out.
3. What is the effect of all the questions, of the lines interrupted by asides, qualifications, parenthetical elements?
4. What words has Hopkins apparently made up? Try to define them from the context of the poem.

Walter Savage Landor (1775–1864)

AGE

Death, though I see him not, is near
And grudges me my eightieth year.
Now, I would give him all those last
For one that fifty have run past.
Ah! he strikes all things, all alike,
But bargains: those he will not strike.

QUESTIONS

1. On what two meanings of the word *strike* does Landor's closing line depend?
2. What advantage is it to this epigram that the play on the word *strike* dawns on us only with the last word of the last line? Suppose the poem had ended in a different word order:

   Ah! all alike he strikes all things,
   But he will not strike bargainings.

   What would be lost?

FOR REVIEW AND FURTHER STUDY

Lewis Carroll
[Charles Lutwidge Dodgson] (1832–1898)

JABBERWOCKY

'Twas brillig, and the slithy toves
    Did gyre and gimble in the wabe:
All mimsy were the borogoves,
    And the mome raths outgrabe.   4

"Beware the Jabberwock, my son!
    The jaws that bite, the claws that catch!
Beware the Jubjub bird, and shun
    The frumious Bandersnatch!"   8

He took his vorpal sword in hand;
    Long time the manxome foe he sought —
So rested he by the Tumtum tree,
    And stood awhile in thought.   12

And, as in uffish thought he stood,
    The Jabberwock, with eyes of flame,
Came whiffling through the tulgey wood,
    And burbled as it came!   16

One, two! One, two! And through and through
    The vorpal blade went snicker-snack!
He left it dead, and with its head
    He went galumphing back.   20

"And hast thou slain the Jabberwock?
    Come to my arms, my beamish boy!
O frabjous day! Callooh, Callay!"
    He chortled in his joy.   24

'Twas brillig, and the slithy toves
    Did gyre and gimble in the wabe:
All mimsy were the borogoves,
    And the mome raths outgrabe.   28

QUESTIONS

1. Look up *chortled* (line 24) in your dictionary and find out its definition and origin.
2. In *Through the Looking-Glass,* Alice seeks the aid of Humpty Dumpty to decipher the meaning of this nonsense poem. *"Brillig,"* he explains, "means four o'clock in the afternoon — the time when you begin *broiling* things for dinner." Does *brillig* sound like any other familiar word?
3. *"Slithy,"* the explanation goes on, "means 'lithe and slimy.' 'Lithe' is the same as 'active.' You see it's like a portmanteau — there are two meanings packed up into one word." *Mimsy* is supposed to pack together both "flimsy" and "miserable." In the rest of the poem, what other portmanteau — or packed suitcase — words can you find?

Wallace Stevens (1879–1955)

METAMORPHOSIS

Yillow, yillow, yillow,
Old worm, my pretty quirk,
How the wind spells out
Sep - tem - ber. . . .   4

Summer is in bones.
Cock-robin's at Caracas.
Make o, make o, make o,
Oto - otu - bre.   8

And the rude leaves fall.
The rain falls. The sky
Falls and lies with the worms.
The street lamps   12

Are those that have been hanged,
Dangling in an illogical
To and to and fro
Fro   Niz - nil - imbo.   16

QUESTIONS

1. Explain the title. Of the several meanings of *metamorphosis* given in a dictionary, which best applies to the process that Stevens sees in the natural world?
2. What metamorphosis is also taking place in the *language* of the poem? How does it continue from line 4 to line 8 to line 16?
3. In the last line, which may recall the thickening drone of a speaker lapsing into sleep, *Niz - nil - imbo* seems not only a pun on the name of a month, but also a portmanteau word into which at least two familiar words are packed. Say it aloud. What are they?
4. What dictionary definitions of the word *quirk* seem relevant to line 2? How can a worm be a quirk? What else in this poem seems quirky?

EXERCISE: *Will the Real Sir Philip Sidney Please Stand Up?*

In each pair of quotations, one is an original passage by a poet, the other an inferior rewording of it. Which is the original? How do you know? In which does the word order become awkward? Which words receive weak substitutes?

1. Sir Philip Sidney

   a. Leave me, O Love, which reachest but to dust,
      And thou, my mind, aspire to higher things . . .

   b. Go away, Love, which but to dust doth reach,
      O mind of mine, fly up to better things . . .

2. Emily Dickinson

   a. Around my life the belt he put –
      And snapped the buckle –

   b. He put the belt around my life –
      I heard the buckle snap –

3. Alexander Pope

   a. The hungry judges soon the sentence sign,
      And wretches hang that jurymen may dine.

   b. To pass the sentence fast is judges' feat,
      And hang men so the jury lunch may eat.

4. John Donne

   a. O angels, blow upon your trumpets now
      You many souls that wait the call, arise!
      Go look around and find your bodies, thou
      May come from all the corners of the skies . . .

b. At the round earth's imagined corners, blow
Your trumpets, angels, and arise, arise
From death, you numberless infinities
Of souls, and to your scattered bodies go . . .

5. Edgar Allan Poe

a. So blend the turrets and shadows there
That all seem pendulous in air,
While from a proud tower in the town
Death looks gigantically down.

b. The turrets and shadows blend so there
They all seem pendants in the air,
While from a tower in the town
Proud Death the giant looks right down.

EXERCISE: *Different Kinds of English*

Read the following poems and see what kinds of diction and word order you find in them. Which poems are least formal in their language and which most formal? Is there any use of vulgate English? Any dialect? What does each poem achieve that its own kind of English makes possible?

Anonymous (American; nineteenth century?)
AS I WAS LAYING ON THE GREEN

As I was laying on the green,
A small English book I seen.
Carlyle's *Essay on Burns* was the edition,
So I left it laying in the same position.

A. R. Ammons (b. 1926)
SPRING COMING

The caryophyllaceae
like a scroungy
frost are
rising through the lawn:
many-fingered as leggy   5
    copepods:
a suggestive delicacy,
lacework, like
the scent of wild plum
    thickets: 10
also the grackles
with their incredible
vertical, horizontal,
reversible
tails have arrived: 15
such nice machines.

William Wordsworth (1770–1850)

My heart leaps up when I behold

My heart leaps up when I behold
  A rainbow in the sky;
So was it when my life began;
So is it now I am a man;
So be it when I shall grow old.   5
  Or let me die!
The Child is father of the Man;
And I could wish my days to be
Bound each to each by natural piety.

William Wordsworth (1770–1850)

Mutability

From low to high doth dissolution climb,
And sink from high to low, along a scale
Of awful notes, whose concord shall not fail;
A musical but melancholy chime,   4
Which they can hear who meddle not with crime,
Nor avarice, nor over-anxious care.
Truth fails not; but her outward forms that bear
The longest date do melt like frosty rime°,   *frozen dew* 8
That in the morning whitened hill and plain
And is no more; drop like the tower sublime
Of yesterday, which royally did wear
His crown of weeds, but could not even sustain
Some casual shout that broke the silent air,
Or the unimaginable touch of Time.   14

Anonymous (American; collected 1936)

Scottsboro

Paper come out — done strewed de news
Seven po' chillun moan deat' house blues,
Seven po' chillun moanin' deat' house blues.
Seven nappy° heads wit' big shiny eye   *kinky*
All boun' in jail and framed to die,
All boun' in jail and framed to die.   6

Messin' white woman — snake lyin' tale
Hang and burn and jail wit' no bail.
Dat hang and burn and jail wit' no bail.
Worse ol' crime in white folks' lan'
Black skin coverin' po' workin' man,
Black skin coverin' po' workin' man.   12

Judge and jury — all in de stan'
Lawd, biggety name for same lynchin' ban',
Lawd, biggety name for same lynchin' ban'.
White folks and nigger in great co't house
Like cat down cellar wit' nohole mouse.
Like cat down cellar wit' nohole mouse.   18

SCOTTSBORO. This folk blues, collected by Lawrence Gellert in *Negro Songs of Protest* (New York, 1936), is a comment on the Scottsboro case. In 1931 nine black youths of Scottsboro, Alabama, were arrested and charged with the rape of two white women. Though eventually, after several trials, they were found not guilty, some of them at the time this song was composed had been convicted and sentenced to death.

4 Saying and Suggesting

DENOTATION AND CONNOTATION

To write so clearly that they might bring "all things as near the mathematical plainness" as possible — that was the goal of scientists according to Bishop Thomas Sprat, who lived in the seventeenth century. Such an effort would seem bound to fail, because words, unlike numbers, are ambiguous indicators. Although it may have troubled Bishop Sprat, the tendency of a word to have multiplicity of meaning rather than mathematical plainness opens broad avenues to poetry.

Every word has at least one **denotation:** a meaning as defined in a dictionary. But the English language has many a common word with so many denotations that a reader may need to think twice to see what it means in a specific context. The noun *field,* for instance, can denote a piece of ground, a sports arena, the scene of a battle, part of a flag, a profession, and a number system in mathematics. Further, the word can be used as a verb ("he fielded a grounder") or an adjective ("field trip," "field glasses").

A word also has **connotations:** overtones or suggestions of additional meaning that it gains from all the contexts in which we have met it in the past. The word *skeleton,* according to a dictionary, denotes "the bony framework of a human being or other vertebrate animal, which supports the flesh and protects the organs." But by its associations, the word can rouse thoughts of war, of disease and death, or (possibly) of one's plans to go to medical school. Think, too, of the difference between "Old Doc Jones" and "Abner P. Jones, M.D." In the mind's eye, the former appears in his shirtsleeves; the latter has a gold nameplate on his door. That some words denote the same thing but have sharply different connotations is pointed out in this anonymous Victorian jingle:

> Here's a little ditty that you really ought to know:
> Horses "sweat" and men "perspire," but ladies only "glow."

The terms *druggist, pharmacist,* and *apothecary* all denote the same occupation, but apothecaries lay claim to special distinction.

Few people care more about the connotations of language than do advertisers, who know that connotations make money. Recently a Boston automobile dealer advertised his secondhand cars not as "used" but as "pre-owned," as if fearing that "used car" would connote an old heap with soiled upholstery and mysterious engine troubles that somebody couldn't put up with. "Pre-owned," however, suggests that the previous owner has taken the trouble of breaking in the car for you. Not long ago prune-packers, alarmed by a slump in sales, sponsored a survey to determine the connotations of prunes in the public consciousness. Asked, "What do you think of when you hear the word *prunes*?" most people replied, "dried up," "wrinkled," or "constipated." Dismayed, the packers hired an advertising agency to create a new image for prunes, in hopes of inducing new connotations. Soon, advertisements began to show prunes in gay, brightly colored settings, in the company of bikinied bathing queens.[1]

In imaginative writing, connotations are as crucial as they are in advertising. Consider this sentence: "A new brand of journalism is being born, or spawned" (Dwight Macdonald writing in *The New York Review of Books*). The last word, by its associations with fish and crustaceans, suggests that this new journalism is scarcely the product of human beings. And what do we make of Romeo's assertion that Juliet "is the sun"? Surely even a lovesick boy cannot mean that his sweetheart is "the incandescent body of gases about which the earth and other planets revolve" (a dictionary definition). He means, of course, that he thrives in her sight, that he feels warm in her presence or even at the thought of her, that she illumines his world and is the center of his universe. Because in the mind of the hearer these and other suggestions are brought into play, Romeo's statement, literally absurd, makes excellent sense. In a famous poem by Blake, both denotation and connotation are indispensable.

William Blake (1757–1827)

LONDON

I wander through each chartered street,
Near where the chartered Thames does flow,
And mark in every face I meet
Marks of weakness, marks of woe.   4

In every cry of every man,
In every infant's cry of fear,
In every voice, in every ban,
The mind-forged manacles I hear.   8

---

[1] For this and other instances of connotation-engineering, see Vance Packard's *The Hidden Persuaders* (New York, 1958), chap. 13.

How the chimney-sweeper's cry
Every black'ning church appalls;
And the hapless soldier's sigh
Runs in blood down palace walls.   12

But most through midnight streets I hear
How the youthful harlot's curse
Blasts the new born infant's tear,
And blights with plagues the marriage hearse.   16

Here are only a few of the possible meanings of four of Blake's
words:

chartered (lines 1, 2)
> Denotations: Established by a charter (a written grant or a certif-
> icate of incorporation), leased or hired.
>
> Connotations: Defined, limited, restricted, channeled, mapped,
> bound by law; bought and sold (like a slave or an inanimate ob-
> ject); Magna Charta; charters given crown colonies by the King.
>
> Other Things in the Poem with Similar Connotations: *Ban;*
> *manacles; chimney-sweeper, soldier, harlot* (all hirelings).
>
> Interpretation of the Lines: The street has had mapped out for
> it the direction in which it must go; the Thames has had laid
> down to it the course it must follow. Street and river are chan-
> neled, imprisoned, enslaved (like every inhabitant of London).

black'ning (line 10)
> Denotation: Becoming black.
>
> Connotations: The darkening of something once light, the de-
> filement of something once clean, the deepening of guilt, the
> gathering of darkness at the approach of night.
>
> Other Things in the Poem with Similar Connotations: Ob-
> jects becoming marked or smudged (*marks of weakness, marks*
> *of woe* in the faces of passers-by; bloodied walls of a palace; mar-
> riage blighted with plagues); the word *appalls* (suggesting not
> only "to overcome with horror" but "to cast a pall or shroud
> over something"); *midnight streets.*
>
> Interpretation of the Line: Literally, every London church grows
> black from soot and hires a chimney-sweeper (a small boy) to
> help clean it. But Blake suggests too that by profiting from the
> suffering of the child laborer, the church is soiling its original
> purity.

Blasts, blights (lines 15–16)
> Denotations: Both *blast* and *blight* mean "to cause to wither" or
> "to ruin and destroy." Both are terms from horticulture. Frost
> *blasts* a bud and kills it; disease *blights* a growing plant.

Connotations: Sickness and death; gardens shriveled and dying; gusts of wind and the ravages of insects; things blown to pieces or rotted and warped.

Other Things in the Poem with Similar Connotations: Faces marked with weakness and woe; the child become a chimney-sweep; the soldier killed by war; blackening church and bloodied palace; young girl turned harlot; wedding carriage transformed into a hearse.

Interpretation of the Lines: Literally, the harlot spreads the plague of syphilis, which, carried into marriage, can cause a baby to be born blind. In a larger and more meaningful sense, Blake sees the prostitution of even one young girl corrupting the entire institution of matrimony and endangering every child.

Some of these connotations are more to the point than others; the reader of a poem nearly always has the problem of distinguishing relevant associations from irrelevant ones. We need to read a poem in its entirety and, when a word leaves us in doubt, look for other things in the poem to corroborate or refute what we think it means. Relatively simple and direct in its statement, Blake's account of his stroll through the city at night becomes an indictment of a whole social and religious order. The indictment could hardly be this effective if it were "mathematically plain," its every word restricted to one denotation clearly spelled out.

Samuel Johnson (1709–1784)

A Short Song of Congratulation

Long-expected one and twenty
  Ling'ring year at last is flown,
Pomp and pleasure, pride and plenty,
  Great Sir John, are all your own.   4

Loosened from the minor's tether;
  Free to mortgage or to sell,
Wild as wind, and light as feather
  Bid the slaves of thrift farewell.   8

Call the Bettys, Kates, and Jennys
  Every name that laughs at care,
Lavish of your grandsire's guineas,
  Show the spirit of an heir.   12

All that prey on vice and folly
  Joy to see their quarry fly,
Here the gamester light and jolly
  There the lender grave and sly.   16

Wealth, Sir John, was made to wander,
  Let it wander as it will;
See the jockey, see the pander,
  Bid them come, and take their fill.   20

When the bonny blade carouses,
  Pockets full, and spirits high,
What are acres? What are houses?
  Only dirt, or° wet or dry.   *either*   24

If the guardian or the mother
  Tell the woes of willful waste,
Scorn their counsel and their pother,
  You can hang or drown at last.   28

QUESTIONS

1. Johnson states in line 24 the connotations that *acres* and *houses* have for the young heir. What connotations might these terms have for Johnson himself?
2. Why are *Bettys, Kates,* and *Jennys* more meaningful names as Johnson uses them than Elizabeths, Katherines, and Genevieves would be?

Wallace Stevens (1879–1955)
DISILLUSIONMENT OF TEN O'CLOCK

The houses are haunted
By white night-gowns.
None are green,
Or purple with green rings,
Or green with yellow rings,   5
Or yellow with blue rings.
None of them are strange,
With socks of lace
And beaded ceintures.
People are not going   10
To dream of baboons and periwinkles.
Only, here and there, an old sailor,
Drunk and asleep in his boots,
Catches tigers
In red weather.   15

QUESTIONS

1. What is lacking in the people who live in these houses? Why should the poet's view of them be a "disillusionment"?
2. What contrast is drawn between the people and the old sailor? What connotations of *white night-gowns* and *sailor* contribute to this contrast?
3. What are *beaded ceintures*? What does the phrase suggest to you?
4. What do the colors suggest?

Robert Herrick (1591–1674)
UPON JULIA'S VOICE

So smooth, so sweet, so silv'ry is thy voice,
As, could they hear, the damned would make no noise,
But listen to thee (walking in thy chamber)
Melting melodious words, to lutes of amber.

QUESTION

Two denotations of the word *amber* are possible: the fossilized resin from which pipestems are sometimes made today and which might have been used to inlay the body of a lute; an alloy of four parts silver and one part gold. In this poem, which denotation makes more sense? Explain Herrick's comparison.

Guy Owen (b. 1925)
THE WHITE STALLION

The Runaway

A white horse came to our farm once
Leaping like dawn the backyard fence.
In dreams I heard his shadow fall
Across my bed. A miracle,   4
I woke beneath his mane's surprise;
I saw my face within his eyes,
The dew ran down his nose and fell
Upon the bleeding window quince. . . .   8

But long before I broke the spell
My father's curses sped him on,
Four flashing hooves that bruised the lawn.
And as I stumbled into dawn   12
I saw him scorn a final hedge,
I heard his pride upon the bridge,
Then through the wakened yard I went
To read the rage the stallion spent.   16

QUESTIONS

1. What do these words in Owen's poem denote: *scorn, pride, wakened?*
2. What do they connote?
3. Does *miracle* in line 4 refer to the sudden appearance of the stallion or to the boy himself? On what evidence do you base your answer?

J. V. Cunningham (b. 1911)
MOTTO FOR A SUN DIAL

I who by day am function of the light
Am constant and invariant by night.

In mathematics, what do the words *function* and *constant* mean?

W. S. Merwin (b. 1927)

DEAD HAND

Temptations still nest in it like basilisks.
Hang it up till the rings fall.

DEAD HAND. The basilisk, a fabled lizard of the Sahara, could crack rock with its look and (according to the Roman poet Lucan) could poison the hand of an attacker so that he died unless he quickly severed his hand from his body. (For more details see Jorge Luís Borges, *The Book of Imaginary Beings*, New York, 1970.)

QUESTIONS

1. What are we told about the owner of the hand?
2. What is suggested?

EXPERIMENT: *Removing Connotations*

Here is a translation from Li Po, a Chinese poet of the eighth century. Try rewriting "The Jewel Stairs' Grievance," into either prose or a new poem, making explicit to a Western reader every idea that, according to Pound, is suggested in the original by connotation. Then compare your noteless and connotationless poem with Pound's poem in its brevity. What, if anything, does this comparison show you about denotation and connotation?

Ezra Pound (1885–1972)

THE JEWEL STAIRS' GRIEVANCE

The jeweled steps are already quite white with dew,
It is so late that the dew soaks my gauze stockings,
And I let down the crystal curtain
And watch the moon through the clear autumn.

THE JEWEL STAIRS' GRIEVANCE. Pound supplies these notes on connotations in the poem: "Jewel stairs, therefore a palace. Grievance, therefore there is something to complain of. Gauze stockings, therefore a court lady, not a servant who complains. Clear autumn, therefore she has no excuse on account of weather. Also she has come early, for the dew has not merely whitened the stairs, but has soaked her stockings. The poem is especially prized because she utters no direct reproach."

ALLUSION

An **allusion** is a reference to any person, place, or thing — fictitious, historical, or actual. Sometimes, to understand an allusion in a poem we have to find out something we might not have known before. Such may be necessary in reading W. S. Merwin's "Dead Hand" (above), with its reference to the basilisk. But usually the poet expects us to bring to his poem some item of common knowledge. When Edgar Allan Poe refers us to "the glory that was Greece / And the grandeur that was Rome," he has a right to assume that we have heard of those places. Similarly, T. S. Eliot said he wrote for the reader who knows Shakespeare and the Bible. (However, in his highly allusive long poem *The Waste Land,* Eliot apparently expected his readers to know a great deal more.)

Allusions have the further value of saving space. By giving a brief introductory quotation from the speech of a damned soul in Dante's *Inferno,* Eliot can suggest that "The Love Song of J. Alfred Prufrock" is to be the confession of a soul in torment, who sees no chance of escape.

EXERCISE: *Catching Allusions*

From your knowledge, supplemented by an encyclopedia if need be, explain the allusions in the following four poems.

Cid Corman (b. 1924)

THE TORTOISE

Always to want to
go back, to correct
an error, ease a

guilt, see how a friend
is doing. And yet   5
one doesnt, except

in memory, in
dreams. The land remains
desolate. Always

the feeling is of   10
terrible slowness
overtaking haste.

John Keats (1795–1821)

ON FIRST LOOKING INTO CHAPMAN'S HOMER

Much have I traveled in the realms of gold,
And many goodly states and kingdoms seen;
Round many western islands have I been
Which bards in fealty to Apollo hold.   4
Oft of one wide expanse had I been told
That deep-browed Homer ruled as his demesne;
Yet did I never breathe its pure serene
Till I heard Chapman speak out loud and bold: 8

Then felt I like some watcher of the skies
When a new planet swims into his ken;
Or like stout Cortez when with eagle eyes
He stared at the Pacific — and all his men
Looked at each other with a wild surmise —
Silent, upon a peak in Darien.   14

John Dryden (1631–1700)
LINES PRINTED UNDER THE ENGRAVED PORTRAIT OF MILTON

Three poets, in three distant ages born,
Greece, Italy, and England did adorn.
The first in loftiness of thought surpassed,
The next in majesty, in both the last:
The force of Nature could no farther go;
To make a third she joined the former two.

LINES PRINTED UNDER THE ENGRAVED PORTRAIT OF MILTON. These lines appeared in
Tonson's folio edition of *Paradise Lost* (1668).

J. V. Cunningham (b. 1911)
FRIEND, ON THIS SCAFFOLD THOMAS MORE LIES DEAD

Friend, on this scaffold Thomas More lies dead
Who would not cut the Body from the Head.

FOR REVIEW AND FURTHER STUDY

Philip Larkin (b. 1922)
AS BAD AS A MILE

Watching the shied core
Striking the basket, skidding across the floor,
Shows less and less of luck, and more and more   3

Of failure spreading back up the arm
Earlier and earlier, the unraised hand calm,
The apple unbitten in the palm.   6

QUESTIONS

1. To what familiar proverb does the title allude? What meaning do you see in
   the fact that a word has been changed in it?
2. What differences in connotation between *apple* and *core* does Larkin put to
   good use?

Robert Herrick (1591–1674)

To Daisies, Not to Shut So Soon

Shut not so soon; the dull-eyed night
  Has not as yet begun
To make a seizure on the light,
  Or to seal up the sun.   4

No marigolds yet closèd are;
  No shadows great appear;
Nor doth the early shepherd's star
  Shine like a spangle here.   8

Stay but till my Julia close
  Her life-begetting eye;
And let the whole world then dispose
  Itself to live or die.   12

Questions

1. Why is Julia's eye called *life-begetting* (line 10)?
2. How would you answer the quibble that the poet is at fault in not mentioning her other eye?
3. What meanings do you find in *dull-eyed* (line 1)? What connotations?
4. *To make a seizure* (line 3) can be a legal term, meaning to claim land or property, as for instance a government might attach land that a citizen thought he had freely inherited. What would this denotation add to the meaning of the poem?
5. Look up *daisy* in your dictionary and see where the word comes from. How does awareness of its derivation help you in reading Herrick's poem?

Timothy Steele (b. 1948)

Epitaph

Here lies Sir Tact, a diplomatic fellow,
Whose silence was not golden, but just yellow.

Questions

1. To what familiar saying does Steele allude?
2. What are the connotations of the colors?

Robert Frost (1874–1963)

Fire and Ice

Some say the world will end in fire,
Some say in ice.
From what I've tasted of desire
I hold with those who favor fire.

But if it had to perish twice,   5
I think I know enough of hate
To say that for destruction ice
Is also great
And would suffice.

1. What connotations of *fire* and *ice* contribute to the richness of Frost's comparison?
2. To whom does Frost allude in line 1? In line 2?

E. E. Cummings (1894–1962)

THE CAMBRIDGE LADIES WHO LIVE IN FURNISHED SOULS

the Cambridge ladies who live in furnished souls
are unbeautiful and have comfortable minds
(also, with the church's protestant blessings
daughters, unscented shapeless spirited)
they believe in Christ and Longfellow, both dead,
are invariably interested in so many things —
at the present writing one still finds
delighted fingers knitting for the is it Poles?   8
perhaps. While permanent faces coyly bandy
scandal of Mrs. N and Professor D
.... the Cambridge ladies do not care, above
Cambridge if sometimes in its box of
sky lavender and cornerless, the
moon rattles like a fragment of angry candy   14

QUESTIONS

1. To which city named Cambridge does Cummings allude? How do you know?
2. What is meant by the double allusion to Christ and Longfellow?
3. In line 3, why does *protestant* lack a capital letter? What does the word denote?
4. What do you understand by the interrupted syntax of *knitting for the is it Poles* (line 8)?
5. What connotations are we to draw from the words *furnished* (line 1), *comfortable* (line 2), *permanent, coyly* (line 9), *lavender* and *cornerless* (line 13)?
6. What do the last four lines tell us about the Cambridge ladies? How can candy be angry?
7. How would you describe the tone of the poem? To what extent have allusion and connotation helped to communicate it?

5 Imagery

Ezra Pound (1885–1972)

The apparition of these faces in the crowd;
Petals on a wet, black bough.

Pound has said he wrote this poem to convey an experience: emerging one day from a train in the Paris subway (*Métro*), he beheld "suddenly a beautiful face, and then another and another." Originally he had described his impression in a poem thirty lines long. In this final version, each line contains an **image,** which, like a picture, may take the place of a thousand words.

Though the term *image* suggests a thing seen, when speaking of images in poetry we generally mean *a word or sequence of words that refers to any sensory experience.* Often this experience is a sight (**visual imagery,** as in Pound's poem), but it may be a sound (**auditory imagery**) or a touch (**tactile imagery,** as a perception of roughness or smoothness). It may be an odor or a taste or perhaps a bodily sensation such as pain, the prickling of gooseflesh, the quenching of thirst. Here are two brief poems containing very little eye appeal. Instead, they embody physical sensations.

William Carlos Williams (1883–1963)

This Is Just to Say

I have eaten
the plums
that were in
the icebox

and which
you were probably
saving
for breakfast

Forgive me
they were delicious
so sweet
and so cold

Taniguchi Buson (1715–1783)

THE PIERCING CHILL I FEEL

The piercing chill I feel:
  my dead wife's comb, in our bedroom,
    under my heel . . .

                     — Translated by Harold G. Henderson

As in this **haiku** (in Japanese, a poem of seventeen syllables) an image can convey — in a flash — understanding. Had he wished, the poet might have spoken of the dead woman, of the contrast between her death and his memory of her, of his feelings toward death in general. But such a discussion probably would be less forceful. Striking his bare foot against the comb, now cold and motionless but associated with the living wife (perhaps worn in her hair), the widower feels a shock as if he had touched the woman's corpse. A literal, physical sense of death is conveyed; the abstraction "death" is understood through the senses. To render the abstract in concrete terms is what poets often try to do; in this attempt, an image can be valuable.

An image may occur in a single word, a phrase, a sentence, or, as in this case, an entire short poem. To speak of the **imagery** of a poem — all its images taken together — is often more useful than to speak of separate images. To divide Buson's haiku into five images — *chill, wife, comb, bedroom, heel* — is possible, for any noun that refers to a visible object or a sensation is an image, but this is to draw distinctions that in themselves mean little and to disassemble a single experience.

Does an image cause a reader to experience a sense impression for himself? Not quite. Reading the word *petals,* no one literally sees petals but is given the occasion to imagine them. The image asks to be seen with the mind's eye. And although "In a Station of the Metro" records what Ezra Pound saw, it is of course not necessary for a poet actually to have lived through a sensory experience in order to write it. Keats may never have seen a newly discovered planet through a telescope, despite the image in his sonnet on Chapman's Homer (p. 63).

It is tempting to think of imagery as mere decoration, particularly when we read Keats, who fills his poems with an abundance of sights, sounds, odors, and tastes. But a successful image is not just a dab of paint or a flashy bauble. When Keats opens "The Eve of St. Agnes" with what have been called the coldest lines in literature, he evokes by a series of images a setting and a mood:

> St. Agnes' eve — Ah, bitter chill it was!
> The owl, for all his feathers, was a-cold;
> The hare limped trembling through the frozen grass,
> And silent was the flock in woolly fold:
> Numb were the Beadsman's fingers, while he told
> His rosary, and while his frosted breath,
> Like pious incense from a censer old,
> Seemed taking flight for heaven, without a death, . . .

Indeed, some literary critics look for much of the meaning of a poem in its imagery, wherein they expect to see the mind of the poet more truly revealed than in whatever he explicitly *tells* us he believes. In his investigation of Wordsworth's "Ode: Intimations of Immortality," the critic Cleanth Brooks devotes his attention to the imagery of light and darkness, which he finds carries on and develops Wordsworth's thought.[1]

"The greatest poverty," wrote Wallace Stevens, "is not to live / In a physical world." In his own poems, Stevens makes us aware of our world's richness. He can take even a common object sold by the pound in supermarkets and, with precise imagery, recall to us what we had forgotten we ever knew about it.

Wallace Stevens (1879–1955)
STUDY OF TWO PEARS

I

Opusculum paedagogum°.	*a little work that teaches*
The pears are not viols,	
Nudes or bottles.	
They resemble nothing else.	4

II

They are yellow forms
Composed of curves
Bulging toward the base.
They are touched red.   8

III

They are not flat surfaces
Having curved outlines.
They are round
Tapering toward the top.   12

---

[1] "Wordsworth and the Paradox of the Imagination," in *The Well Wrought Urn* (New York, 1947).

IV

In the way they are modeled
There are bits of blue.
A hard dry leaf hangs
From the stem.   16

V

The yellow glistens.
It glistens with various yellows,
Citrons, oranges and greens
Flowering over the skin.   20

VI

The shadows of the pears
Are blobs on the green cloth.
The pears are not seen
As the observer wills.   24

Though Shakespeare's Theseus (in *A Midsummer Night's Dream*) accused the poet of being concerned with "airy nothings," the poet is usually very much concerned with what is in front of him. This concern is of use to us. Perhaps, as Alan Watts has remarked, Americans are not the materialists they are sometimes accused of being. How could anyone taking a look at an American city think that its inhabitants deeply cherish material things? Involved in our personal hopes and apprehensions, anticipating the future so hard that much of the time we see the present through a film of thought across our eyes, perhaps we need a poet occasionally to remind us that even the coffee we absentmindedly sip comes in (as Yeats put it) a "heavy spillable cup."

John Keats (1795–1821)
ODE TO A NIGHTINGALE

My heart aches, and a drowsy numbness pains
  My sense, as though of hemlock I had drunk,
Or emptied some dull opiate to the drains
  One minute past, and Lethe-wards had sunk: 4
'Tis not through envy of thy happy lot,
  But being too happy in thine happiness —
    That thou, light-wingèd Dryad° of the trees,   *nymph or spirit*   7
    In some melodious plot
Of beechen green, and shadows numberless,
  Singest of summer in full-throated ease.   10

O for a draught of vintage! that hath been
  Cooled a long age in the deep-delvèd earth,
Tasting of Flora and the country green,
  Dance, and Provençal song, and sunburnt mirth!   14

O for a beaker full of the warm South,
  Full of the true, the blushful Hippocrene,
    With beaded bubbles winking at the brim,.   17
    And purple-stainèd mouth;
That I might drink, and leave the world unseen,
  And with thee fade away into the forest dim: 20

Fade far away, dissolve, and quite forget
  What thou among the leaves hast never known,
The weariness, the fever, and the fret
  Here, where men sit and hear each other groan;   24
Where palsy shakes a few, sad, last grey hairs,
  Where youth grows pale, and specter-thin, and dies;
    Where but to think is to be full of sorrow   27
    And leaden-eyed despairs,
  Where Beauty cannot keep her lustrous eyes,
    Or new Love pine at them beyond to-morrow.   30

Away! away! for I will fly to thee,
  Not charioted by Bacchus and his pards,
But on the viewless wings of Poesy,
  Though the dull brain perplexes and retards: 34
Already with thee! tender is the night,
  And haply the Queen-Moon is on her throne,
    Clustered around by all her starry Fays°;   *Fairies* 37
    But here there is no light,
  Save what from heaven is with the breezes blown
    Through verdurous glooms and winding mossy ways.   40

I cannot see what flowers are at my feet,
  Nor what soft incense hangs upon the boughs,
But, in embalmèd darkness, guess each sweet
  Wherewith the seasonable month endows   44
The grass, the thicket, and the fruit tree wild;
  White hawthorn, and the pastoral eglantine;
    Fast fading violets covered up in leaves;   47
    And mid-May's eldest child,
  The coming musk rose, full of dewy wine,
    The murmurous haunt of flies on summer eves.   50

Darkling° I listen; and, for many a time   *in darkness*
  I have been half in love with easeful Death,
Called him soft names in many a musèd rhyme,
  To take into the air my quiet breath;   54
Now more than ever seems it rich to die,
  To cease upon the midnight with no pain,
    While thou art pouring forth thy soul abroad   57
    In such an ecstasy!
  Still wouldst thou sing, and I have ears in vain —
    To thy high requiem become a sod.   60

Thou wast not born for death, immortal Bird!
 No hungry generations tread thee down;
The voice I hear this passing night was heard
 In ancient days by emperor and clown: 64
Perhaps the self-same song that found a path
 Through the sad heart of Ruth, when, sick for home,
 She stood in tears amid the alien corn;   67
 The same that oft-times hath
Charmed magic casements, opening on the foam
 Of perilous seas, in faery lands forlorn.   70

Forlorn! the very word is like a bell
 To toll me back from thee to my sole self!
Adieu! the fancy cannot cheat so well
 As she is famed to do, deceiving elf.   74
Adieu! adieu! thy plaintive anthem fades
 Past the near meadows, over the still stream,
 Up the hillside; and now 'tis buried deep   77
 In the next valley glades:
Was it a vision, or a waking dream?
 Fled is that music: — Do I wake or sleep?   80

ODE TO A NIGHTINGALE. 4. *Lethe:* River in Hades, a taste of whose waters caused forgetfulness. 16. *Hippocrene:* Fountain sacred to the Muses, on Mt. Helicon, whose waters gave
poetic inspiration. 32. *Bacchus . . . pards:* The god of wine was sometimes depicted riding
in a leopard-drawn chariot. 66. *Ruth:* See the Book of Ruth in the Bible, chap. 2.

QUESTIONS

1. To what extent does Keats employ visual imagery in this poem?
2. What images appeal to senses other than sight?
3. Paraphrase, stanza by stanza, what Keats is saying. Is it possible to divorce
   the meaning of the poem from its imagery? Explain.

[handwritten: not in cronological order to show the shappiness of the bust.]

Elizabeth Bishop (b. 1911)

THE FISH

[handwritten: ✻ Imagery. She takes a fresh look at fish. She makes it ugly & then beautiful.]

[handwritten: 1st section ugly, just a thing]

I caught a tremendous fish
and held him beside the boat
half out of water, with my hook
fast in a corner of his mouth.
He didn't fight.   5
He hadn't fought at all.
He hung a grunting weight,
battered and venerable
and homely. Here and there
his brown skin hung in strips   10
✻ like ancient wall-paper,
and its pattern of darker brown
was like wall-paper:

[handwritten: anthropomorphic — we see him as we see ourselves]

72   Imagery

shapes like full-blown roses
stained and lost through age.   15
He was speckled with barnacles,
fine rosettes of lime,
and infested
with tiny white sea-lice,
and underneath two or three   20
rags of green weed hung down.
While his gills were breathing in
the terrible oxygen
— the frightening gills,
fresh and crisp with blood,   25
that can cut so badly —
I thought of the coarse white flesh
packed in like feathers,
the big bones and the little bones,
the dramatic reds and blacks   30
of his shiny entrails,
and the pink swim-bladder
like a big peony.
I looked into his eyes
which were far larger than mine
but shallower, and yellowed,   35
the irises backed and packed
with tarnished tinfoil
seen through the lenses
of old scratched isinglass.
They shifted a little, but not   40
to return my stare.
— It was more like the tipping
of an object toward the light.
I admired his sullen face,
the mechanism of his jaw,   45
and then I saw
that from his lower lip
— if you could call it a lip —
grim, wet, and weapon-like,
hung five old pieces of fish-line,   50
or four and a wire leader
with the swivel still attached,
with all their five big hooks
grown firmly in his mouth.
A green line, frayed at the end   55
where he broke it, two heavier lines,
and a fine black thread
still crimped from the strain and snap
when it broke and he got away.
Like medals with their ribbons   60
frayed and wavering,
a five-haired beard of wisdom
trailing from his aching jaw.

(Handwritten annotations:)
gross-literal, direct images
2nd section — in virtue of beauty & ugliness. More than just a thing
peony - a flower - about 8" to 12" leaves like camelias & rose-fullness of a pom pom.
metaphor - human imagery
3rd section — human qualities

Imagery 73

I stared and stared
and victory filled up
the little rented boat,
from the pool of bilge
where oil had spread a rainbow
around the rusted engine
to the bailer rusted orange,
the sun-cracked thwarts,
the oarlocks on their strings,
the gunnels — until everything
was rainbow, rainbow, rainbow!
And I let the fish go.

gives clue she is writing about more than just a fish.

oil from the boat & the victory itself.

Probably from an actual experience

4th section: back to just the description of the fish.

a victorious, triumphant humming of courage victory of it, then the bucket & everything of it.

QUESTIONS

1. How many abstract words does this poem contain? How much imagery?
2. What is the speaker's attitude toward the fish? Comment in particular on the imagery of lines 61–64.
3. What attitude do the images of the rainbow of oil (line 69), the orange bailer (bailing bucket, line 71), the *sun-cracked thwarts* (line 72) convey? Does the poet expect us to feel mournful because the boat is in such sorry condition? What is meant by *rainbow, rainbow, rainbow?*
4. How do these images prepare us for the conclusion? Why does the speaker let the fish go?

FOR REVIEW AND FURTHER STUDY

EXPERIMENT: *Writing with Images*

Taking the following poems as examples from which to start rather than as models to be slavishly copied, try to compose a brief poem that consists largely of imagery.

William Carlos Williams (1883–1963)

POEM

As the cat
climbed over
the top of

the jamcloset
first the right
forefoot

carefully
then the hind
stepped down

into the pit of
the empty
flowerpot

T. E. Hulme (1883–1917)

IMAGE

Old houses were scaffolding once
                   and workmen whistling.

Gary Snyder (b. 1930)

FROM "HITCH HAIKU"

They didn't hire him
          so he ate his lunch alone:
the noon whistle

     .   .   .   .

Over the Mindanao Deep
Scrap brass
         dumpt off the fantail
falling six miles

     .   .   .   .

After weeks of watching the roof leak
         I fixed it tonight
by moving a single board

     .   .   .   .

A great freight truck
         lit like a town
through the dark stony desert

     .   .   .   .

Drinking hot saké
         toasting fish on coals
  the motorcycle
out   parked in the rain.

Richard Brautigan (b. 1935)

HAIKU AMBULANCE

A piece of green pepper
  fell
off the wooden salad bowl:
  so what?

Robert Bly (b. 1926)
DRIVING TO TOWN LATE TO MAIL A LETTER

It is a cold and snowy night. The main street is deserted.
The only things moving are swirls of snow.
As I lift the mailbox door, I feel its cold iron.
There is a privacy I love in this snowy night.
Driving around, I will waste more time.

EXERCISE: *Sensing Imagery*

Read the following poems and, for each, try to describe its predominant imagery. Is it visual, auditory, tactile, or what? In which poems do you find more than one kind of imagery?

Sylvia Plath (1932–1963)
CUT

For Susan O'Neill Roe

[handwritten: Quatrains]

What a thrill —
My thumb instead of an onion.
The top quite gone
Except for a sort of a hinge   4

[handwritten: the odd nonrhymes rhyming scheme to lend a nursery rhyme effect]

Of skin,
A flap like a hat,
Dead white.
Then that red plush.   8

Little pilgrim, *[handwritten: her thumb]*
The Indian's axed your scalp. *[handwritten: the nail is the face]*
Your turkey wattle
Carpet rolls   12

Straight from the heart. *[handwritten: the pulse]*
I step on it,
Clutching my bottle
Of pink fizz.   16

A celebration, this is.
Out of a gap
A million soldiers run,
Redcoats, every one.   20

Whose side are they on?
O my
Homunculus, I am ill.
I have taken a pill to kill   24

The thin
Papery feeling.
Saboteur,
Kamikaze man —   28

The stain on your
Gauze Ku Klux Klan
Babushka
Darkens and tarnishes and when   32

The balled
Pulp of your heart
Confronts its small
Mill of silence   36
How you jump —
Trepanned veteran,
Dirty girl,
Thumb stump.   40

Jean Toomer (1894–1967)

REAPERS

Black reapers with the sound of steel on stones
Are sharpening scythes. I see them place the hones
In their hip-pockets as a thing that's done,
And start their silent swinging, one by one.
Black horses drive a mower through the weeds,
And there, a field rat, startled, squealing bleeds,
His belly close to ground. I see the blade,
Blood-stained, continue cutting weeds and shade.

Walt Whitman (1819–1892)

THE DALLIANCE OF THE EAGLES

Skirting the river road, (my forenoon walk, my rest,)
Skyward in air a sudden muffled sound, the dalliance of the eagles,
The rushing amorous contact high in space together,
The clinching interlocking claws, a living, fierce, gyrating wheel,
Four beating wings, two beaks, a swirling mass tight grappling,   5
In tumbling turning clustering loops, straight downward falling,
Till o'er the river pois'd, the twain yet one, a moment's lull,
A motionless still balance in the air, then parting, talons loosing,
Upward again on slow-firm pinions slanting, their separate diverse
     flight,
She hers, he his, pursuing.   10

H. D. [Hilda Doolittle] (1886–1961)

Heat

O wind, rend open the heat,
cut apart the heat,
rend it to tatters.

Fruit cannot drop
through this thick air —   5
fruit cannot fall into heat
that presses up and blunts
the points of pears
and rounds the grapes.

Cut the heat —   10
plough through it,
turning it on either side
of your path.

6 Figures of Speech

WHY SPEAK FIGURATIVELY?

"I will speak daggers to her, but use none," says Hamlet, preparing to confront his mother. His statement makes sense only because we realize that *daggers* is to be taken two ways: literally (denoting sharp, pointed weapons) and nonliterally (referring to something that can be used *like* weapons — namely, words). Reading poetry, we often meet comparisons between two things whose similarity we have never noticed before. When Marianne Moore observes that a fir tree has "an emerald turkey-foot at the top," the result is a pleasure that poetry richly affords: the sudden recognition of likenesses.

A treetop like a turkey-foot, words like daggers — such comparisons are called **figures of speech.** In its broadest definition, a figure of speech may be said to occur whenever a speaker or writer, for the sake of freshness or emphasis, departs from the usual denotations of his words. Certainly, when Hamlet says he will speak daggers, no one expects him to release pointed weapons from his lips, for *daggers* is not to be read solely for its denotation. Its connotations — sharp, stabbing, piercing, wounding — also come to mind, and we see ways in which words and daggers work alike. (Words too can hurt: by striking through pretenses, possibly, or by wounding their hearer's self-esteem.) In the statement "A razor is sharper than an ax," there is no departure from the usual denotations of *razor* and *ax,* and no figure of speech results. Both objects are of the same class; the comparison is not offensive to logic. But in "How sharper than a serpent's tooth it is to have a thankless child," the objects — snake's tooth (fang) and ungrateful offspring — are so unlike that no reasonable comparison may be made between them. To find similarity, we attend to the connotations of *serpent's tooth* — biting, piercing, pain — rather than to its denotations.

Figures of speech are much more than ways of stating what is demonstrably untrue. They do, indeed, state a truth that more literal language cannot.

Alfred, Lord Tennyson (1809–1892)

THE EAGLE

He clasps the crag with crooked hands;
Close to the sun in lonely lands,
Ringed with the azure world, he stands.   3

The wrinkled sea beneath him crawls;
He watches from his mountain walls,
And like a thunderbolt he falls.   6

This brief poem is rich in figurative language. In the first line, the phrase *crooked hands* may surprise us. An eagle does not have hands, we might protest; but the objection would be a quibble, for evidently Tennyson is indicating exactly how an eagle clasps a crag, in the way that human fingers clasp a thing. By implication, too, the eagle is a person. *Close to the sun,* if taken literally, is an absurd exaggeration, the sun being a mean distance of 93,000,000 miles from the earth. For the eagle to be closer to it by the altitude of a mountain is an approach so small as to be insignificant. But figuratively, Tennyson conveys that the eagle stands above the clouds, perhaps silhouetted against the sun, and for the moment belongs to the heavens rather than to the land and sea. The word *ringed* makes a circle of the whole world's horizons and suggests that we see the world from the eagle's height; the sea becomes an aged, sluggish animal; *mountain walls,* possibly literal, also suggests a fort or castle; and finally the eagle himself is likened to a thunderbolt in speed and in power, perhaps also in that his beak is — like our abstract conception of a lightningbolt — pointed. How much of the poem can be taken literally? Only *he clasps the crag, he stands, he watches, he falls.* The rest is made of figures of speech. The result is that, reading Tennyson's poem, we gain a bird's-eye view of sun, sea, and land — and even of bird. Like imagery, figurative language refers us to the physical world.

METAPHOR AND SIMILE

Life, like a dome of many-colored glass,
Stains the white radiance of Eternity.

The first of these lines (from Shelley's "Adonais") is a **simile:** a comparison of two things, indicated by some connective, usually *like, as, than,* or a verb such as *resembles.* The things compared have to be dissimilar in kind for a simile to exist: it is no simile to say "Your fingers are like mine"; it is a literal observation. But to say "Your fingers are like sausages" is to use a simile. Omit the connective — say "Your fingers are sausages" — and the result is a **metaphor,** a statement that one thing *is* something else, which, in a literal sense, it is not. In the second of Shelley's lines, it is *assumed* that Eternity is light or radiance, and we have an **implied metaphor,** one that uses neither a connective nor the verb *to be.* Here are examples:

O, my love is like a red, red rose.	*Simile*
O, my love resembles a red, red rose.	*Simile*
O, my love is redder than a rose.	*Simile*
O, my love is a red, red rose.	*Metaphor*
O, my love has red petals and sharp thorns.	*Implied metaphor*
O, I placed my love into a long-stem vase	*Implied metaphor*
And I bandaged my bleeding thumb.	

Often you can tell a metaphor from a simile by much more than the presence or absence of a connective. In general, a simile refers to only one characteristic that two things have in common, while a metaphor is not plainly limited in the number of resemblances it may indicate. To use the simile "He eats like a pig" is to compare man and animal in one respect: eating habits. But to say "He's a pig" is to use a metaphor that might involve comparisons of appearance and morality as well as of eating habits. We might — if we prefer to classify figures of speech according to what they mean instead of according to words they use — throw over the traditional usage and call the line "My love is like a red, red rose" a metaphor rather than a simile because it conveys not just a single resemblance but many resemblances — of freshness, color (red cheeks and lips), and sweet odor — to name a few.[1]

In everyday speech, simile and metaphor occur frequently. We use metaphors ("She's a doll"), and similes ("The tickets are selling like hotcakes") without being fully conscious of them. If, however, we are aware that words possess literal meanings as well as figurative ones, we do not write *died in the wool* for *dyed in the wool* or *tow the line* for *toe the line,* nor do we use **mixed metaphors** as did the newspaper astrologist who advised Pisceans, "Do everything in your power to bridge the generation gap, even though it is quite a hurdle," or the speaker who urged, "To get ahead, keep your nose to the grindstone, your shoulder to the wheel, your ear to the ground, and your eye on the ball." Perhaps the unintended humor of these statements comes from our seeing that the writer, busy stringing together stale metaphors, was not aware that they had any physical reference.

A word of warning: almost all figurative language is grotesque if we visualize it unimaginatively. "My love is like a red, red rose" ought not call to mind a girl with a scarlet face and a thorny neck. What is wrong with the mixed metaphors we have been considering is that their user has no control over his clichés; they control his mind. But a

---

[1] Preferring such classification, the critic Philip Wheelwright has suggested that, as a manner of speaking, metaphor is often better than simile, for it may differ "in degree of intensity, or in depth of penetration, or in freshness of recombination" (*The Burning Fountain,* Bloomington, Indiana, 1954, p. 84).

good poet can combine incongruous things. He can do so because he selects words carefully and realizes their possible effects on us. In "Thirty Bob a Week," John Davidson gives us a series of metaphors to show what it meant in Victorian England to be a working man with a family to support on a pitifully small wage:

> It's a naked child against a hungry wolf;
>   It's playing bowls upon a splitting wreck;
> It's walking on a string across a gulf
>   With millstones fore-and-aft about your neck;
> But the thing is daily done by many and many a one;
>   And we fall, face forward, fighting, on the deck.

The impossibilities coalesce. Though no less literally absurd than the man with his nose to the grindstone, Davidson's man can be visualized, and his balancing act is meaningful.

A poem may involve a series of comparisons, like Davidson's, or the whole poem may be one extended comparison:

Richard Wilbur (b. 1917)
A SIMILE FOR HER SMILE

Your smiling, or the hope, the thought of it,
Makes in my mind such pause and abrupt ease
As when the highway bridgegates fall,
Balking the hasty traffic, which must sit
On each side massed and staring, while
Deliberately the drawbridge starts to rise: 6

Then horns are hushed, the oilsmoke rarifies,
Above the idling motors one can tell
The packet's smooth approach, the slip,
Slip of the silken river past the sides,
The ringing of clear bells, the dip
And slow cascading of the paddle wheel.   12

How much life metaphors bring to poetry may be seen by comparing two poems by Tennyson and Blake.

Alfred, Lord Tennyson (1809–1892)
FLOWER IN THE CRANNIED WALL

Flower in the crannied wall,
I pluck you out of the crannies,
I hold you here, root and all, in my hand,
Little flower — but if I could understand
What you are, root and all, and all in all,
I should know what God and man is.

How many metaphors does this poem contain? None. Compare it with a briefer poem on a similar theme: the quatrain that begins Blake's "Auguries of Innocence." (We follow here the opinion of W. B. Yeats who, in editing Blake's poems, thought the lines ought to be printed separately.)

William Blake (1757–1827)

To SEE A WORLD IN A GRAIN OF SAND

To see a world in a grain of sand
And a heaven in a wild flower,
Hold infinity in the palm of your hand
And eternity in an hour.

Set beside Blake's poem, Tennyson's — short though it is — seems lengthy. What contributes to the richness of "To see a world in a grain of sand" is Blake's use of a metaphor in every line. And every metaphor is loaded with suggestion. Our world does indeed resemble a grain of sand: in being round, in being stony, in being one of a myriad (the suggestions go on and on). Like Blake's grain of sand, a metaphor holds much, within a small circumference.

Sylvia Plath (1932–1963)

METAPHORS   – A PREGNANT   WOMAN

I'm a riddle in nine syllables,
An elephant, a ponderous house,
A melon strolling on two tendrils.
O red fruit, ivory, fine timbers!
This loaf's big with its yeasty rising.   5
Money's new-minted in this fat purse.
I'm a means, a stage, a cow in calf.
I've eaten a bag of green apples,
Boarded the train there's no getting off.

QUESTIONS

1. To what central fact do all the metaphors in this poem refer?
2. In the first line, what has the speaker in common with a riddle? Why does she say she has *nine* syllables?
3. How would you describe the tone of this poem? (Perhaps the poet expresses more than one attitude.) What attitude is conveyed in the metaphors of an elephant, "ponderous house," "melon strolling on two tendrils"? By the metaphors of red fruit, ivory, fine timbers, new-minted money? By the metaphor in the last line?

Emily Dickinson (1830–1886)

IT DROPPED SO LOW – IN MY REGARD

It dropped so low – in my Regard –
I heard it hit the Ground –
And go to pieces on the Stones
At bottom of my Mind –   4

Yet blamed the Fate that flung it – *less*
Than I denounced Myself,
For entertaining Plated Wares
Upon my Silver Shelf –   8

QUESTIONS

1. What is *it*? What two things are compared?
2. How much of the poem consists of developing and amplifying this comparison?
3. In another version of this poem, lines 5–6 read: "Yet blamed the Fate that fractured – *less* / Than I reviled Myself." Which version do you prefer? Why?

Anonymous (English; 1784 or earlier)

THERE WAS A MAN OF DOUBLE DEED

There was a man of double deed
Who sowed his garden full of seed.   2
When the seed began to grow
'Twas like a garden full of snow,   4
When the snow began to melt
'Twas like a ship without a belt,   6
When the ship began to sail
'Twas like a bird without a tail,   8
When the bird began to fly
'Twas like an eagle in the sky,   10
When the sky began to roar
'Twas like a lion at the door,   12
When the door began to crack
'Twas like a stick across my back,   14
When my back began to smart
'Twas like a penknife in my heart,   16
And when my heart began to bleed
'Twas death and death and death indeed.   18

THERE WAS A MAN OF DOUBLE DEED. This traditional nursery rime may have originated as a chant to the rhythm of a bouncing ball. Its opening lines echo an old proverb: "A man of words and not of deeds is like a garden full of weeds." 6. *belt:* A series of armored plates at a ship's water line.

Does this seem no more than rigmarole or do you find it making any sense? Consider possible meanings of the phrase *double deed* and ways in which the objects joined in similes might be truly similar.

Ruth Whitman (b. 1922)

CASTOFF SKIN

She lay in her girlish sleep at ninety-six,
small as a twig.
Pretty good figure

for an old lady, she said to me once.
Then she crawled away, leaving   5
a tiny stretched transparence

behind her. When I kissed her paper cheek
I thought of the snake,
of his quick motion.

QUESTION

Explain the central metaphor in "Castoff Skin." What other figures of speech does the poem contain?

Robert Graves (b. 1895)

A CIVIL SERVANT

While in this cavernous place employed
    Not once was I aware
Of my officious other-self
    Poised high above me there,   4

My self reversed, my rage-less part,
    A slimy yellowish cone —
Drip, drip; drip, drip — so down the years
    I stalagmized in stone.   8

Now pilgrims to the cave, who come
    To chip off what they can,
Prod me with child-like merriment:
    "Look, look! It's like a man!"   12

QUESTIONS

1. What is the difference between a stalactite and a stalagmite? What does Graves liken to each of them?
2. How are they formed? To what is Graves comparing the process of their formation?

3. What is the theme of the poem?
4. How would you describe the relationship between theme and metaphors in this poem?

Ogden Nash (1902–1971)
Very Like a Whale

One thing that literature would be greatly the better for
Would be a more restricted employment by authors of simile and
    metaphor.   2
Authors of all races, be they Greeks, Romans, Teutons or Celts,
Can't seem just to say that anything is the thing it is but have to go out
    of their way to say that it is like something else.   4
What does it mean when we are told
That the Assyrian came down like a wolf on the fold?   6
In the first place, George Gordon Byron had had enough experience
To know that it probably wasn't just one Assyrian, it was a lot of
    Assyrians.   8
However, as too many arguments are apt to induce apoplexy and thus
    hinder longevity,
We'll let it pass as one Assyrian for the sake of brevity.   10
Now then, this particular Assyrian, the one whose cohorts were gleam-
    ing in purple and gold,
Just what does the poet mean when he says he came down like a wolf
    on the fold?   12
In heaven and earth more than is dreamed of in our philosophy there
    are a great many things,
But I don't imagine that among them there is a wolf with purple and
    gold cohorts or purple and gold anythings.   14
No, no, Lord Byron, before I'll believe that this Assyrian was actually
    like a wolf I must have some kind of proof;
Did he run on all fours and did he have a hairy tail and a big red mouth
    and big white teeth and did he say Woof woof woof?   16
Frankly I think it very unlikely, and all you were entitled to say, at the
    very most,
Was that the Assyrian cohorts came down like a lot of Assyrian cohorts
    about to destroy the Hebrew host.   18
But that wasn't fancy enough for Lord Byron, oh dear me no, he had to
    invent a lot of figures of speech and then interpolate them,
With the result that whenever you mention Old Testament soldiers to
    people they say Oh yes, they're the ones that a lot of wolves dressed
    up in gold and purple ate them.   20
That's the kind of thing that's being done all the time by poets, from
    Homer to Tennyson;
They're always comparing ladies to lilies and veal to venison.   22
How about the man who wrote,
Her little feet stole in and out like mice beneath her petticoat?   24
Wouldn't anybody but a poet think twice
Before stating that his girl's feet were mice?   26

Then they always say things like that after a winter storm
The snow is a white blanket. Oh it is, is it, all right then, you sleep under a
    six-inch blanket of snow and I'll sleep under a half-inch blanket of
    unpoetical blanket material and we'll see which one keeps warm,   28
And after that maybe you'll begin to comprehend dimly
What I mean by too much metaphor and simile.   30

VERY LIKE A WHALE. The title is from *Hamlet* (Act III, scene 2): Feigning madness, Hamlet likens the shape of a cloud to a whale. "Very like a whale," says Polonius, who, to humor his prince, will agree to the accuracy of any figure at all. Nash's art has been described by Max Eastman in *Enjoyment of Laughter* (New York, 1936):

> If you have ever tried to write rimed verse, you will recognize in Nash's writing every naïve crime you were ever tempted to commit — artificial inversions, pretended rimes, sentences wrenched and mutilated to bring the rime-word to the end of the line, words assaulted and battered into riming whether they wanted to or not, ideas and whole dissertations dragged in for the sake of a rime, the metrical beat delayed in order to get all the necessary words in, the metrical beat speeded up unconscionably because there were not enough words to put in.

QUESTIONS

1. Nash alludes to the opening lines of Byron's poem "The Destruction of Sennacherib":

The Assyrian came down like the wolf on the fold,
And his cohorts were gleaming in purple and gold;

and to Sir John Suckling's portrait of a bride in "A Ballad Upon a Wedding":

Her feet beneath her petticoat,
Like little mice stole in and out,
As if they feared the light: . . .

How can these metaphors be defended against Nash's quibbles?
2. What valuable functions of simile and metaphor in poetry is Nash pretending to ignore?

Langston Hughes (1902–1967)

DREAM DEFERRED

What happens to a dream deferred?

Does it dry up
like a raisin in the sun?
Or fester like a sore —
And then run?   5
Does it stink like rotten meat?
Or crust and sugar over —
like a syrupy sweet?

Maybe it just sags
like a heavy load.   10

Or does it explode?

OTHER FIGURES

When Shakespeare asks, in a sonnet,

> O! how shall summer's honey breath hold out
> Against the wrackful siege of batt'ring days,

it might seem at first that he mixes metaphors. How can a *breath* confront the battering ram of an invading army? But it is summer's breath and, by giving it to summer, Shakespeare makes the season a man or woman. It is as if the fragrance of summer were the breath within a person's body, and winter were the onslaught of old age.

Such is one instance of **personification:** a figure of speech in which a thing, an animal, or an abstract term (*truth, nature*) is made human. A personification extends throughout this whole short poem:

James Stephens (1882–1950)
THE WIND

The wind stood up and gave a shout.
He whistled on his fingers and

Kicked the withered leaves about
And thumped the branches with his hand

And said he'd kill and kill and kill,
And so he will and so he will.

This wind is a wild man, and evidently it is not just any autumn breeze but a hurricane or at least a stiff gale. In poems that do not work as well as this one, personification may be employed mechanically. Hollow-eyed personifications stalk through the works of lesser English poets of the eighteenth century: Coleridge has quoted the beginning of such a neoclassical ode, "Inoculation! heavenly Maid, descend!" It is hard for the contemporary reader to be excited by William Collins's "The Passions, An Ode for Music" (1747), which personifies, stanza by stanza, Fear, Anger, Despair, Hope, Revenge, Pity, Jealousy, Love, Hate, Melancholy, and Cheerfulness, and has them listen to Music, until even "Brown Exercise rejoiced to hear, / And Sport leapt up, and seized his beechen spear." However, using a figure of speech from custom rather than from inspiration does not necessarily discredit it. The portrayals of the Seven Deadly Sins in the fourteenth-century poem *The Vision of Piers Plowman* remain memorable: "Thanne come Slothe al bislabered, with two slimy eiyen. . . ." In "Two Sonnets on Fame" John Keats made an abstraction come alive in personifying Fame as "a wayward girl."

Hand in hand with personification often goes **apostrophe:** a way of addressing someone or something invisible or not ordinarily spoken to. In an apostrophe, a poet (in these examples Wordsworth) may address an inanimate object ("Spade! with which Wilkinson hath tilled his lands"), some dead or absent person ("Milton! thou shouldst be living at this hour"), an abstract thing ("Return, Delights!"), or a spirit ("Thou Soul that art the eternity of thought"). More often than not, the poet uses apostrophe to announce a lofty and serious tone. He may even put an "O" in front of it ("O moon!") as, according to W. D. Snodgrass, every poet has a right to do at least once in his life. But apostrophe does not necessarily have to be hifalutin. It is a way of giving body to the intangible, a way of speaking to it person to person, as in the words of a moving American spiritual: "Death, ain't you got no shame?"

Most of us, from time to time, emphasize a point with a statement containing exaggeration: "He's faster than greased lightning," "I've told him a thousand times." We speak, then, not literal truth but use a figure of speech called **overstatement** (or **hyperbole**). Poets too, being fond of emphasis, often exaggerate, sometimes with splendid effect. Instances are Marvell's profession of a love that should grow "Vaster than empires, and more slow" and Burgon's description of Petra: "A rose-red city, half as old as Time." Overstatement can be used also for humorous purposes, as in a fat woman's boast (from a blues song): "Every time I shake, some skinny gal loses her home."[2] The opposite is **understatement,** implying more than is said. Mark Twain in *Life on the Mississippi* recalls how, as an apprentice steamboat-pilot asleep when supposed to be on watch, he was roused by the pilot and sent clambering to the pilot house: "Mr. Bixby was close behind, commenting." Another example is Robert Frost's line "One could do worse than be a swinger of birches" — the conclusion of a poem that has suggested that to swing on a birch tree is one of the most deeply satisfying activities in the world. Because in both overstatement and understatement we notice a discrepancy between what the writer says and what he means, both are forms of verbal irony.

In **metonymy,** the name of a thing is substituted for that of another closely associated with it: we say "The White House decided," and mean the President did. When John Dyer writes in "Grongar Hill,"

A little rule, a little sway,
A sun beam on a winter's day,
Is all the proud and mighty have
Between the cradle and the grave,

we recognize that *cradle* and *grave* signify birth and death. A kind of metonymy, **synecdoche** is the use of a part of a thing to stand for the whole of it or vice versa. We say "He lent a hand," and mean that he lent his entire presence. Similarly, Milton in "Lycidas" refers to greedy clergymen as "blind mouths." Another kind of metonymy is the **trans-**

---

[2] Quoted by LeRoi Jones in *Blues People* (New York, 1963).

ferred epithet: a device of emphasis in which the poet attributes some characteristic of a thing to another thing closely associated with it. When Thomas Gray observes that, in the evening pastures, "drowsy tinklings lull the distant folds," he well knows that sheep's bells do not drowse, but sheep do. When Hart Crane, describing the earth as seen from an airplane, speaks of "nimble blue plateaus," he attributes the airplane's motion to the earth.

Paradox occurs in a statement that at first strikes us as self-contradictory but that on reflection makes some sense. "The peasant," said G. K. Chesterton, "lives in a larger world than the globe-trotter." Here, two different meanings of *larger* are contrasted: "greater in spiritual values" versus "greater in miles." Some paradoxical statements, however, are more than plays on words. They point to situations the writer finds absurd or full of cosmic irony. Fulke Greville, Lord Brooke, sees such a paradox:

> Oh, wearisome condition of humanity,
> Born under one law, to another bound;
> Vainly begot, and yet forbidden vanity,
> Created sick, commanded to be sound.

EXERCISE: *Paradox*

What paradoxes do you find in the following poem? For each, explain the sense that underlies the statement.

Chidiock Tichborne (1558?–1586)

ELEGY, WRITTEN WITH HIS OWN HAND IN THE TOWER BEFORE HIS EXECUTION

My prime of youth is but a frost of cares,
  My feast of joy is but a dish of pain,
My crop of corn is but a field of tares°,   *weeds*
  And all my good is but vain hope of gain: 4
The day is past, and yet I saw no sun,
And now I live, and now my life is done.   6

My tale was heard, and yet it was not told,
  My fruit is fall'n, and yet my leaves are green,
My youth is spent, and yet I am not old,
  I saw the world, and yet I was not seen: 10
My thread is cut, and yet it is not spun,
And now I live, and now my life is done.   12

I sought my death, and found it in my womb,
  I looked for life, and saw it was a shade,
I trod the earth, and knew it was my tomb,
  And now I die, and now I was but made: 16
My glass is full, and now my glass is run,
And now I live, and now my life is done.   18

Ironic poems often will use, together with paradox, a figure known to classical rhetoricians as *paranomasia,* the **pun** or play on words. Asked by a lady to define the difference between men and women, Samuel Johnson replied, "I can't conceive, madam, can you?" As in this example, a pun calls to mind another word (or other words) of the same or similar sound but of different denotation. Puns may be mere quibbles, but at their best they can point to resemblances. The name of a dentist's country home, Tooth Acres, is accurate: quite literally, the land was paid for by patients with aching teeth. In verse and poetry, the use of two or more denotations may be facetious, as in Thomas Hood's ballad of "Faithless Nelly Gray":

> Ben Battle was a soldier bold,
>   And used to war's alarms;
> But a cannon-ball took off his legs,
>   So he laid down his arms!

Or it may be serious, as in these lines on war by E. E. Cummings:

> the bigness of cannon
> is skilful,

(*is skilful* becoming *is kill-ful* when read aloud), or perhaps, as in Shakespeare's song in *Cymbeline,* "Fear no more the heat o' th' sun," both facetious and serious at once:

> Golden lads and girls all must,
> As chimney-sweepers, come to dust.

The effect of the following poem depends on serious punning. To read the poem with understanding, sort out the various meanings of the word *rest.* The title suggests a metaphor: the pulley is man's weariness, with which God draws him home.

George Herbert (1593–1633)
THE PULLEY

> When God at first made man,
> Having a glass of blessings standing by —
> Let us (said he) pour on him all we can;
> Let the world's riches, which dispersèd lie,
>   Contract into a span.   5
>
> So strength first made a way,
> Then beauty flowed, then wisdom, honor, pleasure:
> When almost all was out, God made a stay,
> Perceiving that, alone of all His treasure,
>   Rest in the bottom lay.   10
>
> For if I should (said he)
> Bestow this jewel also on My creature,

He would adore My gifts instead of Me,
And rest in Nature, not the God of Nature:
   So both should losers be.   15

  Yet let him keep the rest,
But keep them with repining restlessness;
Let him be rich and weary, that at least,
If goodness lead him not, yet weariness
   May toss him to My breast.   20

     To sum up: figures of speech are not to be taken literally, but they may direct us to things we can see and touch. By doing so, they can make an abstraction more definite, more clearly apprehensible. By *personifying* an eagle, the poet reminds us that the world of nature and that of men have something in common; by *animizing* the sea, he gives it life. By *metonymy* he can focus our attention on a particular detail in a large, complicated object that otherwise might be a blur to us; by *hyperbole* and *understatement, pun* and *paradox,* he can emphasize the physical actuality in back of his words. By *apostrophe,* he animates the inanimate and makes it listen; he speaks directly to an immediate god or to the revivified dead. Put to such uses, a figure of speech has power. It is more than just a manner of playing with words.

Robert Frost (1874–1963)

Tree at My Window

Tree at my window, window tree,
My sash is lowered when night comes on;
But let there never be curtain drawn
Between you and me.   4

Vague dream-head lifted out of the ground,
And thing next most diffuse to cloud,
Not all your light tongues talking aloud
Could be profound.   8

But, tree, I have seen you taken and tossed,
And if you have seen me when I slept,
You have seen me when I was taken and swept
And all but lost.   12

That day she put our heads together,
Fate had her imagination about her,
Your head so much concerned with outer,
Mine with inner, weather.   16

Questions

1. What is the central metaphor of this poem? Is it explicit or implied?
2. What is meant by *light tongues* (line 7)? What resemblances does this comparison point out?

3. What do you understand from the "inner weather" (line 16) by which the speaker was "taken and swept"?
4. What use does Frost make of personification? What does it contribute to the poem?

Edmund Waller (1606–1687)

On a Girdle

That which her slender waist confined,
Shall now my joyful temples bind;
No monarch but would give his crown,
His arms might do what this has done.   4

It was my heaven's extremest sphere,
The pale° which held that lovely deer;   *enclosure*
My joy, my grief, my hope, my love,
Did all within this circle move!   8

A narrow compass! and yet there
Dwelt all that's good, and all that's fair!
Give me but what this riband bound,
Take all the rest the sun goes round!   12

On a Girdle, 1–2. *That which . . . temples bind:* A courtly lover might bind his brow with a lady's ribbon, to signify he was hers. 5. *extremest sphere:* In Ptolemaic astronomy, the outermost of the concentric spheres that surround the earth. In its wall the farthest stars are set.

Questions

1. To what things is the girdle compared?
2. Explain the pun in line 4. What effect does it have upon the tone of the poem?
3. Why is the effect of this pun different from that of Thomas Hood's play on the same word in "Faithless Nelly Gray" (quoted on p. 91)?
4. What does *compass* denote in line 9?
5. What paradox occurs in lines 9–10?
6. How many of the poem's statements are hyperbolic? Is the compliment he pays his lady too grandiose to be believed? Explain.

John Donne (1572–1631)

A Hymn to God the Father

Wilt Thou forgive that sin where I begun,
    Which is my sin, though it were done before?
Wilt Thou forgive those sins through which I run,
    And do them still, though still I do deplore?
        When Thou hast done, Thou hast not done,
            For I have more.   6

Wilt Thou forgive that sin by which I have won
  Others to sin? and made my sin their door?
Wilt Thou forgive that sin which I did shun
  A year or two, but wallowed in a score?
    When Thou hast done, Thou hast not done,
      For I have more.   12

I have a sin of fear, that when I have spun
  My last thread, I shall perish on the shore;
Swear by Thyself that at my death Thy Sun
  Shall shine as it shines now, and heretofore;
    And, having done that, Thou hast done,
      I have no more.   18

A HYMN TO GOD THE FATHER. According to his biographer Izaak Walton, Donne wrote
this poem during an illness in 1623, which brought him close to death.

QUESTIONS

1. For what different meanings can we read lines 5–6, 11–12, 17–18?
2. Discuss how fairly it can be charged that, because of its puns, Donne's
   poem is not serious.
3. Donne's wife, who had died in 1617, was named Anne More. Do you think
   he is punning on her name? Would that interpretation make sense?

FOR REVIEW AND FURTHER STUDY

Anne Sexton (b. 1928)
YOU ALL KNOW THE STORY OF THE OTHER WOMAN

It's a little Walden.
She is private in her breathbed
as his body takes off and flies,
flies straight as an arrow.
But it's a bad translation.   5
Daylight is nobody's friend.
God comes in like a landlord
and flashes on his brassy lamp.
Now she is just so-so.
He puts his bones back on,   10
turning the clock back an hour.
She knows flesh, that skin balloon,
the unbound limbs, the boards,
the roof, the removable roof.
She is his selection, part time.   15
You know the story too! Look,
when it is over he places her,
like a phone, back on the hook.

1. By her final simile, the poet tries to make sure that any reader who had happened not to know the story of the other woman will know it at the end.
What is this conventional story?
2. What sense do you make of the *it* in line 1? Of the *it* in line 5?
3. Besides these metaphors, what other figures of speech do you find? Comment especially on *breathbed* (line 2).

Elizabeth Jennings (b. 1926)

DELAY

The radiance of that star that leans on me
Was shining years ago. The light that now
Glitters up there my eye may never see
And so the time lag teases me with how   4

Love that loves now may not reach me until
Its first desire is spent. The star's impulse
Must wait for eyes to claim it beautiful
And love arrived may find us somewhere else.   8

QUESTIONS

1. What are the two terms in this metaphor?
2. Why would the metaphor not have been available to a poet in Shakespeare's
time?
3. What is the tone of the poem? How does the speaker feel about the *radiance
of that star* — simply joyous and glad, as we might expect?
4. What connotations has the word *impulse* (line 6)? What is the implied
metaphor here?

Andrew Marvell (1621–1678)

THE DEFINITION OF LOVE

My Love is of a birth as rare
As 'tis for object strange and high:
It was begotten by Despair
Upon Impossibility.   4

Magnanimous Despair alone
Could show me so divine a thing,
Where feeble Hope could ne'er have flown
But vainly flapped its tinsel wing.   8

And yet I quickly might arrive
Where my extended soul is fixed,
But Fate does iron wedges drive,
And always crowds itself betwixt.   12

For Fate with jealous eyes does see
Two perfect loves, nor lets them close:
Their union would her ruin be,
And her tyrannic power depose.   16

And therefore her decrees of steel
Us as the distant poles have placed,
(Though Love's whole world on us doth wheel)
Not by themselves to be embraced,   20

Unless the giddy heaven fall,
And earth some new convulsion tear,
And, us to join, the world should all
Be cramped° into a planisphere.   *forced flat*   24

As lines, so loves oblique may well
Themselves in every angle greet;
But ours, so truly parallel,
Though infinite, can never meet.   28

Therefore the love which us doth bind,
But Fate so enviously debars,
Is the conjunction of the mind,
And opposition of the stars.   32

THE DEFINITION OF LOVE. 24. *planisphere:* A map of the globe projected on a plane surface. 31. *conjunction:* A term from astrology and astronomy, the seeming closeness of two heavenly bodies in the same celestial longitude. 32. *opposition:* A planet is said to be in opposition to the sun when its longitude and the sun's are 180° apart.

QUESTIONS

1. What personifications does Marvell employ? Which of them seems most central?
2. To what is *Hope* compared in lines 7–8?
3. What figure of speech is *decrees of steel* (line 17)? Explain this phrase.
4. What meanings do you find in *oblique* (line 25) and *parallel* (line 27)? To what does Marvell refer?
5. What use is made of hyperbole?

EXERCISE: *Recognizing Figures of Speech*

In each of the following poems, what uses are made of metaphor, simile, personification, apostrophe, metonymy, hyperbole, pun, and paradox? In each metaphor or simile, what two things are compared? In each use of metonymy, what is represented?

Anonymous
(English; time of the Crimean War, 1854–1856)
THE FORTUNES OF WAR, I TELL YOU PLAIN

The fortunes of war, I tell you plain,
Are a wooden leg — or a golden chain.

A. R. Ammons (b. 1926)

Auto Mobile

For the bumps bangs & scratches of
collisive encounters
madam
I through time's ruts and weeds
sought you, metallic, your   5
stainless steel flivver:
I have banged you, bumped
and scratched, side-swiped,
momocked & begommed you &
your little flivver still   10
works so well.

Theodore Roethke (1908–1963)

I Knew a Woman

I knew a woman, lovely in her bones,
When small birds sighed, she would sigh back at them;
Ah, when she moved, she moved more ways than one:
The shapes a bright container can contain!   4
Of her choice virtues only gods should speak,
Or English poets who grew up on Greek
(I'd have them sing in chorus, cheek to cheek).   7

How well her wishes went! She stroked my chin,
She taught me Turn, and Counter-turn, and Stand;
She taught me Touch, that undulant white skin;
I nibbled meekly from her proffered hand;   11
She was the sickle; I, poor I, the rake,
Coming behind her for her pretty sake
(But what prodigious mowing we did make).   14

Love likes a gander, and adores a goose:
Her full lips pursed, the errant note to seize;
She played it quick, she played it light and loose;
My eyes, they dazzled at her flowing knees;   18
Her several parts could keep a pure repose,
Or one hip quiver with a mobile nose
(She moved in circles, and those circles moved).   21

Let seed be grass, and grass turn into hay:
I'm martyr to a motion not my own;
What's freedom for? To know eternity.
I swear she cast a shadow white as stone.   25
But who would count eternity in days?
These old bones live to learn her wanton ways:
(I measure time by how a body sways).   28

Ishmael Reed (b. 1938)

.05

If i had a nickel
For all the women who've
Rejected me in my life
I would be the head of the
World Bank with a flunkie   5
To hold my derby as i
Prepared to fly chartered
Jet to sign a check
Giving India a new lease
On life   10

If i had a nickel for
All the women who've loved
Me in my life i would be
The World Bank's assistant
Janitor and wouldn't need   15
To wear a derby
All i'd think about would
Be going home

A. E. Housman (1859–1936)

FROM THE WASH THE LAUNDRESS SENDS

From the wash the laundress sends
My collars home with raveled ends:
I must fit, now these are frayed,
My neck with new ones London-made.   4

Homespun collars, homespun hearts,
Wear to rags in foreign parts.
Mine at least's as good as done,
And I must get a London one.   8

John Ciardi (b. 1916)

CREDIBILITY

Who could believe an ant in theory?
a giraffe in blueprint?
Ten thousand doctors of what's possible
could reason half the jungle out of being.
I speak of love, and something more,   5
to say we are the thing that proves itself
not against reason, but impossibly true,
and therefore to teach reason reason.

James C. Kilgore (b. 1928)
The White Man Pressed the Locks

Driving down the concrete vein,
Away from the smoky heart,
Through the darkening, blighted body,
Pausing at clotted arteries,
The white man pressed the locks   5
  on all the sedan's doors,
Sped toward the white corpuscles
  in the white arms
  hugging the black city.

Anonymous (English; fifteenth century)
I Sing of a Maiden That Is Makeless

I sing of a maiden	that is makeless°:	*matchless or mateless*
king of alle kinges	to° here sone she ches°.	*to be; chose* 2
He came all so stille	there° his mother was	*where*
as dew in Aprille	that falleth on the grass.	4
He came all so stille	to his motheres bower	
as dew in Aprille	that falleth on the flower.	6
He came all so stille	there his mother lay	
as dew in Aprille	that falleth on the spray.	8
Mother and maiden	was never none but she —	
well may swich° a lady	Godes mother be.	*such* 10

William Shakespeare (1564–1616)
Shall I Compare Thee to a Summer's Day?

Shall I compare thee to a summer's day?
Thou art more lovely and more temperate.
Rough winds do shake the darling buds of May,
And summer's lease hath all too short a date.   4
Sometime too hot the eye of heaven shines,
And often is his gold complexion dimmed;
And every fair from fair sometime declines,
By chance, or nature's changing course, untrimmed.   8
But thy eternal summer shall not fade,
Nor lose possession of that fair thou ow'st°;   *ownest, have*
Nor shall death brag thou wand'rest in his shade,
When in eternal lines to time thou grow'st.   12
  So long as men can breathe or eyes can see,
  So long lives this, and this gives life to thee.   14

7 Song

SINGING AND SAYING

Most poems are more memorable than most ordinary speech, and when music is combined with poetry the result is more memorable still. The differences between speech, poetry, and song may be observed by considering, first of all, this fragment of an imaginary conversation:

> Let's not drink; let's just sit and look at each other. Or put a kiss inside my goblet and I won't want anything to drink.

Forgettable language, we might think; but we can try to make it a little more interesting:

> Drink to me only with your eyes, and I'll pledge my love to you with my
> my eyes;
> Or leave a kiss within the goblet, that's all I'll want to drink.

The passage is closer to poetry, but still has a distance to go. At least we now have a figure of speech — the metaphor that love is wine, implied in the statement that one lover may salute another by lifting an eye as well as by lifting a goblet. But the sound of the words is not yet especially interesting. Here is another try, by Ben Jonson:

> Drink to me only with thine eyes,
> And I will pledge with mine;
> Or leave a kiss but in the cup,
> And I'll not ask for wine.

In these opening lines from Jonson's poem "To Celia," the improvement is noticeable. These lines are poetry; their language has become special. For one thing, the lines rime (with an additional rime sound on *thine*). There is interest, too, in the proximity of the words *kiss* and *cup:* the repetition (or alliteration) of the *k* sound. The rhythm of the lines has become regular; generally every other word (or syllable) is stressed:

> DRINK to me ON-ly WITH thine EYES,
> And I will PLEDGE with MINE;
> OR LEAVE a KISS but IN the CUP,
> And I'LL not ASK for WINE.

All these devices of sound and rhythm, together with metaphor, produce a pleasing effect — more pleasing than the effect of "Let's not drink; let's look at each other." As far as we know, Jonson's famous poem first appeared in a book printed in 1616. But the words became more pleasing still when later set to music:

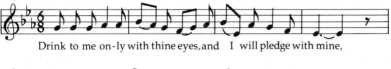

Drink to me on-ly with thine eyes, and   I will pledge with mine,

Or leave a kiss but   in the   cup, and   I'll   not ask for   wine.

In this memorable form, the poem is still alive today.

Ben Jonson (1573?–1637)

To Celia

Drink to me only with thine eyes,
  And I will pledge with mine;
Or leave a kiss but in the cup,
  And I'll not ask for wine.   4
The thirst that from the soul doth rise
  Doth ask a drink divine;
But might I of Jove's nectar sup,
  I would not change for thine.   8

I sent thee late a rosy wreath,
  Not so much honoring thee
As giving it a hope that there
  It could not withered be.   12
But thou thereon didst only breathe,
  And sent'st it back to me;
Since when it grows, and smells, I swear,
  Not of itself but thee.   16

A compliment to a lady has rarely been put in language more graceful, more wealthy with interesting sounds. Other figures of speech besides metaphor make them unforgettable: the hyperbolic tributes to the power of the lady's sweet breath, which can start picked roses growing again, and her kisses, which surpass the nectar of the gods.

This song falls into stanzas — as many poems that resemble songs also do. A **stanza** (Italian for "station," "stopping-place," or "room") is a group of lines whose pattern is repeated throughout the poem. Most songs have more than one stanza. When printed, the stanzas of songs and poems usually are set off from one another by space. Stanzas of songs are indicated by a pause or by the introduction of a refrain, or chorus (a line or lines repeated). The word **verse,** which strictly refers to one line of a poem, is something loosely used to mean a whole stanza: "All join in and sing the second verse!" In speaking of a stanza, whether sung or read, it is customary to indicate by a convenient algebra its **rime scheme,** the order in which rimed words recur. For instance, the rime scheme of this stanza by Herrick is *a b a b*; the first and third lines rime and so do the second and fourth:

> Round, round, the roof doth run;
> And being ravished thus,
> Come, I will drink a tun
> To my Propertius.

Refrains are words, phrases, or lines repeated at intervals in a song or songlike poem. A refrain usually follows immediately after a stanza, and when it does, it is called **terminal refrain.** A refrain whose words change slightly with each recurrence is called an **incremental refrain,** as in "Frankie and Johnny" (p. 117). Sometimes we also hear an **internal refrain:** one that appears within a stanza, generally in a position that stays fixed throughout a poem, as in the ballad "Johnny, I Hardly Knew Ye" (p. 28) and in Yeats's "Long-Legged Fly" (p. 357). Both internal refrains and terminal refrains are used to great effect in the traditional song "The Cruel Mother":

Anonymous (Scottish folk ballad)
THE CRUEL MOTHER

She sat down below a thorn,
  Fine flowers in the valley,
And there she has her sweet babe born
  And the green leaves they grow rarely.   4

"Smile na sae° sweet, my bonny babe,"   *so*
  Fine flowers in the valley,
"And° ye smile sae sweet, ye'll smile me dead."   *if*
  And the green leaves they grow rarely.   8

She's taen out her little pen-knife,
  Fine flowers in the valley,
And twinned° the sweet babe o' its life,   *severed*
  And the green leaves they grow rarely.   12

She's howket° a grave by the light o' the moon,   *dug*
  Fine flowers in the valley,
And there she's buried her sweet babe in
  And the green leaves they grow rarely.   16

As she was going to the church,
  Fine flowers in the valley,

She saw a sweet babe in the porch
And the green leaves they grow rarely.   20

"O sweet babe, and thou were mine,"
Fine flowers in the valley,
"I wad cleed° thee in the silk so fine."   *dress*
And the green leaves they grow rarely.   24

"O mother dear, when I was thine,"
Fine flowers in the valley,
"You did na prove to me sae kind."
And the green leaves they grow rarely.   28

Taken by themselves, the refrain lines might seem mere pretty nonsense. But interwoven with the story of the murdered child, they form a terrible counterpoint. What do they come to mean? Possibly that Nature keeps going about her chores, unmindful of sin and suffering. The effect is an ironic contrast. It is the repetitiveness of a refrain, besides, that helps to give it such power.

Songs tend to be written in language simple enough to be understood on first hearing. Obviously these lines by T. S. Eliot are not meant to be singable, though they have rhythm and rime:

> Polyphiloprogenitive
> The sapient sutlers of the Lord
> Drift across the window-panes.
> In the beginning was the Word.

Recently, however, song-writers have been able to assume that their audiences would pay close attention to their words. Bob Dylan, Leonard Cohen, Phil Ochs, and others have employed words more complicated and difficult than have most previous writers of popular songs, requiring listeners sometimes to play their recordings many times over, with trebles turned up all the way.

Many poems began life as songs but today, their tunes forgotten, survive in poetry anthologies. Shakespeare studded his plays with songs, and many of his contemporaries wrote verse to fit existing tunes. Some poets, themselves musicians (like Thomas Campion), composed both words and music. In Shakespeare's day **madrigals,** short secular songs for three or more voice-parts arranged in counterpoint, enjoyed great favor.

Anonymous (English madrigal; printed 1598)
LADY, WHEN I BEHOLD THE ROSES SPROUTING

Lady, when I behold the roses sprouting,
  Which clad in damask mantles deck the arbors,
  And then behold your lips where sweet Love harbors,
My eyes presents me with a double doubting.

For, viewing both alike, hardly my mind supposes
Whether the roses be your lips, or your lips the roses.

A madrigal by Chidiock Tichborne is given on page 90, and another, the anonymous "Silver Swan," is on page 120.

Some poets who were not composers printed their work in madrigal books for others to set to music. In the seventeenth century, however, poetry and song seem to have fallen away from each other. By the end of the century, much new poetry, other than songs for plays, was written to be printed and to be silently read. Poets who wrote popular songs — like Thomas D'Urfey, compiler of the collection *Pills to Purge Melancholy* — were considered somewhat disreputable. With the notable exceptions of John Gay, who took existing popular tunes for *The Beggar's Opera,* and Robert Burns, who rewrote folk songs or made completely new words for them, few important English poets since Campion have been first-rate song-writers.

Occasionally, a poet has learned a thing or two from music. "But for the opera I could never have written *Leaves of Grass*," said Walt Whitman, who loved that Italian art form for its expansiveness. Coleridge, Hardy, Auden, and many others have learned from folk ballads, and T. S. Eliot patterned his thematically repetitive *Four Quartets* after the structure of a quartet in classical music. "Poetry," said Ezra Pound, "begins to atrophy when it gets too far from music." Still, even in the twentieth century, the poet has been more often a corrector of printer's proofs than a tunesmith or performer.

Some people think that to make a poem and to travel about singing it, as many rock singer-composers now do, is a return to the venerable tradition of the **troubadours,** minstrels of the late Middle Ages. But there are differences. No doubt the troubadours had to please their patrons, but for better or worse their songs were not affected by a stopwatch in a producer's hand or by the technical resources of a sound studio. Bob Dylan has denied that he is a poet, and Paul Simon once told an interviewer, "If you want poetry read Wallace Stevens." Nevertheless, much has been made lately of current song lyrics as poetry.[1] Are rock songs poems? Clearly some, but not all, are. That the lyrics of a song cannot stand the scrutiny of a reader does not necessarily invalidate them, though; song-writers do not usually write in order to be read. Pete Seeger has quoted a saying of his father: "A printed folk song is like a photograph of a bird in flight." Still there is no reason not to read song lyrics. If the words seem rich and interesting, we may possibly increase our enjoyment of them and perhaps be able to sing them

---

[1] See the paperback anthologies *The Poetry of Rock,* edited by Richard Goldstein (New York, 1969), and *Rock Is Beautiful,* edited by Stephanie Spinner (New York, 1970). See also the provocative essay by Robert Christgau, "Rock Lyrics Are Poetry (Maybe)," in *The Age of Rock,* edited by Jonathan Eisen (New York, 1969), and in *Voices of Revelation,* edited by Nancy H. Deane (Boston, 1970).

more accurately. Like most poems and songs of the past, most current songs may end in the trash can of time. And yet, certain memorable rimed and rhythmic lines may live on, especially if music has served them for a base and if singers have given them wide exposure.

Edwin Arlington Robinson (1869–1935)

RICHARD CORY

Whenever Richard Cory went down town,
We people on the pavement looked at him:
He was a gentleman from sole to crown,
Clean favored, and imperially slim.   4

And he was always quietly arrayed,
And he was always human when he talked;
But still he fluttered pulses when he said,
"Good-morning," and he glittered when he walked.   8

And he was rich — yes, richer than a king —
And admirably schooled in every grace:
In fine°, we thought that he was everything   *in short*
To make us wish that we were in his place.   12

So on we worked, and waited for the light,
And went without the meat, and cursed the bread;
And Richard Cory, one calm summer night,
Went home and put a bullet through his head.   16

Paul Simon (b. 1942)

RICHARD CORY

With Apologies to E. A. Robinson

They say that Richard Cory owns
One half of this old town,
With elliptical connections
To spread his wealth around.
Born into Society,   5
A banker's only child,
He had everything a man could want:
Power, grace and style.

Refrain:

But I, I work in his factory
And I curse the life I'm livin'   10
And I curse my poverty

"Richard Cory," by Paul Simon, © 1966, Paul Simon. Used with permission of the publisher.

And I wish that I could be
Oh I wish that I could be
Oh I wish that I could be
Richard Cory. 15

The papers print his picture
Almost everywhere he goes:
Richard Cory at the opera,
Richard Cory at a show
And the rumor of his party 20
And the orgies on his yacht —
Oh he surely must be happy
With everything he's got.   *(Refrain.)*

He really gave to charity,
He had the common touch, 25
And they were grateful for his patronage
And they thanked him very much,
So my mind was filled with wonder
When the evening headlines read:
    "Richard Cory went home last night 30
    And put a bullet through his head."   *(Refrain.)*

RICHARD CORY (PAUL SIMON). If possible, listen to this ballad sung by Simon and Gar-
funkel on *Sounds of Silence* (Columbia recording CL 2469, stereo CS 9269).

Anonymous (Kentucky mountain song)
ON TOP OF OLD SMOKY

On top of old Smoky, all covered with snow,
I lost my true lover for acourtin' too slow. 2
Now, courtin's a pleasure, but parting is grief,
And a false-hearted lover is worse than a thief; 4
For a thief will just rob you and take what you have,
But a false-hearted lover will lead you to the grave; 6
And the grave will decay you, and turn you to dust.
Not one boy in a hundred a poor girl can trust: 8
They'll hug you and kiss you, and tell you more lies
Than the crossties on a railroad, or stars in the skies. 10
So, come all you young maidens, and listen to me:
Never place your affections in a green willow tree; 12
For the leaves they will wither, and the roots they will die.
Your lover will forsake you, and you'll never know why. 14

QUESTION

What figures of speech does this well-known folk song contain? How do they
help make it not only a great song but a poem?

BALLADS AND OTHER POEMS TO SING

Any narrative song, like Paul Simon's "Richard Cory," may be called a **ballad.** In English, some of the most famous ballads are **folk ballads,** loosely defined as anonymous story-songs transmitted orally before they were ever written down. Sir Walter Scott, a pioneer collector of Scottish folk ballads, drew the ire of an old woman whose songs he had transcribed: "They were made for singing and no' for reading, but ye ha'e broken the charm now and they'll never be sung mair." The old singer had a point. Print freezes songs and tends to hold them fast to a single version. However, if Scott and others had not written them down, many would have been lost.

In his monumental work *The English and Scottish Popular Ballads* (1882–1898), the American scholar Francis J. Child winnowed out 305 folk ballads he considered authentic — that is, creations of illiterate or semi-literate people who had preserved them orally. Child, who worked by insight as well as by learning, did such a good job of telling the difference between folk ballads and other kinds that later scholars have added only about a dozen ballads to his count. Often called **Child ballads,** his texts include "The Three Ravens," "Sir Patrick Spence," "The Unquiet Grave," "Edward," "The Cruel Mother," "The Cherry-Tree Carol," and many others still on the lips of singers. Here is one of the best-known Child ballads.

Anonymous (traditional Scottish folk ballad)
BONNY BARBARA ALLAN

It was in and about the Martinmas time,
  When the green leaves were afalling,
That Sir John Graeme, in the West Country,
  Fell in love with Barbara Allan.   4

He sent his men down through the town,
  To the place where she was dwelling:
"O haste and come to my master dear,
  Gin° ye be Barbara Allan."   *if*   8

O hooly°, hooly rose she up,   *slowly*
  To the place where he was lying,
And when she drew the curtain by:
  "Young man, I think you're dying."   12

"O it's I'm sick, and very, very sick,
  And 'tis a' for Barbara Allan." —
"O the better for me ye's never be,
  Tho your heart's blood were aspilling.   16

"O dinna ye mind°, young man, " said she,   *don't you remember*
  "When ye was in the tavern adrinking,
That ye made the health° gae round and round,   *toasts*
  And slighted Barbara Allan?"   20

He turned his face unto the wall,
  And death was with him dealing:
"Adieu, adieu, my dear friends all,
  And be kind to Barbara Allan."   24

And slowly, slowly raise she up,
  And slowly, slowly left him,
And sighing said she could not stay,
  Since death of life had reft him.   ·   28

She had not gane a mile but twa,
  When she heard the dead-bell ringing,
And every jow° that the dead-bell geid,   *stroke*
  It cried, "Woe to Barbara Allan!"   32

"O mother, mother, make my bed!
  O make it saft and narrow!
Since my love died for me today,
  I'll die for him tomorrow."   36

BONNY BARBARA ALLAN. 1. *Martinmas:* Saint Martin's day, November 11.

QUESTIONS

1. In any line does the Scottish dialect cause difficulty? If so, try reading the
   line aloud.
2. Without ever coming out and explicitly calling Barbara hard-hearted, this
   ballad reveals that she is. In which stanza and by what means is her cruelty
   demonstrated?
3. At what point does Barbara evidently have a change of heart? Again, how
   does the poem dramatize this change rather than talk about it?
4. In many American versions of this ballad, noble knight John Graeme becomes an ordinary citizen. The gist of the story is the same, but at the end
   are these further stanzas, incorporated from a different ballad:

   They buried Willie in the old churchyard
     And Barbara in the choir;
   And out of his grave grew a red, red rose,
     And out of hers a briar.

   They grew and grew to the steeple top
     Till they could grow no higher;
   And there they locked in a true love's knot,
     The red rose round the briar.

   Do you think this appendage heightens or weakens the final impact of the
   story? Can the American ending be defended as an integral part of a new
   song? Explain.
5. Paraphrase lines 9, 15–16, 22, 25–28. By putting these lines into prose, what
   has been lost?

As you can see from "Bonny Barbara Allan," in a traditional English or Scottish folk ballad the storyteller speaks of people other than himself. Even if the pronoun "I" occurs, it rarely has much personality. Characters often exchange dialogue, but no one character speaks all the way through. Events move rapidly, perhaps because some of the dull transitional stanzas have been forgotten. The events themselves, as ballad scholar Albert B. Friedman has said, are frequently "the stuff of tabloid journalism — sensational tales of lust, revenge and domestic crime. Unwed mothers slay their newborn babes; lovers unwilling to marry their pregnant mistresses brutally murder the poor women, for which, without fail, they are justly punished."[2] There are also many ballads about people who converse with the dead ("The Unquiet Grave") or with supernatural beings ("Thomas the Rimer") and about gallant knights ("Sir Patrick Spence"), and there are a few humorous ballads, usually about unhappy marriages.

The ballad-spinner has at his disposal a fund of ready-made epithets: steeds are usually "milk-white" or "berry-brown," lips "rosy" or "ruby-red," corpses and graves "clay-cold," beds (like Barbara Allan's) "soft and narrow." At least, these conventional phrases are terse and understandable. Sometimes they add meaning: the king who sends Sir Patrick Spence to his doom drinks "blood-red wine." The clothing, steeds, and palaces of ladies and lords are always luxurious: a queen may wear "grass-green silk" or "Spanish leather" and ride a horse with "fifty silver bells and nine." Such descriptions are naive, for as Friedman points out, ballad-singers were probably peasants imagining what they had seen only from afar: the life of the nobility. This may be why the skin of ladies in folk ballads is ordinarily "milk-white," "lily-white," or "snow-white." In an agrarian society, where most people worked in the fields, not to be suntanned was a sign of gentility.

A favorite pattern of ballad-makers is the so-called **ballad stanza**, four lines rimed *a b c b*, tending to fall into 8, 6, 8, and 6 syllables:

> Clerk Saunders and Maid Margaret
> Walked owre yon garden green,
> And deep and heavy was the love
> That fell thir twa between°.   *between those two*

Though not the only possible stanza for a ballad, this easily singable quatrain has continued to attract poets since the Middle Ages. For an example from a modern folk song, see "Frankie and Johnny" (p. 117): sung or read aloud, such a poem in couplets of long lines will tend to fall into quatrains. **Common meter** is another name sometimes given to the ballad stanza, especially when it occurs in hymns. Other poets besides ballad-singers and hymnists have been fond of it, among them

[2] Introduction to *The Viking Book of Folk Ballads of the English-Speaking World* (New York, 1963).

A. E. Housman and Emily Dickinson. Rime in folk ballads is often rough-and-ready rather than polished and exact: the name Barbara Allan is made to rime with *afalling, dwelling, aspilling, dealing,* and even with *ringing* and *adrinking.*

Obviously, whatever stanza a folk ballad may have is determined not by any printed shape its poet wishes for it but by the demands of music. Here, for instance, is a folk ballad (one of the few Child overlooked) with a stanza much more complicated than the ballad stanza.[3] How would you describe its stanza pattern and, if you know music, how has the tune apparently helped to shape it?

Anonymous (traditional English folk ballad)
STILL GROWING

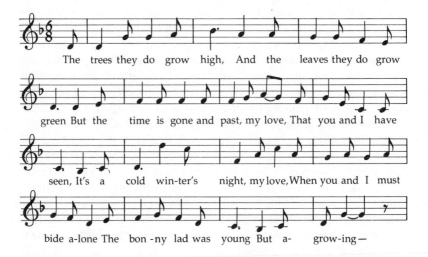

The trees they do grow high, And the leaves they do grow green But the time is gone and past, my love, That you and I have seen, It's a cold win-ter's night, my love, When you and I must bide a-lone The bon -ny lad was young But a- grow-ing —

The trees they do grow high, and the leaves they do grow green;
  The time is gone and past, my love, that you and I have seen:
It's a cold winter's night, my love, when you and I must bide alone.
  The bonny lad was young,
    But a-growing.   5

"O father, dear father, I'm feared you've done me harm
  You've married me a boy and I fear he is too young."
"O daughter, dear daughter, and if you stay at home and wait along o' me
  A lady you shall be,
    While he's a-growing.   10

"We'll send him to the college for one year or two
  And then perhaps in time, my love, a man he will grow.

[3] Collected by Cecil Sharp in *Folksongs from Somerset* (London, 1904–09).

I will buy you a bunch of white ribbons to tie about his bonny, bonny
    waist
  To let the ladies know
    That he's married."   15

At the age of sixteen, he was a married man,
  At the age of seventeen, she brought him a son;
At the age of eighteen, my love, O his grave was growing green,
  And so she put an end
    To his growing.

"I made my love a shroud of the holland so fine,"   20
  And every stitch she put in it the tears came trickling down;
"O once I had a sweetheart, but now I have got never a one
  So fare you well my own true love
    For ever."   25

Telling a long story briefly, as ballads tend to do, "Still Growing" in its fourth stanza so greatly condenses and speeds the action that the effect is startling.

Related to traditional folk ballads but displaying characteristics of their own, **broadside ballads** (so called because they were printed on one sheet of paper) often were set to traditional tunes. Most broadside ballads were an early form of journalism made possible by the development of cheap printing and by the growth of audiences who could read, just barely. Sometimes merely humorous or tear-jerking, often they were rimed accounts of sensational news events. That they were widespread and often scorned in Shakespeare's day is attested by the character of Autolycus in *A Winter's Tale,* an itinerant hawker of ballads about sea monsters and strange pregnancies ("a usurer's wife was brought to bed of twenty money-bags"), who swears to the truth of his merchandise. Although folk ballads occasionally were printed and sold as broadsides and although broadsides occasionally were taken up and in time transformed into folk songs, it is possible to distinguish the two kinds of ballads (as Child did in selecting the ballads he believed to be of folk origin). Here, for instance, is a rather modern broadside ballad about a troubled courtship. How is it different from "Still Growing" and "Bonny Barbara Allan"?

Anonymous
(English broadside ballad; nineteenth century)
SQUIRE AND MILKMAID, OR, BLACKBERRY FOLD

It's of a rich squire in Bristol I'll tell,
There are ladies of honor that love him full well,
But all was in vain, in vain was said,
For he was in love with a charming milkmaid.   4

As the squire and his sister did sit in the hall,
And as they were talking to one and to all,
And as they were singing each other a song,
Pretty Betsy, the milkmaid, came tripping along.   8

Do you want any milk? pretty Betsy did say.
Oh yes, said the squire; step in, pretty maid,
It is you, fair body, that I do adore —
Was there ever a body so wounded me before?   12

Oh! hold your tongue, squire, and let me go free,
Do not make your game on my poverty;
There are ladies of honor more fitter for you
Than I, a poor milkmaid, brought up from the cows.   16

A ring from his finger he instantly drew
And right in the middle he broke it in two,
And half he gave to her, as I have been told,
And they both went a-walking to Blackberry Fold.   20

O Betsy, O Betsy, let me have my will,
So constant a squire I'll prove to you still,
And if you deny me, in this open field,
Why, the first time I'll force, and make you to yield.   24

With hugging and struggling, poor Betsy got free,
Saying, You never shall have your will of me,
I'll protect my own virtue, as I would my life,
And drew from her bosom a large dagger knife.   28

Then with her own weapon she run him quite through
And home to her master like lightning she flew,
Saying, O my dear master, with tears in her eyes,
I have wounded the squire and I'm afraid dead he lies.   32

The coach was got ready, the squire brought home,
The doctor was sent for to heal up the wound,
Poor Betsy was sent for — the gay maiden fair —
Who wounded the squire, drove his heart in a snare.   36

The parson was sent for, this couple to wed,
And she did enjoy the sweet marriage bed.
It's better to be honest if ever so poor,
For he's made her his Lady instead of his whore.   40

QUESTIONS

1. What attitude or attitudes toward love does the author of this broadside take
   for granted? What do you make of his advice to his listeners in the last stanza?
2. Compare his attitude with the attitudes toward love in "Still Growing"
   and "Bonny Barbara Allan." To what do you attribute the differences?
3. "Squire and Milkmaid" uses conventional language: *like lightning she flew*
   (line 30), *gay maiden fair* (line 35), *honest if . . . poor* (line 39; like the saying
   "poor but honest"). How is such language unlike the stock descriptive
   epithets used in folk ballads?

4. Do you suspect that the author of "Squire and Milkmaid" was a highly educated and sophisticated poet or a slightly literate one? Point to evidence.
5. What dramatic irony do you find in the squire's question (line 12)?
6. Do you think "Squire and Milkmaid" totally lacking in those qualities we expect of good poetry? What is there to be said for it?

Clearly, folk ballads are written by people with a different outlook, who approach storytelling differently from those who write broadsides. Folk ballads tend to use stock diction worn smooth by time and tend to be in the ballad stanza; broadsides tend to use more literate clichés and to be written in a straggling **doggerel** (verse full of irregularities due not to skill but to incompetence). Folk ballads tend to be highly dramatic and concentrated, depicting scenes of aristocratic life; broadsides tend to be rather leisurely narratives of strange happenings in a middle-class world. Folk ballads tend to be understated and impersonal; broadsides tend to be extravagantly sentimental, with the narrator often expressing his feelings and telling his hearers how they should feel. Although many broadsides tend to be doggerel, excellent poets have had their work taken up and peddled in the streets, among them Marvell, Rochester, Swift, and Byron.

Because they stick in the mind and because they were inexpensive to publish and to purchase, broadsides in the nineteenth century often were used to convey social or political messages. Some of the best are **protest songs,** like "Song of the Lower Classes" (about 1848) by Ernest Jones. A stanza follows:

We're low — we're low — we're very very low,
　Yet from our fingers glide
The silken flow — and the robes that glow
　Round the limbs of the sons of pride.
And what we get — and what we give —
　We know, and we know our share;
We're not too low the cloth to weave,
　But too low the Cloth to wear!

Compare that stanza with this modern protest ballad:

Woody Guthrie (1912–1967)
Plane Wreck at Los Gatos (Deportee)

The crops are all in and the peaches are rotting,
The oranges are piled in their creosote dumps;
You're flying them back to the Mexican border
To pay all their money to wade back again.　　　　　　　4

Refrain:
Goodbye to my Juan, Goodbye Rosarita;
Adiós mes amigos, Jesús and Marie,
You won't have a name when you ride the big airplane:
All they will call you will be deportee.   8

My father's own father he waded that river;
They took all the money he made in his life;
My brothers and sisters come working the fruit trees
And they rode the truck till they took down and died.   12

Some of us are illegal and some are not wanted,
Our work contract's out and we have to move on;
Six hundred miles to that Mexico border,
They chase us like outlaws, like rustlers, like thieves.   16

We died in your hills, we died in your deserts,
We died in your valleys and died on your plains;
We died neath your trees and we died in your bushes,
Both sides of this river we died just the same.   20

The sky plane caught fire over Los Gatos Canyon,
A fireball of lightning and shook all our hills.
Who are all these friends all scattered like dry leaves?
The radio says they are just deportees.   24

Is this the best way we can grow our big orchards?
Is this the best way we can grow our good fruit?
To fall like dry leaves to rot on my top soil
And be called by no name except deportees?   28

PLANE WRECK AT LOS GATOS (DEPORTEE). This song pays tribute to twenty-eight deported migrant workers killed when the airplane returning them to Mexico crashed on January 28, 1948, near Coalinga, California.

"Plane Wreck at Los Gatos" superficially resembles English broadsides in its recreation of a news event in song. However, it differs from most broadsides (to mention just one way) because the singer, instead of commenting on the action, disappears from view and lets his characters speak for themselves. This is what happens in most Child ballads. In England today, broadside ballads like "Squire and Milkmaid" have been replaced almost entirely by the *News of the World* and other popular newspapers specializing in sex and crime.[4]

Literary ballads, not usually meant for singing, are written by sophisticated poets for book-educated readers who can be expected to enjoy being reminded of folk ballads. They imitate certain features of

[4] A generous collection of broadsides has been assembled by Vivian de Sola Pinto and A. E. Rodway in *The Common Muse: An Anthology of Popular British Ballad Poetry, XVth–XXth Century* (London, 1957). See also *Irish Street Ballads,* edited by Colm O. Lochlainn (New York, 1960), and Olive Woolley Burt, *American Murder Ballads and Their Stories* (New York, 1964).

folk ballads: plot, diction, imagery, figures of speech, or the ballad stanza. Among the most celebrated literary ballads are Keats's "La Belle Dame sans Merci" (p. 228), Scott's "Proud Maisie" (p. 169), and Coleridge's "Rime of the Ancient Mariner."

EXPERIMENT: *Seeing Ballad Traits in Other Poetry*
In the anthology at the back of the book, read the folk ballads "Edward" (p. 309), "The Three Ravens" (p. 311), "Twa Corbies" (p. 312), and "Sir Patrick Spence" (p. 310). With these ballads in mind, examine one or more of the following poems: W. H. Auden, "As I Walked Out One Evening" (p. 380), E. E. Cummings, "All in green went my love riding" (p. 374), Walter de la Mare, "The Listeners" (p. 360), Bob Dylan, "Subterranean Homesick Blues" (p. 418), William Jay Smith, "American Primitive" (p. 394), William Butler Yeats, "Crazy Jane Talks with the Bishop" (p. 355). What characteristics of folk ballads do you find in them?

Some songs in plays help tell a story, though no one thinks them ballads. Many of the songs in Shakespeare's plays, like that of the witches in *Macbeth,* help unfold a plot or set a mood. Lyrics in Shakespeare's plays generally are sung; although in *Cymbeline* (Act IV, scene 2), this one is spoken. While the princess Imogen, disguised as a boy, lies in a deep sleep, her brothers, who do not recognize her, believe her dead and recite these lines over her.

William Shakespeare (1564–1616)
FEAR NO MORE THE HEAT O' TH' SUN

Guiderius: Fear no more the heat o' th' sun
      Nor the furious winter's rages;
      Thou thy worldly task hast done,
        Home art gone, and ta'en thy wages.   4
      Golden lads and girls all must,
      As chimney-sweepers, come to dust.   6

Arviragus: Fear no more the frown o' th' great,
      Thou art past the tyrant's stroke;
      Care no more to clothe and eat,
        To thee the reed is as the oak.   10
      The scepter°, learning, physic°, must   *law; science of*
      All follow this and come to dust.   *medicine*   12

Guiderius: Fear no more the lightning flash,
Arviragus: Nor the all-dreaded thunder-stone°;   *meteorite*
Guiderius: Fear not slander, censure rash,
Arviragus: Thou hast finished joy and moan.   16
Both: All lovers young, all lovers must
      Consign to thee° and come to dust.   *join their signatures* 18
                                        to yours

Guiderius:	No exorciser harm thee!	
Arviragus:	Nor no witchcraft charm thee!	
Guiderius:	Ghost unlaid forbear thee!	
Arviragus:	Nothing ill come near thee!	22
Both:	Quiet consummation have,	
	And renownèd be thy grave!	24

Whether joyful, ironic, or sorrowful, songs convey powerful feelings. No wonder, indeed, that even some of the best poems without tunes tend to resemble them.

Robert Browning (1812–1889)
THE YEAR'S AT THE SPRING

The year's at the spring,
And day's at the morn;
Morning's at seven;
The hillside's dew-pearled;
The lark's on the wing;
The snail's on the thorn;
God's in his heaven —
All's right with the world!

THE YEAR'S AT THE SPRING. In *Pippa Passes,* a long poem in the form of a play, these words sung by an innocent girl are overheard by a man who has just murdered his mistress' husband. The song goads him into committing suicide.

QUESTIONS
1. Would you think this lyric a better poem if you didn't know its context? Why or why not?
2. What discrepancy between the girl's point of view and the poet's do these lines (taken in their context) reveal?

EXPERIMENT: *Setting Words to Music*
Compose a tune for Browning's words and try singing them to it. (A knowledge of musical notation is not necessary.) How easy or difficult is it to set these lines to music? What qualities of the text make for this ease or difficulty?

Anonymous (traditional English song)
THE UNQUIET GRAVE

"The wind doth blow today, my love,
    And a few small drops of rain;
I never had but one true-love,
    In cold grave she was lain.   4

"I'll do as much for my true-love
  As any young man may;
I'll sit and mourn all at her grave
  For a twelvemonth and a day."   8

The twelvemonth and a day being up,
  The dead began to speak:
"Oh who sits weeping on my grave,
  And will not let me sleep?"   12

" 'Tis I, my love, sits on your grave,
  And will not let you sleep;
For I crave one kiss of your clay-cold lips,
  And that is all I seek."   16

"You crave one kiss of my clay-cold lips,
  But my breath smells earthy strong;
If you have one kiss of my clay-cold lips,
  Your time will not be long.   20

" 'Tis down in yonder garden green,
  Love, where we used to walk,
The finest flower that ere° was seen   *ever*
  Is withered to a stalk.   24

"The stalk is withered dry, my love,
  So will our hearts decay;
So make yourself content, my love,
  Till God calls you away."   28

QUESTIONS

1. Why do you suppose the opening two lines of this folk song have been so
   greatly admired?
2. What connection might be drawn between these lines and the withered
   flower in stanza 6?
3. A different version, in which the second speaker is a murdered man, ends:

   "Your lips are cold as clay, dear love,
     Your breath doth smell so strong;
   I am afraid, my pretty, pretty maid,
     Your time will not be long."

   Do you prefer this version?
4. Is this poem a ballad or a lyric? Explain.
5. If this story has a moral, what is it?

Anonymous (American ballad; early twentieth century)
FRANKIE AND JOHNNY

Frankie she was a good woman, Johnny he was her man,
And every silver dollar Frankie made went straight to her Johnny's hand.
He was her man, but he done her wrong.   3

Frankie and Johnny went walking, Johnny in a brand new suit.
"Cost me a hundred," says Frankie, "but don't my Johnny look cute?"
He was her man, but he done her wrong.   6

Frankie went down to the corner, she called for a thimble of gin,
She says to the fat bartender, "Has my lovin' Johnny been in?
I can't believe he's been doing me wrong."   9

"Ain't going to tell you no story, ain't going to tell you no lie,
Mister Johnny was in here 'bout an hour ago with a floozy named Ella Fly.
He is your man, but I believe he's doing you wrong."   12

Frankie ran down to the pawn shop, she didn't go there for fun.
She turned in her doorknob diamonds, she took out a forty-four gun.
He was her man, but he done her wrong.   15

Frankie ran down to the parlor-house, she leaned on the parlor-house bell.
"Stand out of my way, you floozies, or I'll splash you all over Hell!
I want my man, he's been doing me wrong."   18

Frankie looked over the transom, the tears ran out of her eyes.
There was her lovin' Johnny a-lovin' up Ella Fly.
He was her man, but he was doing her wrong.   21

She threw back her red silk kimono, she whipped out that old forty-four.
Rooty-toot-toot, three times she did shoot, right through that hardwood
  door.
He was her man, but he done her wrong.   24

Johnny grabbed off his Stetson, "O Lord no, Frankie, don't shoot!"
But Frankie squeezed the trigger three times more and he fell down like a
  stick of wood.
He was her man, but he done her wrong.   27

The first shot, Johnny staggered; the second shot, he fell;
The third shot took him through the heart and his face started coming out
  in Hell.
He was her man, but he done her wrong.   30

"O roll me over easy, roll me over slow,
Roll me over on my right side, honey, so my heart don't overflow.
I was your man, but I done you wrong."   33

Bring on your rubber-tired hearses, bring on your rubber-tired hacks.
There's eight men going to the burying yard and only seven of 'em coming
  back.
He was her man, but he done her wrong.   36

The judge look hard at the jury, says, "It's plain as plain can be,
This woman put some daylight through her man, it's murder in the
  second degree.
He was her man, and she done him wrong."   39

Now it wasn't murder in the second degree, it wasn't murder in the third,
All Frankie did was drop her man like a hunter drops a bird.
He was her man, but he done her wrong.   42

The jury went out on Frankie, sat under an electric fan,
Came back and said, "You're a free woman, go kill yourself another man
If he does you wrong, if he does you wrong."   45

"O put me away in a dungeon, put me in a cold, cold cell,
Put me where the north wind blows from the southeast corner of Hell.
I shot my man, 'cause he done me wrong."   48

Frankie she heard a rumbling, away down under the ground.
Maybe it was little Johnny where she had shot him down.
He was her man, but he done her wrong.   51

Frankie went out to the burying yard, just to look her Johnny in the face.
"Ain't it hard to see you, Johnny, in this lonesome place?"
He was her man, but he done her wrong.   54

Well, I looked down the lonesome street, Lord, as far off as I could see,
All I could hear was a two-string fiddle playing "Nearer, My God,
        to Thee."
He was her man, but he done her wrong.   57

FRANKIE AND JOHNNY. Hundreds of versions of this ballad exist; this one is a composite
of many. In the 1890's a murder that took place either in St. Louis or in Kansas City,
Missouri, became famous in folk song as the story of Frankie and Albert. About 1911,
vaudeville singers changed Albert's name to Johnny and introduced other elements.
16. *parlor-house:* A brothel fancy enough to have a waiting room.

QUESTIONS

1. How would you describe the tone of this ballad?
2. Compare its account of Frankie's trial with these stanzas from an earlier
   "Frankie and Albert" version:

   They took little Frankie to the courthouse,
   They sat her in a big arm chair.
   She was waiting for the judge to say,
   "We will give her ninety-nine year,
   Because she killed her man in the first degree."

   But the judge he said to the jury,
   "It's plain as plain can be
   Why she shot the man she loved.
   I think she ought to go free
   Because a gambling man won't treat you right."

   Frankie walked out on the scaffold
   As brave as she could be:
   "When I shot the man I loved
   I murdered in the first degree.
   He was my man and I loved him so."

   How is this earlier version different in tone?
3. How can it be claimed that "Frankie and Johnny," like "The Unquiet Grave,"
   is composed in the ballad stanza? It is hardly likely that whoever wrote it
   knew Child ballads. Why do you suppose this stanza has been so popular
   for five hundred years or more?
4. In what ways does "Frankie and Johnny" seem like a broadside ballad?

FOR REVIEW AND FURTHER STUDY

EXERCISE: *Songs or Poems or Both?*

Consider each of the following song lyrics. Which do you think can stand not only to be sung but to be read as poetry? Which probably should not be seen but only heard?

Anonymous (English madrigal; printed 1609)

FA, MI, FA, RE, LA, MI

Fa, mi, fa, re, la, mi,
Begin, my son, and follow me;
    Sing flat, fa mi,
    So shall we well agree.
        Hey tro loly lo.
        Hold fast, good son,
    With hey tro lily lo.
O sing this once again, lustily.

Anonymous (English madrigal; printed 1612)

THE SILVER SWAN, WHO LIVING HAD NO NOTE

The silver swan, who living had no note,
When death approached unlocked her silent throat;
Leaning her breast against the reedy shore,
Thus sung her first and last, and sung no more.
Farewell, all joys; O death, come close mine eyes;
More geese than swans now live, more fools than wise.

Thomas Campion (1567–1620)

ROSE-CHEEKED LAURA, COME

Rose-cheeked Laura, come,
Sing thou smoothly with thy beauty's
Silent music, either other
    Sweetly gracing.   4

Lovely forms do flow
From concent° divinely framèd;   *harmony*
Heav'n is music, and thy beauty's
    Birth is heavenly.   8

These dull notes we sing
Discords need for helps to grace them;
Only beauty purely loving
    Knows no discord,   12

But still moves delight,
Like clear springs renewed by flowing,
Ever perfect, ever in them-
    Selves eternal.   16

Anonymous (American song; twentieth century)
GOOD MORNIN', BLUES

I woke up this mornin' with the blues all round my bed,
Yes, I woke up this morning with the blues all round my bed,
Went to eat my breakfast, had the blues all in my bread.

"Good mornin', blues, blues, how do you do?" (2)
"I'm feelin' pretty well, but, pardner, how are you?"   5

Yes, I woke up this morning, 'bout an hour 'fore day, (2)
Reached and grabbed the pillow where my baby used to lay.

If you ever been down, you know just how I feel, (2)
Feel like an engine, ain't got no drivin' wheel.

If I feel tomorrow, like I feel today, (2)   10
I'll stand right here, look a thousand miles away.

If the blues was whisky, I'd stay drunk all the time, (2)
Stay drunk, baby, just to wear you off my mind.

I got the blues so bad, it hurts my feet to walk, (2)
I got the blues so bad, it hurts my tongue to talk.   15

The blues jumped a rabbit, run him a solid mile, (2)
When the blues overtaken him, he hollered like a newborn child.

GOOD MORNIN', BLUES. This folk song has been adapted by Alan Lomax from a version by singer Huddie Ledbetter (Leadbelly). The number (2) indicates a line to be sung twice.

Ern Alpaugh (b. 1914)
Dewey G. Pell (b. 1917)
SWINGING CHICK

Swinging chick
You know she does the trick
Sho ba ba dee ba
She's so swinging
Always singing   5
She's my swinging chick

Swinging chick
Boy are we ever nice and thick
When she starts to doin' that swing and sway
The man in the moon's gotta get out of her way   10

Oh, swinging chick
Sho ba ba·dee ba
She's my swing it
Pick it up and fling it
Swinging hum-a-dinging chick   15

John Lennon (b. 1940)
Paul McCartney (b. 1942)

ELEANOR RIGBY

Ah, look at all the lonely people!
Ah, look at all the lonely people!

Eleanor Rigby
Picks· up the rice in the church where a wedding has been,
Lives in a dream,   5
Waits at the window
Wearing the face that she keeps in a jar by the door.
Who is it for?

All the lonely people,
Where do they all come from?   10
All the lonely people,
Where do they all belong?

Father McKenzie,
Writing the words of a sermon that no one will hear,
No one comes near   15
Look at him working,
Darning his socks in the night when there's nobody there.
What does he care?

All the lonely people
Where do they all come from?   20
All the lonely people
Where do they all belong?

Eleanor Rigby
Died in the church and was buried along with her name.
Nobody came.   25
Father McKenzie,
Wiping the dirt from his hands as he walks from the grave,
No one was saved.

All the lonely people,
Where do they all come from?   30

All the lonely people,
Where do they all belong?

Ah, look at all the lonely people!
Ah, look at all the lonely people!

Leonard Cohen (b. 1934)

SUZANNE

Suzanne takes you down
to her place near the river,
you can hear the boats go by
you can stay the night beside her.
And you know that she's half crazy   5
but that's why you want to be there
and she feeds you tea and oranges
that come all the way from China.
Just when you mean to tell her
that you have no gifts to give her,   10
she gets you on her wave-length
and she lets the river answer
that you've always been her lover.
     And you want to travel with her,
     you want to travel blind   15
     and you know that she can trust you
     because you've touched her perfect body
     with your mind.

Jesus was a sailor
when he walked upon the water   20
and he spent a long time watching
from a lonely wooden tower
and when he knew for certain
only drowning men could see him
he said All men will be sailors then   25
until the sea shall free them,
but he himself was broken
long before the sky would open,
forsaken, almost human,
he sank beneath your wisdom like a stone.   30
     And you want to travel with him,
     you want to travel blind
     and you think maybe you'll trust him
     because he touched your perfect body
     with his mind.   35

Suzanne takes your hand
and she leads you to the river,
she is wearing rags and feathers
from Salvation Army counters.
The sun pours down like honey   40
on our lady of the harbor
as she shows you where to look
among the garbage and the flowers,
there are heroes in the seaweed
there are children in the morning,   45
they are leaning out for love
they will lean that way forever
while Suzanne she holds the mirror.
   And you want to travel with her
   and you want to travel blind   50
   and you're sure that she can find you
   because she's touched her perfect body
   with her mind.

8 Sound

Songs usually contain rime and other devices of repeated sounds. By such devices, as well as by the accompanying tune, song lyrics show that sung language is special language, different from that of ordinary conversation. In the next two chapters, on *sound* and *rhythm*, we shall look closely at a few of these devices, so valuable both to song lyrics and to songlike (but spoken) poetry.

SOUND AS MEANING

Isak Dinesen, in a memoir of her life on a plantation in East Africa, tells how some Kikuyu tribesmen reacted to their first hearing of rimed verse:

> The Natives, who have a strong sense of rhythm, know nothing of verse, or at least did not know anything before the times of the schools, where they were taught hymns. One evening out in the maize-field, where we had been harvesting maize, breaking off the cobs and throwing them on to the ox-carts, to amuse myself, I spoke to the field laborers, who were mostly quite young, in Swahili verse. There was no sense in the verses, they were made for the sake of rime — "Ngumbe na-penda chumbe, Malaya mbaya. Wakamba na-kula mamba." The oxen like salt — whores are bad — The Wakamba eat snakes. It caught the interest of the boys, they formed a ring round me. They were quick to understand that meaning in poetry is of no consequence, and they did not question the thesis of the verse, but waited eagerly for the rime, and laughed at it when it came. I tried to make them themselves find the rime and finish the poem when I had begun it, but they could not, or would not, do that, and turned away their heads. As they had become used to the idea of poetry, they begged: "Speak again. Speak like rain." Why they should feel verse to be like rain I do not know. It must have been, however, an expression of applause, since in Africa rain is always longed for and welcomed.[1]

What the tribesmen had discovered is that poetry, like music, appeals to the ear. However limited it may be in comparison with the sound of an orchestra — or a tribal drummer — the sound of words in itself gives

[1] *Out of Africa* (New York, 1937).

pleasure. However, we might doubt Isak Dinesen's assumption that "meaning in poetry is of no consequence." "Hey nonny-nonny" and such nonsense has a place in song lyrics and other poems, and we might take pleasure in hearing rimes in Swahili; but most good poetry has meaningful sound as well as musical sound. Certainly the words of a song have an effect different from that of wordless music: they go along with their music and, by making statements, add more meaning. The French poet Isodore Isou, founder of a literary movement called *lettrisme*, maintained that poems can be written not only in words but in letters (sample lines: *xyl, xyl, / prprali dryl / znglo trpylo pwi*). But the sound of letters alone, without denotation and connotation, has not been enough to make Letterist poems memorable. In the response of the Kikuyu tribesmen, there may have been not only the pleasure of hearing sounds but also the agreeable surprise of finding that things not usually associated had been brought together.

More powerful when in the company of meaning, not apart from it, the sounds of consonants and vowels can contribute greatly to a poem's effect. The sound of *s*, which can suggest the swishing of water, has rarely been used more accurately than in Surrey's line "Calm is the sea, the waves work less and less." When, in a poem, the sound of words working together with meaning pleases mind and ear, the effect is **euphony**, as in the following lines from Tennyson's "Come down, O maid":

> Myriads of rivulets hurrying through the lawn,
> The moan of doves in immemorial elms,
> And murmuring of innumerable bees.

Its opposite is **cacophony**: a harsh, discordant effect. It too is chosen for the sake of meaning. We hear it in Milton's scornful reference in "Lycidas" to corrupt clergymen whose songs "Grate on their scrannel pipes of wretched straw." (Read that line and one of Tennyson's aloud and see which requires lips, teeth, and tongue to do more work.) But note that although Milton's line is harsh in sound, the line (when we meet it in his poem) is pleasing because it is artful. Pope has illustrated both euphony and cacophony in his *Essay on Criticism,* insisting that sound must echo sense:

> Soft is the strain when Zephyr gently blows,
> And the smooth stream in smoother numbers° flows;   *metrical rhythm*
> But when loud surges lash the sounding shore,
> The harsh, rough verse should like the torrent roar . . .

Not merely sound but also rhythm contributes to the effect of this passage.

Is the sound in each of those examples identical with meaning? Not quite. In Tennyson's lines, for instance, the cooing of doves is not *exactly* a moan. As John Crowe Ransom has pointed out, the sound would be almost the same but the meaning entirely different in "The murdering of innumerable beeves." While it is true that the consonant sound *sl-* will often begin a word that conveys ideas of wetness and smoothness — *slick, slimy, slippery, slush* — we are so used to hearing it in words that convey nothing of the kind — *slave, sledgehammer, sleeve, slow* — that it is doubtful that the sound all by itself communicates anything very definite. Asked to nominate the most beautiful word in the English language, a wit once suggested not *sunrise* or *silvery* but *syphilis.*

Relating sound more closely to meaning, the device called **onomatopoeia** is an attempt to represent a thing or action by a word that imitates the sound associated with it: *zoom, whiz, crash, bang, ding-dong, pitter-patter, yakety-yak.* Onomatopoeia is often effective in poetry, as in Emily Dickinson's line about the fly with its "uncertain stumbling Buzz," in which the nasal sounds *n, m, ng* and the sibilants *c, s,* help make a droning buzz, and in Robert Lowell's transcription of a bird-call, "yuck-a, yuck-a, yuck-a" (in "Falling Asleep over the Aeneid").

Like the Kikuyu tribesmen, others who care for poetry have discovered in the sound of words something of the refreshment of cool rain. Dylan Thomas, telling how he began to write poetry, said that from early childhood words were to him "as the notes of bells, the sounds of musical instruments, the noises of wind, sea, and rain, the rattle of milkcarts, the clopping of hooves on cobbles, the fingering of branches on the window pane, might be to someone, deaf from birth, who has miraculously found his hearing."[2] For readers, too, the sound of words can have a magical spell, most powerful when it points to meaning. James Weldon Johnson in *God's Trombones* has told of an old-time preacher who began his sermon, "Brothers and sisters, this morning I intend to explain the unexplainable — find out the indefinable — ponder over the imponderable — and unscrew the inscrutable!" The repetition of sound in *unscrew* and inscrutable has appeal, but the magic of the words is all the greater if they lead us to imagine the mystery of all Creation as an enormous screw that the preacher's mind, like a screw-driver, will loosen. Though the sound of a word or the meaning of a word may have value all by itself, both become more memorable, when taken together.

William Butler Yeats (1865–1939)
WHO GOES WITH FERGUS?

Who will go drive with Fergus now,
And pierce the deep wood's woven shade,
And dance upon the level shore?

[2] "Notes on the Art of Poetry," *The Texas Quarterly,* 1961; reprinted in *Modern Poetics,* James Scully, ed. (New York, 1965).

Young man, lift up your russet brow,
And lift your tender eyelids, maid,
And brood on hopes and fear no more.   6

And no more turn aside and brood
Upon love's bitter mystery;
For Fergus rules the brazen cars,
And rules the shadows of the wood,
And the white breast of the dim sea
And all dishevelled wandering stars.   12

WHO GOES WITH FERGUS? *Fergus:* Irish king who gave up his throne to be a wandering
poet.

QUESTIONS

1. In what lines do you find euphony? ·
2. In what line do you find cacophony?
3. How do the sounds of these lines stress what is said in them?

EXERCISE: *Listening to Meaning*

Read aloud the following brief poems. In the sounds of which particular words
are meanings well captured? In which poems do you find onomatopoeia?

John Updike (b. 1932)
WINTER OCEAN

Many-maned scud-thumper, tub
of male whales, maker of worn wood, shrub-
ruster, sky-mocker, rave!
portly pusher of waves, wind-slave.

Frances Cornford (1886–1960)
THE WATCH

I wakened on my hot, hard bed,
Upon the pillow lay my head;   2
Beneath the pillow I could hear
My little watch was ticking clear.   4
I thought the throbbing of it went
Like my continual discontent.   6
I thought it said in every tick:
I am so sick, so sick, so sick.   8
O death, come quick, come quick, come quick,
Come quick, come quick, come quick, come quick!   10

William Wordsworth (1770–1850)

A Slumber Did My Spirit Seal

A slumber did my spirit seal;
    I had no human fears —
She seemed a thing that could not feel
    The touch of earthly years.   4

No motion has she now, no force;
    She neither hears nor sees;
Rolled round in earth's diurnal course,
    With rocks, and stones, and trees.   8

Gerard Manley Hopkins (1844–1889)

Pied Beauty

Glory be to God for dappled things —
    For skies of couple-color as a brinded° cow;
        For rose-moles all in stipple upon trout that swim;
Fresh-firecoal chestnut-falls; finches' wings;
    Landscape plotted and pieced — fold, fallow, and plow;   5
    And áll trádes, their gear and tackle and trim°.   *equipment*

All things counter, original, spare, strange;
    Whatever is fickle, freckled (who knows how?)
        With swift, slow; sweet, sour; adazzle, dim;
He fathers-forth whose beauty is past change:
            Praise him.   10

ALLITERATION AND ASSONANCE

Listening to a symphony in which themes are repeated throughout each movement, we enjoy both their recurrence and their variation. We take similar pleasure in the repetition of a phrase or a single chord. Something like this pleasure is afforded us frequently in poetry.

Analogies between poetry and wordless music, it is true, tend to break down when carried far, since poetry — to mention a single difference — has denotation. But like musical compositions, poems have patterns of sounds. Among such patterns long popular in English poetry is **alliteration,** which has been defined as a succession of similar sounds. Alliteration occurs in the repetition of the same consonant sound at the beginning of successive words — "round and round the rugged rocks the ragged rascal ran" — or inside the words, as in Milton's description of the gates of Hell:

> On a sudden open fly
> With impetuous recoil and jarring sound

The infernal doors, and on their hinges grate
Harsh thunder, that the lowest bottom shook
Of Erebus.

The former kind is called **initial alliteration,** the latter **internal alliteration** or **hidden alliteration.** We recognize alliteration by sound, not by spelling: *know* and *nail* alliterate, *know* and *key* do not. In a line by E. E. Cummings, "colossal hoax of clocks and calendars," the sound of *x* within *hoax* alliterates with the *cks* in clocks. Incidentally, the letter *r* does not *always* lends itself to cacophony: elsewhere in *Paradise Lost* Milton said that

Heaven opened wide
Her ever-during gates, harmonious sound
On golden hinges moving . . .

By itself, a letter-sound has no particular meaning. This is a truth forgotten by people who would attribute the effectiveness of Milton's lines on the Heavenly Gates to, say, "the mellow *o*'s and liquid *l* of *harmonious* and *golden*." Mellow *o*'s and liquid *l*'s occur also in the phrase "moldy cold oatmeal," which may have a quite different effect. Meaning depends on larger units of language than letters of the alphabet.

Today good prose writers usually avoid alliteration; in the past, some cultivated it. "There is nothing more swifter than time, nothing more sweeter," wrote John Lyly in *Euphues* (1579), and he went on — playing especially with the sounds of *v, n, t, s, l,* and *b* — "we have not, as Seneca saith, little time to live, but we lose much; neither have we a short life by nature, but we make it shorter by naughtiness." Poetry, too, formerly contained more alliteration than it usually contains today. In Old English verse, each line was held together by alliteration, a basic pattern still evident in the fourteenth century, as in the following description of the world as a "fair field" in *Piers Plowman:*

A *f*eir *f*eld *f*ul of *f*olk *f*ond I ther bi-twene,
Of alle *m*aner of *m*en, the *m*ene and the riche . . .

(For a modern imitation of Old English verse, see Richard Wilbur's "Junk," p. 396.) Most poets nowadays save alliteration for special occasions. They may use it to give emphasis, as Edward Lear does: "*F*ar and *f*ew, *f*ar and *f*ew, / Are the *l*ands where the Jumblies *l*ive." With its aid they can point out the relationship between two things placed side by side, as in Pope's line on things of little worth: "The courtier's *p*romises, and sick man's *p*rayers." Alliteration, too, can be a powerful aid to memory. It is hard to forget such tongue twisters as "Peter Piper picked a peck of pickled peppers," or common expressions like "green as grass," "tried and true," and "from stem to stern." In fact, because alliteration directs our attention to something, it had best be used neither thoughtlessly nor merely for decoration, lest it call attention to emptiness. A case in point may be a line by Philip James Bailey, a reaction to a lady's weeping: "I saw, but *spared* to *speak*." If the poet chose the word *spared* for any meaningful reason other than that it alliterates with *speak*, the reason is not clear.

As we have seen, to repeat the sound of a consonant is to produce alliteration, but to repeat the sound of a *vowel* is to produce **assonance**. Like alliteration, assonance may occur either initially — "*all* the *awful augu*ries"[3] — or internally — Spenser's "Her goodly *eyes* like sapphires sh*i*ning br*i*ght, / Her forehead *i*vory wh*i*te . . ." and it can help make common phrases unforgettable: "*ea*ger b*ea*ver," "h*o*ly sm*o*ke." Like alliteration, it slows the reader down and focuses his attention.

EXPERIMENT: *Reading for Assonance*

Try reading aloud as rapidly as possible the following poem by Tennyson. From the difficulties you encounter, you may be able to sense the slowing effect of assonance. Then read the poem aloud a second time, with consideration.

Alfred, Lord Tennyson (1809–1892)
THE SPLENDOR FALLS ON CASTLE WALLS

The splendor falls on castle walls
    And snowy summits old in story;
The long light shakes across the lakes,
    And the wild cataract leaps in glory.   4
Blow, bugle, blow, set the wild echoes flying,
Blow, bugle; answer, echoes, dying, dying, dying.   6

O hark, O hear! how thin and clear,
    And thinner, clearer, farther going!
O sweet and far from cliff and scar
    The horns of Elfland faintly blowing!   10
Blow, let us hear the purple glens replying:
Blow, bugle; answer, echoes, dying, dying, dying.   12

O love, they die in yon rich sky,
    They faint on hill or field or river;
Our echoes roll from soul to soul,
    And grow for ever and for ever.   16
Blow, bugle, blow, set the wild echoes flying,
And answer, echoes, answer, dying, dying, dying.   18

---

[3] Some prefer to call the repetition of an initial vowel-sound by the name of alliteration: "apt alliteration's artful aid."

A. E. Housman (1859–1936)

EIGHT O'CLOCK

He stood, and heard the steeple
  Sprinkle the quarters on the morning town.
One, two, three, four, to market-place and people
  It tossed them down.   4

Strapped, noosed, nighing his hour,
  He stood and counted them and cursed his luck;
And then the clock collected in the tower
  Its strength, and struck.   8

QUESTIONS

1. Why does the protagonist in this brief drama curse his luck? What is his situation?
2. For so short a poem, "Eight O'Clock" carries a great weight of alliteration. What patterns of initial alliteration do you find? What patterns of internal alliteration? What effect is created by all this heavy emphasis?

Alexander Pope (1688–1744)

INTENDED FOR SIR ISAAC NEWTON IN WESTMINSTER ABBEY

Nature and Nature's laws lay hid in night.
God said, *Let Newton be!* and all was light.

QUESTIONS

1. What patterns of alliteration and assonance does Pope employ?
2. How are they useful to his poem?

J. C. Squire (1884–1958)

IT DID NOT LAST

It did not last: the Devil, howling *Ho!*
Let Einstein be! restored the status quo.

EXERCISE: *Hearing How Sound Helps*

Which of these translations of the same passage from Petrarch do you think is better poetry? Why? What do assonance and alliteration have to do with your preference?

1. Love that liveth and reigneth in my thought,
  That built his seat within my captive breast,

Clad in the arms wherein with me he fought,
Oft in my face he doth his banner rest.
— Henry Howard, Earl of Surrey (1517?–1547)

2. The long love that in my thought doth harbor,
And in mine heart doth keep his residence,
Into my face presseth with bold pretense
And therein campeth, spreading his banner.
— Sir Thomas Wyatt (1503?–1542)

RIME

Isak Dinesen's natives, to whom rime was a new phenomenon, recognized at once that rimed language is special language. So do we, for, although much English poetry is unrimed, rime is one means to set poetry apart from ordinary conversation and bring it closer to music. A **rime** (or rhyme), defined most narrowly, occurs when two or more words or phrases contain an identical or similar vowel-sound, usually accented, and the consonant-sounds (if any) that follow the vowel-sound are identical: *hay* and *sleigh, prairie schooner* and *piano tuner*.[4] From these examples it will be seen that rime depends not on spelling but on sound.

To be excellent, rime ought to surprise. It is all very well that a reader may anticipate which vowel-sound is coming next, for patterns of rime give him pleasure by satisfying his expectations; but riming becomes dull clunking if, at the end of each line, the reader can predict the word that will end the next. Hearing many a jukebox song for the first time, a listener can do so: *charms* lead to *arms, skies above* to *love*. As Alexander Pope observes of the habits of dull rimesters,

Where'er you find "the cooling western breeze,"
In the next line it "whispers through the trees";
If crystal streams "with pleasing murmurs creep,"
The reader's threatened (not in vain) with "sleep" . . .

But who — given the opening line of this children's jingle — could predict the lines that follow?

Anonymous (English; twentieth century)
JULIUS CAESAR

Julius Caesar,
The Roman geezer,
Squashed his wife with a lemon-squeezer.

---

[4] Some definitions of *rime* would apply the term to the repetition of any identical or similar sound, not only a vowel-sound. In this sense, assonance is a kind of rime; so is alliteration (called **initial rime**).

Here rimes combine things unexpectedly. Robert Herrick, too, made good use of rime to indicate a startling contrast:

> Then while time serves, and we are but decaying,
> Come, my Corinna, come, let's go a-Maying.

Though good rimes seem fresh, not all will startle, and probably few will call to mind things so unlike as *May* and *decay, Caesar* and *lemon-squeezer*. Some masters of rime often link words that, taken out of context, might seem common and unevocative. Here, for instance, is Pope's comment on a trifling and effeminate courtier:

> Yet let me flap this bug with gilded wings,
> This painted child of dirt, that stinks and stings;
> Whose buzz the witty and the fair annoys,
> Yet wit ne'er tastes, and beauty ne'er enjoys:
> So well-bred spaniels civilly delight
> In mumbling of the game they dare not bite.
> Eternal smiles his emptiness betray,
> As shallow streams run dimpling all the way.

Pope's rime-words are not especially memorable — and yet these lines are, because (among other reasons) they rime. Wit may be driven home without rime, but it is rime that rings the doorbell when she arrives. Admittedly, some rimes wear thin from too much use. More difficult to use freshly than before the establishment of Tin Pan Alley, rimes such as *moon, June, croon* seem leaden and to ring true would need an extremely powerful context. *Death* and *breath* are a rime that poets have used with wearisome frequency; another is *birth, earth, mirth*. And yet we cannot exclude these from the diction of poetry, for they might be the very words a poet would need in order to say something new and original. This poem by Blake remains fresher than its rimes (if we took them out of context) would suggest:

William Blake (1757–1827)
THE ANGEL THAT PRESIDED O'ER MY BIRTH

The Angel that presided o'er my birth
Said, "Little creature, formed of Joy and Mirth,
Go love without the help of any thing on earth."

What matters to rime is freshness — not of a word but of the poet's way of seeing.

Good poets, said John Dryden, learn to make their rime "so properly a part of the verse, that it should never mislead the sense, but itself be led and governed by it." The comment may remind us that skillful rime — unlike poor rime — is never a distracting ornament. "Rime the rudder is of verses, / With which, like ships, they steer their courses," wrote the seventeenth-century poet Samuel Butler. Like other patterns of sound, rime can help a poet to group his ideas, emphasize particular words, and weave a poem together. It can start reverberations between words and can point to connections of meaning.

To have an **exact rime,** sounds following the vowel sound have to be the same: *red* and *bread, wealthily* and *stealthily, walk to her* and *talk to her.* If final consonant sounds are the same but the vowel sounds are different, the result is **slant rime,** also called **near rime, off rime,** or **partial rime:** *stone* riming with *sun, moon, rain, green, gone, thin.* By not satisfying the reader's expectation of an exact chime, but instead giving him a clunk, a slant rime can help a poet say some things more meaningfully. It works especially well for disappointed let-downs, negations, and denials, as in Blake's couplet:

> He who the ox to wrath has moved
> Shall never be by woman loved.

Consonance, a kind of slant rime, occurs when the rimed words or phrases have the same consonant sounds but a different vowel, as in *chitter* and *chatter.* It is used in a traditional nonsense poem, "The Cutty Wren": "'O where are you going?' says *Milder* to *Malder.*" (W. H. Auden wrote a variation on it that begins, "'O where are you going?' said *reader* to *rider,*" thus keeping the consonance.)

End rime, as its name indicates, comes at the ends of lines, **internal rime** within them. Most rime tends to be end rime. Few recent poets have used internal rime so heavily as Wallace Stevens in the beginning of "Bantams in Pine-Woods": "Chieftain Iffucan of Azcan in caftan / Of tan with henna hackles, halt!" (lines also heavy on alliteration). A poet may employ both end rime and internal rime in the same poem, as in Robert Burns's satiric ballad "The Kirk's Alarm":

> Orthodox, Orthodox, wha believe in John Knox,
>> Let me sound an alarm to your conscience:
> There's a heretic blast has been blawn i' the wast°,   *west*
>> "That what is not sense must be nonsense."

Masculine rime is a rime of one-syllable words (*jail, bail*) or (in words of more than one syllable) stressed final syllables: *di-VORCE, re-MORSE,* or *horse, re-MORSE.* **Feminine rime** is a rime of two or more syllables, with stress on a syllable other than the last: *TUR-tle, FER-tile,* or (to take an example from Byron) *in-tel-LECT-u-al, hen-PECKED you all.* Often it lends itself to comic verse, but can occasionally be valuable to serious poems, as in Wordsworth's "Resolution and Independence":

> We poets in our youth begin in gladness,
> But thereof come in the end despondency and madness.

or as in Anne Sexton's "Eighteen Days Without You":

> and of course we're not married, we are a pair of scissors
> who come together to cut, without towels saying His. Hers.

In English, serious poems containing feminine rimes of three syllables have been attempted, notably by Thomas Hood in "The Bridge of Sighs":

> Take her up tenderly,
> Lift her with care;
> Fashioned so slenderly,
> Young, and so fair!

But the pattern is hard to sustain without lapsing into unintended comedy, as in the same poem:

> Still, for all slips of hers,
> One of Eve's family —
> Wipe those poor lips of hers,
> Oozing so clammily.

It works better when comedy is meant:

Hilaire Belloc (1870–1953)
THE HIPPOPOTAMUS

I shoot the Hippopotamus
  with bullets made of platinum,
Because if I use leaden ones
  his hide is sure to flatten 'em.

In **eye rime,** spellings look alike but pronunciations differ — *rough* and *dough, idea* and *flea.* Strictly speaking, eye rime is not rime at all.

In recent years American poetry has seen a great erosion of faith in rime, with Louis Simpson, James Wright, Robert Lowell, W. S. Merwin, and others quitting it for open forms. Indeed, it has been suggested that rime in the English language is exhausted. Such a view may be a reaction against the wearing-thin of rimes by overuse or the mechanical and meaningless application of a rime scheme. Yet anyone who listens to children skipping rope in the street, making up rimes to delight themselves as they go along, may doubt that the pleasures of rime are ended; and certainly the practice of Yeats and Emily Dickinson, to name only two, suggests that the possibilities of slant rime may be nearly infinite. If successfully employed, as it has been at times by a majority of English-speaking poets whose work we care to save, rime runs through its poem like a spine: the creature moves by means of it.

(Slant (Internal) rhymes) *[handwritten at top]*

Gerard Manley Hopkins (1844–1889)

GOD'S GRANDEUR *Alliteration the throughout the poem.* *[handwritten]*   *Italian sonnet* *[handwritten]*

The world is charged with the grandeur of God. a *The world is filled with the grandeur of god.* *[handwritten]*
  It will flame out, like shining from shook foil; b
  It gathers to a greatness, like the ooze of oil b
Crushed. Why do men then now not reck his rod? a
Generations have trod, have trod, have trod; a
  And all is seared with trade; bleared, smeared with toil; b *man doesn't care* *[handwritten]*
  And wears man's smudge and shares man's smell: the soil b *about nature* *[handwritten]*
Is bare now, nor can foot feel, being shod. a   8
they have ruined everything with machines etc... *[handwritten]*
And for all this, nature is never spent; c
  There lives the dearest freshness deep down things; d
  And though the last lights off the black West went c *we can't feel because we wear* *[handwritten]*
  Oh, morning, at the brown brink eastward, springs —d *shoes, we cover ourselves* *[handwritten]*
Because the Holy Ghost over the bent c
  World broods with warm breast and with ah! bright wings. d
even though we did this nature's never worn out. constantly renewing itself. *[handwritten]*

QUESTIONS

1. In a letter Hopkins explained _shook foil_ (line 2): "I mean foil in its sense of *moving* leaf or tinsel . . . Shaken goldfoil gives off broad glares like sheet lightning *comes* and also, and this is true of nothing else, owing to its zigzag dints and *after word* creasings and network of small many cornered facets, a sort of fork lightning *not true* too." What do you think he meant by _ooze of oil_ (line 3)? Is this phrase an *ooze's* example of alliteration?
2. What instances of internal rime does the poem contain? How would you *ooze of* describe their effects? *pedal*
3. Point out some of the poet's uses of alliteration and assonance. Does he go *is ringing* too far in his heavy use of devices of sound, or would you defend his practice?
assonance 'ws & b's also Holy Ghosts the long o's'. *[handwritten]*

Emanuel Morgan [Witter Bynner] (1881–1968)

OPUS 6

If I were only dafter
  I might be making hymns
To the liquor of your laughter
  And the lacquer of your limbs.   4

But you turn across the table
  A telescope of eyes,
And it lights a Russian sable
  Running circles in the skies . . .   8

Till I go running after,
  Obeying all your whims —
For the liquor of your laughter
  And the lacquer of your limbs.   12

1. This deliberately baffling poem was attributed to the Pittsburgh bohemian Emanuel Morgan by Witter Bynner, who invented him. (For an entertaining history of this 1916 literary prank, see William Jay Smith, *The Spectra Hoax,* Wesleyan University Press, 1961.) In what demonstrations of sound effects do these lines revel?
2. How do you account for this poem's being comic in effect, while Hopkins's "God's Grandeur," though more heavily laden with devices of sound, is not?

READING POEMS ALOUD

Thomas Moore's "The light that lies in women's eyes" — a line rich in internal rime, alliteration, and assonance — is harder to forget than "The light burning in the gaze of a woman." Because of sound, it is possible to remember the obscure line Christopher Smart wrote while in an insane asylum: "Let Ross, house of Ross rejoice with the Great Flabber Dabber Flat Clapping Fish with hands." Such lines, striking as they are even when read silently, become still more effective when said out loud. Reading poems aloud is a way to understand them. For this reason, you will do well to practice the art of lending poetry your voice.

Before trying to read a poem aloud to other people, understand its meaning as thoroughly as possible. If you know what the poet is saying and his attitude toward it, you will be able to find an appropriate tone of voice and to give each part of the poem a proper emphasis.

Except in the most informal situations and in some class exercises, read a poem to yourself before trying it on an audience. No actor goes before the footlights without first having studied his script, and the language of poems usually demands even more consideration than the language of most contemporary plays. Prepare your reading in advance. Check pronunciations you are not sure of. Underline things to be emphasized.

Read deliberately, more slowly than you would read aloud from a newspaper. Keep in mind that you are saying something to somebody. Don't race through the poem as if you are eager to get it over with.

Don't lapse into singsong. A poem may have a definite swing, but swing should never be exaggerated at the cost of sense. If you understand what the poem is saying and utter the poem as if you do, the temptation to fall into such a mechanical intonation should not occur. Observe the punctuation, making slight pauses for commas, longer pauses for full stops (periods, question marks, exclamation points).

If the poem is rimed, don't raise your voice and make the rimes stand out unnaturally. They should receive no more volume than other words in the poem, though a faint pause at the end of each line will call the listener's attention to them. This advice is contrary to a school that holds that, reading aloud a line that does not end in any punctuation, one should not pause but run it together with the line following. However, from such a reading, a listener may not be able to identify the rimes; besides, the line, that valuable unit of rhythm, is destroyed.

In some older poems rimes that look like slant rimes may have been exact rimes in their day:

> Still so perverse and opposite,
> As if they worshiped God for spite.
> — Samuel Butler, *Hudibras* (1663)

> Soft yielding minds to water glide away,
> And sip, with nymphs, their elemental tea.
> — Alexander Pope, "The Rape of the Lock" (1714)

You may wish to establish a consistent policy toward such shifting usage: is it worthwhile to distort current pronunciation for the sake of the rime?

Listening to a poem, especially an unfamiliar poem, places considerable demands on the hearers' attention. Seldom read poetry aloud uninterruptedly to anyone for more than a few minutes at a time. Robert Frost, a master at reading to audiences, would intersperse his poems with many silences and seemingly casual comments, shrewdly giving the poems a chance to sink in.

You may find it helpful to listen to recordings of some poets reading their poems. Not all read their own work well, but there is much to be relished in both the highly dramatic reading styles of Dylan Thomas and Ezra Pound and the quiet underplay of Frost. You need feel no obligation to imitate the poet's reading of a poem. You must feel about the poem in your own way in order to read it with conviction and spontaneity.

FOR REVIEW AND FURTHER STUDY

EXERCISE: *Reading for Sound and Meaning*

Read the following poems aloud. (Shakespeare's is a song lyric.) What devices of sound — alliteration, assonance, onomatopoeia, rime, slant rime, internal rime — do you find in each? Point out euphony or cacophony. Try to explain what the sound contributes to the total effect of the poem and how it reinforces what the poet is saying.

William Shakespeare (1564–1616)

IT WAS A LOVER AND HIS LASS

It was a lover and his lass,
  With a hey, and a ho, and a hey nonny no,
That o'er the green corn fields did pass
  In spring time, the only pretty ring time,
  When birds do sing, hey ding a ding a ding:
Sweet lovers love the spring.   6

Between the acres of the rye,
  With a hey, and a ho, and a hey nonny no,
These pretty country fools would lie,
  In spring time, the only pretty ring time,
  When birds do sing, hey ding a ding a ding:
  Sweet lovers love the spring.   12

This carol they began that hour,
  With a hey, and a ho, and a hey nonny no,
How that a life was but a flower
  In spring time, the only pretty ring time,
  When birds do sing, hey ding a ding a ding:
  Sweet lovers love the spring.   18

Then pretty lovers take the time
  With a hey, and a ho, and a hey nonny no,
For love is crownèd with the prime
  In spring time, the only pretty ring time,
  When birds do sing, hey ding a ding a ding:
  Sweet lovers love the spring.   24

Robert Herrick (1591–1674)

Delight in Disorder

A sweet disorder in the dress
Kindles in clothes a wantonness.   2
A lawn° about the shoulders thrown   *linen*
Into a fine distractión;   4
An erring lace, which here and there
Enthralls the crimson stomacher;   6
A cuff neglectful, and thereby
Ribbons to flow confusedly;   8
A winning wave, deserving note,
In the tempestuous petticoat;   10
A careless shoestring, in whose tie
I see a wild civility;   12
Do more bewitch me than when art
Is too precise in every part.   14

John Milton (1608–1674)

Rivers arise; whether thou be the son

Rivers arise; whether thou be the son
Of utmost *Tweed*, or *Oose*, or gulfy *Dun*,
Or *Trent*, who like some earth-born giant spreads
His thirty arms along th' indented meads,   4
Or sullen *Mole* that runneth underneath,
Or *Severn* swift, guilty of maiden's death,   6
Or rocky *Avon*, or of sedgy *Lee*,
Or coaly *Tine*, or ancient hallowed *Dee*,   8

Or *Humber* loud, that keeps the Scythian's name,
Or *Medway* smooth, or royal towered *Thame.*

RIVERS ARISE. This affectionate list of English rivers is one of several verses (collectively titled "At a Vacation Exercise") Milton wrote to be spoken at a college entertainment in June 1628. It appears to have been addressed to a fellow student named Rivers. 6. *maiden:* Sabrina, daughter of King Locrine, was supposed to have drowned herself in the Severn. (See Milton's "Comus," lines 824–858.) 9. *the Scythian:* According to Spenser, the Humber was named for a Scythian king whom it had drowned.

Leigh Hunt (1784–1859)
RONDEAU

Jenny kissed me when we met,
  Jumping from the chair she sat in;
Time, you thief, who love to get
  Sweets into your list, put that in: 4
Say I'm weary, say I'm sad,
  Say that health and wealth have missed me,
Say I'm growing old, but add,
  Jenny kissed me.   8

Emanuel diPasquale (b. 1943)
RAIN

Like a drummer's brush,
the rain hushes the surface of tin porches.

Charles Reznikoff (b. 1894)
HOW SHALL WE MOURN YOU WHO ARE KILLED AND WASTED

How shall we mourn you who are killed and wasted,
sure that you would not die with your work unended,
as if the iron scythe in the grass stops for a flower?

A. E. Housman (1859–1936)
WITH RUE MY HEART IS LADEN

With rue my heart is laden
  For golden friends I had,
For many a rose-lipt maiden
  And many a lightfoot lad.
         4
By brooks too broad for leaping
  The lightfoot boys are laid;
The rose-lipt girls are sleeping
  In fields where roses fade.   8

9 Rhythm

STRESSES AND PAUSES

A rhythm is produced by a series of recurrences: the returns and departures of the seasons, the repetitions of an engine's stroke, the beats of the heart. A rhythm may be produced by the recurrence of a sound (the throb of a drum, a telephone's busy-signal), but rhythm and sound are not identical. A totally deaf man at a parade can sense rhythm from the motions of the marchers' arms and feet, from the shaking of the pavement as they tramp. Rhythms inhere in the motions of the moon and stars, even though they move without a sound.

In poetry, several kinds of recurrent *sound* are possible, including (as we saw in the last chapter) rime, alliteration, and assonance. But most often when we speak of the **rhythm** of a poem we mean the recurrence of stresses and pauses in it. When we hear a poem read aloud, stresses and pauses are, of course, part of its sound. However, it is possible to be aware of rhythms in poems read silently.

A **stress** (or **accent**) is a greater amount of force given to one syllable in speaking than is given to another. We favor a stressed syllable with a little more breath and emphasis, with the result that it comes out slightly louder, higher in pitch, or longer in duration than other syllables. In this manner we place a stress on the first syllable of words such as *eagle, impact, open,* and *statue,* and on the second syllable in *cigar, mystique, precise,* and *until.* Each word in English carries at least one stress, except (usually) for the articles *a, an,* and *the,* and one-syllable prepositions: *at, by, for, from, of, to, with.* Even these, however, take a stress once in a while: "Get WITH it!" "You're not THE John Lennon?" One word by itself is seldom long enough for us to notice a rhythm in it. Usually a sequence of at least a few words is needed for stresses to establish their pattern: a line, a passage, a whole poem.

Rhythms affect us powerfully. We are lulled by a hammock's sway, awakened by an alarm clock's repeated yammer. Long after we come home from a beach, the rising and falling of waves and tides continue in memory. How powerfully the rhythms of poetry also move us may be felt in folk songs of railroad workers and chain gangs whose words were chanted in time to the lifting and dropping of a sledgehammer, and in verse that marching soldiers shout, putting a stress on every word that coincides with a footfall:

> Your LEFT! TWO! THREE! FOUR!
> Your LEFT! TWO! THREE! FOUR!
> You LEFT your WIFE and TWEN-ty-one KIDS
> And you LEFT! TWO! THREE! FOUR!
> You'll NEV-er get HOME to-NIGHT!

Strong rhythms may be seen in most Mother Goose rimes, to which children have been responding for hundreds of years. This rime is for an adult to chant while jogging a child up and down on his knee:

> Here goes my lord
> A trot, a trot, a trot, a trot!
> Here goes my lady
> A canter, a canter, a canter, a canter!
> Here goes my young master
> Jockey-hitch, jockey-hitch, jockey-hitch, jockey-hitch!
> Here goes my young miss
> An amble, an amble, an amble, an amble!
> The footman lags behind to tipple ale and wine
> And goes gallop, a gallop, a gallop, to make up his time.

More than one rhythm occurs in these lines, as the make-believe horse changes pace. How do these rhythms differ? From one line to the next, the interval between stresses lengthens or grows shorter. In "a TROT a TROT a TROT a TROT," the stress falls on every other syllable. But in the middle of the line "A CAN-ter a CAN-ter a CAN-ter a CAN-ter," the stress falls on every third syllable. When stresses recur at fixed intervals as in these lines, the resulting pattern is called a **meter**. The line "A trot a trot a trot a trot" is in **iambic** meter, a pattern of alternate unstressed and stressed syllables.[1] Of all patterns of rhythm in the English language, this one is most familiar; most of our traditional poetry is written in it and ordinary speech tends to resemble it. Most poems, less obvious in rhythm than nursery rimes are, rarely stick to their meters with such jog-trot regularity.

Stresses embody meanings. Whenever two or more fall side by side or whenever they far outnumber unstressed (or **slack**) syllables, the poet is placing emphasis on his words just as surely as if he had underlined them.

Consider the following hard-hitting lines from John Donne, in

---

[1] Another kind of meter is possible, in which the intervals between stresses vary. This is **accentual** meter, not often found in contemporary poetry. It is discussed in the second section of this chapter.

which accent marks have been placed, dictionary-fashion, to indicate the stressed syllables:

Bat'ter my heart', three'-per'soned God', for You'
As yet' but knock', breathe', shine', and seek' to mend';
That I may rise' and stand', o'er'throw' me, and bend'
Your force' to break', blow', burn', and make' me new'.

Unstressed syllables, too, can direct our attention to what the poet means. In a line containing few stresses and a great many unstressed syllables, he can achieve an effect not of power and force but of hesitation and uncertainty. Yeats asks in "Among School Children" what young mother, if she could see her baby grown to be an old man, would think him

A com'pen·sa'tion for the pang' of his birth'
Or the un·cer'tain·ty of his set'ting forth'?

When unstressed syllables recur in pairs, the result is a rhythm that trips and bounces, as in Robert Service's rollicking line:

A bunch' of the boys' were whoop'ing it up' in the Mal'a·mute sa·loon' . . .

or in Poe's lines — also light but probably supposed to be serious:

For the moon' nev'er beams' with·out bring'ing me dreams'
Of the beau'ti·ful An'na·bel Lee'.

Apart from the words that convey it, the rhythm of a poem has no meaning. There are no essentially sad rhythms, nor any essentially happy ones. But some rhythms enforce certain meanings better than others do. The bouncing rhythm of Service's line seems fitting for an account of a merry night in a Klondike saloon, but it may be distracting when encountered in Poe's wistful elegy.

EXERCISE: *Appropriate and Inappropriate Rhythms*

In each of the following passages, decide whether rhythm enforces meaning and tone or works against these elements and consequently against the poem's effectiveness.

1. Alfred, Lord Tennyson, "Break, break, break"

Break, break, break,
On thy cold gray stones, O Sea!

2. Edgar Allan Poe, "Ulalume"

Then my heart it grew ashen and sober
As the leaves that were crispèd and sere —
As the leaves that were withering and sere,

And I cried: "It was surely October
On *this* very night of last year
That I journeyed — I journeyed down here —
That I brought a dread burden down here —
On this night of all nights in the year,
Ah, what demon has tempted me here?"

3. A. A. Milne, "Disobedience"

James James
Morrison Morrison
Weatherby George Dupree
Took great
Care of his Mother,
Though he was only three.
James James
Said to his Mother,
"Mother," he said, said he;
"You must never go down to the end of the town, if you don't go down
with me."

4. Thomas Middleton, song from *Chaste Maid in Cheapside*

Weep eyes, break heart!
My love and I must part.

5. Eliza Cook, "Song of the Sea-Weed"

Many a lip is gaping for drink,
  And madly calling for rain;
And some hot brains are beginning to think
  Of a messmate's opened vein.

6. William Shakespeare, song from *The Tempest*

The master, the swabber, the boatswain, and I,
The gunner and his mate
Loved Moll, Meg, and Marian, and Margery,
But none of us cared for Kate;
For she had a tongue with a tang
Would cry to a sailor "Go hang!" —
She loved not the savor of tar nor of pitch
Yet a tailor might scratch her where'er she did itch;
Then to sea, boys, and let her go hang!

Rhythms in poetry are due not only to stresses but also to pauses. "Every nice ear," observed Alexander Pope (*nice* meaning "finely tuned"), "must, I believe, have observed that in any smooth English verse of ten syllables, there is naturally a pause either at the fourth, fifth, or sixth syllable." Such a light but definite pause within a line is called a **cesura** (or caesura), "a cutting." More liberally than Pope, we apply the name to any pause in a line of any length, after any word in the line. In studying a poem, we often indicate a cesura by double lines (‖). Usually, a cesura will occur at a mark of punctuation, but there can be a cesura even if no punctuation is present. Sometimes you will find it at the end of a phrase or clause or, as in these lines by William Blake, after an internal rime:

And priests in black gowns ‖ were walking their rounds
And binding with briars ‖ my joys and desires.

Lines of ten or twelve syllables (as Pope knew) tend to have just one cesura, though sometimes there are more:

Cover her face: ‖ mine eyes dazzle: ‖ she died young.

Pauses also tend to recur at more prominent places — namely, after each line. At the end of a verse (from *versus,* "a turning"), the reader's eye, before turning to go on to the next line, makes a pause, however brief. If a line ends in a full pause — usually indicated by some mark of punctuation — we call it **end-stopped.** All the lines in this stanza by Theodore Roethke are end-stopped:

Let seed be grass, and grass turn into hay:
I'm martyr to a motion not my own;
What's freedom for? To know eternity.
I swear she cast a shadow white as stone.
But who would count eternity in days?
These old bones live to learn her wanton ways:
(I measure time by how a body sways).[2]

A line that does not end in punctuation and that therefore is read with only a slight pause after it is called **run-on;** the running-on of its thought into the next line is **enjambment.** A run-on line gives us only part of a phrase, clause, or sentence. All these lines from Robert Browning's "My Last Duchess' are run-on lines, despite the fact that the lines are pairs of rimes:

Sir, 'twas not
Her husband's presence only, called that spot
Of joy into the Duchess' cheek: perhaps
Frà Pandolf chanced to say "Her mantle laps
Over my lady's wrist too much," or "Paint
Must never hope to reproduce the faint
Half-flush that dies along her throat." Such stuff
Was courtesy, she thought . . .

A passage in run-on lines has a rhythm different from that of a passage like Roethke's in end-stopped lines. When emphatic pauses occur in the quotation from Browning, they fall within a line rather than at the end of one. The passage by Roethke and that by Browning are in lines of the same meter (iambic) and the same length (ten syllables). What makes the big difference in their rhythms is enjambment, or lack of it.

---

[2] The complete poem, "I Knew a Woman," appears on page 97.

To sum up: rhythm is recurrence. In poems, it is made of stresses and pauses. The poet can produce it by doing any of several things: making the intervals between his stresses fixed or varied, long or short; indicating pauses (cesuras) within his lines; end-stopping lines or running them over; writing in short or long lines. Rhythm in itself cannot convey meaning. And yet if a poet's words have meaning, their rhythm must be one with it.

Gwendolyn Brooks (b. 1917)
WE REAL COOL

The Pool Players.
Seven at the Golden Shovel.

We real cool. We
Left school. We   2

Lurk late. We
Strike straight. We   4

Sing sin. We
Thin gin. We   6

Jazz June. We
Die soon.   8

QUESTION
Describe the rhythms of this poem. By what techniques are they produced?

Robert Frost (1874–1963)
NEVER AGAIN WOULD BIRDS' SONG BE THE SAME

He would declare and could himself believe
That the birds there in all the garden round
From having heard the daylong voice of Eve
Had added to their own an oversound,   4
Her tone of meaning but without the words.
Admittedly an eloquence so soft
Could only have had an influence on birds
When call or laughter carried it aloft.   8
Be that as may be, she was in their song.
Moreover her voice upon their voices crossed
Had now persisted in the woods so long
That probably it never would be lost.   12
Never again would birds' song be the same.
And to do that to birds was why she came.   14

QUESTIONS

1. Who is *he?*
2. In reading aloud line 9, do you stress *may?* (Do you say "as MAY be" or "as may BE"?) What guide do we have to the poet's wishes here?
3. Which lines does Frost cast mostly or entirely into monosyllables? How would you describe the impact of these lines?
4. In his *Essay on Criticism,* Alexander Pope made fun of poets who wrote mechanically, without wit: "And ten low words oft creep in one dull line." Do you think this criticism applicable to Frost's lines of monosyllables? Explain.

Ben Jonson (1573?–1637)

SLOW, SLOW, FRESH FOUNT, KEEP TIME WITH MY SALT TEARS

Slow, slow, fresh fount, keep time with my salt tears;
  Yet slower yet, oh faintly, gentle springs;
List to the heavy part the music bears,
    Woe weeps out her division° when she sings.   *a part in a song*   4
      Droop herbs and flowers,
      Fall grief in showers;
      Our beauties are not ours;   7
        Oh, I could still,
Like melting snow upon some craggy hill,
  Drop, drop, drop, drop,
Since nature's pride is now a withered daffodil.   11

SLOW, SLOW, FRESH FOUNT. The nymph Echo sings this lament over the youth Narcissus in Jonson's play *Cynthia's Revels.* In mythology, Nemesis, goddess of vengeance, to punish Narcissus for loving his own beauty, caused him to pine away and then transformed him into a narcissus (another name for a *daffodil,* line 11).

QUESTIONS

1. Read the first line aloud rapidly. Why is it difficult to do so?
2. Which lines rely most heavily on stressed syllables?
3. In general, how would you describe the rhythm of this poem? How is it appropriate to what is said?

Robert Lowell (b. 1917)

AT THE ALTAR

I sit at a gold table with my girl
Whose eyelids burn with brandy. What a whirl   2
Of Easter eggs is colored by the lights,
As the Norwegian dancer's crystalled tights   4
Flash with her naked leg's high-booted skate,
Like Northern Lights upon my watching plate.   6

The twinkling steel above me is a star;
I am a fallen Christmas tree. Our car   8
Races through seven red-lights — then the road
Is unpatrolled and empty, and a load   10
Of ply-wood with a tail-light makes us slow.
I turn and whisper in her ear. You know   12
I want to leave my mother and my wife,
You wouldn't have me tied to them for life . . .   14
Time runs, the windshield runs with stars. The past
Is cities from a train, until at last   16
Its escalating and black-windowed blocks
Recoil against a Gothic church. The clocks   18
Are tolling. I am dying. The shocked stones
Are falling like a ton of bricks and bones   20
That snap and splinter and descend in glass
Before a priest who mumbles through his Mass   22
And sprinkles holy water; and the Day
Breaks with its lightning on the man of clay,   24
Dies amara valde. Here the Lord
Is Lucifer in harness: hand on sword,   26
He watches me for Mother, and will turn
The bier and baby-carriage where I burn.   28

AT THE ALTAR. In a public reading of this poem, Robert Lowell made some remarks cited
by George P. Elliott in *Fifteen Modern American Poets* (New York, 1956). Lit up like a
Christmas tree, the speaker finds himself in a Boston nightclub, watching a skating
floorshow. Then he and his girl drive (or does he only dream they drive?) to a church
where a priest saying a funeral Mass sprinkles a corpse with holy water. 23. *the Day:* The
Day of Judgment. 25. *Dies amara valde:* "Day bitter above all others," a phrase from a
funeral hymn, the *Dies Irae,* in which sinners are warned to fear God's wrath. 28. *baby-
carriage:* The undertaker's silver dolly, supporting a coffin.

QUESTIONS

1. Which lines in this poem are end-stopped?
2. What effects does Lowell obtain by so much enjambment?
3. What besides enjambment contributes to the rhythm of the poem?
4. How is this rhythm appropriate to what the poet is saying? Explain.

EXERCISE: *Two Kinds of Rhythm*

The following compositions in verse have lines of similar length, yet they differ
greatly in rhythm. Explain how they differ and why.

Sir Thomas Wyatt (1503?–1542)

WITH SERVING STILL

With serving still°   *continually*
    This have I won,
For my goodwill
    To be undone;   4

And for redress
  Of all my pain,
Disdainfulness
  I have again;   8

And for reward
  Of all my smart
Lo, thus unheard,
  I must depart!   12

Wherefore all ye
  That after shall
By fortune be,
  As I am, thrall,   16

Example take
  What I have won,
Thus for her sake
  To be undone!   20

Dorothy Parker (1893–1967)

Résumé

Razors pain you;
Rivers are damp;
Acids stain you;
And drugs cause cramp.   4
Guns aren't lawful;
Nooses give;
Gas smells awful;
You might as well live.   8

METER

To enjoy the rhythms of a poem, no special knowledge of meter is
necessary. All you need do is pay attention to stresses and where they
fall; and you will perceive the basic pattern, if there is any. However,
there is nothing occult about the study of meter. Most people find they
can master its essentials in no more time than it takes to learn a complicated game such as chess. If you take the time, you will then have the
pleasure of knowing what is happening in the rhythms of many a fine
poem, and pleasurable knowledge may even deepen your insight into
poetry.

Far from being artificial constructions found only in the minds of
poets, meters occur in the most everyday speech and prose. As the
following example will show, they may need only a poet to recognize
them. The English satirist Max Beerbohm, after contemplating the title
page of his first book, took his pen and added two more lines.

Max Beerbohm (1872–1956)

On the Imprint of the First English Edition of "The Works of Max Beerbohm"

"London: John Lane, *The Bodley Head*
New York: Charles Scribner's Sons."
This plain announcement, nicely read,
Iambically runs.

In everyday life, nobody speaks or writes in perfect iambic rhythm, except in occasional brief remarks: "a HAM on RYE." (As we have seen, iambic rhythm consists of a series of syllables alternately unstressed and stressed.) Poets rarely speak in it for very long either, and seldom with exactitude. If you read aloud Max Beerbohm's lines, you will hear an iambic rhythm but not an absolutely invariable one. And yet all of us speak with a rising and falling of stress somewhat like iambic meter. Perhaps, as the poet and scholar John Thompson has maintained, "The iambic metrical pattern has dominated English verse because it provides the best symbolic model of our language."[3]

A meter is not a detailed description of actual speech but a pattern for a poet's speech to depart from or to follow. To make ourselves aware of this pattern, we can **scan** a line or a poem by indicating the stresses in it. **Scansion,** the art of so doing, is not just a matter of pointing to syllables; it is also a matter of listening to a poem and making sense of it. To scan a poem is one way to indicate how to read it aloud; in order to see where stresses fall, you have to see the places where the poet wishes to put emphasis. That is why, when scanning a poem, you may find yourself suddenly understanding it. Sometimes different readers may not agree on the scansion of a poem because they do not agree on the meaning of the poem itself.

An objection might be raised against scanning: isn't it too simple to pretend that all language (and poetry) can be divided neatly into stressed syllables and unstressed syllables? Indeed it is. As the linguist Otto Jespersen has said, "In reality there are infinite gradations of stress, from the most penetrating scream to the faintest whisper."[4] However, the idea in scanning a poem is not to reproduce the sound of a human voice. For that we would do better to buy a tape recorder. To scan a poem, rather, is to make a diagram of the stresses (and absences of stress) we find in it. Various marks are used in scansion; in this book we use ´ for a stressed syllable and ˘ for an unstressed syllable. Some

[3] *The Founding of English Metre* (New York, 1966), p. 12.
[4] "Notes on Metre," *Linguistica* (Copenhagen, 1933); reprinted in *The Structure of Verse: Modern Essays on Prosody*, edited by Harvey Gross (New York, 1966).

scanners, wishing a little more precision, also use the **half-stress** (ˇ); this device can be helpful in many instances when a syllable usually not stressed comes at a place where it takes some emphasis, as in the last syllable in a line:

ˇ ́ ˇ ́ ˇ ́ ˇ ˇ ́ˇˋ
Bound each to each with nat·u·ral pi·e·ty.

Here, with examples, are some of the principal meters we find in English poetry. For each is given its basic **foot,** or molecule (usually one stressed and one or two unstressed syllables):

1. **Iambic** (foot: the **iamb,** ˇ ́):
   ˇ ́ ˇ ́ ˇ ́   ́ ˇ ́ ˇ ́ ˇ ́
   The fall·ing out of faith·ful friends, re·new·ing is of love

2. **Anapestic** (foot: the **anapest,** ˇ ˇ ́):
   ˇˇ ́ ˇ ˇ ́ ˇ ˇ ́
   I am mon·arch of all I sur·vey

3. **Trochaic** (foot: the **trochee,** ́ ˇ):
   ́ ˇ ́ ˇ ́ ˇ ́ ˇ
   Dou·ble, dou·ble, toil and trou·ble

4. **Dactylic** (foot: the **dactyl,** ́ ˇ ˇ):
   ́   ˇ ˇ ́ ˇ ˇ
   Take her up ten·der·ly

Iambic and anapestic meters are called **rising** meters because their movement rises from unstressed syllable (or syllables) to stress; trochaic and dactylic meters are called **falling.** In the twentieth century, the bouncing meters — anapestic and dactylic — have been used more often for comic verse than for serious poetry. Called feet, though they contain no unaccented syllables, are the **monosyllabic foot** (́) and the **spondee** (́ ́). Meters are not ordinarily made up of them; if one were, it would be like the steady impact of nails being hammered into a board — no pleasure to hear or to dance to. But inserted now and then, they can lend emphasis and variety to a meter, as Yeats well knew when he broke up the predominantly iambic rhythm of "Who Goes with Fergus?" (p. 127) with the line,

ˇ ˇ ́ ́ ˇ ˇ ́ ́
And the white breast of the dim sea,

in which occur two spondees.

Metrical patterns are classified also by line lengths: **trochaic monometer,** for instance, is a line one trochee long, as in this anonymous brief comment on microbes:

Adam
Had 'em.

A frequently heard metrical description is **iambic pentameter:** a line of five iambs, a pattern especially familiar because it occurs in all blank verse (such as Shakespeare's plays and Milton's *Paradise Lost*), heroic couplets, and sonnets. The customary names for line lengths are:

monometer	one foot
dimeter	two feet
trimeter	three feet
tetrameter	four feet
pentameter	five feet
hexameter	six feet
heptameter	seven feet
octameter	eight feet

Lines of more than eight feet are possible but, to the listening ear, tend to break up into shorter lengths.

When Yeats chose the spondees *white breast* and *dim sea*, he was doing what poets who write in meter do frequently for variety — using a foot other than the expected one. Often such a substitution will be made at the very beginning of a line, as in the third line of this passage from Christopher Marlowe's *Tragical History of Doctor Faustus:*

Was this the face that launched a thou·sand ships
And burnt the top·less tow'rs of Il·i·um?
Sweet Hel·en, make me im·mor·tal with a kiss.

How, we might wonder, can that last line be called iambic at all? But it is, just as a waltz that includes an extra step or two, or leaves a few steps out, remains a waltz. In the preceding lines the basic iambic pentameter is established, and though in the third line the pattern is varied from, it does not altogether disappear but continues for a while to run on in the reader's mind, where, if the poet does not stay away from it for too long, it will be when he chooses to come back to it.

Like a basic dance step, a metrical pattern is not to be slavishly adhered to. The fun in reading a metrical poem often comes from watching the poet continually departing from his pattern, giving a few kicks of his heels to display a bit of joy or ingenuity, coming down with a few bangs for emphasis, and then easing back into his basic step again. Because meter is orderly and the rhythms of living speech are unruly, poets can play one against the other, in a sort of counterpoint. Robert Frost, a master at pitting a line of iambs against a very natural-sounding and irregular sentence, declared, "I am never more pleased than when I can get these into strained relation. I like to drag and break the intonation across the meter as waves first comb and then break stumbling on a shingle."[5]

[5] Letter to John Cournos in 1914, *Selected Letters of Robert Frost*, edited by Lawrance Thompson (New York, 1964), p. 128.

Evidently Frost's skilled effects would be lost to any reader who, scanning a Frost poem or reading it aloud, distorted its rhythms to fit the words exactly to the meter. With rare exceptions, a good poem can be read and scanned the way we would speak its sentences if they were ours. This, for example, is an unreal scansion:

That's my last Duch·ess paint·ed on the wall.

— because no speaker of English would say that sentence in that way. We are likely to stress *That's* and *last*.

Departure from metrical pattern is not merely desirable in poetry, it is usually a necessity: woe be to the poet who fails to depart from it often enough. Allowing the beat of his words to slip into mechanical regularity, the poet sets his poem marching robot-like right over a precipice. Luckily, few poets, except writers of greeting cards, favor rhythms that go "a TROT a TROT a TROT a TROT" for very long. Robert Frost told an audience one time that if when writing a poem he found its rhythm becoming monotonous, he knew that the poem was going wrong and that he himself didn't believe what it was saying.

As readers, our only test of whether a poem is telling the truth is to see whether its rhythm seems right for it. Sometimes a poet will seek metrical monotony for deliberate effect. Words fall meaningfully in Macbeth's famous statement of world-weariness: "Tomorrow and tomorrow and tomorrow . . ." and in the opening lines of Thomas Gray's famous "Elegy":

The cur·few tolls the knell of part·ing day,

The low·ing herd wind slow·ly o'er the lea,

The plow·man home·ward plods his wear·y way,

And leaves the world to dark·ness and to me.

Here the almost unvarying iambic rhythm seems appropriate to convey the tolling of a bell and the weary setting down of one foot after the other.

Besides the two rising meters (iambic, anapestic) and the two falling meters (trochaic, dactylic), English poets have another valuable meter. It is **accentual meter,** in which the poet does not write in feet (as in the other meters) but instead counts accents (stresses). The idea is to have the same number of stresses in every line. The poet may place them anywhere he likes and may include practically any number of unstressed syllables, which do not count. In "Christabel," for instance, Coleridge keeps four stresses to a line, though the first line has only eight syllables and the last line has eleven:

There is not wind e·nough to twirl

The one red leaf, the last of its clan,

That dan·ces as of ten as dance it can,

Háng·ing so líght, and háng·ing so hígh,

On the tóp·most twíg that looks úp at the ský.

The history of accentual meter is long and honorable. Old English poetry was written in a kind of accentual meter, but its line was more rule-bound than Coleridge's: four stresses arranged two on either side of a cesura, plus alliteration of three of the stressed syllables. In "Junk" (p. 396), Richard Wilbur revives the pattern:

An áxe án·gles ‖ from my néigh·bor's ásh·can . . .

Many poets, from the authors of Mother Goose rimes to Gerard Manley Hopkins, have sometimes found accentual meters congenial, even preferable to **accentual-syllabic** meters, the other kind.

It has been charged that the importation of Greek names for meters and the classical notion of feet was an unsuccessful attempt to make a Parthenon out of English wattles. The charge is open to debate, but at least it is certain that Greek names for feet cannot mean to us what they meant to Aristotle. Greek and Latin poetry is measured not by stressed and unstressed syllables but by long and short vowel sounds. An iamb in classical verse is one short vowel followed by a long vowel. Such a meter constructed on the principle of vowel length is called a **quantitative** meter. Campion's "Rose-cheeked Laura" (p. 120) was an attempt to demonstrate it in English, but probably we enjoy the rhythm of the poem's well-placed stresses whether or not we notice its pattern of vowel sounds.

Less popular among poets today than formerly, the use of meter endures. Major poets from Shakespeare through Yeats have fashioned their poems by it, and if we are to read their work closely and sensitively, we need to be aware of it. One argument in favor of meter is expressed in an old jazz song: "It don't mean a thing if you ain't got that swing." Or, as critic Paul Fussell, Jr., has put it: "No element of a poem is more basic — and I mean physical — in its effect upon the reader than the metrical element, and perhaps no technical triumphs reveal more readily than the metrical the poet's sympathy with that universal human nature . . . which exists outside his own."[6]

Walter Savage Landor (1775–1864)

ON SEEING A HAIR OF LUCRETIA BORGIA

Borgia, thou once wert almost too august
And high for adoration; now thou'rt dust.
All that remains of thee these plaits unfold,
Calm hair, meandering in pellucid gold.

---

[6] *Poetic Meter and Poetic Form* (New York, 1965), p. 110.

1. Who was Lucretia Borgia and when did she live? What connotations that add meaning to Landor's poem has her name?
2. What does *meander* mean? How can a hair meander?
3. Scan the poem, indicating stressed syllables. What is the basic meter of most of the poem? What happens to this meter in the last line? Note especially *meandering in pel-*. How many light, unstressed syllables are there in a row? Does rhythm in any way reinforce what Landor is saying?

Percy Bysshe Shelley (1792–1822)

A DIRGE

Rough wind, that moanest loud
　Grief too sad for song;
Wild wind, when sullen cloud
　Knells all the night long;　　　　　　　　　　　　　　4
Sad storm, whose tears are vain,
Bare woods, whose branches strain,
Deep caves and dreary main —
　Wail, for the world's wrong!　　　　　　　　　　　　8

QUESTION

What kind of meter is "A Dirge" written in?

EXERCISE: *Meaningful Variation*

At what place or places in each of these passages does the poet depart from his basic iambic meter? How does each departure help him underscore his meaning?

1. John Dryden, "Mac Flecknoe" (speech of Flecknoe, prince of Nonsense, referring to Thomas Shadwell, poet and playwright)

   Shadwell alone of all my sons is he
   Who stands confirmed in full stupidity.
   The rest to some faint meaning make pretense,
   But Shadwell never deviates into sense.

2. Alexander Pope, *An Essay on Criticism*

   A needless Alexandrine ends the song
   That, like a wounded snake, drags its slow length along.

3. Henry King, "The Exequy" (an apostrophe to his wife)

   'Tis true, with shame and grief I yield,
   Thou like the van° first tookst the field,　　　　　　*vanguard*
   And gotten hath the victory
   In thus adventuring to die
   Before me, whose more years might crave
   A just precedence in the grave.
   But hark! my pulse like a soft drum
   Beats my approach, tells thee I come;

And slow howe'er my marches be,
I shall at last sit down by thee.

4. Henry Wadsworth Longfellow, "Mezzo Cammin"

Half-way up the hill, I see the Past
Lying beneath me with its sounds and sights, —
A city in the twilight dim and vast,
With smoking roofs, soft bells, and gleaming lights, —
And hear above me on the autumnal blast
The cataract of Death far thundering from the heights.

5. Wallace Stevens, "Sunday Morning"

Deer walk upon our mountains, and the quail
Whistle about us their spontaneous cries;
Sweet berries ripen in the wilderness;
And, in the isolation of the sky,
At evening, casual flocks of pigeons make
Ambiguous undulations as they sink,
Downward to darkness, on extended wings.

FOR REVIEW AND FURTHER STUDY

Experiment: *Reading for Rhythm*

Some latter-day critics have called Sir Thomas Wyatt a careless poet because
some of his lines appear faltering and metrically inconsistent; others have
thought he knew what he was doing. It is uncertain whether the final *e*'s in English spelling were still pronounced in Wyatt's day as they were in Chaucer's,
but if they were, perhaps Wyatt has been unjustly blamed. In the text below,
spellings have been modernized except in words where the final *e* would make
a difference in rhythm. To sense how it matters, try reading the poem aloud
leaving out the final *e*'s and then putting them in wherever indicated. Sound
them like the *a* in *sofa*. Which way of reading the poem do you prefer? Why?

Sir Thomas Wyatt (1503?–1542)

They flee from me that sometime did me sekë

They flee from me that sometime did me sekë
    With naked fotë° stalking in my chamber.   *foot*
I have seen them gentle, tame and mekë
    That now are wild, and do not remember
    That sometime they put themself in danger   5
To take bread at my hand; and now they range
Busily seeking with a continual change.   7

Thanked be fortune, it hath been otherwise
    Twenty times better; but once in speciàll,
In thin array, after a pleasant guise,
    When her loose gown from her shoulders did fall,
    And she me caught in her armës long and small,   12
Therewith all sweetly did me kiss,
And softly said, *Dear heart, how like you this?*   14

It was no dremë: I lay broadë waking.
  But all is turned thorough° my gentleness   *through*
Into a strangë fashion of forsaking;
  And I have leave to go of her goodness,
  And she also to use newfangleness°.   *to seek novelty*   19
But since that I so kindëly° am served   *naturally (according to woman's*
I would fain knowë what she hath deserved.   *nature)*   21

EXERCISE: *Recognizing Rhythms*

Which of the following poems contain meters? In which are the rhythms varying or alternating? What is it that produces the rhythm of each poem? What
elements besides rhythm give each poem its total effect?

Gerard Manley Hopkins (1844–1889)
INVERSNAID

This darksome burn°, horseback brown,   *brook*
His rollrock highroad roaring down,
In coop° and in comb° the fleece of his foam   *hollow; ravine*
Flutes and low to the lake falls home.   4

A windpuff-bonnet of fáwn-fróth
Turns and twindles over the broth
Of a pool so pitchblack, féll-frówning,
It rounds and rounds Despair to drowning.   8

Degged° with dew, dappled with dew   *sprinkled*
Are the groins of the braes that the brook treads through,
Wiry heathpacks, flitches° of fern,   *ragged clumps*
And the beadbonny ash that sits over the burn.   12

What would the world be, once bereft
Of wet and of wildness? Let them be left,
O let them be left, wildness and wet;
Long live the weeds and the wilderness yet.   16

INVERSNAID is a hilly place in Scotland lying along Loch Lomond. 6. *twindles:* W. H.
Gardner, who has edited Hopkins's poems, thinks this word may be a coinage made up
of *dwindles* and *twists.*

Alfred, Lord Tennyson (1809–1892)
DARK HOUSE, BY WHICH ONCE MORE I STAND

Dark house, by which once more I stand
  Here in the long unlovely street,
  Doors, where my heart was used to beat
So quickly, waiting for a hand,   4

A hand that can be clasped no more —
Behold me, for I cannot sleep,
And like a guilty thing I creep
At earliest morning to the door.   8

He is not here; but far away
The noise of life begins again,
And ghastly through the drizzling rain
On the bald street breaks the blank day.   12

DARK HOUSE. This poem is one part of the series *In Memoriam,* an elegy for Tennyson's
friend Arthur Henry Hallam.

William Carlos Williams (1883–1963)
THE DESCENT OF WINTER (SECTION 10/30)

To freight cars in the air

all the slow
    clank, clank
    clank, clank
moving above the treetops   5

the
    wha, wha
of the hoarse whistle

    pah,   pah,   pah
    pah, pah, pah, pah, pah   10
    piece and piece
    piece and piece
moving still trippingly
through the morningmist

long after the engine   15
has fought by
            and disappeared
in silence
            to the left

Walt Whitman (1819–1892)
BEAT! BEAT! DRUMS!

Beat! beat! drums! — blow! bugles! blow!
Through the windows — through doors — burst like a ruthless force,
Into the solemn church, and scatter the congregation,
Into the school where the scholar is studying;

Leave not the bridegroom quiet — no happiness must he have now with
    his bride, 5
Nor the peaceful farmer any peace, ploughing his field or gathering his
    grain,
So fierce you whirr and pound you drums — so shrill you bugles blow.

Beat! beat! drums! — blow! bugles! blow!
Over the traffic of cities — over the rumble of wheels in the streets;
Are beds prepared for sleepers at night in the houses? no sleepers must
    sleep in those beds, 10
No bargainer's bargains by day — no brokers or speculators — would
    they continue?
Would the talkers be talking? would the singer attempt to sing?
Would the lawyer rise in the court to state his case before the judge?
Then rattle quicker, heavier drums — you bugles wilder blow.

Beat! beat! drums! — blow! bugles! blow! 15
Make no parley — stop for no expostulation,
Mind not the timid — mind not the weeper or prayer,
Mind not the old man beseeching the young man,
Let not the child's voice be heard, nor the mother's entreaties,
Make even the trestles to shake the dead where they lie awaiting the
    hearses. 20
So strong you thump O terrible drums — so loud you bugles blow.

10 Closed Form, Open Form

Of late, poets and critics debating the relative merits of "closed form" and "open form" have worn out many miles of typewriter ribbon. Writing in **closed form,** a poet follows or discovers some sort of pattern: a meter or a rime-scheme or the structure of a sonnet with its fourteen iambic pentameter lines. Along with William Butler Yeats, who believed that a successful poem will "come shut with a click, like a closing box," the contemporary poet who writes in rime and meter apparently strives for some kind of perfection: seeking, perhaps, to lodge his words so securely in the best possible order that no word can be budged without a worsening.

The poet who writes in **open form** (sometimes dubbed "free verse") seeks no such final click of perfection. More often than not, he will speak of the writing of poetry as a process, rather than as a quest for an absolute. Presumably, he believes that he discovers the form of his poem while in the act of writing it. Free to use white space for emphasis, able to shorten or lengthen his lines to accommodate whatever he is saying, the poet lets his poem choose its shape as it goes along, moving as naturally as water flows downhill, adjusting to its terrain, engulfing obstacles.

These differing persuasions, here much simplified, will be examined in this chapter, along with some poems written in accord with them. In general, most American poets these days prefer open form to closed. Most new poems printed in literary magazines today are rimeless and unmetered. But although less popular than they were, rime and meter are still in evidence. Most poetry of the past is poetry in closed form. The reader who seeks a wide understanding of poetry will wish to consider both closed and open varieties.

CLOSED FORM

Form, as a general idea, is the design of a thing as a whole, the configuration of all its parts. No poem can escape having some kind of form, whether its line-lengths are as various as broomstraws, or all in hexameter. To put it another way: if you were to listen to a poem read aloud in a language completely unknown to you, or if you saw the poem printed in that foreign language, whatever element of the poem you could see or hear would be the form of it.[1]

Poems written in closed form tend to have regular recurrences of rhythm and sound, and seen on the page, they tend to look even and symmetrical. Closed form helps make some poems more easily memorable. The **epic** poems of nations — long narratives tracing the adventures of popular heroes: the Greek *Iliad* and *Odyssey*, the French *Song of Roland*, the Spanish *Cid* — tend to occur in patterns of fairly consistent line length or number of stresses because these works were sometimes transmitted orally. Sung to the music of a lyre or chanted to a drumbeat, they may have been easier to memorize because of their patterns. If a singer forgot something, his song would have a noticeable hole in it, so rime or fixed meter probably helped prevent an epic from deteriorating when passed along from one singer to another. It is no coincidence that so many English playwrights of Shakespeare's day favored iambic pentameter. Companies of actors, often called upon to perform a different play daily, could count on a fixed line length to aid their burdened memories.

Some poets complain that closed form is a straitjacket, a limit to free expression. Some other poets, however, feel that, like fires held fast in a narrow space, thoughts stated in a tightly binding form may take on a heightened intensity. "Limitation makes for power," according to one contemporary practitioner of closed form, Richard Wilbur; "the strength of the genie comes of his being confined in a bottle." At times, to be sure, a poet does well not to allow himself to say what first comes to mind. Compelled by some strict pattern to arrange and rearrange his words, delete, and exchange them, the poet must focus on them his keenest attention and may stand a chance of discovering words more meaningful than the ones he started out with. And at times, in obedience to a rime scheme, the poet may surprise himself by saying something he had not expected to say at all. He is like a blindfolded man walking down a dark road, his hand in the hand of an inexorable guide. With the conscious portion of his mind, he may wish to express what he thinks would be a good idea. But having written a line ending in *year*, he must follow it with another ending in *atmosphere, beer, bier, bombardier, cashier, deer, friction-gear, frontier*, or some other rime that otherwise might not have entered his head. That is why he may find, in rime schemes and stanza patterns, mighty allies and valuable disturbers of the unconscious. As Rolfe Humphries has said about a strict form: "It makes you think of better things than you would all by yourself."

---

[1] For a good summary of the several different uses of the term *form* in criticism of poetry, see the article "Form" by G. N. G. Orsini in *Princeton Encyclopedia of Poetry and Poetics* ed. Preminger, Warnke, and Hardison (Princeton, 1965). In the same reference book, see also the article on "Free Verse" by William Carlos Williams.

By suggesting a pattern, then shying away from it, a poet can startle us pleasurably.

Stevie Smith (1902–1971)

I Remember

It was my bridal night I remember,
An old man of seventy-three
I lay with my young bride in my arms,
A girl with t.b.   4
It was wartime, and overhead
The Germans were making a particularly heavy raid on Hampstead.   6
What rendered the confusion worse, perversely
Our bombers had chosen that moment to set out for Germany.   8
Harry, do they ever collide?
I do not think it has ever happened,
Oh my bride, my bride.   11

This poem keeps pulling rugs out from under us. From its opening, we might expect some rollicking, roughly metrical ballad or song, but then the short fourth line draw us up with a jolt. At least, any reader still hoping for a conventional ballad might tell himself, line 4 rimes. However, the passage introducing the bombers (lines 5–8) shatters any such anticipation. Far from songlike, these prosaic lines sprawl, end in far-out feminine rimes (*overhead* and *Hampstead, perversely* and *Germany*), and bring to mind the artful outrages of Ogden Nash.[2] With the bride's question, the poem unexpectedly returns to medium-length lines, and the rime that clicks it shut (*collide, bride*) is masculine and exact once more. Miss Smith's poem, though full of surprises, has less anarchy than order in it.

Patterns of sound and rhythm can be striven after in a dull mechanical way, for which reason many poets today think them dangerous. Swinburne, who loved alliterations and tripping meters, had enough detachment to poke fun at his own excessive patterning:

> From the depth of the dreamy decline of the dawn through a notable
> nimbus of nebulous noonshine,
> Pallid and pink as the palm of the flag-flower that flickers with fear of
> the flies as they float,
> Are the looks of our lovers that lustrously lean from a marvel of mystic
> miraculous moonshine,
> These that we feel in the blood of our blushes that thicken and threaten
> with throbs through the throat?

[2] See Nash's poem on page 86. Such outrages have been christened **Nashers** by Lewis Turco, who even perceives a pattern in them: "Nashers are lines or couplets, usually long, of flat free verse or prose with humorous, often multisyllabic endings utilizing wrenched rhymes" (*The Book of Forms: A Handbook of Poetics*, New York, 1968).

This is bad, but bad deliberately. If any good at all, a poem in a fixed pattern, such as a sonnet, is created not only by the craftsman's chipping away at it but by the explosion of a sonnet-shaped idea in his mind. Viewed mechanically, as so many empty boxes somehow to be filled up, stanzas can impose the most hollow sort of discipline, and a poem written in these stanzas becomes no more than finger-exercise. This comment (although on fiction) may be appropriate:

Roy Campbell (1901–1957)
ON SOME SOUTH AFRICAN NOVELISTS

You praise the firm restraint with which they write —
  I'm with you there, of course.
They use the snaffle and the curb all right;
  But where's the bloody horse?

But some of the finest poems in English are distinguished simultaneously by the firm restraint of form and by towering passion. For Shakespeare or Blake, a strict form may be a means to put in order and thereby contain the thoughts and emotions that throng within. Such poets are powerful horsemen upon a sturdy horse.

The best-known one-line pattern for a poem in English is **blank verse:** unrimed iambic pentameter. (This pattern is not a stanza: stanzas have more than one line.) Most portions of Shakespeare's plays are in blank verse, and so are Milton's *Paradise Lost,* Tennyson's "Ulysses," certain dramatic monologues of Browning and Frost, and thousands of other poems. Here is a poem in blank verse that startles us by dropping out of its pattern in the final line. Keats appears to have written it late in his life to his fiancée Fanny Brawne.

John Keats (1795–1821)
THIS LIVING HAND, NOW WARM AND CAPABLE

This living hand, now warm and capable
Of earnest grasping, would, if it were cold
And in the icy silence of the tomb,
So haunt thy days and chill thy dreaming nights
That thou wouldst wish thine own heart dry of blood   5
So in my veins red life might stream again,
And thou be conscience-calmed — see here it is —
I hold it towards you.

The **couplet** is a two-line stanza, usually rimed. Its lines often tend to be equal in length, whether short or long. Here are two examples:

Blow,
Snow!

As I in hoary winter's night stood shivering in the snow,
Surprised I was with sudden heat which made my heart to glow.

(Actually, any pair of rimed lines that contains a complete thought is called a couplet, even if it is not a stanza, such as the *couplet* that ends a sonnet by Shakespeare.) Unlike other stanzas, couplets are often printed solid, not separated by white space. This practice is usual in printing the **heroic couplet** — or **closed couplet** — two rimed lines of iambic pentameter, the first ending in a light pause, the second more heavily end-stopped. George Crabbe, in *The Parish Register,* described a shotgun wedding:

Next at our altar stood a luckless pair,
Brought by strong passions and a warrant there:
By long rent cloak, hung loosely, strove the bride,
From every eye, what all perceived, to hide;
While the boy bridegroom, shuffling in his place,
Now hid awhile and then exposed his face.
As shame alternately with anger strove
The brain confused with muddy ale to move,
In haste and stammering he performed his part,
And looked the rage that rankled in his heart.

Though employed by Chaucer, the heroic couplet was named from its later use by Dryden and others in poems, translations of classical epics, and verse plays of epic heroes. It continued in favor through most of the eighteenth century. Much of our pleasure in reading good heroic couplets comes from the seemingly easy precision with which a skilled poet unites statements and strict pattern. In doing so, he may place a pair of words, phrases, clauses, or sentences side by side in agreement or similarity, forming a **parallel,** or in contrast and opposition, forming an **antithesis.** The effect is neat. For such skill in manipulating parallels and antitheses, John Denham's lines on the river Thames were much admired:

O could I flow like thee, and make thy stream
My great example, as it is my theme!
Though deep, yet clear; though gentle, yet not dull;
Strong without rage, without o'erflowing full.

These lines were echoed by Pope, ridiculing a poetaster, in two heroic couplets in *The Dunciad:*

Flow, Welsted, flow! like thine inspirer, Beer:
Though stale, not ripe; though thin, yet never clear;
So sweetly mawkish, and so smoothly dull;
Heady, not strong; o'erflowing, though not full.

Reading long poems in so exact a form, one may feel like a spectator at a ping-pong match unless the poet skillfully keeps varying his rhythms. (Among much else, this skill distinguishes the work of

Dryden and Pope from that of a lockstep horde of coupleteers who followed them.) One way of escaping such metronome-like monotony is to keep the cesura (see p. 145) shifting about from place to place — now happening early in a line, now happening late — and at times unexpectedly to hurl in a second or third cesura. Try working through George Crabbe's lines (on p. 165) and observe where the cesuras fall.

The **tercet** is a three-line stanza that, if rimed, usually keeps to one rime sound. **Terza rima,** the form Dante employs for *The Divine Comedy,* is made of tercets linked together by the rime scheme *a b a, b c b, c d c, d e d, e f e,* and so on. Harder to do in English than in Italian with its greater resources of riming words, the form nevertheless has been managed by Shelley in "Ode to the West Wind" (with the aid of some slant rimes):

> Make me thy lyre, even as the forest is:
> What if my leaves are falling like its own!
> The tumult of thy mighty harmonies
>
> Will take from both a deep, autumnal tone,
> Sweet though in sadness. Be thou, spirit fierce,
> My spirit! Be thou me, impetuous one!

The workhorse of English stanzas is the **quatrain,** used for more rimed poems than any other form. It comes in many line lengths, and sometimes contains lines of varying length, as in the *ballad stanza* (see Chapter Seven).

Longer and more complicated stanzas are, of course, possible, but couplet, tercet, and quatrain have been called the building blocks of our poetry because most longer stanzas are made up of them. What short stanzas does John Donne mortar together to make the longer stanza of his "Song"?

John Donne (1572–1631)

SONG

> Go and catch a falling star
>   Get with child a mandrake root,
> Tell me where all past years are,
>   Or who cleft the Devil's foot,
> Teach me to hear mermaids singing,
>   Or to keep off envy's stinging,
>   And find
>   What wind
> Serves to advance an honest mind.

If thou be'st borne to strange sights,
  Things invisible to see,
Ride ten thousand days and nights,
  Till age snow white hairs on thee,
Thou, when thou return'st, wilt tell me
  All strange wonders that befell thee,
    And swear
    Nowhere
Lives a woman true, and fair.

If thou findst one, let me know,
  Such a pilgrimage were sweet —
Yet do not, I would not go,
  Though at next door we might meet;
Though she were true, when you met her,
  And last, till you write your letter,
    Yet she
    Will be
False, ere I come, to two, or three.

Recently in vogue has been **syllabic verse,** usually stanzaic, in which the poet establishes a pattern of a certain number of syllables to a line. Either rimed or rimeless, syllabic verse has been hailed as a way for the poet to escape "the tyranny of the iamb" and discover less conventional rhythms, since, if he takes as his line length an *odd* number of syllables, then iambs, being feet of *two* syllables, cannot fit perfectly into it. Offbeat victories have been scored in syllabics by such poets as W. H. Auden, W. D. Snodgrass, Donald Hall, Thom Gunn, Henri Coulette, and Marianne Moore. Here is a well-known syllabic poem:

Dylan Thomas (1914–1953)
Fern Hill

Now as I was young and easy under the apple boughs
About the lilting house and happy as the grass was green,
      The night above the dingle° starry,   *wooded valley*
        Time let me hail and climb
      Golden in the heydays of his eyes,
And honored among wagons I was prince of the apple towns
And once below a time I lordly had the trees and leaves
        Trail with daisies and barley
      Down the rivers of the windfall light.   9

And as I was green and carefree, famous among the barns
About the happy yard and singing as the farm was home,

In the sun that is young once only,
Time let me play and be
Golden in the mercy of his means,
And green and golden I was huntsman and herdsman, the calves
Sang to my horn, the foxes on the hills barked clear and cold,
And the sabbath rang slowly
In the pebbles of the holy streams.   18

All the sun long it was running, it was lovely, the hay
Fields high as the house, the tunes from the chimneys, it was air
And playing, lovely and watery
And fire green as grass.
And nightly under the simple stars
As I rode to sleep the owls were bearing the farm away,
All the moon long I heard, blessed among stables, the nightjars
Flying with the ricks, and the horses
Flashing into the dark.   27

And then to awake, and the farm, like a wanderer white
With the dew, come back, the cock on his shoulder: it was all
Shining, it was Adam and maiden,
The sky gathered again
And the sun grew round that very day.
So it must have been after the birth of the simple light
In the first, spinning place, the spellbound horses walking warm
Out of the whinnying green stable
On to the fields of praise.   36

And honored among foxes and pheasants by the gay house
Under the new made clouds and happy as the heart was long,
In the sun born over and over,
I ran my heedless ways,
My wishes raced through the house high hay
And nothing I cared, at my sky blue trades, that time allows
In all his tuneful turning so few and such morning songs
Before the children green and golden
Follow him out of grace,   45

Nothing I cared, in the lamb white days, that time would take me
Up to the swallow thronged loft by the shadow of my hand,
In the moon that is always rising,
Nor that riding to sleep
I should hear him fly with the high fields
And wake to the farm forever fled from the childless land.
Oh as I was young and easy in the mercy of his means,
Time held me green and dying
Though I sang in my chains like the sea.   54

Notice that syllabics do not prevent a poet from riming or keep him from falling into meter if he wants to (as Thomas does in his last line).

For many readers, patterns of rhythm and rime continue to appeal. Part of the pleasure of reading a good poem in closed form comes from the way the poet makes words fall into a graceful accommodation: it is the pleasure of watching any hard thing done well — a pirouette in a dance, a basket scored from the far side of the court. Such a discipline can help a poet to sing well, with Dylan Thomas, who "sang in [his] chains like the sea."

Sir Walter Scott (1771–1832)

Proud Maisie

Proud Maisie is in the wood,
　Walking so early;
Sweet Robin sits on the bush,
　Singing so rarely.　　　　　　　　　　　　　　　　　　　　　　　　4

"Tell me, thou bonny bird,
　When shall I marry me?" —
"When six braw° gentlemen　　　　　　　　　　　　　　　　*brave*
　Kirkward° shall carry ye."　　　　　　　　　　*to the church*　8

"Who makes the bridal bed,
　Birdie, say truly?" —
"The gray-headed sexton
　That delves the grave duly.　　　　　　　　　　　　　　　　　12

"The glow-worm o'er grave and stone
　Shall light thee steady;
The owl from the steeple sing,
　'Welcome, proud lady.'"　　　　　　　　　　　　　　　　　　16

Questions

1. What comparisons are drawn between a wedding and a funeral?
2. How is the particular stanza form of this poem useful to the poet in setting things side by side?
3. How is the pattern of the poem ballad-like? What other elements (besides pattern) in "Proud Maisie" remind you of folk ballads?
4. Describe the effect of the closing slant rime.

Ronald Gross (b. 1935)

Yield

Yield.
No Parking.
Unlawful to Pass.
Wait for Green Light.
Yield.

Stop.
Narrow Bridge.
Merging Traffic Ahead.
Yield.

Yield.

QUESTIONS

1. This poem by Ronald Gross is a "found poem." After reading it, how would
you define **found poetry?**
2. Does "Yield" have a theme? If so, how would you state it?
3. What makes "Yield" mean more than traffic signs ordinarily mean to us?

EXPERIMENT: *Finding a Poem*

In a newspaper, magazine, catalogue, textbook, or advertising throwaway,
find a sentence or passage that (with a little artistic manipulation on your
part) shows promise of becoming a poem. Copy it into lines like poetry, being
careful to place what seem to be the most interesting words at the ends of lines
to give them greatest emphasis. According to the rules of found poetry, you
may excerpt, delete, repeat, and rearrange elements but not add anything.
What does this experiment tell you about poetic form? About ordinary prose?

THE SONNET AND OTHERS

Ronald Gross, who produces his "found poetry" by arranging prose
from such unlikely places as traffic signs and news stories into poem-
like lines, has told of making a discovery:

> As I worked with labels, tax forms, commercials, contracts, pin-up
> captions, obituaries, and the like, I soon found myself rediscovering all
> the traditional verse forms in found materials: ode, sonnet, epigram,
> haiku, free verse. Such finds made me realize that these forms are not
> mere artifices, but shapes that language naturally takes when carrying
> powerful thoughts or feelings.[3]

Though Gross is a playful experimenter, he hits upon a serious
truth. Traditional verse forms like sonnets and haiku are not neces-

---

[3] "Speaking of Books: Found Poetry," *The New York Times Book Review*, June 11, 1967.
Inspired by pop artists who reveal fresh vistas in Brillo boxes and comic strips, found
poetry has had a recent vogue. Earlier practitioners include William Carlos Williams,
whose long poem *Paterson* (New York, 1946–1951) quotes historical documents and
statistics. Prose, said Williams in a letter, can be a "laboratory" for poetry: "It throws up
jewels which may be cleaned and grouped." Such a jewel may be the sentence Rosmarie
Waldrop found in *The Joy of Cooking* and grouped as free verse:

Abalone, like inkfish,
needs prodigious pounding
if it has died in a state
of tension.

(*The Relaxed Abalone; or, What-You-May-Find*, Providence, R.I., 1970.) See also Gross's
Pop Poems (New York, 1967).

sarily a lot of empty pillowcases for a poet to stuff with words. At best, in the hands of an excellent poet, they can be shapes into which passionate language grows naturally.

We are speaking now of *forms* (in the plural): genres or kinds of poems. And when we speak, as Gross does, of "traditional verse forms," we usually mean **fixed forms** and exclude "free verse." A poem in a fixed form has familiar and agreed-upon elements inherited from other poems. Perhaps it has a certain fixed number of lines, an expected verse pattern or stanza pattern, a special way of arranging its ideas. Perhaps it also employs certain **conventions,** or customary subjects, attitudes, and figures of speech. For example, in the medieval French fixed form called the **ballade** (no relation to the ballad), there has to be a short last stanza containing an address to a prince. Ill done, a ballade can be rigid and overly precious, but the form has served some master poets well (see "The Complaint of Chaucer to His Purse," p. 313).

In our poetry, the **sonnet** is probably the fixed form that has attracted for the longest time the largest number of great practitioners. The name implies much more than simply "fourteen iambic pentameter lines." Originally an Italian form (*sonnetto:* "little song"), it owes much of its prestige to Petrarch (1304–1374), who wrote in it of his longing for his unattainable Laura. So great was the vogue for sonnets in England at the end of the sixteenth century that a gentleman courtier might have been thought a boor if he could not write a decent sonnet when his lady demanded one. Not content to adopt only the *pattern* of the sonnet, poets also assumed its conventional mask of the suffering lover, imitated Petrarch's similes, and invented others. The result was a great surplus of Petrarchan **conceits,** or comparisons (from the Italian *concetto:* concept, idea, bright thought). A lady's eyes were suns, her hair gold wires, her lips coral, her cheeks roses or cherries. A lover's heart was a storm-tossed ship, love the star he steered by. The lover was a fleeing deer hunted by love, and, in a favorite hyperbole, his tears were rain, his sighs gales. Contrary to what you might expect, fine poems were written with the aid of these conventions (see some of the poems in this book by Wyatt, Shakespeare, Jonson, Sidney, Drayton, Herrick, and Campion). In the following sonnet, Shakespeare, who helped himself generously from the Petrarchan stockpile, pokes fun at poets who use such figures of speech thoughtlessly:

William Shakespeare (1564–1616)
MY MISTRESS' EYES ARE NOTHING LIKE THE SUN

My mistress' eyes are nothing like the sun;
Coral is far more red than her lips' red;
If snow be white, why then her breasts are dun;
If hairs be wires, black wires grow on her head.   4

I have seen roses damasked red and white,
But no such roses see I in her cheeks;
And in some perfumes is there more delight
Than in the breath that from my mistress reeks.   8
I love to hear her speak, yet well I know
That music hath a far more pleasing sound;
I grant I never saw a goddess go:
My mistress, when she walks, treads on the ground.   12
    And yet, by heaven, I think my love as rare
    As any she°, belied with false compare.   *woman*   14

Not long after English poets imported the sonnet in the middle of
the sixteenth century, they worked out their own rime scheme — one
easier for them to follow than Petrarch's, which calls for a greater
number of riming words than English can readily come up with. (In
Italian, according to an exaggerated report, practically everything
rimes.) In the preceding sample of an **English sonnet,** sometimes called
a **Shakespearean sonnet,** the rimes cohere in four clusters: *a b a b,
c d c d, e f e f, g g*. Because a rime scheme tends to shape the poet's statements to it, the English sonnet has three places where the procession of
thought is likely to turn in another direction. Within its form, a poet
may pursue one idea throughout the three quatrains and then in the
couplet whip out a surprise ending. Suddenly even an absolute farewell
can yield to hope:

Michael Drayton (1563–1631)
SINCE THERE'S NO HELP, COME LET US KISS AND PART

Since there's no help, come let us kiss and part;
Nay, I have done, you get no more of me,
And I am glad, yea, glad with all my heart
That thus so cleanly I myself can free;   4
Shake hands for ever, cancel all our vows,
And when we meet at any time again,
Be it not seen in either of our brows
That we one jot of former love retain.   8
Now at the last gasp of Love's latest breath,
When, his pulse failing, Passion speechless lies,
When Faith is kneeling by his bed of death,
And Innocence is closing up his eyes,   12
    Now if thou wouldst, when all have given him over,
    From death to life thou mightst him yet recover.   14

Less frequently met in English poetry, the **Italian sonnet,** or
Petrarchan sonnet, follows the rime scheme *a b b a a b b a* in its first
eight lines, the **octave,** and then adds new rime sounds in the last six

lines, the **sestet.** The sestet may rime *c d c d c d, c d e c d e, c d c c d c,* or in almost any other variation that does not end in a couplet. This organization into two parts sometimes helps arrange the poet's thoughts. In his octave, the poet may state a problem, and then in his sestet, may offer a resolution. A lover, for example, may lament all octave long that his loved one neglects him, then in line 9 begin to foresee some outcome: he'll die, or accept unhappiness, or trust that the lady will change her mind.

Elizabeth Barrett Browning (1806–1861)

G RIEF

I tell you, hopeless grief is passionless;
   That only men incredulous of despair,
   Half-taught in anguish, through the midnight air
Beat upward to God's throne in loud access   4
Of shrieking and reproach. Full desertness
   In souls, as countries, lieth silent-bare
   Under the blanching, vertical eye-glare
Of the absolute Heavens. Deep-hearted man, express   8
Grief for the Dead in silence like to death:
   Most like a monumental statue set
In everlasting watch and moveless woe   11
Till itself crumble to the dust beneath.
   Touch it: the marble eyelids are not wet —
If it could weep, it could arise and go.   14

In this Italian sonnet, the division in thought comes a bit early — in the middle of line 8. Few English-speaking poets who have used the form seem to feel strictly bound by it.

"The sonnet," in the view of Robert Bly, a modern critic, "is where old professors go to die." And yet the use of the form by such twentieth-century poets as Yeats, Frost, Auden, Thomas, Pound, Cummings, Snodgrass, Berryman, and Lowell suggests that it may be far from exhausted. Like the hero of the popular ballad "Finnegan's Wake," literary forms (though not professors) declared dead have a habit of springing up again.

E XERCISE

Find other sonnets in this book. Which are English in form? Which are Italian? Which are variations on either form or combinations of the two? You may wish to try your hand at writing both kinds of sonnet and experience the difference for yourself.

Oscar Wilde said that a cynic is "a man who knows the price of everything and the value of nothing." Such a terse, pointed statement is called an epigram. In poetry, however, an **epigram** is a form: "A short poem ending in a witty or ingenious turn of thought, to which the rest of the composition is intended to lead up" (according to the *Oxford English Dictionary*). Often it is a malicious gibe with an unexpected stinger in the final line:

John Donne (1572–1631)
ANTIQUARY

If in his study he hath so much care
To hang all old strange things, let his wife beware.

Cultivated by the Roman poet Martial — for whom the epigram was a short poem, sometimes satiric but not always — this form has been especially favored by English poets who love Latin. Few characteristics of the English epigram seem fixed. Its pattern tends to be brief and rimed, its tone playfully merciless.

Martial (A.D. 40?–102?)
YOU SERVE THE BEST WINES ALWAYS, MY DEAR SIR

You serve the best wines always, my dear sir,
And yet they say your wines are not so good.
They say you are four times a widower.
They say . . . A drink? I don't believe I would.
— Translated by J. V. Cunningham

Sir John Harrington (1561?–1612)
OF TREASON

Treason doth never prosper; what's the reason?
For if it prosper, none dare call it treason.

John Wilmot, Earl of Rochester (1647–1680)
IMPROMPTU ON CHARLES II

God bless our good and gracious King,
  Whose promise none relies on;
Who never said a foolish thing,
  Nor ever did a wise one.

The king replied that his words were his own, his deeds were his courtiers'.

William Blake (1757–1827)
HER WHOLE LIFE IS AN EPIGRAM

Her whole life is an epigram: smack smooth°, and   *perfectly smooth*
   neatly penned,
Platted° quite neat to catch applause, with a sliding   *plaited, woven*
   noose at the end.

E. E. Cummings (1894–1962)
A POLITICIAN

a politician is an arse upon
which everyone has sat except a man

John Frederick Nims (b. 1914)
VISITING POET

"The famous bard, he comes! The vision nears!"
Now heaven protect your booze. Your wife. Your ears.

EXPERIMENT: *Expanding an Epigram*
Rewrite any of the preceding epigrams, taking them out of rime and adding a few more words to them. See if your revisions have nearly the same effect as the originals.

EXERCISE: *Reading for Couplets*
Read all the sonnets by Shakespeare in this book. How do the final couplets of some of them resemble epigrams? Does this diminish their effect of "seriousness"?

     In English the only other fixed form to rival the sonnet and the epigram in favor is the **limerick:** five anapestic lines usually riming *a a b b a.*

    There was an old man of Pantoum
    Who kept a live sheep in his room.
       "It reminds me," he said,
       "Of a loved one long dead,
    But I never can quite recall whom."

The limerick was made popular by Edward Lear (1812–1888), English humorist and painter, whose own practice was to make the last line echo the first: "That oppressive old man of Pantoum."

EXPERIMENT: *Contriving a Clerihew*

The **clerihew,** a fixed form named for its inventor, Edmund Clerihew Bentley (1875–1956), has straggled behind the limerick in popularity. Here are four examples: how would you define the form and what are its rules? Who or what is its conventional subject matter? Try writing your own example.

James Watt
Was the hard-boiled kind of Scot:
He thought any dream
Sheer waste of steam.
— W. H. Auden

Sir Christopher Wren
Said, "I am going to dine with some men.
If anybody calls
Say I am designing St. Paul's."
— Edmund Clerihew Bentley

Etienne de Silhouette
(It's a good bet)
Has the shadiest claim
To fame.
— Cornelius J. Ter Maat

Dylan Thomas
Showed early promise.
His name's no dimmer, man,
On old Bob Zimmerman.
— T. O. Maglow

EXERCISE: *Seeing a Fixed Form's Rules*

When Dylan Thomas wrote a poem addressed to his father, who he felt had grown tame in old age, he cast it into a **villanelle: a fixed form of French** courtly origin. From this example, sum up its rules. In obeying them, does Thomas commit himself to write nothing more than what a villanelle so easily can be — an elaborate and trivial exercise?

Dylan Thomas (1914–1953)

Do Not Go Gentle into That Good Night

Do not go gentle into that good night,
Old age should burn and rave at close of day;
Rage, rage against the dying of the light.

3

Though wise men at their end know dark is right,
Because their words had forked no lightning they
Do not go gentle into that good night.

6

Good men, the last wave by, crying how bright
Their frail deeds might have danced in a green bay,
Rage, rage against the dying of the light.

9

Individuals - people who enjoyed lived too soon.

Wild men who caught and sang the sun in flight,
And learn, too late, they grieved it on its way,
Do not go gentle into that good night.

varies to a simple from common statement.

Grave men, near death, who see with blinding sight
Blind eyes could blaze like meteors and be gay,
Rage, rage against the dying of the light.   15

And you, my father, there on the sad height,
Curse, bless, me now with your fierce tears, I pray. *the two first rimes*
Do not go gentle into that good night. *have to close*
Rage, rage against the dying of the light. *the poem.*   19

Edgar Lee Masters (1869–1950)

PETIT, THE POET

Seeds in a dry pod, tick, tick, tick,
Tick, tick, tick, like mites in a quarrel —
Faint iambics that the full breeze wakens —
But the pine tree makes a symphony thereof.
Triolets, villanelles, rondels, rondeaus.   5
Ballades by the score with the same old thought:
The snows and the roses of yesterday are vanished;
And what is love but a rose that fades?
Life all around me here in the village:
Tragedy, comedy, valor and truth,   10
Courage, constancy, heroism, failure —
All in the loom, and, oh, what patterns!
Woodlands, meadows, streams and rivers —
Blind to all of it all my life long.
Triolets, villanelles, rondels, rondeaus,   15
Seeds in a dry pod, tick, tick, tick,
Tick, tick, tick, what little iambics,
While Homer and Whitman roared in the pines!

QUESTIONS

1. The speaker is a local poet of the village that Masters celebrates in *Spoon River Anthology*. What does his name suggest?
2. Summarize Petit's criticism of his own work. Does he mean that major poetry cannot be written in iambs?
3. Like the *villanelle*, just seen in the example by Dylan Thomas, the other fixed forms mentioned are those of French courtly verse. For a *ballade*, see Chaucer's "Complaint" (p. 313). For a *rondeau* (so called, though it is not one strictly according to the French pattern), see Leigh Hunt's "Rondeau" (p. 141). What is a *rondel*? A *triolet*?

OPEN FORM

Poetry in open form follows no pattern. In fact, its lines may look as if scattered about by accident. On inspection, we will often find this apparent disarray to be deliberate. Here is an unchaotic example:

Denise Levertov (b. 1923)
SIX VARIATIONS (PART III)

Shlup, shlup, the dog
as it laps up
water
makes intelligent
music, resting
now and then to take breath in irregular
measure.

Wittily, the poet has cast her observations into an appropriate form. Now and again, her run-on sentence interrupts itself by line breaks at which anyone reading it aloud can pause for breath. Idea, sound, and rhythm are all one. The result is an "intelligent music."

Some poets, usually beginners, think such verse easy to write. On the contrary, if he cares about capturing his reader's attention and keeping it, the poet working in open form probably has to work harder than the metrical poet. Lacking the powerful (some would say hypnotic) devices of rime and meter, he has to discover by his own unaided wits words that can speak for themselves. As W. H. Auden has put it: "The poet who writes 'free verse' is like Robinson Crusoe on his desert island: he must do all his cooking, laundry and darning for himself. In a few exceptional cases this manly independence produces something original and impressive, but more often the result is squalor — dirty sheets on the unmade bed and empty bottles on the unswept floor."[4]

"Writing free verse," said Robert Frost, who distrusted it, "is like playing tennis with the net down." And yet, high scores can be made in such an unconventional game, provided it can be kept from straggling all over the court. On his side, the poet writing in open form has several advantages. For one thing, he has white space to do with as he will. He can arrange words in visual groupings. If he likes, he can even set one word alone on a line — where it will stand out far more apparently than it would in a line of pentameter. He also can break his lines wherever he likes to indicate pauses. In this way, if his ear is keen, he may discover subtle rhythms of great variety.

No one seems entirely happy with the name "free verse," handed

[4] *The Dyer's Hand* (New York, 1962), p. 22.

down from a nineteenth-century French anti-classicist movement, *vers libre*. Various substitute names have been suggested: organic poetry, composition by field, raw (as against cooked) poetry, open form poetry. "But what does it matter what you call it?" remark the editors of an anthology called *Naked Poetry*. The best poems of the last twenty years "don't rhyme (usually) and don't move on feet of more or less equal duration (usually). That nondescription moves toward the only technical principle they all have in common."[5]

And yet many poems in open form have much more in common than absences and lacks. One positive principle has been Ezra Pound's famous suggestion that poets "compose in the sequence of the musical phrase, not in the sequence of the metronome" — good advice, perhaps, even for poets who write inside fixed forms. In Charles Olson's influential theory of **projective verse,** the poet composes by listening to his own breathing. On paper, he indicates the rhythms of his poem by using a little white space or a lot, a slight indentation or a deep one, depending on whether he wishes to denote a short pause or a long. Words can be grouped in clusters on the page (usually no more words than a lungful of air can accommodate). Heavy cesuras are sometimes shown by breaking a line in two and lowering the second part of it.[6] (An Olson poem appears on page 192.)

To the poet working in open form, no less than to the poet writing a sonnet, line length can be valuable. Walt Whitman, who loved to expand vast sentences for line after line, knew well that an impressive rhythm can accumulate if the poet will keep his long lines approximately the same length, causing a pause to recur at about the same interval after every line. Sometimes, too, Whitman repeats the same word at each line's opening. An instance is the masterful sixth section of "When Lilacs Last in the Dooryard Bloom'd," an elegy for Abraham Lincoln:

> Coffin that passes through lanes and streets,
> Through day and night with the great cloud darkening the land,
> With the pomp of the inloop'd flags with the cities draped in black,
> With the show of the States themselves as of crape-veil'd women standing,
> With processions long and winding and the flambeaus of the night,
> With the countless torches lit, with the silent sea of faces and the unbared heads,
> With the waiting depot, the arriving coffin, and the somber faces,
> With dirges through the night, with the thousand voices rising strong and solemn,

[5] Stephen Berg and Robert Mezey, foreword to *Naked Poetry: Recent American Poetry in Open Forms* (Indianapolis, 1969).
[6] See Olson's essays "Projective Verse" and "Letter to Elaine Feinstein" in *Selected Writings,* edited by Robert Creeley (New York, 1966). Olson's letters to Cid Corman are fascinating: *Letters for Origin, 1950–1955,* edited by Albert Glover (London, 1970).

With all the mournful voices of the dirges pour'd around the coffin,
The dim-lit churches and the shuddering organs — where amid these you
    journey,
With the tolling tolling bells' perpetual clang,
Here, coffin that slowly passes,
I give you my sprig of lilac.

There is music in such solemn, operatic arias. Whitman's lines echo another model: the Hebrew **psalms** or sacred songs as translated in the King James Bible. In Psalm 150, repetition also occurs inside of lines:

> Praise ye the Lord. Praise God in his sanctuary: praise him in the firmament of his power.
> Praise him for his mighty acts: praise him according to his excellent greatness.
> Praise him with the sound of the trumpet: praise him with the psaltery and harp.
> Praise him with the timbrel and dance: praise him with stringed instruments and organs.
> Praise him upon the loud cymbals: praise him upon the high sounding cymbals.
> Let every thing that hath breath praise the Lord. Praise ye the Lord.

In Biblical Psalms, we are in the presence of (as Robert Lowell has said) "supreme poems, written when their translators merely intended prose and were forced by the structure of their originals to write poetry."[7]

Whitman was a more deliberate craftsman than he let his readers think, and to anyone interested in writing in open form, his work will repay close study. He knew that repetitions of any kind often make memorable rhythms, as in this passage from "Song of Myself," with every line ending on an *-ing* word (a stressed syllable followed by an unstressed syllable):

> Here and there with dimes on the eyes walking,
> To feed the greed of the belly the brains liberally spooning,
> Tickets buying, taking, selling, but in to the feast never one going,
> Many sweating, ploughing, thrashing, and then the chaff for payment
>   receiving,
> A few idly owning, and they the wheat continually claiming.

Much more than simply repetition, of course, went into the music of those lines — the internal rime *feed, greed,* the use of assonance, the trochees that begin the third and fourth lines, whether or not they were calculated.

In such classics of open form poetry, sound and rhythm are positive forces. When speaking a poem in open form, you often may find that it makes a difference for the better if you pause at the end of each line. Try pausing there, however briefly, but whatever you do don't let your voice drop. Read just as you would normally read a sentence

---

[7] "On Freedom in Poetry," in Berg and Mezey, *Naked Poetry*.

in prose (except for the pauses, of course). Why do the pauses matter? Open form poetry usually has no meter to lend it rhythm. *Some* lines in an open form poem, as we have seen in Whitman's "dimes on the eyes" passage, do fall into metrical feet; sometimes the whole poem does. Usually lacking meter's aid, however, open form, in order to have more and more noticeable rhythms, has need of all the recurring pauses it can get. When reading their own work aloud, open form poets like Robert Creeley and Allen Ginsberg often pause very definitely at each line break. Such a habit makes sense only in reading artful poems. There are also many artless poets. Unaware that line breaks set rhythms in motion and throw more emphasis on the last word of a line, they stop and start their lines just any place, for no apparent reason except to make their poems look like poems.

No law requires a poet to split his thoughts into lines at all, if he has no special reason to. Arthur Rimbaud, Rainer Maria Rilke, T. S. Eliot, St.-John Perse, Karl Shapiro, Robert Duncan, and others have written **prose poems,** in which, without caring that eye-appeal and some of the rhythm of line structure may be lost, the poet prints his words in a block like a prose paragraph. For an example, see Shapiro's "The Dirty Word" (p. 386).

E. E. Cummings (1894–1962)
Buffalo Bill's

Buffalo Bill's
defunct
    who used to
    ride a watersmooth-silver
                stallion   5
and break onetwothreefourfive pigeonsjustlikethat
                          Jesus

he was a handsome man
                and what i want to know is
how do you like your blueeyed boy   10
Mister Death

Question
Cummings' poem would look like this if given conventional punctuation and set in a solid block like prose:

> Buffalo Bill's defunct, who used to ride a water-smooth silver stallion and break one, two, three, four, five pigeons just like that. Jesus, he was a handsome man. And what I want to know is: "How do you like your blue-eyed boy, Mister Death?"

If this were done, by what characteristics would it still be recognizable as poetry? But what would be lost?

The great majority of poems appearing at present in American literary magazines are in open form. "Farewell, pale skunky pentameters (the only honest English meter, gloop! gloop!)," Kenneth Koch has gleefully exclaimed. Many poets have sought reasons for turning away from patterns and fixed forms. Some hold that it is wrong to fit words into any pattern that already exists and instead believe in letting a poem seek its own shape as it goes along. (Traditionalists might say that that is what all good poems do anyway: sonnets rarely know they are going to be sonnets until the third line has been written. However, there is no doubt that the sonnet form already exists at least in the back of the poet's head if he has ever read sonnets.) Some open form poets offer a historical motive: they want to reflect the nervous, staccato, disconnected pace of our bumper-to-bumper society. Others see open form as an attempt to suit thoughts and words to a more spontaneous order than traditional verse forms allow. "Better," says Gary Snyder, quoting from Zen, "the perfect, easy discipline of the swallow's dip and swoop, 'without east or west.'"[8]

Emily Dickinson (1830–1886)

VICTORY COMES LATE

Victory comes late –
And is held low to freezing lips –
Too rapt with frost
To take it –
How sweet it would have tasted –   5
Just a Drop –
Was God so economical?
His Table's spread too high for Us –
Unless We dine on tiptoe –
Crumbs – fit such little mouths –   10
Cherries – suit Robins –
The Eagle's Golden Breakfast strangles – Them –
God keep His Oath to Sparrows –
Who of little Love – know how to starve –

QUESTIONS

1. In this specimen of poetry in open form, can you see any other places at which the poet might have broken off any of her lines? To place a word last in a line gives it a greater emphasis; she might, for instance, have ended line 12 with *Breakfast* and begun a new line with the word *strangles*. Do you think she knows what she is doing here or does the pattern of this poem seem decided by whim? Discuss.

[8] "Some Yips & Barks in the Dark," in Berg and Mezey, *Naked Poetry.*

2. Read the poem aloud. Try pausing for a fraction of a second at every dash. Is there any justification for her unorthodox punctuation?

William Carlos Williams (1883–1963)

THE DANCE

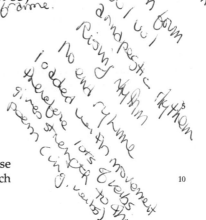

In Breughel's great picture, The Kermess,
the dancers go round, they go round and
around, the squeal and the blare and the
tweedle of bagpipes, a bugle and fiddles
tipping their bellies (round as the thick-
sided glasses whose wash they impound)
their hips and their bellies off balance
to turn them. Kicking and rolling about
the Fair Grounds, swinging their butts, those
shanks must be sound to bear up under such
rollicking measures, prance as they dance
in Breughel's great picture, The Kermess.   10

THE DANCE. Pieter Breughel (1520?–1569), a Flemish painter known for his scenes of peasant activities, represented in "The Kermess" a celebration on the feast day of a local patron saint.

QUESTIONS

1. Scan this poem and try to describe the effect of its rhythms.
2. Williams, widely admired for his free verse, insisted for many years that what he sought was a form not in the least bit free. What effect does he achieve by ending lines on such weak words as the articles *and* and *the*? By splitting *thick-* / *sided*? By splitting a prepositional phrase with the break at the end of line 8? By using line breaks to split *those* and *such* from what they modify? What do you think he is trying to convey?
3. Is there any point in his making line 12 a repetition of the opening line?
4. If possible, look at a reproduction of Breughel's painting "The Kermess" (also called "Peasants Dancing"). Aware that the rhythms of dancers, the rhythms of a painting, and the rhythms of a poem are not all the same, can you put in your own words what Breughel's dancing figures have in common with Williams's descriptions of them?

Robert Herrick (1591–1674)

UPON A CHILD THAT DIED

Here she lies, a pretty bud,
Lately made of flesh and blood.
Who as soon fell fast asleep
As her little eyes did peep.
Give her strewings, but not stir
The earth that lightly covers her.

Saint Geraud [Bill Knott] (b. 1940)

POEM

The only response
to a child's grave is
to lie down before it and play dead

QUESTION

What differences do you find between the effect of Herrick's poem and that of Saint Geraud's? Try to explain how the pattern (or lack of pattern) in each poem contributes to these differences.

Stephen Crane (1871–1900)

THE HEART

In the desert
I saw a creature, naked, bestial,
Who, squatting upon the ground,
Held his heart in his hands,
And ate of it.   5

I said, "Is it good, friend?"
"It is bitter — bitter," he answered;
"But I like it
Because it is bitter,
And because it is my heart."   10

Walt Whitman (1819–1892)

CAVALRY CROSSING A FORD

A line in long array where they wind betwixt green islands,
They take a serpentine course, their arms flash in the sun — hark to the
    musical clank,
Behold the silvery river, in it the splashing horses loitering stop to drink,
Behold the brown-faced men, each group, each person a picture, the
    negligent rest on the saddles,
Some emerge on the opposite bank, others are just entering the ford —
    while,
Scarlet and blue and snowy white,
The guidon flags flutter gayly in the wind.

QUESTIONS

The following nit-picking questions are intended to help you see exactly what makes these two open form poems by Crane and Whitman so different in their music.

1. What devices of sound occur in Whitman's phrase *silvery river* (line 3)? Where else in his poem do you find these devices?

2. Does Crane use any such devices? Try picking out, for instance, all syllables that end with the sound of the letter *t*. (There are a surprising number for a poem so short.)
3. In number of syllables, Whitman's poem is almost twice as long as Crane's. Which poem has more pauses in it? (Count pauses at the ends of lines, at marks of punctuation.)
4. Read the two poems aloud. In general, how would you describe the effect of their sounds and rhythms? Is Crane's poem necessarily an inferior poem for having less music?

Gary Gildner (b. 1938)

FIRST PRACTICE

After the doctor checked to see
we weren't ruptured,
the man with the short cigar took us
under the grade school,
where we went in case of attack   5
or storm, and said
he was Clifford Hill, he was
a man who believed dogs
ate dogs, he had once killed
for his country, and if   10
there were any girls present
for them to leave now.
           No one
left. OK, he said, he said I take
that to mean you are hungry
men who hate to lose as much   15
as I do. OK. Then
he made two lines of us
facing each other,
and across the way, he said,
is the man you hate most   20
in the world,
and if we are to win
that title I want to see how.
But I don't want to see
any marks when you're dressed,   25
he said. He said, *Now*.

QUESTIONS

1. What do you make of Hill and his world-view?
2. How does the speaker reveal his own view? Why, instead of quoting Hill directly ("This is a dog-eat-dog world"), does he call him *a man who believed dogs ate dogs* (lines 8–9)?
3. What effect is made by breaking off and lowering *No one* at the end of line 12?
4. What rimes occur? What is gained by having a rime on the poem's last word?

5. For the sake of understanding how right the form of Gildner's poem is for it, imagine the poem in meter and a rime scheme:

Then he made two facing lines of us
And he said, Across the way,
Of all the men there are in the world
Is the man you most want to slay,

And if we are to win that title, he said,
I want you to show me how.
But I don't want to see any marks when you're dressed,
He said. Go get him. *Now*.

Why would that rewrite be so unfaithful to what Gildner is saying?
6. How would you answer someone who argued, "This can't be a poem — its subject is ugly and its language isn't beautiful"?

EXPERIMENT: *Destroying Open Form*

Take any poem in open form you consider artful and rewrite or retype it into a solid paragraph. Then read it aloud, without pauses except for full stops and other punctuation, as you would read prose. What good reasons for the arrangement of lines in the original does such abuse reveal?

To work on, see any poems in the anthology by any of the following poets: Imamu Amiri Baraka, Lucille Clifton, Robert Creeley, Kenneth Fearing, Allen Ginsberg, David Ignatow, Denise Levertov, W. S. Merwin, Marianne Moore, Marge Piercy, Ezra Pound, Theodore Roethke, W. D. Snodgrass, Gary Snyder, William Stafford, James Tate, Keith Waldrop, Walt Whitman, William Carlos Williams.

FOR REVIEW AND FURTHER STUDY

Wallace Stevens (1879–1955)

THIRTEEN WAYS OF LOOKING AT A BLACKBIRD

I

Among twenty snowy mountains,
The only moving thing
Was the eye of the blackbird.

II

I was of three minds,
Like a tree   5
In which there are three blackbirds.

III

The blackbird whirled in the autumn winds.
It was a small part of the pantomime.

IV

A man and a woman
Are one.   10
A man and a woman and a blackbird
Are one.

V

I do not know which to prefer,
The beauty of inflections
Or the beauty of innuendoes,   15
The blackbird whistling
Or just after.

VI

Icicles filled the long window
With barbaric glass.
The shadow of the blackbird   20
Crossed it, to and fro.
The mood
Traced in the shadow
An indecipherable cause.

VII

O thin men of Haddam,   25
Why do you imagine golden birds?
Do you not see how the blackbird
Walks around the feet
Of the women about you?

VIII

I know noble accents   30
And lucid, inescapable rhythms;
But I know, too,
That the blackbird is involved
In what I know.

IX

When the blackbird flew out of sight,   35
It marked the edge
Of one of many circles.

X

At the sight of blackbirds
Flying in a green light,
Even the bawds of euphony   40
Would cry out sharply.

XI

He rode over Connecticut
In a glass coach.
Once, a fear pierced him,
In that he mistook   45
The shadow of his equipage
For blackbirds.

XII

The river is moving.
The blackbird must be flying.

XIII

It was evening all afternoon.   50
It was snowing
And it was going to snow.
The blackbird sat
In the cedar-limbs.

THIRTEEN WAYS OF LOOKING AT A BLACKBIRD. 25. *Haddam:* This Biblical-sounding name
is that of a town in Connecticut.

QUESTIONS

1. What is the speaker's attitude toward the men of Haddam? What attitude —
   or failure of comprehension — toward their world does he condemn? What
   attitude toward this world does he suggest they lack? What is implied by
   calling them *thin* (line 25)?
2. What do the landscapes of winter contribute to the poem's effectiveness? If
   instead Stevens had chosen images of summer lawns, what would have been
   lost?
3. In which sections of the poem does Stevens suggest that a unity exists between human being and blackbird, between blackbird and the entire natural
   world? Can we say that Stevens "philosophizes"? What role does imagery
   play in the poet's statement of his ideas?
4. What sense can you make of Part X? Make an enlightened guess.
5. Consider any one of the thirteen parts. What patterns of sound and rhythm
   do you find in it? What kind of structure does it have?
6. If the thirteen parts were arranged in some different order, would the poem
   be just as good? Or can we find a justification for its beginning with Part I
   and ending with Part XIII?
7. Does the poem seem an arbitrary combination of thirteen separate poems?
   Or is there any reason to call it a whole?

Alexander Pope (1688–1744)

ATTICUS

How did they fume, and stamp, and roar, and chafe!
And swear, not Addison himself was safe.   2
   Peace to all such! but were there one whose fires
True genius kindles, and fair fame inspires;   4
Blest with each talent, and each art to please,
And born to write, converse, and live with ease,   6
Should such a man, too fond to rule alone,
Bear, like the Turk, no brother near the throne,   8
View him with scornful, yet with jealous eyes,
And hate for arts that caused himself to rise;   10
Damn with faint praise, assent with civil leer,
And, without sneering, teach the rest to sneer;   12
Willing to wound, and yet afraid to strike,
Just hint a fault, and hesitate dislike;   14
Alike reserved to blame, or to commend,
A timorous foe, and a suspicious friend;   16

Dreading e'en fools, by flatterers besieged,
And so obliging, that he ne'er obliged;   18
Like Cato, give his little Senate laws,
And sit attentive to his own applause: 20
While wits and Templars every sentence raise,
And wonder with a foolish face of praise —   22
Who but must laugh, if such a man there be?
Who would not weep, if Atticus were he?   24

ATTICUS. In this selection from "An Epistle to Dr. Arbuthnot," Pope has been referring to
dull versifiers and their angry reception of his satiric thrusts at them. With *Peace to all
such!* (line 3) he turns to his celebrated portrait of a rival man of letters, Joseph Addison.
19. *Cato:* Roman senator about whom Addison had written a tragedy. 21. *Templars:*
London lawyers who dabbled in literature.

QUESTIONS

1. What positive virtues, in Pope's view, does Addison lack?
2. What effects does the form of the heroic couplet have upon Pope's organization of his argument?
3. What antitheses are contained in these couplets, either within a line or
   between two lines? What parallels?

Henry Taylor (b. 1942)
REMEMBERING KEVAN MACKENZIE

Once upon a time I spent a summer
At a camp for children far from here,
Teaching riding to young boys and girls.
I taught them to make a horse go straight,
The way to make a horse stand still.
They grew and danced like weeds before my eyes.   6

Now there remains in my mind's eye
One face of all the faces of that summer;
It smiles at me, and I sit here
Wondering what's become of all the girls
That Kevan MacKenzie hounded straight
To earth, and may be chasing still.   12

Every week there was a dance, and still
I can recall the roll of those girls' eyes
As they hunted love, the first of summer:
Kevan, refusing to dance, stood straight
By the wall and dared the girls
To rout him from his sanctuary here.   18

Later he began to dress with care, and here
I remember the guarded gleam in his eye
As he came through the door and went straight
For the oldest and prettiest girl,
While with that stare that disturbs me still
The young girls hunted the first love of summer.   24

In the arms of that tall breath of summer
He danced, and looked her waist in the eye.
I whispered then, "Be cheerful, girls,
The sunshine boys are here."
When the music at last grew still,
The tall girl smiled, once more stood straight.   30

The days of dancing and love rode straight
To the last long week of that summer.
When I said goodbye to my boys and girls
I stood among them with tears in my eyes,
While Kevan MacKenzie, smiling still,
Said, "You must be glad to get out of here."   36

Now I sit here in another summer
And rising straight in my mind's eye
Kevan and his girls are dancing still.   39

QUESTIONS

1. This poem is in the fixed form of a **sestina**. What are its rules?
2. How skillfully does the poet make us forget that these rules exist?

EXERCISE: *Trying to See the Logic of Open Form Verse*

Read the following poems in open form silently to yourself, noticing what
each poet does with white space, repetitions, line breaks, and indentations.
Then read the poems aloud, trying to indicate by slight pauses where lines
end and also pausing slightly at any space inside a line. Can you see any
reasons for the poet's placing his words in this arrangement rather than in a
prose paragraph? Do any of these poets seem to care also about visual effect?
(As is the case with other kinds of poetry, there may not be any obvious logical
reason for everything that happens in these poems.)

E. E. Cummings (1894–1962)

IN JUST-

in Just-
spring   when the world is mud-
luscious the little
lame balloonman

whistles   far   and wee   5

and eddieandbill come
running from marbles and
piracies and it's
spring

when the world is puddle-wonderful   10

the queer
old balloonman whistles
far   and   wee
and bettyandisbel come dancing

from hop-scotch and jump-rope and   15

it's
spring
and
    the

        goat-footed   20

balloonMan   whistles
far
and
wee

Donald Finkel (b. 1929)
GESTURE

My arm sweeps down
    a pliant arc
        whatever I am
            streams through my
                negligent wrist: 5
the poem
        uncoils
            like a
                whip, and
snaps   10
softly   an inch from your enchanted face.

John Haines (b. 1924)
THE CAULIFLOWER

I wanted to be a cauliflower,
all brain and ears,
thinking on the origin of gardens
and the divinity of him
who carefully binds my leaves.   5

With my blind roots touched
by the songs of the worms,
and my rough throat throbbing
with strange, vegetable sounds,
perhaps I'd feel the parting stroke   10
of a butterfly's wing . . .

Not like my cousins, the cabbages,
whose heads, tightly folded,
see and hear nothing of this world,
dreaming only on the yellow   15
and green magnificence
that is hardening within them.

Charles Olson (1910–1970)

LA CHUTE

my drum, hollowed out thru the thin slit,
carved from the cedar wood, the base I took
when the tree was felled

o my lute, wrought from the tree's crown

my drum, whose lustiness   5
was not to be resisted
                    my lute,
from whose pulsations
not one could turn away

                                    They   10
are where the dead are, my drum fell
where the dead are, who
will bring it up, my lute
who will bring it up where it fell in the face of them
where they are, where my lute and drum have fallen?   15

11 Poems for the Eye

WORD SHAPES

Let us look at a famous poem with a distinctive visible shape. In the seventeenth century, ingenious poets trimmed their lines into the silhouettes of altars and crosses, pillars and pyramids. Here is one. Is it anything more than a demonstration of ingenuity?

George Herbert (1593–1633)

EASTER WINGS

Lord, who createdst man in wealth and store,
   Though   foolishly   he   lost   the   same,
      Decaying   more   and   more
         Till   he   became
           Most poor;   5
          With thee
       Oh,   let   me   rise
   As   larks,   harmoniously,
 And   sing   this   day   thy   victories;
Then shall the fall further the flight in me.   10

My tender age in sorrow did begin;
  And still with sicknesses and shame
    Thou didst so punish sin,
       That   I   became
         Most thin.
         With thee   15
       Let   me   combine,
    And feel this day thy victory;
 For if I imp my wing on thine,
Affliction shall advance the flight in me.
                                     20

In line 19, *imp* is a term from falconry meaning to repair the wing of an injured bird by grafting feathers into it. As if to make its wing shapes all the more apparent, the poem originally was printed sideways, its lines running vertically.

If we see it merely as a picture, we will have to admit that Herbert's word design does not go far. It renders with difficulty shapes that a sketcher's pencil could set down in a flash. The pencil sketch might have more detail, might be more accurate. Was Herbert's effort wasted? It might have been, were there not more to his poem than meets the eye. The mind, too, is engaged by the visual pattern, by the realization in line 15, for instance, that the words *most thin* are given emphasis by their narrow form. Here, visual pattern points out meaning. Heard aloud, too, "Easter Wings" takes on additional depths. Its rimes, its pattern of rhythm are perceptible. It gives pleasure as any poem in a symmetrical stanza may do: by establishing a pattern that leads the reader to anticipate when another rime or a pause will arrive and then fulfilling his expectation.

How can we tell the difference between poetry and prose? Legend has it that a schoolboy, asked this puzzler on a test, made an inspired reply. "Poetry," he wrote, "is when the lines don't come out even to the right-hand side of the page." He may not have realized that by the poet's turning back to the left margin a pattern of rhythm is formed. But he knew at least one truth: a printed poem has a shape addressed to the eye.

Ever since the invention of the alphabet, poems have existed not only as rhythmic sounds upon the air but also as visual patterns: arrangements of lines upon two-dimensional surfaces. Beginning to write a poem, the poet finds his blank page lying in wait, much like a painter's canvas. At times he may try to be a graphic artist and to entertain the eye as well as the ear. To at least some extent, our pleasure in silently reading a poem comes from looking at the way a poet adorns his empty page with words set in type. We notice how he indents lines, how he uses white space to set off certain words and place them in positions of emphasis.

Since Herbert's time, writers have continued to make fresh visual experiments. Notable among these are Lewis Carroll's rimed mouse's tail in *Alice in Wonderland* and the *Calligrammes* of Guillaume Apollinaire, who arranged words into the shapes of falling rain, a necktie, and the Eiffel Tower. Here is a shaped poem of more recent inspiration:

John Hollander (b. 1929)

Skeleton key

Opening and starting key for a
1954 Dodge junked last year.

O with what key
shall I unlock this
heart Tight in a coffer
of chest something awaits a
jab a click a sharp turn yes an
opening Out with it then Let it
pour into forms it molds itself
Much like an escape of dreaming
prisoners taking shape out in a
relenting air in bright volumes
unimaginable even amid anterior
blacknesses let mine run out in
the sunny roads Let them be
released by modulations
of point by bend of
line too tiny for
planning out back
in hopeful dark
times or places
How to hold on
to a part flat
or wide enough
to grasp was
not too hard
formerly and
patterned
edges cut
themselves
What midget
forms shall
fall in
line or
row beyond
this wall
of self A
key can
open a car
Why not me
O let me
get in

Evidently the shape of Hollander's car key agrees with what is said in it. A whole poem, of course, does not need to be such a verbal silhouette to have meaningful appearances. In part of a longer poem, William Carlos Williams has conveyed the way a bellhop runs downstairs:

```
ta tuck a
        ta tuck a
                ta tuck a
                        ta tuck a
                                ta tuck a
```

This is not only good onomatopoeia and an accurate description of a rhythm; the steplike appearance of the lines goes together with their meaning.

As poets who work in open form demonstrate, white space is valuable to indicate pauses, for rhythm and for emphasis. But the appearance on the page of a more traditional poem is not accidental. By arranging his lines in stanza shapes, the poet at the same time arranges his thoughts and delineates a sound pattern. He may use indentation, too, to show which lines rime.

Sometimes an unconventional-looking poem represents no familiar object but is an attempt to make the eye follow an unaccustomed path, as in this experiment by E. E. Cummings.

E. E. Cummings (1894–1962)

R-P-O-P-H-E-S-S-A-G-R

```
                        r-p-o-p-h-e-s-s-a-g-r
             who
a)s w(e loo)k
upnowgath
             PPEGORHRASS
                        eringint(o-
aThe):l
       eA
         !p:
S                                              a
             (r
   rIvInG         .gRrEaPsPhOs)
                        to
rea(be)rran(com)gi(e)ngly
,grasshopper;
```

However startling it may be to eyes accustomed to poems in conventional line arrangements, this experiment is not a shaped poem. What matters is the grasshopperish leaps and backtracks that our eyes must make in unscrambling letters and words, rearranging them into a more usual order.

Though too much importance can be given to the visual element of poetry and though many poets seem hardly to care about it, it can be another dimension that sets apart poetry from prose. It is at least arguable that some of Walt Whitman's long-line, page-filling descriptions of the wide ocean, open landscapes, and broad streets of his America, which meet the eye as wide expanses of words, would lose something — besides what would be lost in rhythm — if couched in lines three or four syllables long.

The way a poem looks, while significant, is hardly enough in itself to make a poem succeed. To pour just any old words into a silhouette of the Taj Mahal would be as likely to result in a dismal poem as to arrange them into the pattern of a sonnet. Like other good poems, good shaped poems appeal not only to sight but to our other faculties, and they depend upon sound, rhythm, imagery, denotation, and connotation. May Swenson, a poet who has written poems of both kinds, has insisted that for her the visual arrangement of a poem can be discovered only after the poem's "whole language structure and behavior" have been completed: "What the poems say or show, their way of doing it with *language,* is the main thing."[1] Clearly, if a poem has other virtues, its visual pattern can be one more means for the poet to speak to us, striking both eye and mind.

May Swenson (b. 1919)
STONE GULLETS

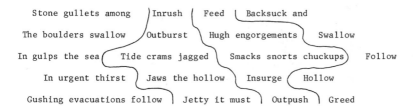

QUESTIONS

1. What do the three curving lines drawn into this poem suggest?
2. Besides depicting something, do they have any other uses to the poem?
3. Read "Stone Gullets" aloud. By what other devices (besides visual ones) does the poet communicate meanings?

[1] From an explanatory note at the end of her book of poems, *Iconographs* (New York: 1970).

Robert Herrick (1591–1674)

Upon Prew His Maid

In this little urn is laid
Prudence Baldwin (once my maid)
From whose happy spark here let
Spring the purple violet.

QUESTIONS

1. What possible meanings has the phrase *this little urn?*
2. What sense do you make of *happy spark?* What metaphor binds together lines 3 and 4? What characteristics do *spark* and *violet* have in common?
3. What does the visual appearance of this well-wrought poem have to do with the meaning of it?

CONCRETE POETRY

Poets who write in English have sometimes envied poets who write in Chinese, a language in which a word often looks like the thing it represents. Consider this Chinese poem:

Wang Wei (701–761)

BIRD-SINGING STREAM

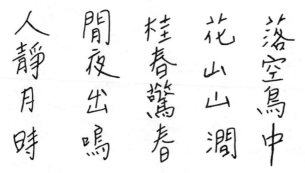

Substituting English words for ideograms, the poem becomes:

man	leisure	cassia	flower	fall
quiet	night	spring	mountain	empty
moon	rise	startle	mountain	bird
at times	sing	spring	stream	middle

Even without the aid of English crib-notes, all of us can read some Chinese if we can recognize a picture of a man. What resemblances can you see between any of the other ideograms and the things they stand for?[2]

Wai-lim Yip, the poet and critic who provided the Chinese text and translation, has also translated the poem into more usual English word order, still keeping close to the original sequence of ideas:

Man at leisure. Cassia flowers fall.
Quiet night. Spring mountain is empty.
Moon rises. Startles — a mountain bird.
It sings at times in the spring stream.

One envious Western poet was Ezra Pound, who included a few Chinese ideograms in his *Cantos* as illustrations. From the scholar Ernest Fenollosa, Pound said he had come to understand why a language written in ideograms "simply *had to stay poetic;* simply couldn't help being and staying poetic in a way that a column of English type might very well not stay poetic."[3] For a poet, obviously it is an advantage to have a language whose words strike the eye with their concreteness even before the poet has made anything out of them.

From time to time, English-speaking poets have tried to remind us of the appearance of words and letters. E. E. Cummings, in a poem that begins "mOOn Over tOwns mOOn," has reveled in the fact that O's are moon-shaped. In recent years, there has been a widespread movement called **Concrete poetry,** which, in the words of a prominent Concretist, Eugene Wildman, "aims, in general, at the ideogrammatic state."[4]

Though practitioners of the art disagree over its definition, what most Concretists seem to do is make designs out of letters and words. They may do as did the German artist Reinhard Döhl and construct a silhouette shaped like an apple out of the word apple repeated seventy-nine times, with the word *worm* in the middle.[5] They may wield typography like a brush dipped in paint, using such techniques as blow-up, montage, and superimposed elements (the same words printed many times on top of the same impression, so that the result is blurriness). They may even keep words in a usual order, perhaps employing white space as freely as any writer of open form verse. According to Mary Ellen Solt, an American Concretist, we can tell a Concrete poem by its "concentration upon the physical material from which the poem or text is made."[6] Still another practitioner, Richard Kostelanetz, has suggested

---

[2] To help you compare English and Chinese, the ideograms in the Chinese original have been arranged in Western word-order. (Ordinarily, in Chinese, the ideogram for "man" would appear at the upper right.)

[3] *The ABC of Reading* (Norfolk, Conn., 1960), p. 22.

[4] Introduction to *The Chicago Review Anthology of Concretism* (Chicago, 1967).

[5] Included in *Anthology of Concrete Poetry,* edited by Emmett Williams (New York, 1967).

[6] Introduction to her anthology *Concrete Poetry: A World View* (Bloomington, Ind., 1969).

that a more accurate name for Concrete poetry might be "word-imagery." He sees it occupying an area somewhere between conventional poetry and visual art.[7]

What makes Concretism look foolish or impossible to understand to those who approach it as if it ought to be traditional poetry may be that Concretists often use words without placing them in context with any other words. Aram Saroyan has a Concrete poem consisting of a page, blank except for one word: *oxygen.*

Much Concrete poetry is clearly "something to look at rather than to read," Louis Untermeyer has said unsympathetically. And yet certain Concrete poems can please as good poems always do: by their connotations, figures of speech, sounds, and metaphors — not to mention their rewards to the eye.

Ian Hamilton Finlay (b. 1925)

THE HORIZON OF HOLLAND

Like E. E. Cummings's grasshoppers (p. 196), Finlay's verbal windmills make us search out a familiar word order. But in Finlay's poem our pleasure lies not only in puzzling out a sentence ("The horizon of Holland is all ears"), but also in beholding a shape that strikes the eye and in making a connection between it and an image that the title brings to mind. This is something other than what happens in a shaped poem such as "Skeleton key" (p. 195) and "Easter Wings" (p. 193), where individual letters of the alphabet are not in themselves especially important.

Admittedly, some Concrete poems mean less than meets the eye. In this fact, they seem more rigidly confined to the printed page than shaped poems such as "Easter Wings." A good shaped poem, though it would lose much if heard and not seen, still might be a satisfying poem. That many pretentious doodlers have taken up Concretism may

---

[7] Introduction to his anthology *Imaged Words and Worded Images* (New York, 1970).

have caused a *Time* writer to sneer: did Joyce Kilmer miss all that much by never having seen a poem lovely as a

```
      t
     ttt
    rrrrr
   rrrrrrr
  eeeeeeeee
     ???
```

However, like other structures of language, Concrete poems evidently can have the effect of poetry, if written by poets. Whether or not it ought to be dubbed "poetry," this art can do what poems traditionally have done: use language in delightful ways that reveal meanings to us.

Edwin Morgan (b. 1920)
SIESTA OF A HUNGARIAN SNAKE

s sz sz SZ sz SZ sz ZS zs ZS zs zs z

QUESTIONS
1. Does the sound of its consonants matter?
2. What do you suppose Morgan is trying to indicate by reversing the order of the two letters in mid line?
3. What, if anything, about this snake seems Hungarian?

Dorthi Charles (b. 1950)
CONCRETE CAT

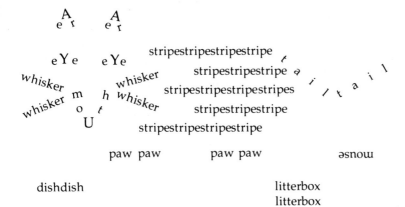

1. What does this writer indicate by capitalizing the *a* in *ear*? The *y* in *eye*? The *u* in *mouth*? By using spaces between the letters in the word *tail*?
2. Why is the word *mouse* upside down?
3. What possible pun might be seen in the cat's middle stripe?
4. What is the tone of "Concrete Cat"? How is it made evident?
5. Do these words seem chosen for their connotations or only for their denotations? Would you call this work of art a poem?

EXPERIMENT: *Do It Yourself*

Make a Concrete poem of your own. If you need inspiration, pick some familiar object or animal and try to find words that look like it. For more ideas, study the typography of a magazine or newspaper; cut out interesting letters and numerals and try pasting them into arrangements. What (if anything) do your experiments tell you about familiar letters and words? You might also find it helpful to read a book of Concrete poetry. Some are mentioned in this chapter.

12 Symbol and Allegory

SYMBOL

The national flag is supposed to bestir our patriotic feelings. When a black cat crosses his path, a superstitious man shivers, foreseeing bad luck. To each of these, by custom, our society expects a standard response. A flag, a black cat's crossing one's path — each is a **symbol:** a visible object or action that suggests some further meaning in addition to itself. In literature, a symbol might be the word *flag* or the words *a black cat crossed his path* or every description of flag or cat in an entire novel, story, play, or poem.

A flag and the crossing of a black cat may be called **conventional symbols,** since they can have a conventional or customary effect on us. Conventional symbols are also part of the language of poetry, as we know when we meet the red rose, emblem of love, in a lyric, or the Christian cross in the devotional poems of George Herbert. More often, however, symbols in literature have no conventional, long-established meaning, but particular meanings of their own. In Melville's novel *Moby Dick,* to take a rich example, whatever we associate with the great white whale is *not* attached unmistakably to white whales by custom. Though Melville tells us that men have long regarded whales with awe and relates Moby Dick to the celebrated fish that swallowed Jonah, the reader's response is to one particular whale, the creature of Herman Melville. Only the experience of reading the novel in its entirety can give Moby Dick his particular meaning.

We should say *meanings,* for as Eudora Welty has observed, it is a good thing Melville made Moby Dick a whale, a creature large enough to contain all that critics have found in him. A symbol in literature, if not conventional, has more than just one meaning. In "The Raven," by Edgar Allan Poe, the appearance of a strange black bird in the narrator's study is sinister; and indeed, if we take the poem seriously, we may even respond with a sympathetic shiver of dread. Does the bird mean death, fate, melancholy, the loss of a loved one, knowledge in the service of evil? All these, perhaps. Like any well-chosen symbol, Poe's raven sets going within the reader an unending train of feelings and associations.

We miss the value of a symbol, however, if we think it can mean absolutely anything we wish. If a poet has any control over our reactions, his poem will guide our responses in a certain direction.

T. S. Eliot (1888–1965)

THE BOSTON EVENING TRANSCRIPT

The readers of the *Boston Evening Transcript*
Sway in the wind like a field of ripe corn.

When evening quickens faintly in the street,
Wakening the appetites of life in some
And to others bringing the *Boston Evening Transcript*,   5
I mount the steps and ring the bell, turning
Wearily, as one would turn to nod good-bye to La Rochefoucauld,
If the street were time and he at the end of the street,
And I say, "Cousin Harriet, here is the *Boston Evening Transcript*."

The newspaper, whose name Eliot purposely repeats so monotonously, indicates what this poem is about. Now defunct, the *Transcript* covered in detail the slightest activity of Boston's leading families and was noted for the great length of its obituaries. Eliot, then, uses the newspaper as a symbol for an existence of boredom, fatigue (*Wearily*), petty and unvarying routine (since an evening newspaper, like night, arrives on schedule). The *Transcript* evokes a way of life without zest or passion, for, opposed to people who read it, Eliot sets people who do not: those whose desires revive, not expire, when the working day is through. Suggestions abound in the ironic comparison of the *Transcript*'s readers to a cornfield late in summer. To mention only a few: the readers sway because they are sleepy; they vegetate; they are drying up; each makes a rattling sound when turning his page. It is not necessary that we know the remote and similarly disillusioned friend to whom the speaker might nod: La Rochefoucauld, whose cynical *Maxims* entertained Parisian society under Louis XIV (sample: "All of us have enough strength to endure the misfortunes of others"). We understand that the nod is symbolic of an immense weariness of spirit. We know nothing about Cousin Harriet, whom the speaker addresses, but imagine from the greeting she inspires that she is probably a bore.

If Eliot wishes to say that certain Bostonians lead lives of sterile boredom, why does he couch his meaning in symbols? Why doesn't he tell us directly what he means? These questions imply two assumptions not necessarily true: first, that Eliot has a message to impart; second, that he is concealing it. We have reason to think that Eliot did not usually have a message in mind when beginning a poem, for as he once told a critic: "The conscious problems with which one is concerned in the actual writing are more those of a quasi musical nature . . . than of a conscious exposition of ideas." A poet sometimes discovers what he has to say while in the act of saying it. And it may be that in his *Transcript* poem, Eliot is saying exactly what he means. By communicating his meaning through symbols instead of statements, he may be choosing the only kind of language appropriate to an idea of great subtlety and complexity. (The paraphrase "Certain Bostonians are bored" hardly begins to describe the poem in all its possible meaning.) And by his use of symbolism, Eliot affords us the pleasure of finding our own entrances to his poem. Another great strength of a symbol is that, like some figures of speech, it renders the abstract in concrete terms, and, like any other image, refers to what we can perceive — an object like a newspaper, a gesture like a nod. Eliot might, like Robert Frost, have called himself a "synecdochist." Frost explained: "Always a larger significance. A little thing touches a larger thing."

This power of suggestion that a symbol contains is, perhaps, its greatest advantage. Sometimes, as in the following poem by Emily Dickinson, a symbol will lead us from a visible object to something whose dimensions are too vast to be perceived.

Emily Dickinson (1830–1886)
THE LIGHTNING IS A YELLOW FORK

The Lightning is a yellow Fork
From Tables in the sky
By inadvertent fingers dropt
The awful Cutlery   4

Of mansions never quite disclosed
And never quite concealed
The Apparatus of the Dark
To ignorance revealed.   8

If the lightning is a fork, then whose are the fingers that drop it, the table from which it slips, the household to which it belongs? The poem implies this question without giving an answer. An obvious answer is "God," but can we be sure? We are left wondering, too, about these partially lighted mansions: if our vision were clearer, what would we behold?[1]

"But how am I supposed to know a symbol when I see one?" The

---

[1] In its suggestion of an infinite realm that mortal eyes cannot quite see, but whose nature can be perceived fleetingly through things visible, Emily Dickinson's poem, by coincidence, resembles the work of late-nineteenth-century French poets called **Symbolists.** To a Symbolist the shirt-tail of Truth is continually seen disappearing around a corner. With their Neoplatonic view of ideal realities existing in a great beyond, whose corresponding symbols are the perceptible cats that bite us and tangible stones we stumble over, French poets such as Charles Baudelaire, Jules Laforgue, and Stéphane Mallarmé were profoundly to affect poets writing in English, notably Yeats (who said a poem "entangles . . . a part of the Divine essence") and Eliot..But we consider in this chapter symbolism as an element in certain poems, not Symbolism, the literary movement.

best approach is to read poems closely, taking comfort in the likelihood that it is better not to notice symbols at all than to find significance in every literal stone and huge meanings in every thing. In looking for the symbols in a poem, pick out all the references to concrete objects — newspapers, black cats, twisted pins. Consider these with special care. Note any that the poet emphasizes by detailed description, by repetition, or by placing at the very beginning or end of the poem. Ask: what is the poem about, what does it add up to? If, when the poem is paraphrased, the paraphrase depends primarily upon the meaning of certain concrete objects, these richly suggestive objects may be the symbols.

There are some things a literary symbol usually is *not*. A symbol is not an abstraction. Such terms as *truth, death, love,* and *justice* cannot work as symbols (unless personified, as in the traditional figure of Justice holding a scale). Most often, a symbol is something we can see in the mind's eye: a newspaper, a lightning bolt, a gesture of nodding good-bye.

In narratives, a well-developed character who speaks much dialogue and is not the least bit mysterious is usually not a symbol. But watch out for an executioner in a black hood; a character, named for a Biblical prophet, who does little but utter a prophecy; a trio of old women who resemble the Three Fates. (It has been argued, with good reason, that Milton's fully rounded character of Satan in *Paradise Lost* is a symbol embodying evil and man's pride, but a narrower definition of symbol is more frequently useful.) A symbol *may* be a part of a person's body (the baleful eye of the murder victim in Poe's story "The Tell-Tale Heart") or a look, a voice, a mannerism.

A symbol usually is not the second term of a metaphor. In the line "The lightning is a yellow fork," the symbol is the lightning, not the fork.

Sometimes a symbol addresses a sense other than sight: the sound of a mysterious harp at the end of Chekhov's play *The Cherry Orchard;* or, in William Faulkner's tale "A Rose for Emily," the odor of decay that surrounds the house of the last survivor of a town's leading family — suggesting not only physical dissolution but also the decay of a social order. A symbol is a special kind of image, for it exceeds the usual image in the richness of its connotations. The dead wife's cold comb in the haiku of Buson (discussed on p. 67) works symbolically, suggesting among other things the chill of the grave, the contrast between the living and the dead.

Holding a narrower definition than that used in this book, some readers of poetry prefer to say that a symbol is always a concrete object, never an act. They would deny the label "symbol" to Ahab's breaking his tobacco pipe before setting out to pursue Moby Dick (suggesting, perhaps, his determination to allow no pleasure to distract him from the chase) or to any large motion (as Ahab's whole quest). This distinction, while confining, does have the merit of sparing one from seeing all motion to be possibly symbolic. Some would call Ahab's gesture not a symbol but a **symbolic act.**

To sum up: a symbol radiates hints or casts long shadows (to use Henry James's metaphor). We are unable to say it "stands for" or "represents" a meaning. It evokes, it suggests, it manifests. It demands no single necessary interpretation, such as the interpretation a driver gives to a red traffic light. Rather, like Emily Dickinson's lightning bolt, it points toward an indefinite meaning, which may lie in part beyond the reach of words. In a symbol, as Thomas Carlyle said in *Sartor Resartus,* "the Infinite is made to blend with the Finite, to stand visible, and as it were, attainable there."

Emily Dickinson (1830–1886)
I heard a Fly buzz – when I died

I heard a Fly buzz – when I died –
The Stillness in the Room
Was like the Stillness in the Air –
Between the Heaves of Storm –   4

The Eyes around – had wrung them dry –
And Breaths were gathering firm
For that last Onset – when the King
Be witnessed – in the Room –   8

I willed my Keepsakes – Signed away
What portion of me be
Assignable – and then it was
There interposed a Fly –   12

With Blue – uncertain stumbling Buzz –
Between the light – and me –
And then the Windows failed – and then
I could not see to see –   16

Questions

1. Why is the poem written in the past tense? Where is the speaker at present?
2. What do you understand from the repetition of the word *see* in the last line?
3. What does the poet mean by *Eyes around* (line 5), *that last Onset* (line 7), *the King* (line 7), and *What portion of me be / Assignable* (lines 10–11)?
4. In line 13, how can a sound be called *Blue* and *stumbling*?
5. What further meaning might *the Windows* (line 15) suggest, in addition to denoting the windows of the room?
6. What connotations of the word *fly* seem relevant to an account of a death?
7. Summarize your interpretation of the poem. What does the fly mean?

Thomas Hardy (1840–1928)

NEUTRAL TONES

We stood by a pond that winter day,
And the sun was white, as though chidden of God,
And a few leaves lay on the starving sod;
— They had fallen from an ash, and were gray.   4

Your eyes on me were as eyes that rove
Over tedious riddles of years ago;
And some words played between us to and fro
  On which lost the more by our love.   8

The smile on your mouth was the deadest thing
Alive enough to have strength to die;
And a grin of bitterness swept thereby
  Like an ominous bird a-wing. . . .   12

Since then, keen lessons that love deceives,
And wrings with wrong, have shaped to me
Your face, and the God-curst sun, and a tree,
  And a pond edged with grayish leaves.   16

QUESTIONS

1. Sum up the story told in this poem. In lines 1–12, what is the dramatic situation? What has happened in the interval between the experience related in these lines and the reflection in the last stanza?
2. What meanings do you find in the title?
3. Explain in your own words the metaphor in line 2.
4. What connotations appropriate to this poem does the *ash* (line 4) have, that *oak* or *maple* would lack?
5. What visible objects in the poem function symbolically? What actions or gestures?

ALLEGORY

If we read of a ship, its captain, its sailors, and the rough seas, and we realize we are reading about a commonwealth and how its rulers and workers keep it going even in difficult times, then we are reading an **allegory.** Closely akin to symbolism, allegory is a description — usually narrative — in which persons, places, and things are employed in a continuous system of equivalents.

Although more strictly limited in its suggestions than symbolism, allegory need not be thought inferior. Few poems continue to interest readers more than Dante's allegorical *Divine Comedy.* Sublime evidence of the appeal of allegory may be found in Christ's use of the **parable:** a brief narrative — usually allegorical but sometimes not — that teaches a moral.

Matthew 13:24–30 (Authorized or King James Version, 1611)
THE PARABLE OF THE GOOD SEED

The kingdom of heaven is likened unto a man which sowed good seed in his field:
But while men slept, his enemy came and sowed tares among the wheat, and went his way.
But when the blade was sprung up, and brought forth fruit, then appeared the tares also.
So the servants of the householder came and said unto him, Sir, didst not thou sow good seed in thy field? From whence then hath it tares?
He said unto them, An enemy hath done this. The servants said unto him, Wilt thou then that we go and gather them up?
But he said, Nay; lest while ye gather up the tares, ye root up also the wheat with them.
Let both grow together until the harvest: and in the time of harvest I will say to the reapers, Gather ye together first the tares, and bind them in bundles to burn them: but gather the wheat into my barn.

The sower is the Son of man, the field is the world, the good seed are the children of the Kingdom, the tares are the children of the wicked one, the enemy is the devil, the harvest is the end of the world, the reapers are angels. "As therefore the tares are gathered and burned in the fire; so shall it be in the end of this world" (Matthew 13:36–42).

Usually, as in this parable, the meanings of an allegory are plainly labeled or thinly disguised. In John Bunyan's allegorical narrative *The Pilgrim's Progress,* it is clear that the hero Christian, on his journey through places with such pointed names as Vanity Fair, the Valley of the Shadow of Death, and Doubting Castle, is the soul, traveling the road of life on his way toward Heaven. An allegory, when carefully built, is systematic. It makes one principal comparison, the working out of whose details may lead to further comparisons, then still further comparisons: Christian, thrown by Giant Despair into the dungeon of Doubting Castle, escapes by means of a key called Promise. Such a complicated design may take great length to unfold, as does that of Spenser's *Faerie Queene;* however, the method of allegory may be seen in a poem as short as this:

Sir Walter Raleigh (1552?–1618)
WHAT IS OUR LIFE? A PLAY OF PASSION

What is our life? A play of passion,
Our mirth the music of division.
Our mothers' wombs the tiring-houses° be,   *attiring-houses*
Where we are dressed for this short comedy.   4
Heaven the judicious sharp spectator is,
That sits and marks still who doth act amiss.

Our graves that hide us from the searching sun
Are like drawn curtains when the play is done.   8
Thus march we, playing, to our latest rest,
Only we die in earnest, that's no jest.

Like the basic metaphor of *The Pilgrim's Progress* — life is a pilgrimage
— that of Raleigh's poem represents an abstract concept in terms of
something tangible: all the world's a theater, life is a play, mirth is the
musical interlude, wombs are dressing-rooms, and so on. Some people
prefer to say that allegories in literature are always long and that
Raleigh's poem develops one sustained simile.

An object in allegory is like a bird whose cage is clearly lettered
with its identity — "RAVEN, *Corvus corax;* habitat of specimen, Maine."
A symbol, by contrast, is a bird with piercing eyes that mysteriously
appears one evening in your library. It is there; you can touch it. But
what does it mean? You look at it. It continues to look at you.

Whether an object in literature is a symbol, part of an allegory, or
no such thing at all, it has at least one sure meaning. Moby Dick is first
a whale, the *Boston Evening Transcript* a newspaper. Besides deriving a
multitude of intangible suggestions from the title symbol in Eliot's long
poem *The Waste Land*, its readers cannot fail to carry away a sense of the
land's physical appearance: a river choked with sandwich papers and
cigarette ends, London Bridge "under the brown fog of a winter dawn."
A virtue of *The Pilgrim's Progress* is that its walking abstractions are no
mere abstractions but are also human: Giant Despair is a henpecked
husband. The most vital element of a literary work may pass us by,
unless before seeking further depths in a thing, we look to the thing
itself.

Sir Philip Sidney (1554–1586)

You that with allegory's curious frame

You that with allegory's curious frame
  Of others' children changelings use to make,
  With me those pains, for God's sake, do not take;
  I list not° dig so deep for brazen fame.   *I do not choose to*   4
When I say Stella, I do mean the same
  Princess of beauty for whose only sake
  The reins of love I love, though never slake,
  And joy therein, though nations count it shame.   8
I beg no subject to use eloquence,
  Nor in hid ways do guide philosophy;
  Look at my hands for no such quintessence,
But know that I in pure simplicity   12
  Breathe out the flames which burn within my heart,
  Love only reading unto me this art.   14

Robert Frost (1874–1963)

DEPARTMENTAL

An ant on the tablecloth
Ran into a dormant moth
Of many times his size.
He showed not the least surprise.
His business wasn't with such.   5
He gave it scarcely a touch,
And was off on his duty run.
Yet if he encountered one
Of the hive's enquiry squad
Whose work is to find out God   10
And the nature of time and space,
He would put him onto the case.
Ants are a curious race;
One crossing with hurried tread
The body of one of their dead   15
Isn't given a moment's arrest —
Seems not even impressed.
But he no doubt reports to any
With whom he crosses antennae,
And they no doubt report   20
To the higher up at court.
Then word goes forth in Formic:
"Death's come to Jerry McCormic,
Our selfless forager Jerry.
Will the special Janizary°   *soldier*   25
Whose office it is to bury
The dead of the commissary
Go bring him home to his people.
Lay him in state on a sepal.
Wrap him for shroud in a petal.   30
Embalm him with ichor of nettle.
This is the word of your Queen."
And presently on the scene
Appears a solemn mortician;
And taking formal position   35
With feelers calmly atwiddle,
Seizes the dead by the middle,
And leaving him high in air,
Carries him out of there.
No one stands round to stare.   40
It is nobody else's affair.

It couldn't be called ungentle.
But how thoroughly departmental.

1. Why do you suppose that in his book *A Further Range,* Frost included "Departmental" in a section of poems called "Taken Doubly"?
2. Is this narrative a parable? Has it a moral? If so, what?

FOR REVIEW AND FURTHER STUDY

EXERCISE: *Symbol Hunting*

After reading each of the following poems, decide which of these descriptions is most nearly accurate:

1. The poem treats a concrete object as its central symbol.
2. The whole poem draws one extended metaphor or simile.
3. The poem does neither of these things.

Wallace Stevens (1879–1955)
ANECDOTE OF THE JAR

I placed a jar in Tennessee,
And round it was, upon a hill.
It made the slovenly wilderness
Surround that hill.   4

The wilderness rose up to it,
And sprawled around, no longer wild.
The jar was round upon the ground
And tall and of a port in air.   8

It took dominion everywhere.
The jar was gray and bare.
It did not give of bird or bush,
Like nothing else in Tennessee.   12

William Shakespeare (1564–1616)
LO, AS A CAREFUL HOUSEWIFE RUNS TO CATCH

Lo, as a careful housewife runs to catch
One of her feathered creatures broke away,
Sets down her babe, and makes all swift dispatch
In pùrsuit of the thing she would have stay;   4
Whilst her neglected child holds her in chase,
Cries to catch her whose busy care is bent
To follow that which flies before her face,
Not prizing her poor infant's discontent: 8
So runn'st thou after that which flies from thee,
Whilst I thy babe chase thee afar behind;

But if thou catch thy hope, turn back to me,
And play the mother's part, kiss me, be kind: 12
   So will I pray that thou mayst have thy "Will,"
   If thou turn back and my loud crying still.   14

Mina Loy (1881–1966)

OMEN OF VICTORY

Women in uniform

relaxed for tea

under a shady garden tree

discover

a dove's feather

fallen in the sugar.

Theodore Roethke (1908–1963)

NIGHT CROW

When I saw that clumsy crow
Flap from a wasted tree,
A shape in the mind rose up:
Over the gulfs of dream
Flew a tremendous bird
Further and further away   6
Into a moonless black,
Deep in the brain, far back.   8

John Donne (1572–1631)

A BURNT SHIP

Out of a fired ship which by no way
But drowning could be rescued from the flame
Some men leaped forth, and ever as they came
Near the foe's ships, did by their shot decay;   4
So all were lost, which in the ship were found,
   They in the sea being burnt, they in the burnt ship drowned.   6

Robert Frost (1874–1963)

THE SILKEN TENT

She is as in a field a silken tent
At midday when a sunny summer breeze
Has dried the dew and all its ropes relent,
So that in guys it gently sways at ease,   4

And its supporting central cedar pole,
That is its pinnacle to heavenward
And signifies the sureness of the soul,
Seems to owe naught to any single cord,   8
But strictly held by none, is loosely bound
By countless silken ties of love and thought
To everything on earth the compass round,
And only by one's going slightly taut   12
In the capriciousness of summer air
Is of the slightest bondage made aware.   14

Walt Whitman (1819–1892)

A NOISELESS PATIENT SPIDER

A noiseless patient spider,
I mark'd where on a little promontory it stood isolated,
Mark'd how to explore the vacant vast surrounding,
It launch'd forth filament, filament, filament, out of itself,
Ever unreeling them, ever tirelessly speeding them.   5

And you O my soul where you stand,
Surrounded, detached, in measureless oceans of space,
Ceaselessly musing, venturing, throwing, seeking the spheres to connect
     them,
Till the bridge you will need be form'd, till the ductile anchor hold,
Till the gossamer thread you fling catch somewhere, O my soul.   10

13 Myth

TRADITIONAL MYTH

Poets have long been fond of retelling **myths,** narrowly defined as traditional stories of immortal beings. Such stories taken collectively may also be called **myth** or **mythology.** In one of the most celebrated collections of myth ever assembled, the *Metamorphoses,* the poet Ovid has told — to take one example from many — how Phaeton, child of the sun god, rashly tried to drive his father's fiery chariot on its daily round, lost control of the horses, and caused disaster both to himself and to the world. Our use of the term *myth* in discussing poetry, then, differs from its use in expressions such as "the myth of communism" and "the myth of democracy." In these examples, myth, in its broadest sense, is any idea people believe in, whether true or false. Nor do we mean — to take another familiar use of the word — a cock-and-bull story: "Judge Rapp doesn't roast speeders alive; that's just a *myth.*" In the following discussion, myth will mean — as critic Northrop Frye has put it — "the imitation of actions near or at the conceivable limits of desire." Myths tell us of the exploits of the gods — their battles, the ways in which they live, love, and perhaps suffer — all on a scale of magnificence larger than our life. We envy their freedom and power; they enact our wishes and dreams. Whether we believe in them or not, their adventures are myths: Ovid, it seems, placed no credence in the stories he related, for he declared, "I prate of ancient poets' monstrous lies."

And yet it is characteristic of a myth that it *can* be believed. Throughout history, myths have accompanied religious doctrines and rituals. They have helped sanction or recall to men the reasons for religious observances. A sublime instance is the New Testament account of the Last Supper. Because of it and its record of the words of Jesus, "This do in remembrance of Me," Christians have continued to re-enact the offering and partaking of the body and blood of their Lord, under the appearances of bread and wine. It is essential to recall that, just because a myth narrates the acts of a god, we do not necessarily mean by the term a false or fictitious narrative. When we speak of the "myth of Islam" or "the Christian myth," we do so without implying either belief or disbelief. Myths can also help sanction customs and institutions other than religious ones. At the same time the baking of bread was introduced to ancient Greece — one theory goes — there was introduced the myth of Demeter, goddess of grain, who had kindly sent her emissary Triptolemus to teach man this valuable art — thus helping to persuade the distrustful that bread was a good thing. Some myths seem made to divert and regale, not to sanction anything. Such may be the story of the sculptor Pygmalion, who fell in love with his statue of a woman; so exquisite was his work, so deep was his feeling, that Aphrodite brought the statue to life. And yet perhaps the story goes deeper than mere diversion: perhaps it is a way of saying that works of art achieve a reality of their own, that love can transform or animate its object.

How does a myth begin? Several theories have been proposed, none universally accepted. One is that myth is a way in which primitive man explains to himself some natural phenomenon. In this view, myth is rudimentary science. Winter comes and the vegetation perishes because Persephone, child of Demeter, must return to the underworld for four months every year. This theory, as classical scholar Edith Hamilton has pointed out, may lead us to think incorrectly that Greek mythology was the creation of a primitive people. Tales of the gods of Mount Olympus may reflect an earlier inheritance, but Greek myths known to us were transcribed in an era of high civilization. Anthropologists have questioned whether primitive people generally find beauty in the mysteries of nature. "From my own study of living myths among savages," wrote Bronislaw Malinowski, "I should say that primitive man has to a very limited extent the purely artistic or scientific interest in nature; there is but little room for symbolism in his ideas and tales; and myth, in fact, is not an idle rhapsody . . . but a hardworking, extremely important cultural force."[1] Such a practical function was seen by Sir James Frazer in *The Golden Bough:* myths were originally expressions of man's hope that nature would be fertile. Still another theory is that, once upon a time, heroes of myth were human prototypes. The Greek philosopher Euhemerus declared myths to be tales of real persons, which poets had exaggerated. Most present-day historians of myth would seek no general explanation but would say that different myths probably have different origins.

Poets have many coherent mythologies on which to draw; perhaps those most frequently consulted by British and American poets are the classical, the Christian, the Norse, and folk myth of the American frontier (embodying the deeds of superhuman characters such as Paul

---

[1] *Myth in Primitive Psychology* (New York, 1926); reprinted in *Magic, Science and Religion* (New York, 1954), p. 97.

Bunyan). Some poets have taken inspiration from other myths as well: T. S. Eliot's *The Waste Land,* for example, is enriched by allusions to Buddhism and to pagan vegetation-cults.

As a tour through any good art museum will demonstrate, myth pervades much of the graphic art of Western civilization. In literature, one evidence of its continuing value to recent poets and storytellers is the frequency with which myths — both primitive and civilized — are retold. William Faulkner's story "The Bear" recalls tales of Indian totem animals; John Updike's novel *The Centaur* presents the horse-man Chiron as a modern high school teacher; Hart Crane's poem "For the Marriage of Faustus and Helen" unites two figures of different myths, who dance to jazz; T. S. Eliot's plays bring into the drawing-room the myths of Alcestis (*The Cocktail Party*) and the Eumenides (*The Family Reunion*); Jean Cocteau's film *Orphée* shows us Eurydice riding to the underworld with an escort of motorcycles. Popular interest in such works may testify to the profound appeal myths continue to hold for us. Like any other large body of knowledge that can be alluded to, myth offers the poet an instant means of communication — if his reader also knows the particular myth cited. Writing "Lycidas," John Milton could depend upon his readers — mostly persons of similar classical learn-ing — to understand him without footnotes. Today, a poet referring to a traditional myth must be sure to choose a reasonably well-known one, or else write as well as T. S. Eliot, whose work has compelled his readers to single out his allusions and look them up. Like other varieties of poetry, myth is a kind of knowledge, not at odds with scientific knowledge but existing in addition to it.

D. H. Lawrence (1885–1930)
BAVARIAN GENTIANS

Not every man has gentians in his house
in Soft September, at slow, sad Michaelmas.

Bavarian gentians, big and dark, only dark
darkening the daytime, torch-like with the smoking blueness of Pluto's
    gloom,
ribbed and torch-like, with their blaze of darkness spread blue   5
down flattening into points, flattened under the sweep of white day
torch-flower of the blue-smoking darkness, Pluto's dark-blue daze,
black lamps from the halls of Dis, burning dark blue,
giving off darkness, blue darkness, as Demeter's pale lamps give off light,
lead me then, lead the way.   10

Reach me a gentian, give me a torch!
let me guide myself with the blue, forked torch of this flower
down the darker and darker stairs, where blue is darkened on blueness

even where Persephone goes, just now, from the frosted September
to the sightless realm where darkness is awake upon the dark   15
and Persephone herself is but a voice
or a darkness invisible enfolded in the deeper dark
of the arms Plutonic, and pierced with the passion of dense gloom,
among the splendor of torches of darkness, shedding darkness on the
    lost bride and her groom.

BAVARIAN GENTIANS. 4. *Pluto:* Roman name for Hades, in Greek mythology the ruler of
the underworld, who abducted Persephone to be his bride. Each spring Persephone returns to earth and is welcomed by her mother Demeter, goddess of fruitfulness; each
winter she departs again, to dwell with her husband below. 8. *Dis:* Pluto's realm.

QUESTIONS

1. Read this poem aloud. What devices of sound do you hear in it?
2. What characteristics of gentians appear to remind Lawrence of the story of
   Persephone? What significance do you attach to the poem's being set in
   September? How does the fact of autumn matter to the gentians and to
   Persephone?

Thomas Hardy (1840–1928)
THE OXEN

Christmas Eve, and twelve of the clock.
    "Now they are all on their knees,"
An elder said as we sat in a flock
    By the embers in hearthside ease.   4

We pictured the meek mild creatures where
    They dwelt in their strawy pen,
Nor did it occur to one of us there
    To doubt they were kneeling then.   8

So fair a fancy few would weave
    In these years! Yet, I feel,
If someone said on Christmas Eve,
    "Come; see the oxen kneel   12

"In the lonely barton° by yonder coomb°   *farmyard; a hollow*
    Our childhood used to know,"
I should go with him in the gloom,
    Hoping it might be so.   16

THE OXEN. This ancient belief has had wide currency among peasants and farmers of
Western Europe. Some also say that on Christmas eve the beasts can speak.

QUESTIONS

1. What body of myth is Hardy's subject and what are his speaker's attitudes
   toward it? Perhaps, in Hardy's view, the pious report about oxen is only
   part of it.
2. Read this poem aloud and notice its sound and imagery. What contrast do
   you find between the sounds of the first stanza and the sounds of the last

stanza? Which words make the difference? What images enforce a contrast in tone between the beginning of the poem and its ending?

3. G. K. Chesterton, writing as a defender of Christian faith, called Hardy's writings "the mutterings of the village atheist." See other poems by Hardy (particularly "Channel Firing," p. 346). What do you think Chesterton might have meant? Can "The Oxen" be called a hostile mutter?

William Wordsworth (1770–1850)
THE WORLD IS TOO MUCH WITH US

The world is too much with us; late and soon,
Getting and spending, we lay waste our powers;
Little we see in Nature that is ours;
We have given our hearts away, a sordid boon!   4
This Sea that bares her bosom to the moon;
The winds that will be howling at all hours,
And are up-gathered now like sleeping flowers;
For this, for everything, we are out of tune;   8
It moves us not. — Great God! I'd rather be
A Pagan suckled in a creed outworn;
So might I, standing on this pleasant lea,
Have glimpses that would make me less forlorn;
Have sight of Proteus rising from the sea;
Or hear old Triton blow his wreathèd horn.   14

QUESTIONS

1. In this sonnet by Wordsworth what condition does the poet complain about? To what does he attribute this condition?
2. How does it affect him as an individual?

PERSONAL MYTH

When Plato in *The Republic* relates the Myth of Er, he introduces supernatural characters he himself originated. Poets, too, have been inspired to make up myths of their own, for their own purposes. "I must create a system or be enslaved by another man's," said William Blake, who in his "prophetic books" peopled the cosmos with supernatural beings having names like Los, Urizen, and Vala (side by side with recognizable figures from the Old Testament and New Testament). This kind of system-making probably has advantages and drawbacks. T. S. Eliot, in his essay on Blake, wishes that the author of *The Four Zoas* had accepted traditional myths, and he compares Blake's thinking to a piece of homemade furniture whose construction diverted valuable energy from the writing of poems. Others have found Blake's untraditional cosmos an achievement — notably William Butler Yeats, himself the author of an elaborate personal mythology. Although we need not know all of Yeats's mythology to enjoy his poems, to know of its existence can make a few great poems deeper for us and less difficult.

William Butler Yeats (1865–1939)

THE SECOND COMING

(at the end of WWI)

open form

Turning and turning in the widening gyre°   *spiral*
The falcon cannot hear the falconer;
Things fall apart; the center cannot hold;
Mere anarchy is loosed upon the world,
The blood-dimmed tide is loosed, and everywhere   5
The ceremony of innocence is drowned;
The best lack all conviction, while the worst
Are full of passionate intensity.

Surely some revelation is at hand;
Surely the Second Coming is at hand;   10
The Second Coming! Hardly are those words out
When a vast image out of *Spiritus Mundi*
Troubles my sight: somewhere in sands of the desert
A shape with lion body and the head of a man,
A gaze blank and pitiless as the sun,   15
Is moving its slow thighs, while all about it
Reel shadows of the indignant desert birds.
The darkness drops again; but now I know
That twenty centuries of stony sleep
Were vexed to nightmare by a rocking cradle,   20
And what rough beast, its hour come round at last,
Slouches towards Bethlehem to be born?

What kind of Second Coming does Yeats expect? Evidently it is not to be a Christian one. Yeats saw human history as governed by the turning of a Great Wheel, whose phases influence events and determine men's personalities — rather like the signs of the Zodiac in astrology. Every two thousand years comes a horrendous moment: the Wheel completes a turn; one civilization ends and another begins. Strangely, a new age is always announced by birds and by acts of violence. Thus the Greek-Roman world arrives with the descent of Zeus in swan's form and the burning of Troy, the Christian era with the descent of the Holy Spirit — traditionally depicted as a dove — and the Crucifixion. In 1919 when Yeats wrote "The Second Coming," his Ireland was in the midst of turmoil and bloodshed; the Western Hemisphere had been severely shaken by World War I. A new millennium seemed imminent. What sphinxlike, savage deity would next appear, with birds proclaiming it angrily? Yeats thinks he imagines it emerging from *Spiritus Mundi,* Soul of the World, a collective unconscious from which a man (since his individual soul touches it) receives dreams, nightmares, and racial memories.[2]

[2] Yeats fully explains his system in *A Vision* (New York, 1938; paperbound reprint, 1961).

It is hard to say whether a poet who discovers his own myth does so to have something to live by or to have something to write about. Robert Graves, who professes his belief in a White Goddess ("Mother of All Living, the ancient power of love and terror"), has said that he has written poetry in a trance, inspired by his Goddess-Muse.[3] Luckily, we do not have to know a poet's religious affiliation before we can read his poems. Perhaps most personal myths that enter poems are not acts of faith but works of art: stories that resemble traditional mythology.

More recently the late English scholar and storyteller J. R. R. Tolkien has transcribed the mythology of an ancient world of elves, wizards, and hobbits in his trilogy *The Lord of the Rings*. This fictive world contains, besides heroes, creatures as disgusting as the Mewlips, about whom Tolkien has written in rime:

> The shadows where the Mewlips dwell
>   Are dark and wet as ink,
> And slow and softly rings their bell,
>   As in the slime you sink.

Myths, as the Mewlips remind us, can be invented playfully.

In constructing a whole private myth — as Tolkien did — a poet may help himself to tradition. To complete his symbol of the Great Wheel, Yeats drew upon Eastern religion, occultism, and Rosicrucianism. Robert Graves has found evidence of the worship of the White Goddess dating back, in his opinion, to the Old Stone Age. Blake accepted at least part of the Biblical account of the fallen angels, but his version gives a characteristic twist to it. Defying God, Satan had the good fortune to win his rebellion, but being crafty, he gave out the false news of his own defeat and proceeded to govern under the name of the Almighty he had displaced. Whether as playful as Tolkien or as earnest as Blake, whether creating a single goddess or a whole pantheon, poets have sometimes based remarkable poems on individual mythologies.

John Heath–Stubbs (b. 1918)

A Charm Against the Toothache

Venerable Mother Toothache
Climb down from the white battlements,
Stop twisting in your yellow fingers
The fourfold rope of nerves;
And tomorrow I will give you a tot of whisky   5
To hold in your cupped hands,

---

[3] See Graves's *The White Goddess* (New York, 1948; paperback edition, 1958), or for a terser statement of his position, see his lecture "The Personal Muse" in *On Poetry: Collected Talks and Essays* (New York, 1969).

A garland of anise-flowers,
And three cloves like nails.
And tell the attendant gnomes
It is time to knock off now,   10
To shoulder their little pick-axes,
Their cold-chisels and drills.
And you may mount by a silver ladder
Into the sky, to grind
In the cracked polished mortar   15
Of the hollow moon.

By the lapse of warm waters,
And the poppies nodding like red coals,
The paths on the granite mountains,
And the plantation of my dreams.   20

QUESTIONS

1. This poem shows us a poet inventing his own mythology. What powers and
   characteristics does he attribute to Mother Toothache? What facts of common
   experience does she help account for?
2. In what ways does the poem recall any myths and rituals that already exist?
3. What is the tone of the poem?

Edward Allen (b. 1948)

THE BEST LINE YET

In Stamford, at the edge of town, a giant statue stands:
An iron eagle sternly clasps the crag with crooked hands.
His pedestal is twenty feet, full thirty feet is he.
His head alone weighs many times as much as you or me.   4
All day, all night he keeps his watch and never stirs a feather.
His frowning brow glares straight ahead into the foulest weather.
They say this noble bird will spread his iron wings and fly
The day a virgin graduates from Stamford Senior High.   8
O, evil day when he shall rise above the peaceful town,
Endanger airplanes, frighten children, drop foul tonnage down!
So let not this accipiter° desert his silent vigil,   *bird of prey*
But yield to me my darling, Stamford's finest, Susan Kitchell.   12

QUESTIONS

1. How would you describe the tone of this myth-making poem (written when
   the author was a high school student)? Is it humorous, half-serious, or serious? How is the tone indicated?
2. What does it have in common with John Heath-Stubbs's "A Charm Against
   the Toothache" (page 221)?

William Butler Yeats (1865–1939)

LEDA AND THE SWAN

A sudden blow: the great wings beating still
Above the staggering girl, her thighs caressed
By the dark webs, her nape caught in his bill,
He holds her helpless breast upon his breast.   4

How can those terrified vague fingers push
The feathered glory from her loosening thighs?
And how can body, laid in that white rush,
But feel the strange heart beating where it lies?   8

A shudder in the loins engenders there
The broken wall, the burning roof and tower
And Agamemnon dead.
                              Being so caught up,
So mastered by the brute blood of the air,
Did she put on his knowledge with his power
Before the indifferent beak could let her drop?   14

QUESTIONS

1. According to Greek mythology, the god Zeus in the form of a swan descended upon Leda, a Spartan queen. Among the offspring of this union were Clytemnestra, Agamemnon's unfaithful wife who conspired in his murder, and Helen, on whose account the Trojan war was fought. What does a knowledge of these allusions contribute to our understanding of the poem's last two lines?
2. The slant rime *up / drop* (lines 11, 14) may seem accidental or inept. Is it? Would this poem have ended nearly so well if Yeats had made an exact rime like *up / cup* or *stop / drop?*
3. Do the words *staggering* (line 2) and *loosening* (line 6) keep to the basic meter of the poem or depart from it? How does rhythm express meaning in these lines?
4. How does "Leda and the Swan" reflect Yeats's personal mythology? Compare it with "The Second Coming" (p. 220).

ARCHETYPES

Earlier, looking at symbols, we saw that certain concrete objects in poetry can convey suggestions to which we respond without quite being able to tell why. Such, perhaps, are Emily Dickinson's forked lightning bolt dropped from celestial tables and her buzzing fly that arrives with death. Indefinite power may be present also in an **archetype** (Greek: "first-molded"), which can mean "an original model or pattern from which later things are made." The word acquired a special denotation through the work of the Swiss psychologist Carl Gustav Jung (1875–1961). Recently, it has occurred so frequently in literary criticism that students of poetry may wish to be aware of it.

An archetype, in Jung's view, is generally a story, character, symbol, or situation that recurs again and again in worldwide myth, literature, and dream. Some of these — as defined by Jung and others — might be figures such as the cruel mother (Cinderella's stepmother, the White Goddess), the creature half human and half animal (centaurs, satyrs, mermaids), the beautiful garden (Eden, Arcadia, the myth of the Golden Age), the story of the hero who by slaying a monster delivers a country from its curse (the romance of Parsifal, the Old English heroic narrative *Beowulf*, the myth of Perseus, the legend of Saint George and the dragon, most Hollywood monster movies), the story of the beast who yearns for the love of a woman (the fairy tale of "Beauty and the Beast," the movie *King Kong*), the story of the fall from innocence and initiation into life (the account in Genesis of the departure from Eden, J. D. Salinger's novel *The Catcher in the Rye*).

Like Sigmund Freud, Jung saw myth as an aid to the psychiatrist seeking to understand his patients' dreams. But Jung went further and postulated the existence of a "collective unconscious" or racial memory in which archetypes lie. "These fantasy-images," said Jung, referring to archetypal dreams not traceable to anything a patient himself has ever experienced, "correspond to certain *collective* (not personal) structural elements in the human psyche in general, and, like the morphological elements of the human body, are *inherited*. . . . The archetype — let us never forget this — is a psychic organ present in all of us."[4]

What this means to the study of poetry is that, if we accept Jung's view, poems containing recognizable archetypes are likely to stir us more profoundly than those that do not. Archetypes being our inheritance from what Shakespeare called "the dark backward and abysm of time," most people can perceive them and respond to them. Some critics have found Jung's theory helpful in fathoming poems. In *Archetypal Patterns in Poetry* (1934), Maud Bodkin found similar archetypes in such dissimilar poems as "Kubla Khan" and *Paradise Lost*. Recently the French critic Paul Ginestier has discovered common archetypes in certain classical myths and in modern poetry dealing with the machine.[5]

Recall Yeats's poem "The Second Coming," only one manifestation of the monstrous Sphinx in literature. There are clear resemblances between the *Spiritus Mundi* in Yeats's poem and Jung's idea of the collective unconscious. As early as 1900, Yeats felt sure of the existence of symbols much like archetypes:

> Any one who has any experience of any mystical state of the soul knows how there float up in the mind profound symbols, whose meaning, if indeed they do not delude one into the dream that they are meaningless,

---

[4] "The Psychology of the Child Archetype," in *Psyche and Symbol*, edited by Violet S. de Laszlo (New York, 1958), pp. 117, 123.
[5] *The Poet and the Machine*, translated by Martin B. Friedman (Chapel Hill, N.C., 1961).

one does not perhaps understand for years. Nor I think has any one, who has known that experience with any constancy, failed to find some day, in some old book or on some old monument, a strange or intricate image that had floated up before him, and to grow perhaps dizzy with the sudden conviction that our little memories are but part of some great Memory that renews the world and men's thoughts age after age, and that our thoughts are not, as we suppose, the deep, but a little foam upon the deep.[6]

Not all psychologists and students of literature agree with Jung. Some maintain that archetypes, because they tend to disappear with the disintegration of a culture in which they had prospered, are transmitted by word of mouth, not by racial memory.[7] Jung himself, in *Psychology and Religion,* tells of one tribal medicine man who confessed he had stopped having dreams after his tribe had been given a District Commissioner. All poets are not so fond of the notion of great Memory as Yeats was. Recently the English poet Philip Larkin has spoken for himself, and no doubt for others:

As a guiding principle I believe that every poem must be its own sole freshly created universe, and therefore have no belief in "tradition" or a common myth-kitty. . . . To me the whole of the ancient world, the whole of classical and biblical mythology means very little, and I think that using them today not only fills poems full of dead spots but dodges the writer's duty to be original.[8]

Larkin is probably reacting against bookishness. However, even readers who take no stock in Jung's theories may find *archetype* a useful name for something that, since antiquity, has exerted appeal to makers of myth — including some poets and storytellers.

Anonymous (traditional Scottish folk ballad)
THOMAS THE RIMER

True Thomas lay on Huntlie bank,
  A ferlie° he spied wi' his ee,   *wondrous thing*
And there he saw a lady bright,
  Come riding down by the Eildon Tree.   4

Her shirt was o' the grass-green silk,
  Her mantle o' the velvet fine,
At ilka tett° of her horse's mane   *every lock*
  Hang fifty siller bells and nine.   8

[6] "The Philosophy of Shelley's Poetry," *Essays and Introductions* (New York, 1961), pp. 78–79.
[7] See J. S. Lincoln, *The Dream in Primitive Cultures* (London, 1935), p. 24.
[8] Statements made on two different occasions, quoted by John Press, *A Map of Modern English Verse* (New York, 1969), pp. 258–59.

True Thomas, he pulled aff his cap,
   And louted° low down to his knee: *bowed*
"All hail, thou mighty Queen of Heaven!
   For thy peer on earth I never did see."   12

"O no, O no, Thomas," she said,
   "That name does not belang to me;
I am but the queen of fair Elfland,
   That am hither come to visit thee.   16

"Harp and carp°, Thomas," she said,   *sing ballads*
   "Harp and carp along wi' me,
And if ye dare to kiss my lips,
   Sure of your body I will be."   20

"Betide me weal, betide me woe,
   That weird° shall never daunton me";   *fate*
Syne° he has kissed her rosy lips,   *then*
   All underneath the Eildon Tree.   24

"Now, ye maun° go wi' me," she said,   *must*
   "True Thomas, ye maun go wi' me,
And ye maun serve me seven years,
   Thro weal or woe, as may chance to be."   28

She mounted on her milk-white steed,
   She's taen True Thomas up behind,
And aye° whene'er her bridle rung,   *always*
   The steed flew swifter than the wind.   32

O they rade on, and farther on —
   The steed gaed swifter than the wind —
Until they reached a desart wide,
   And living land was left behind.   36

"Light down, light down, now, True Thomas,
   And lean your head upon my knee;
Abide and rest a little space,
   And I will shew you ferlies three.   40

"O see ye not yon narrow road,
   So thick beset with thorns and briars?
That is the path of righteousness,
   Though after it but few enquires.   44

"And see not ye that braid° braid road,   *broad*
   That lies across that lily leven°?   *lovely lawn*
That is the path of wickedness,
   Though some call it the road to heaven.   48

"And see not ye that bonny road,
   That winds about the ferny brae°?   *hillside*

That is the road to fair Elfland,
   Where thou and I this night maun gae.   52

"But, Thomas, ye maun hold your tongue,
   Whatever ye may hear or see,
For, if you speak word in Elfyn land,
   Ye'll ne'er get back to your ain countrie."   56

O they rade on, and farther on,
   And they waded thro rivers aboon the knee,
And they saw neither sun nor moon,
   But they heard the roaring of the sea.   60

It was mirk° mirk night, and there was nae stern° light,   *murky; star*
   And they waded thro red blude to the knee;
For a' the blude that's shed on earth
   Rins thro the springs o' that countrie.   64

Syne they came on to a garden green,
   And she pu'd an apple frae a tree:
"Take this for thy wages, True Thomas,
   It will give the tongue that can never lie."   68

"My tongue is mine ain," True Thomas said;
   "A gudely gift ye wad gie to me!
I neither dought° to buy or sell,   *would be able*
   At fair or tryst° where I may be.   *market* 72

"I dought neither speak to prince or peer,
   Nor ask of grace from fair ladye":
"Now hold thy peace," the lady said,
   "For as I say, so must it be."   76

He has gotten a coat of the even cloth,
   And a pair of shoes of velvet green,
And till seven years were gane and past
   True Thomas on earth was never seen.   80

THOMAS THE RIMER. Thomas of Erceldoune, popularly called True Thomas or Thomas the Rimer, was an actual Scottish minstrel of the thirteenth century. He was said to have received the power of prophecy as a gift from the queen of the elves.

QUESTIONS

1. From what kinds of traditional myth does the poem derive? Point out Christian and pagan elements.
2. What impression do we receive of the queen? Is she benevolent or sinister? What popular attitudes toward the supernatural might this characterization reveal?
3. What do you make of the magic apple in lines 66–68? What other celebrated apples does it recall?
4. What statements seem ironies?

John Keats (1795–1821)

La Belle Dame sans Merci

O what can ail thee, knight-at-arms,
  Alone and palely loitering?
The sedge has withered from the lake,
  And no birds sing.   4

O what can ail thee, knight-at-arms,
  So haggard and so woe-begone?
The squirrel's granary is full,
  And the harvest's done.   8

I see a lily on thy brow
  With anguish moist and fever dew,
And on thy cheek a fading rose
  Fast withereth too.   12

"I met a lady in the meads,
  Full beautiful — a faery's child;
Her hair was long, her foot was light,
  And her eyes were wild.   16

"I made a garland for her head,
  And bracelets too, and fragrant zone°;   *belt, sash*
She looked at me as she did love,
  And made sweet moan.   20

"I set her on my pacing steed,
  And nothing else saw all day long,
For sidelong would she bend, and sing
  A faery's song.   24

"She found me roots of relish sweet,
  And honey wild, and manna dew,
And sure in language strange she said —
  'I love thee true!'   28

"She took me to her elfin grot,
  And there she wept and sighed full sore,
And there I shut her wild wild eyes
  With kisses four.   32

"And there she lullèd me asleep,
  And there I dreamed — ah! woe betide!
The latest dream I ever dreamed
  On the cold hill's side.   36

"I saw pale kings and princes too,
  Pale warriors, death-pale were they all;
They cried — 'La Belle Dame sans Merci
  Hath thee in thrall!'   40

"I saw their starved lips in the gloam,
  With horrid warning gapèd wide,
And I awoke and found me here,
  On the cold hill's side.   44

"And this is why I sojourn here,
  Alone and palely loitering,
Though the sedge is withered from the lake
  And no birds sing."   48

LA BELLE DAME SANS MERCI. Keats borrowed this title, "The Lovely Merciless Beauty,"
from a medieval French poem. The text given above is his earliest version.

QUESTIONS

1. What happens in this ballad? What is indicated by the contrast between the
   imagery from nature in lines 17, 18, 25, and 26 and that in lines 3–4, 7–8, 44,
   and 47–48? How do you interpret the knight's *latest dream* (line 35)?
2. What do we know about this beautiful lady without pity? What supernatural
   powers does she possess?
3. In what respects does she resemble the Queen of Elfland in the ballad of
   "Thomas the Rimer"? In what respects does she differ?
4. What other *dames sans merci* do you find in other poems in this book? In
   what respects are they similar? In what respects, if any, is Keats's lady an
   individual?
5. What other relentless beauties with supernatural powers do you know from
   myth, folklore, literature, movies, or television? In what respects, if any, do
   they resemble the *Belle Dame* or Thomas the Rimer's queen?

FOR REVIEW AND FURTHER STUDY

John Milton (1608–1674)

LYCIDAS

*In this monody the author bewails a learned friend, unfortunately drowned in his passage
from Chester on the Irish Seas, 1637. And by occasion foretells the ruin of our corrupted
clergy then in their height.*

Yet once more, O ye laurels, and once more,
Ye myrtles brown°, with ivy never sere,   *dark*
I come to pluck your berries harsh and crude°,   *immature*
And with forced fingers rude

LYCIDAS. Milton's "learned friend" was Edward King, scholar and poet, a fellow student
at Cambridge, who had planned to enter the ministry. In calling him Lycidas, Milton
employs a conventional name for a young shepherd in **pastoral poetry** (which either
portrays the world of shepherds with some realism, as in Virgil's *Eclogues,* or makes it a
prettified Eden, as in Marlowe's "The Passionate Shepherd to His Love"). A *monody,* in
the epigraph, is a song for a single voice. 1–2. *laurels, myrtles:* Evergreens in the crowns
traditionally bestowed upon poets.

Shatter your leaves before the mellowing year.   5
Bitter constraint and sad occasion dear
Compels me to disturb your season due;
For Lycidas is dead, dead ere his prime,
Young Lycidas, and hath not left his peer.
Who would not sing for Lycidas? he knew   10
Himself to sing, and build the lofty rhyme.
He must not floàt upon his wat'ry bier
Unwept, and welter° to the parching wind,   *toss about*
Without the meed° of some melodious tear.   *tribute*
   Begin, then, Sisters of the Sacred Well   15
That from beneath the seat of Jove doth spring,
Begin, and somewhat loudly sweep the string.
Hence with denial vain and coy excuse:
So may some gentle Muse°   *poet*
With lucky words favor my destined urn,   20
And, as he passes, turn,
And bid fair peace be to my sable shroud!
For we were nursed upon the self-same hill,
Fed the same flocks, by fountain, shade, and rill;
   Together both, ere the high lawns appeared   25
Under the opening eyelids of the Morn,
We drove a-field, and both together heard
What time the gray-fly winds° her sultry horn,   *sounds*
Batt'ning° our flocks with the fresh dews of night,   *feeding*
Oft till the star that rose at evening bright   30
Toward Heav'n's descent had sloped his westering wheel.
Meanwhile the rural ditties were not mute,
Tempered to the oaten° flute,   *made of an oat stalk*
Rough satyrs danced, and fauns with cloven heel
From the glad sound would not be absent long;   35
And old Damoetas loved to hear our song.
   But, O the heavy change, now thou art gone,
Now thou art gone, and never must return!
Thee, Shepherd, thee the woods and desert caves,
With wild thyme and the gadding° vine o'ergrown,   *wandering*
And all their echoes mourn.   41
The willows, and the hazel copses green,
Shall now no more be seen
Fanning their joyous leaves to thy soft lays.
As killing as the canker to the rose,   45
Or taint-worm to the weanling herds that gaze,
Or frost to flowers, that their gay wardrobe wear
When first the white thorn blows°;   *blossoms*
Such, Lycidas, thy loss to shepherd's ear.
   Where were ye, Nymphs, when the remorseless deep   50
Closed o'er the head of your loved Lycidas?
For neither were ye playing on the steep

36. *Damoetas:* Perhaps some Cambridge tutor.

Where your old bards, the famous Druids, lie,
Nor on the shaggy top of Mona high,
Nor yet where Deva spreads her wizard stream.   55
Ay me! I fondly° dream!   *foolishly*
"Had ye been there" — for what could that have done?
What could the Muse herself that Orpheus bore,
The Muse herself, for her enchanting son,
Whom universal Nature did lament,   60
When, by the rout° that made the hideous roar,   *mob*
His gory visage down the stream was sent,
Down the swift Hebrus to the Lesbian shore?
    Alas! what boots it° with uncessant care   *what good does it do*
To tend the homely, slighted, shepherd's trade,   65
And strictly meditate the thankless Muse?
Were it not better done, as others use°,   *do*
To sport with Amaryllis in the shade,
Or with the tangles of Neaera's hair?
Fame is the spur that the clear spirit doth raise   70
(That last infirmity of noble mind)
To scorn delights and live laborious days;
But the fair guerdon when we hope to find,
And think to burst out into sudden blaze,
Comes the blind Fury with th' abhorrèd shears,   75
And slits the thin-spun life. "But not the praise,"
Phoebus replied, and touched my trembling ears:
"Fame is no plant that grows on mortal soil,
Nor in the glistering° foil   *glittering*
Set off to the world, nor in broad rumor° lies,   *reputation*   80
But lives and spreads aloft by those pure eyes
And perfect witness of all-judging Jove;
As he pronounces lastly on each deed,
Of so much fame in Heav'n expect thy meed."
    O fountain Arethuse, and thou honored flood,   85
Smooth-sliding Mincius, crowned with vocal reeds,
That strain I heard was of a higher mood:
But now my oat proceeds,
And listens to the Herald of the Sea,
That came in Neptune's plea.   90
He asked the waves, and asked the felon winds,
What hard mishap hath doomed this gentle swain?
And questioned every gust of rugged wings

53. *Druids*: Priests and poets of the Celts in pre-Christian Britain. 54. *Mona*: Roman name for the Isle of Man, near which King was drowned. 55. *Deva*: The River Dee, flowing between England and Wales. Its shifts in course were said to augur good luck for one country or the other. 68–69. *Amaryllis, Neaera*: Conventional names for shepherdesses. 70. *the clear spirit doth raise*: Doth raise the clear spirit. 77. *touched . . . ears*: Gesture signifying "Remember!" 79. *foil*: A setting of gold or silver leaf, used to make a gem appear more brilliant. 85–86. *Arethuse, Mincius*: A fountain and river near the birthplaces of Theocritus and Virgil, respectively, hence recalling the most celebrated writer of pastorals in Greek and the most celebrated in Latin. 90. *in Neptune's plea*: Bringing the sea-god's plea, "not guilty."

That blows from off each beakèd promontory:
They knew not of his story;   95
And sage Hippotades their answer brings,
That not a blast was from his dungeon strayed:
The air was calm, and on the level brine
Sleek Panope with all her sisters played.
It was that fatal and perfidious bark,   100
Built in th' eclipse, and rigged with curses dark,
That sunk so low that sacred head of thine.
  Next, Camus, reverend sire, went footing slow,
His mantle hairy, and his bonnet sedge,
Inwrought with figures dim, and on the edge   105
Like to that sanguine flower inscribed with woe.
"Ah! who hath reft," quoth he, "my dearest pledge?"
Last came, and last did go,
The pilot of the Galilean lake;
Two massy keys he bore of metals twain   110
(The golden opes, the iron shuts amain°).   *with force*
He shook his mitered locks, and stern bespake: —
"How well could I have spared for thee, young swain,
Enow° of such, as for their bellies' sake,   *enough*
Creep, and intrude, and climb into the fold!   115
Of other care they little reck'ning make
Than how to scramble at the shearers' feast,
And shove away the worthy bidden guest.
Blind mouths! that scarce themselves know how to hold
A sheep-hook, or have learned aught else the least   120
That to the faithful herdsman's art belongs!
What recks it them? What need they? they are sped°;   *prosperous*
And, when they list°, their lean and flashy songs   *so incline*
Grate on their scrannel° pipes of wretched straw;   *feeble, harsh*
The hungry sheep look up, and are not fed,   125
But, swoll'n with wind and the rank mist they draw,
Rot inwardly, and foul contagion spread;
Besides what the grim wolf with privy° paw   *stealthy*
Daily devours apace, and nothing said;
But that two-handed engine at the door   130
Stands ready to smite once, and smite no more."

99. *Panope:* A sea nymph. Her name means "one who sees all." 101. *eclipse:* Thought to be an omen of evil fortune. 103. *Camus:* Spirit of the river Cam and personification of Cambridge University. 109–112. *pilot:* Saint Peter, once a fisherman in Galilee, to whom Christ gave the *keys* of Heaven (Matthew 16:19). As first Bishop of Rome, he wears the miter, a bishop's emblematic head-covering. 115. *fold:* The Church of England. 120. *sheep-hook:* A bishop's staff or crozier, which resembles a shepherd's crook. 128. *wolf:* Probably the Church of Rome. Jesuits in England at the time were winning converts. 130. *two-handed engine:* This disputed phrase may refer (among other possibilities) to the punishing sword of The Word of God (Revelation 19:13–15 and Hebrews 4:12). Perhaps Milton sees it as a lightning bolt, as does Spenser, to whom Jove's wrath is a "three-forked engine" (*Faerie Queene*, VIII, 9). 131. *smite once . . . no more:* Because, in the proverb, lightning never strikes twice in the same place?

Return, Alpheus; the dread voice is past
That shrunk thy streams; return, Sicilian Muse,
And call the vales, and bid them hither cast
Their bells and flow'rets of a thousand hues.   135
Ye valleys low, where the mild whispers use°   *resort*
Of shades, and wanton winds, and gushing brooks,
On whose fresh lap the swart star sparely looks,
Throw hither all your quaint enameled eyes,
That on the green turf suck the honied showers,   140
And purple all the ground with vernal flowers.
Bring the rathe° primrose that forsaken dies,   *early*
The tufted crow-toe, and pale jessamine,
The white pink, and the pansy freaked° with jet,   *streaked*
The glowing violet,   145
The musk-rose, and the well-attired woodbine,
With cowslips wan that hang the pensive head,
And every flower that sad embroidery wears;
Bid amaranthus all his beauty shed,
And daffadillies fill their cups with tears,   150
To strew the laureate hearse where Lycid lies.
For so, to interpose a little ease,
Let our frail thoughts dally with false surmise,
Ay me! whilst thee the shores and sounding seas
Wash far away, where'er thy bones are hurled;   155
Whether beyond the stormy Hebrides,
Where thou, perhaps, under the whelming tide
Visit'st the bottom of the monstrous° world;   *full of sea monsters*
Or whether thou, to our moist vows° denied,   *prayers*
Sleep'st by the fable of Bellerus old,   160
Where the great Vision of the guarded mount
Looks toward Namancos and Bayona's hold°:   *stronghold*
Look homeward, angel, now, and melt with ruth°;   *pity*
And, O ye dolphins, waft the hapless youth.
    Weep no more, woeful shepherds, weep no more,   165
For Lycidas, your sorrow, is not dead,
Sunk though he be beneath the wat'ry floor:
So sinks the day-star in the ocean bed
And yet anon repairs his drooping head,
And tricks° his beams, and with new-spangled ore°   *arrays; gold*
Flames in the forehead of the morning sky: 171
So Lycidas sunk low, but mounted high,
Through the dear might of Him that walked the waves,
Where, other groves and other streams along,

133. *Sicilian Muse:* Who inspired Theocritus, a native of Sicily. 138. *swart star:* Sirius, at
its zenith in summer, was thought to turn vegetation black. 153. *false surmise:* Futile hope
that the body of Lycidas could be recovered. 160. *Bellerus:* Legendary giant of Land's End,
the far tip of Cornwall. 161. *guarded mount:* Saint Michael's Mount, off Land's End, said
to be under the protection of the archangel. 162. *Namancos, Bayona:* On the coast of Spain.
164. *dolphins:* In Greek legend, these kindly fish carried the spirits of the dead to the
Blessed Isles.

With nectar pure his oozy locks he laves,   175
And hears the unexpressive nuptial song,
In the blest kingdoms meek of Joy and Love.
There entertain him all the Saints above,
In solemn troops, and sweet societies,
That sing, and singing in their glory move,   180
And wipe the tears forever from his eyes.
Now, Lycidas, the shepherds weep no more;
Henceforth thou art the Genius° of the shore,   *guardian spirit*
In thy large recompense, and shalt be good
To all that wander in that perilous flood.   185

Thus sang the uncouth° swain to th' oaks and rills,   *rustic (or little-known)*
While the still Morn went out with sandals gray;
He touched the tender stops of various quills°,   *reeds of a shepherd's pipe*
With eager thought warbling his Doric lay:
And now the sun had stretched out all the hills,   190
And now was dropped into the western bay.
At last he rose, and twitched° his mantle blue: *donned*
Tomorrow to fresh woods and pastures new.

176. *unexpressive nuptial song:* Inexpressibly beautiful song for the marriage feast of the
Lamb (Revelation 19:9). 189. *Doric lay:* Pastoral poem. Doric is the dialect of Greek employed by Theocritus.

Questions and Exercises

1. With the aid of an encyclopedia or a handbook of classical mythology (such
   as Bulfinch's *Mythology*, Edith Hamilton's *Mythology*, or H. J. Rose's *Handbook of Greek Mythology*) learn more about the following myths or mythical
   figures and places to which Milton alludes:

   Line 15 Sisters of the Sacred Well (Muses)
        16 seat of Jove (Mount Olympus)
        58 the Muse . . . that Orpheus bore (Calliope)
     61–63 (the death of Orpheus)
        75 Fury with the . . . shears (Atropos, one of the three Fates)
        77 Phoebus
        89 Herald of the Sea (Triton)
        90 Neptune
        96 Hippotades
       106 (Hyacinthus)
       132 Alpheus

   Then reread Milton's poem. As a result of your familiarity with these myths,
   what details become clear?
2. Read the parable of the Good Shepherd (John 10:1–18). What relationships
   does Milton draw between the Christian idea of the shepherd and pastoral
   poetry?
3. "With these trifling fictions [allusions to classical mythology]," wrote Samuel
   Johnson about "Lycidas," "are mingled the most awful and sacred truths,
   such as ought never to be polluted with such irreverend combinations."
   Does this mingling of paganism and Christianity detract from Milton's
   poem? Discuss.
4. In "Lycidas" does Milton devise any new myth or myths of his own?

Ishmael Reed (b. 1938)

I Am a Cowboy in the Boat of Ra

"The devil must be forced to reveal any such physical evil (potions, charms, fetishes, etc.) still outside the body and these must be burned." — Rituale Romanum, *published 1947, endorsed by the coat of arms and introduction letter from Francis Cardinal Spellman*

I am a cowboy in the boat of Ra,
sidewinders in the saloons of fools
bit my forehead   like   O
the untrustworthiness of Egyptologists
Who do not know their trips. Who was that   5
dog-faced man? they asked, the day I rode
from town.

School marms with halitosis cannot see
the Nefertiti fake chipped on the run by slick
germans, the hawk behind Sonny Rollins' head or   10
the ritual beard of his axe; a longhorn winding
its bells thru the Field of Reeds.

I am a cowboy in the boat of Ra. I bedded
down with Isis, Lady of the Boogaloo, dove
down deep in her horny, stuck up her Wells-Far-ago   15
in daring midday get away. "Start grabbing the
blue," i said from top of my double crown.

I am a cowboy in the boat of Ra. Ezzard Charles
of the Chisholm Trail. Took up the bass but they
blew off my thumb. Alchemist in ringmanship but a   20
sucker for the right cross.

I am a cowboy in the boat of Ra. Vamoosed from
the temple i bide my time. The price on the wanted
poster was a-going down, outlaw alias copped my stance
and moody greenhorns were making me dance; while my mouth's   25
shooting iron got its chambers jammed.

I am a cowboy in the boat of Ra. Boning-up in
the ol West i bide my time. You should see
me pick off these tin cans whippersnappers. I
write the motown long plays for the comeback of   30
Osiris. Make them up when stars stare at sleeping
steer out here near the campfire. Women arrive
on the backs of goats and throw themselves on
my Bowie.

I am a cowboy in the boat of Ra. Lord of the lash,   35
the Loup Garou Kid. Half breed son of Pisces and
Aquarius. I hold the souls of men in my pot. I do
the dirty boogie with scorpions. I make the bulls
keep still and was the first swinger to grape the taste.

I am a cowboy in his boat. Pope Joan of the   40
Ptah Ra. C/mere a minute willya doll?
Be a good girl and
Bring me my Buffalo horn of black powder
Bring me my headdress of black feathers
Bring me my bones of Ju-Ju snake   45
Go get my eyelids of red paint.
Hand me my shadow
I'm going into town after Set

I am a cowboy in the boat of Ra
look out Set   here i come Set   50
to get Set   to sunset Set
to unseat Set   to Set down Set
                         usurper of the Royal couch
                         imposter RAdio of Moses' bush
                         party pooper O hater of dance   55
                         vampire outlaw of the milky way

I AM A COWBOY IN THE BOAT OF RA. *Ra:* The Egyptian sun god. 9. *Nefertiti:* Queen of Egypt, subject of a painted limestone head displayed in the Staatliche Museum, Berlin. 14. *Isis:* Cow-horned Egyptian goddess of fertility, wife of Osiris. 30. *motown:* A recording company. 31 *Osiris:* God of the lower world whose periodic rebirths were said to cause seeds to sprout and the Nile to rise. 36. *Loup Garou:* French for *werewolf.* 40. *Pope Joan:* Heroine of a novel of the same name by Emmanuel Rhoidès and of another novel by Lawrence Durrell, an adaptation of the same story. Disguised as a man, Pope Joan is elected by the College of Cardinals. 41. *Ptah:* Egyptian god, protector of artists and artisans. 48. *Set:* God of night, evil brother who murdered Osiris. In Egyptian myth, Set and Osiris are perpetually in conflict: desert versus fertile soil, darkness versus light.

QUESTIONS

1. As the preceding notes may indicate, there is much more to this poem than verbal fireworks. How many different myths does Reed draw from? What references does he make to superstitions, alchemy, science-fiction, astrology?
2. What similarities does Reed find between Egyptian mythology and cowboy stories?
3. What is the effect of all the puns? Pick them out.
4. Explain the allusion to Moses in line 54. What connection might there be between Moses and Ra? How might *Field of Reeds* (line 12) also recall the history of Moses?
5. Read this poem aloud. What lines in particular use meaningful sound effects?
6. All in all, does Reed's poem seem a statement of traditional myth or a statement of a personal mythology?

14 Telling Good from Bad

IMPRECISIONS

"The bulk of English poetry is bad," a critic[1] has said, referring to all verse printed over the past six hundred years, not only that which survives in anthologies. As his comment reminds us, excellent poetry is at least as scarce as gold. Though the reader who seeks it for himself can expect to pan through much shale, such labor need not discourage him from prospecting. Only the naïve reader assumes, "This poem must be good, or else why would it appear in a leading magazine?" Only the reader whose mind is coasting in neutral says, "Who knows if this poem is good? Who cares? It all depends upon your point of view." Open-minded, skeptical, and alert, the critical reader will make his own evaluations.

Why do we call some poems "bad"? We are not talking about their moral implications. Rather, we mean that, for one or more of many possible reasons, the poem has failed to move us or to engage our sympathies. Instead, it has made us doubt that the poet is in control of his language and his vision; perhaps it has aroused our antipathies or unwittingly appealed to our sense of the comic, though the poet is serious. Some poems can be said to succeed despite burdensome faults. But in general such faults are symptoms of deeper malady: some weakness in a poem's basic conception or in the poet's competence.

Nearly always, a bad poem reveals only a dim and distorted awareness of its probable effect on an alert reader. Perhaps the sound of words may clash with what a poem is saying, as in the jarring last word of this opening line of a tender lyric (author unknown, quoted by Richard Wilbur): "Come into the tent, my love, and close the flap." Perhaps a metaphor may fail by calling to mind more differences than similarities, as in Emily Dickinson's lines "Our lives are Swiss – / So still – so cool." A bad poem usually overshoots or falls short of its mark by the poet's thinking too little or too much. Thinking much, he con-

[1] Christopher Adams in the preface to his anthology, *The Worst English Poets* (London, 1958).

trives such an excess of ingenuity as that quoted by Alexander Pope in *Peri Bathous,* or *Of the Art of Sinking in Poetry:* a hounded stag who "Hears his own feet, and thinks they sound like more; / And fears the hind feet will o'ertake the fore." Thinking little, he writes redundantly, as Wordsworth in "The Thorn": "And they had fixed the wedding-day, / The morning that must wed them both."

In a poem that has a rime scheme or a set line length, when all is well, pattern and structure move inseparably with the rest of their poem, the way a tiger's skin and bones move with their tiger. But sometimes, in a poem that fails, the poet evidently has had difficulty in persuading his statements to fit a formal pattern. English poets have long felt free to invert word order for a special effect, but the poet having trouble keeping to a rime scheme may invert words for no apparent reason but convenience. Needing a rime for *barge,* he ends his next line with a *policedog large* instead of *a large policedog.* Another sign of trouble is a profusion of adjectives. If a line of iambic pentameter reads, "Her lovely skin, like dear sweet white old silk," we suspect the poet of stuffing the line to make it long enough. Whenever two or more adjectives stand together (in poetry or in good prose), they need to be charged with meaning. No one suspects Matthew Arnold of padding the last line of "To Marguerite": "The unplumbed, salt, estranging sea."

Because, over his dead body, even a poet's slightest and feeblest efforts may be collected, some lines in the canon of celebrated bards make us wonder, "How could he have written this?" Wordsworth, Shelley, Whitman, and Browning are among the great whose failures can be painful, and lapses of awareness may occur even in poems that, taken entire, are excellent. To be unwilling to read them, though, would be as ill advised as to refuse to see Venice just because the Grand Canal is said to contain impurities. The seasoned reader of poetry thinks no less of Tennyson for having written, "Form, Form, Riflemen Form! . . . Look to your butts, and take good aims!" The collected works of a duller poet may contain no such lines of unconscious double meaning, but neither do they contain, perhaps, any poem as good as "Ulysses." If the duller poet never had a spectacular failure, it may be because he never dared take risks.

We flatter ourselves if we think all imprecise poetry the work of times gone by. Poetry editors of current magazines find that about nine hundred out of a thousand unsolicited poems are, at a glance, unworthy of a second reading. Although an editor may have nightmares in which he ignorantly rejects the poems of some new Gerard Manley Hopkins or Emily Dickinson, he sends them back with a printed "thank you" slip, then turns to the hundred that look interesting. How does he winnow them so quickly? Often, inept poems fall into familiar categories. At one extreme is the poem written entirely in conventional diction, dimly echoing lines from Shakespeare, Wordsworth, and the Bible, but garbling and flattening them. Couched in a rhythm that ticks along like a metronome, this kind of poem shows no sign that its author has ever taken a hard look at any particular concrete objects that can be tasted, handled, and felt. It employs loosely and thoughtlessly the most abstract of words: *love, beauty, life, death, time, eternity.* Littered with oldfashioned contractions (*'tis, o'er, where'er*), it may end in a simple platitude or preachment, as if the poet expected us to profit from his wisdom and moral superiority. George Orwell's complaint against much contemporary writing (not only poetry) is applicable: "As soon as certain topics are raised" — and one thinks of such standard topics for poetry as spring, a first kiss, and stars — "the concrete melts into the abstract and no one seems able to think of turns of speech that are not hackneyed." Writers, Orwell charged, too often make their sentences out of tacked-together phrases "like the sections of a prefabricated henhouse."[2] Versifiers often do likewise.

At the opposite extreme is the poem that displays no acquaintance with poetry of the past but manages, instead, to fabricate its own clichés. Slightly paraphrased, a manuscript once submitted to *The Paris Review* began:

Vile
     rottenflush
         o   — *screaming* —
         f CORPSEBLOOD!!   ooze
STRANGLE my
     eyes . . .   H E L L's
        O, ghastly   stench * * !!!

At most, such a work has only a private value. The writer has vented his personal frustrations upon words, instead of kicking stray dogs. In its way, "Vile Rottenflush" is as self-indulgent as the oldfangled "first kiss in spring" kind of poem. Both offend, both inspire distrust. "I dislike," said John Livingston Lowes, "poems that black your eyes, or put up their mouths to be kissed."

As jewelers tell which of two diamonds is fine by seeing which scratches the other, two poems may be tested by comparing them. This method works only on poems similar in length and kind: an epigram cannot rival an epic. Most poems we meet are neither sheer trash nor obvious masterpieces. Since, however, good diamonds to be proven need softer ones to scratch, in this chapter you will find a few clear-cut gems and a few clinkers. "In poetry," said Ronsard, "mediocrity is the greatest vice."

[2] "Politics and the English Language," from *Shooting an Elephant and Other Essays* (New York, 1945).

Anonymous (English; about 1900)
O MOON, WHEN I GAZE ON THY BEAUTIFUL FACE

O Moon, when I gaze on thy beautiful face,
Careering along through the boundaries of space,
The thought has often come into my mind
If I ever shall see thy glorious behind.

O MOON. Sir Edmund Gosse, the English critic (1849–1928), offered this quatrain as the
work of his maidservant, but there is reason to suspect him of having written it.

QUESTIONS
1. To what fact of astronomy does the last line refer?
2. Which words seem chosen with too little awareness of their denotations and
   connotations?
3. Even if you did not know that these lines probably were deliberately bad,
   how would you argue with someone who maintained that the opening *O*
   in the poem was admirable as a bit of concrete poetry? (See the quotation
   from E. E. Cummings on page 199.)

Grace Treasone (publ. 1963)
LIFE

Life is like a jagged tooth
that cuts into your heart;
fix the tooth and save the root,
and laughs, not tears, will start.

William Ernest Henley (1849–1903)
MADAM LIFE'S A PIECE IN BLOOM

Madam Life's a piece in bloom
   Death goes dogging everywhere:
She's the tenant of the room,
   He's the ruffian on the stair.   4

You shall see her as a friend,
   You shall bilk him once or twice;
But he'll trap you in the end,
   And he'll stick you for her price.   8

With his kneebones at your chest,
   And his knuckles in your throat,
You would reason — plead — protest!
   Clutching at her petticoat;   12

But she's heard it all before,
   Well she knows you've had your fun,
Gingerly she gains the door,
   And your little job is done.   16

1. Try to paraphrase the two preceding poems. What is the theme of each?
2. Which statement of theme do you find more convincing? Why?
3. Which poem is the more consistent in working out its metaphor?

Stephen Tropp (b. 1930)

MY WIFE IS MY SHIRT

My wife is my shirt
I put my hands through her armpits
slide my head through her mouth
& finally button her blood around my hands

QUESTIONS

1. How consistently is the metaphor elaborated?
2. Why can this metaphor be said to work in exactly the opposite way from a personification?
3. A paraphrase might discover this simile: "My wife is as intimate, familiar, and close to me as the shirt on my back." If this is the idea and the poem is supposed to be a love poem, how precisely is its attitude expressed?

EXERCISE: *Seeing What Went Wrong*

Here is a small anthology of bad moments in poetry. For what reasons does each selection fail? In which passages do you attribute the failure to inappropriate sound or diction? To awkward word order? To inaccurate metaphor? To excessive overstatement? To forced rime? To monotonous rhythm? To redundancy? To simple-mindedness or excessive ingenuity?

1. From Sir Richard Blackmore's *Paraphrase of the Book of Job:*

   I cannot stifle this gigantic woe,
   Nor on my raging grief a muzzle throw.

2. "I'm Glad," in its entirety, author unknown:

   I'm glad the sky is painted blue,
   And the earth is painted green,
   With such a lot of nice fresh air
   All sandwiched in between.

3. A lover's lament from Harry Edward Mills's *Select Sunflowers:*

   I see her in my fondest moods,
       She haunts the parlor hallway;
   And yet her form my clasp eludes,
       Her lips my kisses alway.

4. A suffering swain makes a vow, from "the poem of a young tradesman" quoted by Coleridge in *Biographia Literaria:*

   No more will I endure love's pleasing pain,
   Or round my heart's leg tie his galling chain.

5. From an elegy for Queen Victoria by one of her Indian subjects:

   Dust to dust, and ashes to ashes,
   Into the tomb the Great Queen dashes.

6. The opening lines of Alice Meynell's "The Shepherdess":

She walks — the lady of my delight —
A shepherdess of sheep.

7. From a juvenile poem of John Dryden, "Upon the Death of the Lord Hastings" (a victim of smallpox):

Blisters with pride swelled; which through's flesh did sprout
Like rose-buds, stuck i' th'lily-skin about.
Each little pimple had a tear in it,
To wail the fault its rising did commit . . .

8. A poet discusses the pity he feels for the newborn, from J. W. Scholl's *The Light-Bearer of Liberty:*

Gooing babies, helpless pygmies,
Who shall solve your Fate's enigmas?
Who shall save you from Earth's stigmas?

9. A metaphor from Edgar A. Guest's "The Crucible of Life":

Sacred and sweet is the joy that must come
From the furnace of life when you've poured off the scum.

10. A stanza composed by Samuel Johnson as a deliberately bad example:

I put my hat upon my head
And walked into the Strand;
And there I met another man
Whose hat was in his hand.

11. A lover describes his lady, from Thomas Holley Chivers's "Rosalie Lee":

Many mellow Cydonian suckets,
  Sweet apples, anthosmial, divine,
From the ruby-rimmed beryline buckets,
  Star-gemmed, lily-shaped, hyaline:
Like the sweet golden goblet found growing
  On the wild emerald cucumber-tree,
Rich, brilliant, like chrysoprase glowing,
  Was my beautiful Rosalie Lee.

12. Lines on a sick gypsy, author unknown, quoted in *The Stuffed Owl, an Anthology of Bad Verse,* edited by D. B. Wyndham Lewis and Charles Lee:

There we leave her,
There we leave her,
Far from where her swarthy kindred roam,
In the Scarlet Fever,
Scarlet Fever,
Scarlet Fever Convalescent Home.

SENTIMENTALITY

Sentimentality is the failure of a writer who implies that he feels great emotion but who fails to give us sufficient grounds for sharing it. His emotion may be an anger greater than its object seems to call for, as in these lines to a girl who caused scandal (the exact nature of her act never being specified): "The gossip in each hall / Will curse your name . . . /

Go! better cast yourself right down the falls!"[3] Or it may be an enthusiasm quite unwarranted by its subject: in *The Fleece* John Dyer temptingly describes the pleasures of life in a workhouse for the poor. The sentimental poet is especially prone to tenderness. Great tears fill his eyes at a glimpse of an aged grandmother sitting by a hearth. For all he knows, she may be the well-to-do manager of a casino in Las Vegas, who would be startled to find herself an object of pity, but the sentimentalist seems not to care to know much about the lady herself. He employs her as a general excuse for feeling maudlin. Any other conventional object will serve him as well: a faded valentine, the strains of an old song, a baby's cast-off pacifier. A celebrated instance of such emotional self-indulgence is "The Old Oaken Bucket," by Samuel Woodworth, a stanza of which goes:

How sweet from the green, mossy brim to receive it,
    As, poised on the curb, it inclined to my lips!
Not a full-blushing goblet could tempt me to leave it,
    Tho' filled with the nectar that Jupiter sips.
And now, far removed from the loved habitation,
    The tear of regret will intrusively swell,
As fancy reverts to my father's plantation,
    And sighs for the bucket that hung in the well.

As a symbol, the bucket might conceivably be made to hold the significance of the past and the speaker's regret at being caught in the destroying grip of time. But the staleness of the phrasing and imagery (Jove's nectar, *tear of regret*) suggests that the speaker is not even seeing the actual physical bucket, and the tripping meter of the lines is inappropriate to an expression of tearful regret. Perhaps the poet's nostalgia is genuine. We need not doubt it; indeed, as Keith Waldrop has put it, "a bad poem is always utterly and profoundly sincere." However sincere in his feelings, the sentimental poet is insincere in his art — otherwise, he might take the trouble to write a better poem or at least to burn the one he wrote. By the vagueness of his language and the monotony of his rhythms, Woodworth fails to persuade us that we ought to care. Wet-eyed and sighing for a bucket, he achieves not pathos but **bathos:** a description that can move us to laughter instead of tears.[4]

Tears, of course, can be shed for good reason. A piece of sentimentality is not to be confused with a well-wrought poem whose tone is tenderness. At first glance, the following poem by Burns might strike you as sentimental. If so, your suspicions are understandable, for it is a

---

[3] Ali S. Hilmi, "The Preacher's Sermon," in *Verse at Random* (Larnaca, Cyprus, 1953).
[4] *Bathos* in poetry can also mean an abrupt fall from the sublime to the trivial or incongruous. A sample, from Nicholas Rowe's play *The Fair Penitent:* "Is it the voice of thunder, or my father?" Another, from John Close, a minor Victorian: "Around their heads a dazzling halo shone, / No need of mortal robes, or any hat." When, however, such a letdown is used for a *desirable* effect of humor or contrast, it is usually called an **anticlimax:** as in Alexander Pope's lines on the queen's palace, "Here thou, great Anna! whom three realms obey, / Dost sometimes counsel take — and sometimes tea."

rare poet who can speak honestly or effectively on the theme that love grows deeper as lovers grow old. Many a popular song-writer has seen the process of aging as valuable: "Darling, I am growing old, / Silver threads among the gold." According to such songs, to grow decrepit is a privilege. What is fresh in Burns's poem, however, is that no attempt is made to gloss over the ravages of age and the inevitability of death. The speaker expresses no self-pity, no comment *about* her feelings, only a simple account of what has befallen her and her John and what is still to follow.

Robert Burns (1759–1796)

JOHN ANDERSON MY JO, JOHN

John Anderson my jo°, John,	*dear*
When we were first acquent°,	*acquainted*
Your locks were like the raven,	
Your bonny brow was brent°;	*unwrinkled* 4
But now your brow is beld°, John,	*bald*
Your locks are like the snaw;	
But blessings on your frosty pow°,	*head*
John Anderson my jo.	8
John Anderson my jo, John,	
We clamb the hill thegither;	
And mony a canty° day, John,	*happy*
We've had wi' ane anither:	12
Now we maun° totter down, John,	*must*
And hand in hand we'll go,	
And sleep thegither at the foot,	
John Anderson my jo.	16

EXERCISE: *Fine or Shoddy Tenderness*

Which of the following poems, if any, do you find sentimental? Which would you defend? Why? At least one kind of evidence to look for is minute, detailed observation of physical objects. In a successful poem, the poet is likely at least occasionally to notice the world beyond his own skin; in a sentimental poem, this world is likely to be ignored while the poet contemplates his feelings. So that the poet's reputation (or lack of reputation) will not distract you, the poems are printed without by-lines.

THE BULL CALF

The thing could barely stand. Yet taken
from his mother and the barn smells
he still impressed with his pride,
with the promise of sovereignty in the way
his head moved to take us in.   5
The fierce sunlight tugging the maize from the ground
licked at his shapely flanks.
He was too young for all that pride.
I thought of the deposed Richard II.

"No money in bull calves," Freeman had said.
The visiting clergyman rubbed the nostrils
now snuffing pathetically at the windless day.
"A pity," he sighed.
My gaze slipped off his hat toward the empty sky
that circled over the black knot of men,   15
over us and the calf waiting for the first blow.

Struck,
the bull calf drew in his thin forelegs
as if gathering strength for a mad rush . . .
tottered . . . raised his darkening eyes to us,   20
and I saw we were at the far end
of his frightened look, growing smaller and smaller
till we were only the ponderous mallet
that flicked his bleeding ear
and pushed him over on his side, stiffly,   25
like a block of wood.

Below the hill's crest
the river snuffled on the improvised beach.
We dug a deep pit and threw the dead calf into it.
It made a wet sound, a sepulchral gurgle,   30
as the warm sides bulged and flattened.
Settled, the bull calf lay as if asleep,
one foreleg over the other,
bereft of pride and so beautiful now,
without movement, perfectly still in the cool pit,   35
I turned away and wept.

The Old Arm-Chair

I love it, I love it! and who shall dare
To chide me for loving that old arm-chair?
I've treasured it long as a sainted prize,
I've bedewed it with tears, I've embalmed it with sighs,   4
'Tis bound by a thousand bands to my heart;
Not a tie will break, not a link will start.
Would you know the spell? — a mother sat there!
And a sacred thing is that old arm-chair.   8

In childhood's hour I lingered near
The hallowed seat with listening ear;
And gentle words that mother would give
To fit me to die and teach me to live.   12
She told me that shame would never betide
With truth for my creed, and God for my guide;
She taught me to lisp my earliest prayer,
As I knelt beside that old arm-chair.   16

I sat and watched her many a day,
When her eyes grew dim, and her locks were gray;

And I almost worshipped her when she smiled,
And turned from her Bible to bless her child.   20
Years rolled on, but the last one sped, —
My idol was shattered, my earth-star fled!
I learned how much the heart can bear,
When I saw her die in her old arm-chair.   24

'Tis past, 'tis past! but I gaze on it now,
With quivering breath and throbbing brow;
'Twas there she nursed me, 'twas there she died,
And memory flows with a lava tide.   28
Say it is folly, and deem me weak,
Whilst scalding drops start down my cheek;
But I love it, I love it! and cannot tear
My soul from a mother's old arm-chair.   32

PIANO

Softly, in the dusk, a woman is singing to me;
Taking me back down the vista of years, till I see
A child sitting under the piano, in the boom of the tingling strings
And pressing the small, poised feet of a mother who smiles as she sings.   4

In spite of myself, the insidious mastery of song
Betrays me back, till the heart of me weeps to belong
To the old Sunday evenings at home, with winter outside
And hymns in the cozy parlor, the tinkling piano our guide.   8

So now it is vain for the singer to burst into clamor
With the great black piano appassionato. The glamor
Of childish days is upon me, my manhood is cast
Down in the flood of remembrance, I weep like a child for the past.   12

TEARS, IDLE TEARS, I KNOW NOT WHAT THEY MEAN

Tears, idle tears, I know not what they mean,
Tears from the depth of some divine despair
Rise in the heart, and gather to the eyes,
In looking on the happy autumn-fields,
And thinking of the days that are no more.   5

Fresh as the first beam glittering on a sail,
That brings our friends up from the under-world,
Sad as the last which reddens over one
That sinks with all we love below the verge;
So sad, so fresh, the days that are no more.   10

Ah, sad and strange as in dark summer dawns
The earliest pipe of half-awakened birds
To dying ears, when unto dying eyes
The casement slowly grows a glimmering square;
So sad, so strange, the days that are no more.   15

Dear as remembered kisses after death,
And sweet as those by hopeless fancy feigned
On lips that are for others; deep as love,
Deep as first love, and wild with all regret;
O Death in Life, the days that are no more.   20

PARODY

A sentimental poem is particularly vulnerable to **parody:** a kind of literary composition in which one writer pokes fun at another by imitating him. A parody has a definite attitude toward its original. In skilled hands, it can be a terse, forceful, and detailed evaluation. Generally the parodist imitates the characteristic tone, form, diction, and other features of the original but applies them to ludicrously inappropriate matter, as in E. B. White's take-off on Walt Whitman's "A Classic Waits for Me," which employs the rhetoric of the chest-thumping bard in a pledge of allegiance to a mail-order book club.[5] Rather than fling abuse at his original, the skilled parodist imitates it with understanding, perhaps with affection. The many inadequate parodies of T. S. Eliot's difficult poem *The Waste Land* show the parodists mocking what they do not understand, and their effect is not to illuminate the original but to belittle it. Parody can be aimed at good and bad poems, but there are poems of such splendor and dignity that no parodist seems able to touch them without looking like a small dog defiling a cathedral, and there are poems so illiterate that parody would be squandered on them. In the following original by T. E. Brown, what failings does the parodist jump upon? (*God wot* is an archaism for "God knows.")

T. E. Brown (1830–1897)
My Garden

A garden is a lovesome thing,
    God wot!
Rose plot,
Fringed pool,
Ferned grot —
The veriest school
Of peace; and yet the fool
Contends that God is not —
Not God! in gardens! when the eve
    is cool?
Nay, but I have a sign;
'Tis very sure God walks in mine.

J. A. Lindon (b. 1914)
My Garden

A garden is a *lovesome* thing?
    What rot!
Weed plot,
Scum pool,
Old pot,
Snail-shiny stool
In pieces; yet the fool
Contends that snails are not —
Not snails! in gardens! when the
    eve is cool?
Nay, but I see their trails!
'Tis very sure *my* garden's full of
    snails!

[5] For this and other specimens, see the anthology *Parodies,* edited by Dwight Macdonald (New York, 1960).

Hugh Kingsmill
[Hugh Kingsmill Lunn] (1889–1949)
WHAT, STILL ALIVE AT TWENTY-TWO

What, still alive at twenty-two,
A clean, upstanding chap like you?
Sure, if your throat 'tis hard to slit,
Slit your girl's, and swing for it.   4

Like enough, you won't be glad
When they come to hang you, lad:
But bacon's not the only thing
That's cured by hanging from a string.   8

So, when the spilt ink of the night
Spreads o'er the blotting-pad of light,
Lads whose job is still to do
Shall whet their knives, and think of you.   12

QUESTIONS

1. A. E. Housman considered this the best of many parodies of his poetry.
   Read his poems in this book, particularly "To an Athlete Dying Young" and
   "Terence, this is stupid stuff" (pp. 352–354). What characteristics of theme,
   form, and language does Hugh Kingsmill's parody convey?
2. What does Kingsmill exaggerate?

Kenneth Koch (b. 1925)
MENDING SUMP

"Hiram, I think the sump is backing up.
The bathroom floor boards for above two weeks
Have seemed soaked through. A little bird, I think,
Has wandered in the pipes, and all's gone wrong."
"Something there is that doesn't hump a sump,"   5
He said; and through his head she saw a cloud
That seemed to twinkle. "Hiram, well," she said,
"Smith is come home! I saw his face just now
While looking through your head. He's come to die
Or else to laugh, for hay is dried-up grass   10
When you're alone." He rose, and sniffed the air.
"We'd better leave him in the sump," he said.

QUESTIONS

1. What poet is the object of this parody? Which of his poems are echoed in it?
2. Koch gains humor by making outrageous statements in the tone and language of his original. Looking at other poems in this book by the poet being
   parodied, how would you describe their tone? Their language?

3. Suppose, instead of casting his parody into blank verse, Koch had written:

"Hiram, the sump is backing up.
The bathroom floor boards
For above two weeks
Have been soaking through. A little bird,
I think, has wandered in
The pipes, and all's gone wrong."

Why would the biting edge of his parody have been blunted?
4. What, by the way, is a *sump*?

EXPERIMENT: *Writing a Parody*

Write a parody of Walt Whitman, Emily Dickinson, Thomas Hardy, or any other modern poet whose work interests you and whose forms you feel skillful enough to imitate. In preparation, read all the poet's work included in this book; see also his collected poems; then carefully evaluate the poet's strengths and weaknesses. You may find it simplest to choose one particular poem as the model for your parody, or you may wish to echo many poems. In either case, it might be helpful to select a subject or theme characteristic of the poet.

FOR REVIEW AND FURTHER STUDY

Rod McKuen (b. 1933)

THOUGHTS ON CAPITAL PUNISHMENT

There ought to be capital punishment for cars
that run over rabbits and drive into dogs
and commit the unspeakable, unpardonable crime
of killing a kitty cat still in his prime.

Purgatory, at the very least   5
          should await the driver
    driving over a beast.

Those hurrying headlights coming out of the dark
that scatter the scampering squirrels in the park
should await the best jury that one might compose   10
of fatherless chipmunks and husbandless does.

And then found guilty, after too fair a trial
should be caged in a cage with a hyena's smile
or maybe an elephant with an elephant gun
should shoot out his eyes when the verdict is done.   15

There ought to be something, something that's fair
to avenge Mrs. Badger as she waits in her lair
for her husband who lies with his guts spilling out
cause he didn't know what automobiles are about.

Hell on the highway, at the very least   20
        should await the driver
driving over a beast.

Who kills a man kills a bit of himself
But a cat too is an extension of God.

William Stafford (b. 1914)
TRAVELING THROUGH THE DARK

Traveling through the dark I found a deer
dead on the edge of the Wilson River road.
It is usually best to roll them into the canyon:
that road is narrow; to swerve might make more dead.   4

By glow of the tail-light I stumbled back of the car
and stood by the heap, a doe, a recent killing;
she had stiffened already, almost cold.
I dragged her off; she was large in the belly.   8

My fingers touching her side brought me the reason —
her side was warm; her fawn lay there waiting,
alive, still, never to be born.
Beside that mountain road I hesitated.   12

The car aimed ahead its lowered parking lights;
under the hood purred the steady engine.
I stood in the glare of the warm exhaust turning red;
around our group I could hear the wilderness listen.   16

I thought hard for us all — my only swerving —
then pushed her over the edge into the river.   18

QUESTIONS

1. Compare these poems by Rod McKuen and William Stafford. How are they
   similar in subject?
2. Explain Stafford's title. Who are all those traveling through the dark?
3. Comment on McKuen's use of language: how consistent is it? Consider
   especially: *unspeakable, unpardonable crime* (line 3), *kitty cat* (4), *scatter the
   scampering squirrels* (9), and *cause he didn't know* (19).
4. Compare the meaning of Stafford's last two lines and McKuen's last two.
   Does either poem have a moral? Can either poem be said to moralize?
5. How just is McKuen's justice? How well does the punishment fit the crime?
6. Which poem might be open to the charge of sentimentality? Why?

EXERCISE: *Making Comparisons*

Here are three poems roughly similar in theme and dramatic situation. Compare them and try to describe their relative effectiveness. In any of them, is
there a skillful flight or a definite floundering? If so, how do you account for it?
(The names of the poets are omitted.)

Janet Waking

Beautifully Janet slept
Till it was deeply morning. She woke then
And thought about her dainty-feathered hen,
To see how it had kept.   4

One kiss she gave her mother,
Only a small one gave she to her daddy
Who would have kissed each curl of his shining baby;
No kiss at all for her brother.   8

"Old Chucky, Old Chucky!" she cried,
Running on little pink feet upon the grass
To Chucky's house, and listening. But alas,
Her Chucky had died.   12

It was a transmogrifying° bee   *change-working*
Came droning down on Chucky's old bald head
And sat and put the poison. It scarcely bled,
But how exceedingly   16

And purply did the knot
Swell with the venom and communicate
Its rigor! Now the poor comb stood up straight
But Chucky did not.   20

So there was Janet
Kneeling on the wet grass, crying her brown hen
(Translated far beyond the daughters of men)
To rise and walk upon it.   24

And weeping fast as she had breath
Janet implored us, "Wake her from her sleep!"
And would not be instructed in how deep
Was the forgetful kingdom of death.   28

Mary and Her Dead Canary

Sad Words to a Jovial Air

I weep when the gay are around me,
I'm sad when my slumbers have bound me;
And perchance, ye'll smile to know
That in dreams I often go
    To the weeping willow drooping, where my Jimmie lies so low.   5

O, the robin's songs in the wildwood!
They were love in the heart of my childhood.
Yet far sweeter then they
Was the music of the lay
    That my Jimmie used to sing, till his life fled away.   10

It was sad, oh, so fondly to love him,
And to look while the earth fell above him.
Thus, my Jimmie, will it be,
As it ever is with me,
    That the things I love the dearest, best, will wither first, like thee.   15

Is there one, who hath tears, one only,
Who could weep for my sorrow so lonely?
Such a friend I'd fondly crave,
Who could feel the griefs I have,
    And would with me shed a tear-drop on my dead Canary's grave.   20

SPRING AND FALL

To a Young Child

Márgarét, are you grieving   *are you crying over the changing of the seasons.*
Over Goldengrove unleaving°?   *shedding its leaves*   2
Leáves, like the things of man, you   *can you with your young*
With your fresh thoughts care for, can you?   *thoughts for these leaves as if they were human.*   4
Ah! ás the heart grows older   6
It will come to such sights colder
By and by, nor spare a sigh   *mulch*   *as you get older*
Though worlds of wanwood leafmeal lie;   *lots* *the wood*   *you will still weep*
And yet you will weep and know why.   *for these things but you'll know why.*   9
Now no matter, child, the name: 11
Sórrow's spríngs áre the same.   *the sources of sorrow are the same.*
Nor mouth had, no nor mind, expressed
What heart heard of, ghost° guessed: *spirit*   13
It ís the blight man was born for,   *you mourn for your self because you know*   15
It is Margaret you mourn for.   *that you are going to die*

about the process of dying
mortality
loss of innocence
life & death.

[marginal notes, left side:] why do you have intellectual? why you feel... do you have a soul

15 Knowing Excellence

How can we tell an excellent poem from any other? To give reasons for excellence in poetry is harder than to give reasons for failure in poetry (so often due to familiar, old-hat sorts of imprecision and sentimentality). A bad poem tends to be stereotyped, an excellent poem unique. In judging either, we can have no absolute pre-existing specifications. A poem is not a simple mechanism like an electric toaster that an inspector in a factory can test by a check-off list. It has to be judged on the basis of what it evidently is trying to be and how well it succeeds in its effort. Nor is excellence simply due to regularity and symmetry. For the sake of meaning, a competent poet often will depart from a pattern. There is satisfaction, said Robert Frost, in things not mechanically straight: "We enjoy the straight crookedness of a good walking stick."

To judge a poem, we first have to understand it. At least, we need to understand it *almost* all the way; there is, to be sure, a poem such as Hopkins's "The Windhover" (p. 349), which most readers probably would call excellent even though its meaning is still being debated. While it is a good idea to give a poem at least a couple of considerate readings before judging it, sometimes our first encounter with a poem starts turning into an act of evaluation. Moving along into the poem, becoming more deeply involved in it, we may begin forming an opinion. In general, the more a poem contains for us to understand, the more rewarding we are likely to find it. This does not mean that an obscure and highly demanding poem is always to be preferred to a relatively simple one. Difficult poems can be pretentious and incoherent, but there is something to be said for the poem complicated enough to leave us something to discover on our fifteenth reading (unlike most limericks, which yield their all at a single look). Here is such a poem, one not readily fathomed and exhausted.

William Butler Yeats (1865–1939)

SAILING TO BYZANTIUM

That is no country for old men. The young
In one another's arms, birds in the trees
— Those dying generations — at their song,
The salmon-falls, the mackerel-crowded seas,   4
Fish, flesh, or fowl, commend all summer long
Whatever is begotten, born, and dies.
Caught in that sensual music all neglect
Monuments of unaging intellect.   8

An aged man is but a paltry thing,
A tattered coat upon a stick, unless
Soul clap its hands and sing, and louder sing
For every tatter in its mortal dress,   12
Nor is there singing school but studying
Monuments of its own magnificence;
And therefore I have sailed the seas and come
To the holy city of Byzantium.   16

O sages standing in God's holy fire
As in the gold mosaic of a wall,
Come from the holy fire, perne in a gyre°,   *spin down in a spiral*
And be the singing-masters of my soul.   20
Consume my heart away; sick with desire
And fastened to a dying animal
It knows not what it is; and gather me
Into the artifice of eternity.   24

Once out of nature I shall never take
My bodily form from any natural thing,
But such a form as Grecian goldsmiths make
Of hammered gold and gold enameling   28
To keep a drowsy Emperor awake;
Or set upon a golden bough to sing
To lords and ladies of Byzantium
Of what is past, or passing, or to come.   32

SAILING TO BYZANTIUM. Byzantium was the capital of the Byzantine Empire, the city now called Istanbul. Yeats means, though, not merely the physical city. Byzantium is also a name for his conception of paradise.

Though *salmon-falls* (line 4) suggests Yeats's native Ireland, the poem, as we find out in line 25, is about escaping from the entire natural world. If the poet desires this escape, then probably the *country* mentioned in the opening line is no political nation but the cycle of birth and death in which human beings are trapped; and, indeed, the poet says his heart is "fastened to a dying animal." Imaginary landscapes, it would seem, are merging with the historical Byzantium. Lines 17–18 refer to mosaic images, adornments of the Byzantine cathedral of St. Sophia, in which the figures of saints are inlaid against backgrounds of gold. The clockwork bird of the last stanza is also a reference to something actual. Yeats noted: "I have read somewhere that in the Emperor's palace at Byzantium was a tree made of gold and silver, and artificial birds that sang." This description of the role the poet would seek — that of a changeless, immortal singer — directs us back to the earlier references to music and singing. Taken all together, they point toward the central metaphor of the poem: the craft of poetry can be a kind of singing. One kind of everlasting monument is a great poem. To study masterpieces of poetry is the only "singing school" — the only way to learn to write a poem.

We have no more than skimmed through a few of this poem's suggestions, enough to show that, out of allusion and imagery, Yeats has woven at least one elaborate metaphor. Surely one thing the poem achieves is that, far from merely puzzling us, it makes us aware of relationships between what a man can imagine and his physical world. There is the statement that a man's heart is bound to the body that perishes, and yet it is possible for him to see his consciousness for a moment independent of flesh, to sing with joy at the very fact that his body is crumbling from under him. Expressing a similar view of mortality, the Japanese artist Hokusai has shown a withered tree letting go of its few remaining leaves, while under it two graybeards shake with laughter. Like Hokusai's view, that of Yeats is by no means simple. Much of the power of his poem comes from the physical terms with which he states the ancient quarrel between body and spirit, body being a "tattered coat upon a stick." There is all the difference in the world between the work of the poet like Yeats whose eye is on the living thing and whose mind is awake and passionate, and that of the slovenly poet whose dull eye and sleepy mind focus on nothing more than some book he hastily read long ago. The former writes a poem as if he would die if he did not, the latter as if he thinks it might be a nice idea to write something.

Yeats's poem has the three qualities essential to beauty, according to the definition of Thomas Aquinas: wholeness, harmony, and radiance. The poem is all one; its parts move in peace with one another; it shines with emotional intensity. There is an orderly progression going on in it: from the speaker's statement of his discontent with the world of "sensual music," to his statement that he is quitting this world, to his prayer that the sages will take him in, and his vision of future immortality. And the images of the poem relate to one another — *dying generations* (line 3), *dying animal* (line 22), and the undying golden bird (lines 27–32) — to mention just one series of related things. "Sailing to Byzantium" is not the kind of poem that has, in Pope's words, "One simile, that solitary shines / In the dry desert of a thousand lines." Rich in figurative language, Yeats's whole poem develops a metaphor, with further metaphors as its tributaries.

"Sailing to Byzantium" has a theme that matters to us. What human being does not long, at times, to shed his timid, imperfect flesh, to live in a state of absolute joy, unperishing? Being human, perhaps we too are stirred by Yeats's prayer: "Consume my heart away, sick with desire / And fastened to a dying animal. . . ." If it is true that in poetry (as Ezra Pound declared) "Only emotion endures," then Yeats's poem ought to endure. (No reasons to be moved by a poem, however, can be of much use. If you happen not to feel moved by this particular poem, just try another — but then come back to "Sailing to Byzantium" after a while.)

Most excellent poems, it might be argued, contain significant themes, as does "Sailing to Byzantium." But the presence of such a theme is not enough to render a poem excellent. That classic tear-jerker "The Old Arm-Chair" (p. 245) expresses in its way, too, faith in a kind of immortality. Not theme alone makes an excellent poem, but how a theme is stated.

Yeats's poem, some would say, is the match of any lyric in our language. Some might call it inferior to an epic (to Milton's *Paradise Lost,* say, or to the *Iliad*), but this is to lead us into a different argument: whether certain genres are innately better than others. Such an argument usually leads to a dead end. Evidently, *Paradise Lost* has greater range, variety, matter, length, and ambitiousness. But any poem — whether an epic or an epigram — may be judged by how well it fulfills the design it undertakes. God, who created both fleas and whales, pronounced all good. Fleas, like manmade epigrams, have no reason to feel inferior.

EXERCISE: *Two Poems to Compare*

Here are two poems with a similar theme. Which contains more qualities of excellent poetry? Decide whether the other is bad or whether it may be praised for achieving something different.

Arthur Guiterman (1871–1943)

ON THE VANITY OF EARTHLY GREATNESS

The tusks that clashed in mighty brawls
Of mastodons, are billiard balls.   2

The sword of Charlemagne the Just
Is ferric oxide, known as rust.   4

The grizzly bear whose potent hug
Was feared by all, is now a rug.   6

Great Caesar's bust is on the shelf,
And I don't feel so well myself.   8

Percy Bysshe Shelley (1792–1822)

OZYMANDIAS

I met a traveler from an antique land
Who said: Two vast and trunkless legs of stone
Stand in the desert. Near them, on the sand,
Half sunk, a shattered visage lies, whose frown,
And wrinkled lip, and sneer of cold command,   5
Tell that its sculptor well those passions read
Which yet survive, stamped on these lifeless things,
The hand that mocked° them and the heart that fed;   *imitated*
And on the pedestal these words appear:
"My name is Ozymandias, king of kings: 10
Look on my works, ye Mighty, and despair!"
Nothing beside remains. Round the decay
Of that colossal wreck, boundless and bare
The lone and level sands stretch far away.   14

Some people believe that they can tell the excellence of a poem by the moral uplift of its message. By this standard, Longfellow's "A Psalm of Life" is certainly notable for its cheerful exhortations, "Life is real! Life is earnest!" and for its conclusion,

> Let us, then, be up and doing,
>   With a heart for any fate;
> Still achieving, still pursuing,
>   Learn to labor and to wait.

Such a view was more common a century ago than it now is. Recent critics have felt that Longfellow elsewhere wrote much better poetry. Their complaint is not that a poem must not preach but that a poem must do much more besides preaching. "We must love one another or die," said W. H. Auden. "The woods are lovely, dark and deep, / But I have promises to keep," said Robert Frost. No less than Longfellow's "Life is real! Life is earnest!" each of these statements takes a moral stand. In their contexts, however, Auden and Frost's lines — unlike Longfellow's — work with the emotional power and richness of connotation we expect of poetry.

Some excellent poems of the past will remain sealed to us unless we are willing to sympathize with their conventions. Pastoral poetry, for instance — Marlowe's "Passionate Shepherd" and Milton's "Lycidas" — asks us to accept certain conventions and situations that may seem old-fashioned: idle swains, oaten flutes. We are under no grim duty, of course, to admire poems whose conventions do not appeal to us. But there is no point in blaming a poet for playing the particular game he wishes to play, or for observing its rules.

One way to notice the literary conventions of an age, past or present, is to see how its poets translate the Greek and Roman classics. For his version of the *Iliad* (1720), Alexander Pope accepted the prevailing poetic diction, designed to exclude coarse lowly words and keep poetry lofty. He elected to write in heroic couplets, then thought to be the English verse form most appropriate to an epic. From Book 14 (lines 469–92), here is Pope's rendition of the temporary felling of Hector, the Trojan leader:

> Then back the disappointed Trojan drew,
> And cursed the lance that unavailing flew:
> But 'scaped not Ajax; his tempestuous hand
> A pond'rous stone up-heaving from the sand
> (Where heaps, laid loose beneath the warrior's feet,
> Or° served to ballast, or to prop the fleet),   *either*
> Tossed round and round, the missive° marble flings;   *intended for*
> On the raised shield the falling ruin rings,   *sending*
> Full on his breast and throat with force descends;
> Nor deadened there its giddy fury spends,
> But, whirling on, with many a fiery round,
> Smokes in the dust, and ploughs into the ground.
> As when the bolt, red-hissing from above,
> Darts on the consecrated plant of Jove,
> The mountain-oak in flaming ruin lies,
> Black from the blow, and smokes of sulphur rise:
> Stiff with amaze the pale beholders stand,
> And own the terrors of th' almighty hand!
> So lies great Hector prostrate on the shore;
> His slackened hand deserts the lance it bore;
> His foll'wing shield the fallen chief o'erspread;
> Beneath his helmet, dropped his fainting head;
> His load of armor, sinking to the ground,
> Clanks on the field: a dead and hollow sound.

To repackage Homer's epic in the couplets' series of little boxes, Pope had to invent some thoughts and leave out others. His poetic diction, clearly, is not ours: we avoid contractions like *pond'rous* and *'scaped* and might prefer not to call a flung rock a *missive marble*. But Pope had an eye for a word rich in suggestion: "His slackened hand *deserts* the lance it bore" (as though the hand of the unconscious hero were a soldier fleeing). And his lines have a vigorous music: the *red-hissing* bolt, the armor that *sinking, clanks*. Pope's achievement was to make *The Iliad* come alive for readers of his day as no English translator had done before. (In the next century, John Keats, who shunned heroic couplets, much preferred George Chapman's version of 1612 — as Keats tells us in his sonnet, on page 63.) Compare the effect of Pope's well-groomed, chiming couplets with the effect of this same episode in the words of a recent translator, Richmond Lattimore (1951), who takes fewer lines to tell the story than Pope does, but longer ones:

> And Hektor, in anger
> because his weapon had been loosed from his hand in a vain cast,

to avoid death shrank into the host of his own companions.
But as he drew away huge Telamonian Aias
caught up a rock; there were many, holding-stones for the fast ships,
rolled among the feet of the fighters; he caught up one of these
and hit him in the chest next the throat over his shield rim,
and spun him around like a top with the stroke, so that he staggered
in a circle; as a great oak goes down root-torn under
Zeus father's stroke, and a horrible smell of sulphur uprises
from it, and there is no courage left in a man who stands by
and looks on, for the thunderstroke of great Zeus is a hard thing;
so Hektor in all his strength dropped suddenly in the dust, let
fall the spear from his hand, and his shield was beaten upon him,
and the helm, and his armor elaborate with bronze clashed over him.

Now, there, exclaims the modern reader, there's the way Homer ought to sound — none of that poetic diction stuff! But Lattimore's excellent version chooses its own particular conventions. In its long run-on sentence full of monosyllables, Lattimore's description of how the rock struck Hector (*hit him in the chest next the throat over his shield rim, / and spun him around like a top*) recalls the style of modern writers on war and prize-fighting, among them Ernest Hemingway. "I have used," Lattimore has said, "the plainest language I could find which might be adequate, and mostly this is the language of contemporary prose." It is not that Lattimore is right in his practice and Pope is wrong or vice versa. For having both *Iliads,* our literature is richer and more various.

Excellent poetry might be easier to recognize if each poet had a fixed position on the slopes of Mount Parnassus, but from one century to the next, the reputations of some poets have taken humiliating slides or have made impressive clambers. We decide for ourselves which poems to call excellent, but we admit that readers of the future may reverse our opinions. Most of us no longer would share this popular view of Walt Whitman, by one of his contemporaries:

> Walt Whitman (1819–1892), by some regarded as a great poet; by others, as no poet at all. Most of his so-called poems are mere catalogues of things, without meter or rime, but in a few more regular poems and in lines here and there he is grandly poetical, as in "O Captain! My Captain!"[1]

There is nothing to do but commit ourselves and praise or blame and, if need be, let time erase our error. In a sense, all readers of poetry are constantly re-examining the judgments of the past by choosing those poems they care to go on reading.

[1] J. Willis Westlake, A.M., in *Common-school Literature, English and American, with Several Hundred Extracts to be Memorized* (Philadelphia, 1898).

Walt Whitman (1819–1892)

O Captain! My Captain!

O Captain! my Captain! our fearful trip is done,
The ship has weather'd every rack, the prize we sought is won,   2
The port is near, the bells I hear, the people all exulting,
While follow eyes the steady keel, the vessel grim and daring;   4
      But O heart! heart! heart!
       O the bleeding drops of red,
        Where on the deck my Captain lies,
        Fallen cold and dead.   8

O Captain! my Captain! rise up and hear the bells;
Rise up — for you the flag is flung — for you the bugle trills,   10
For you bouquets and ribbon'd wreaths — for you the shores a-crowding,
For you they call, the swaying mass, their eager faces turning;   12
      Here Captain! dear father!
       This arm beneath your head!
        It is some dream that on the deck,
        You've fallen cold and dead.   16

My Captain does not answer, his lips are pale and still,
My father does not feel my arm, he has no pulse nor will,   18
The ship is anchor'd safe and sound, its voyage closed and done,
From fearful trip the victor ship comes in with object won;   20
      Exult O shores, and ring O bells!
       But I with mournful tread,
        Walk the deck my Captain lies,
        Fallen cold and dead.   24

O CAPTAIN! MY CAPTAIN! Written soon after the death of Abraham Lincoln, this was, in Whitman's lifetime, by far the most popular of his poems.

QUESTIONS

1. Compare this with other Whitman poems. (See another elegy for Lincoln, "When Lilacs Last in the Dooryard Bloom'd," quoted in part on page 179.) In what ways is "O Captain! My Captain!" uncharacteristic of his works? Do you agree with J. Willis Westlake that this is one of the few occasions on which Whitman is "grandly poetical"?
2. Comment on the appropriateness to its subject of the poem's rhythms.
3. Do you find any evidence in this poem that an excellent poet wrote it?

     In the end, we have to admit that the critical principles set forth in this chapter are all very well for admiring excellent poetry we already know, but they cannot be carried like a yardstick in the hand, to go out looking for it. As Ezra Pound said in his *ABC of Reading*, "A classic is classic not because it conforms to certain structural rules, or fits certain definitions (of which its author had quite probably never heard). It is classic because of a certain eternal and irrepressible freshness."
     The best poems, like "Sailing to Byzantium," may offer a kind of

religious experience. In the eighth decade of the twentieth century, some of us rarely set foot outside a man-made environment. Whizzing down four-lane superhighways, we observe lakes and trees in the distance. In a way our cities are to us as anthills are to ants, as Frost reminds us in "Departmental." No less than anthills, they are "natural" structures. But the "unnatural" world of school or business is, as Wordsworth says, too much with us. Locked in the shells of our ambitions, our self-esteem, we forget our kinship to earth and sea. We fabricate self-justifications. But a great poem shocks us into another order of perception. It points beyond language to something still more essential. It ushers us into an experience so moving and true that we feel (to quote King Lear) "cut to the brain." In bad or indifferent poetry, words are all there is.

William Blake (1757–1827)

THE LITTLE BLACK BOY

My mother bore me in the southern wild,
And I am black, but O! my soul is white;
White as an angel is the English child,
But I am black, as if bereaved of light.   4

My mother taught me underneath a tree,
And sitting down before the heat of day,
She took me on her lap and kissèd me,
And pointing to the east, began to say: 8

"Look on the rising run: there God does live,
And gives his light, and gives his heat away;
And flowers and trees and beasts and men receive
Comfort in morning, joy in the noonday.   12

"And we are put on earth a little space,
That we may learn to bear the beams of love;
And these black bodies and this sunburnt face
Is but a cloud, and like a shady grove.   16

"For when our souls have learned the heat to bear,
The cloud will vanish; we shall hear his voice,
Saying: 'Come out from the grove, my love and care,
And round my golden tent like lambs rejoice.'"   20

Thus did my mother say, and kissèd me;
And thus I say to little English boy:
When I from black and he from white cloud free,
And round the tent of God like lambs we joy,   24

I'll shade him from the heat, till he can bear
To lean in joy upon our Father's knee;
And then I'll stand and stroke his silver hair,
And be like him, and he will then love me.   28

1. Summarize the metaphor that extends throughout this poem. What stands for what?
2. Do you find the various parts of this extended metaphor consistent with one another? Is this a well unified or a badly unified poem?
3. What is the speaker's attitude toward the fact that he is black? Is he sorry, glad, or both? Justify your answer by pointing to particulars in the poem.
4. In *A Child's Garden of Verses,* Robert Louis Stevenson makes a little white English child say:

   Little Indian, Sioux or Crow,
   Little frosty Eskimo,
   Little Turk or Japanee,
   Oh! don't you wish that you were me? . . .
   You have curious things to eat,
   I am fed on proper meat;
   You must dwell beyond the foam,
   But I am safe and live at home.

   How would you compare this attitude with that of Blake's little boy toward the English child? Which attitude do you find the more attractive?
5. The mutual love of a black child and a white child is a subject that sometimes has lent itself to sentimentality (for instance, Harriet Beecher Stowe's treatment of Topsy the slave girl and Little Eva in *Uncle Tom's Cabin*). Is Blake's treatment of this subject sentimental? Discuss and explain.

John Keats (1795–1821)

BRIGHT STAR! WOULD I WERE STEADFAST AS THOU ART

Bright star! would I were steadfast as thou art —
  Not in lone splendor hung aloft the night,
And watching, with eternal lids apart,
  Like nature's patient, sleepless Eremite°   *hermit* 4
The moving waters at their priest-like task
  Of pure ablution round earth's human shores,
Or gazing on the new soft-fallen mask
  Of snow upon the mountains and the moors —   8
No — yet still steadfast, still unchangeable,
  Pillowed upon my fair love's ripening breast,
To feel for ever its soft fall and swell,
  Awake for ever in a sweet unrest,   12
Still, still to hear her tender-taken breath,
And so live ever — or else swoon to death.   14

QUESTIONS

1. Stars are conventional symbols for love and a loved one. (Love, Shakespeare tells us in a sonnet, "is the star to every wandering bark.") In this sonnet, why is it not possible for the star to have this meaning? How does Keats use it?
2. What seems concrete and particular in the speaker's observations?

3. Suppose Keats had said *slow and easy* instead of *tender-taken* in line 13? What would have been lost?
4. Many readers have been bothered by the latter half of the last line. Does it lose your sympathy? If so, why? If not, how do you defend it?

Carl Sandburg (1878–1967)

Fog

The fog comes
on little cat feet.
It sits looking
over harbor and city
on silent haunches
and then moves on.

Question

In lines 15–22 of "The Love Song of J. Alfred Prufrock" (p. 368), T. S. Eliot also likens fog to a cat. Compare Sandburg's lines and Eliot's. Which passage tells us more about fogs and cats?

FOR REVIEW AND FURTHER STUDY

Joseph Skipsey (1832–1903)

Get Up!

"Get up!" the caller calls, "Get up!"
  And in the dead of night,
To win the bairns their bite and sup,
  I rise a weary wight.   4

My flannel dudden° donned, thrice o'er   *clothing*
  My birds are kissed, and then
I with a whistle shut the door
  I may not ope again.   8

GET UP! Text from *The Forsaken Garden* edited by John Heath-Stubbs and David Wright (London, 1950), an anthology of Victorian poetry not included in *The Oxford Book of Victorian Verse.* From childhood, Skipsey spent much of his life in the coal mines of North Shielding, England.

Questions

1. Is this statement sentimental and full of self-pity?
2. In its diction, this poem mingles dialect words (*bairns, dudden*) with "poetic" contractions (*o'er, ope*) and an archaism (*wight*). Does this inconsistency negate the poem's success? Why or why not?

3. Skipsey's poem, rarely reprinted, is no longer in the limelight. Do you think its merits commend it to be restored, or has the curtain of time been rung down on it mercifully?

Mark Alexander Boyd (1563–1601)

FRA BANK TO BANK, FRA WOOD TO WOOD I RIN

Fra bank to bank, fra wood to wood I rin°	*run*
Ourhailit° with my feeble fantasie	*overcome*
Like til° a leaf that fallis from a tree	*to*
Or til a reed ourblawin with the wind,	4
Two gods guides me, the ane of them is blin,	
Yea, and a bairn° brocht up in vanitie,	*child*
The next a wife ingenrit° of the sea	*engendered*
And lichter nor° a dauphin° with her fin.	*than; dolphin* 8
Unhappy is the man for evermair	
That tills the sand and sawis° in the air,	*sows* 10
But twice unhappier is he, I lairn,	
That feidis° in his heart a mad desire	*feeds*
And follows on a woman throw the fire	
Led by a blind and teachit by a bairn.	14

QUESTIONS

1. Explain the allusions in lines 5–8.
2. What has Boyd's poem in common with other love poetry in the Petrarchan tradition (discussed on pp. 171–173)?
3. Ezra Pound has called this the most beautiful sonnet in the English language. What is there in it to admire?

J. V. Cunningham (b. 1911)

EPITAPH

When I shall be without regret
And shall mortality forget,
When I shall die who lived for this,
I shall not miss the things I miss.
And you who notice where I lie
Ask not my name. It is not I.

QUESTION

To an anthology (*Poet's Choice*, edited by Paul Engle and Joseph Langland, New York, 1962), J. V. Cunningham contributed this note:

I like this poem because it is all denotation and no connotation; because it has only one level of meaning; because it is not ironic, paradoxical, complex, or subtle; and because the meter is monotonously regular.

He might have added that neither does it contain any image, symbol, allegory, or allusion. What does it have to recommend it?

EXERCISE: *Seeing Order and Unity*

The following puzzle is meant not as a parlor game but as a way to see the structure of a poem. It mistreats a masterpiece little in size but sinewy enough to survive. Here is the garbled text of a poem of Wordsworth. Without looking up the original, try to determine the order in which the stanzas ought to be read. You will need to remove two unnecessary stanzas by Poe. What has determined the order you have given the stanzas? What have you left out and why is it extraneous?

LUCY LEE

She lived unknown, and few could know
    When Lucy ceased to be;
But she is in her grave, and, oh,
    The difference to me!   4

She dwelt among the untrodden ways
    Beside the springs of Dove,
A maid whom there were none to praise
    And very few to love: 8

Ah, broken is the golden bowl!
    The spirit flown forever!
Let the bell toll! — a saintly soul
    Floats on the Stygian river;   12

A violet by a mossy stone
    Half hidden from the eye!
— Fair as a star, when only one
    Is shining in the sky.   16

And so, all the night-tide, I lie down by the side
Of my darling — my darling — my life and my bride,
    In the sepulchre there by the sea,
    In her tomb by the sounding sea.   20

                                    — Edgar Allan Wordsworth

Fred Emerson Brooks (publ. 1894)

PAT'S OPINION OF FLAGS

Every man in the world thinks his banner the best,
        And his national song
        Is often too long,
Yet in praising his flag he makes sport of the rest,
Though there's many a truth that is spoken in jest,   5
        Save wid malice prepense
        There should be no offense.   7

There's the Hawaiian kingdom stuck out in the ocean;
     'Twas made as a site
     For the seabirds to light;
There they worship their colors wid colored devotion,
And they never have war, but internal commotion,   12
     For those islands contain, O,
     Queen Lilli's volcano.   14

       . . .

There's the flag of the Chinese, as everywan knows,
     Cut three-cornered wid care,
     Like they'd no cloth to spare;
Yet they seem to have plenty when makin' their clothes;
Havin' no fashion plate, they've cut big, I suppose;   19
     Hangin' loose roundabout
     So the fleas will drop out.   21

You can judge of those men by the wardrobe they wear:
     They don't look to get fits
     For a "dollar six bits."
Their flag was made yellow, as people declare,
Because they've the smallpox so much over there;   26
     Be warned, if ye're wise,
     By the dragon it flies.   28

But one of the prettiest flags that I know
     Is the great oroflam
     Of our old Uncle Sam;
Wid the red and white bars all laid out in a row,
And a nice pasture blue for the bright stars to grow;   33
     Wid the eagle above
     And around it the dove.   35

Of the Star-spangled Banner alone, it is said
     She has earned this renown —
     She was niver pulled down.
With the green on my grave and that flag overhead
I think I'll rest aisy! But wait till I'm dead!   40
     Wid that flag in the sky
     I'm in no haste to die.   42

Anthony Hecht (b. 1923)

JAPAN

It was a miniature country once
To my imagination; Home of the Short,
And also the academy of stunts
     Where acrobats are taught   4
     The famous secrets of the trade:
     To cycle in the big parade   6

While spinning plates upon their parasols,
Or somersaults that do not touch the ground,
   Or tossing seven balls
In Most Celestial Order round and round.   10

A child's quick sense of the ingenious stamped
All their invention: toys I used to get
At Christmastime, or the peculiar, cramped
   Look of their alphabet.   14
   Fragile and easily destroyed,
   Those little boats of celluloid   16
Driven by camphor round the bathroom sink,
And delicate the folded paper prize
   Which, dropped into a drink
Of water, grew up right before your eyes.   20

Now when we reached them it was with a sense
Sharpened for treachery compounding in their brains
Like mating weasels; our Intelligence
   Said: The Black Dragon reigns   24
   Secretly under yellow skin,
   Deeper than dyes of atabrine   26
And deadlier. The War Department said:
Remember you are Americans; forsake
   The wounded and the dead
At your own cost; remember Pearl and Wake.   30

And yet they bowed us in with ceremony,
Told us what brands of Sake were the best,
Explained their agriculture in a phony
   Dialect of the West,   34
   Meant vaguely to be understood
   As a shy sign of brotherhood   36
In the old human bondage to the facts
Of day-to-day existence. And like ants,
   Signaling tiny pacts
With their antennae, they would wave their hands.   40

At last we came to see them not as glib
Walkers of tightropes, worshipers of carp,
Nor yet a species out of Adam's rib
   Meant to preserve its warp   44
   In Cain's own image. They had learned
   That their tough eye-born goddess burned   46
Adoring fingers. They were very poor.
The holy mountain was not moved to speak.
   Wind at the paper door
Offered them snow out of its hollow peak.   50

Human endeavor clumsily betrays
Humanity. Their excrement served in this;
For, planting rice in water, they would raise
   Schistosomiasis   54

Japonica, that enters through
The pores into the avenue   56
And orbit of the blood, where it may foil
The heart and kill, or settle in the brain.
    This fruit of their nightsoil
Thrives in the skull, where it is called insane.   60

Now the quaint early image of Japan
That was so charming to me as a child
Seems like a bright design upon a fan,
    Of water rushing wild   64
    On rocks that can be folded up,
    A river which the wrist can stop   66
With a neat flip, revealing merely sticks
And silk of what had been a fan before,
    And like such winning tricks,
It shall be buried in excelsior.   70

JAPAN. 24. *The Black Dragon:* Militarist organization that had urged the expansion of the
Japanese empire. 26. *atabrine:* A drug used against malaria. A side effect of it is that it
gives a yellow tinge to the user's skin. 30. *Pearl and Wake:* Pearl Harbor and Wake Island,
attacked by the Japanese on December 7, 1941. Wake fell after a prolonged defense by a
small garrison of Marines. 54–55. *Schistosomiasis Japonica:* A disease caused by parasitic
worms in the bloodstream.

QUESTIONS

1. The preceding two poems by Brooks and Hecht have something in common:
   an American speaker's view of foreigners. Who is the speaker in each poem?
2. Pat opens with an apology for what he is about to say. Do you find this apology satisfactory? Why or why not?
3. Consider Pat's attitude toward flags in Brooks's lines 15–17 and his attitude
   toward Old Glory in the last two stanzas. What contradiction do you notice
   between these two attitudes?
4. A word worth knowing is *jingoism,* from a patriotic ditty sung in English
   music halls in 1878, when a British fleet was sent into Turkish waters to resist Russian advances: "We don't want to fight, but by jingo, if we do / We've
   got the ships, we've got the men, and got the money, too!" For what reasons
   might Brooks's poem be called jingoistic?
5. In Hecht's poem, what is the speaker's attitude toward the Japanese at the
   beginning of the poem? At the end? What changes it?
6. What is the effect of Hecht's references to medicine and disease? How does
   the speaker feel toward victims of Schistosomiasis Japonica? Compare this
   with Pat's reference to smallpox (line 33).
7. What is the theme of each poem? To what extent does each poet make us see
   his theme in concrete terms, using imagery and detailed observation?
8. These two poems point toward a larger topic for discussion. How might the
   excellence of a poet's work be said to relate to his ability to understand and
   sympathize? Can you think of any other poets whose work exhibits (or fails
   to exhibit) such understanding and sympathy?

16 Alternatives

THE POET'S REVISIONS

"He / Who casts to write a living line must sweat, / . . . and strike the second heat / Upon the Muse's anvil," wrote Ben Jonson. Indeed, few if any immortal poems can have been perfected with the first blow. The labor of revising seems the usual practice of most bards (other than the Bard of Avon, if we believe the famous rumor that in "whatsoever he penned, he never blotted out line"). As a result, a poet may leave us two or more versions of a poem — perhaps (as Robert Graves has said of his work drafts) "hatched and cross-hatched by puzzling layers of ink."

We need not, of course, rummage the poet's wastebasket in order to see his accomplishment. If we wish, we can follow a suggestion of the critic Austin Warren: take any fine poem and make changes in it. Then compare the changes to the original. We may then realize why the poet wrote what he did instead of anything else. However, there is a certain undeniable pleasure in watching a poem go through its growth stages. Some readers have claimed that the study of successive versions gives them insight into the process by which poems come to be. More important to a reader whose concern is to read poems with appreciation, we stand to learn something about the rightness of a finished poem from seeing what alternatives occurred to the poet himself. To a critic who protested two lines in "The Thorn," a painfully flat description of an infant's grave,

> I've measured it from side to side;
> 'Tis three feet long and two feet wide

Wordsworth retorted, "They ought to be liked." However, he thought better of them and later made this change:

> Though but of compass small, and bare
> To thirsty suns and parching air.

A novice poet who regards his first draft as inviolable sometimes loses interest in his poem if anyone suggests he do more work on it.

Others have found high excitement in the task. "Months of re-writing! What happiness!" exclaimed William Butler Yeats in a letter to a friend. In fact, Yeats so much enjoyed revision that late in life he kept trying to improve the poems of his youth. The end results seem more youthful and spontaneous than the originals. A merciless self-critic, Yeats discarded lines that a lesser poet would have been grateful for. In some cases his final version was practically a new poem:

William Butler Yeats (1865–1939)

The Old Pensioner

I had a chair at every hearth,
When no one turned to see
With "Look at that old fellow there;
And who may he be?"
And therefore do I wander on,
And the fret is on me.   6

The road-side trees keep murmuring —
Ah, wherefore murmur ye
As in the old days long gone by,
Green oak and poplar tree!
The well-known faces are all gone,
And the fret is on me.   *(1890 text)*   12

The Lamentation of the Old Pensioner

Although I shelter from the rain
Under a broken tree
My chair was nearest to the fire
In every company
That talked of love or politics,
Ere Time transfigured me.   6

Though lads are making pikes again
For some conspiracy,
And crazy rascals rage their fill
At human tyranny,
My contemplations are of Time
That has transfigured me.   12

There's not a woman turns her face
Upon a broken tree,
And yet the beauties that I loved
Are in my memory;
I spit into the face of Time
That has transfigured me.   *(1939 text)*   18

1. "The Old Pensioner" is this poem's first printed version; "Lamentation," its last. From the original, what elements has Yeats in the end retained?
2. What does the final version add to our knowledge of the old man (his character, attitudes, circumstances)?
3. Compare in sound and rhythm the refrain in the "Lamentation" with the original refrain.
4. Why do the statements in the final version seem to follow one another more naturally, and the poem as a whole seem more tightly woven together?

Yeats's practice seems to document the assertion of critic A. F. Scott that "the work of correction is often quite as inspired as the first onrush of words and ideas." Yeats made a revealing comment on his methods of revision:

> In dream poetry, in "Kubla Khan," . . . every line, every word can carry its unanalyzable, rich associations; but if we dramatize some possible singer or speaker we remember that he is moved by one thing at a time, certain words must be dull and numb. Here and there in correcting my early poems I have introduced such numbness and dullness, turned, for instance, the "curd-pale moon" into the "brilliant moon," that all might seem, as it were, remembered with indifference, except some one vivid image. When I began to rehearse a play I had the defects of my early poetry; I insisted upon obvious all-pervading rhythm. Later on I found myself saying that only in those lines or words where the beauty of the passage came to its climax, must rhythm be obvious.[1]

In changing words for "dull and numb" ones, in breaking up and varying rhythms, Yeats evidently is trying for improvement not necessarily in a particular line, but in an entire poem.

Not all revisions are successful. An instance might be the alterations Keats made in "La Belle Dame sans Merci," in which the stanza with the "wild wild eyes" and the exactly counted kisses,

> She took me to her elfin grot,
>   And there she wept and sighed full sore,
> And there I shut her wild wild eyes
>   With kisses four.

was scrapped in favor of:

> She took me to her elfin grot,
>   And there she gazed and sighèd deep,
> And there I shut her wild sad eyes —
>   So kissed to sleep.

When Mark Antony begins his funeral oration, "Friends, Romans, countrymen: lend me your ears," Shakespeare makes him ask something quite different from the modernized version in one high school

[1] "Dramatis Personae, 1896–1902," in *The Autobiography of William Butler Yeats* (New York, 1953).

English textbook: "Friends, Romans, countrymen: listen to me." Strictly speaking, any revised version of a poem is a different poem, even if its only change is a single word.

EXERCISE: *Early and Late Versions*

In each of the following pairs, which details of the revised version show an improvement of the earlier one? Exactly what makes the poet's second thoughts seem better (if you agree that they are)? Italics indicate words of one text not found in the other. Notice that in some cases, the poet has also changed word order.

1. William Blake, "London" (complete poem given on page 57), first two lines:

   a. I wander through each *dirty* street,
      Near where the *dirty* Thames does flow

   b. I wander through each *chartered* street,
      Near where the *chartered* Thames does flow

2. William Blake, "London," last stanza:

   a. But most the midnight harlot's curse
      From every *dismal* street I hear,
      Weaves around the marriage hearse
      And blasts the new born infant's tear.   (*first draft, 1793*)

   b. But most *through* midnight streets I hear
      How the *youthful* harlot's curse
      Blasts the new born infant's tear
      And *blights with plagues* the marriage hearse.   (*1794 version*)

3. Samuel Taylor Coleridge, "The Rime of the Ancient Mariner," from Part III:

   a. With *never a* whisper *in* the Sea
         Off *darts* the Specter-*ship;*
      While clombe above the Eastern bar
      The hornèd Moon, with one bright star
         Almost atween the tips.   5

      One after one by the hornèd Moon
      (*Listen, O Stranger! to me*)
      Each turn'd his face with a ghastly pang
      And curs'd me with his *ee.*   (*1799 version*)   9

   b. *The Sun's rim dips; the stars rush out:*
      At one stride comes the dark;
      With *far-heard* whisper, o'er the sea,
      Off *shot* the specter *bark.*   4

      We listened and looked sideways up!
      Fear at my heart, as at a cup,
      My life-blood seemed to sip!
      The stars were dim, and thick the night,
      The steerman's face by his lamp gleamed white;
      From the sails the dew did drip —
      Till clomb above the eastern bar
      The hornèd Moon, with one bright star
      Within the nether tip.   13

One after one, by the *star-dogged* Moon,
  Too quick for groan or sigh,
Each turned his face with a ghastly pang
And cursed me with his *eye.*   (*1817 version*)

4. Edward FitzGerald, *The Rubáiyát of Omar Khayyám,* a quatrain:

a. *For in and out, above, about, below,*
  '*Tis nothing but a* Magic Shadow-show,
    Play'd in a Box whose Candle is the Sun,
  Round *which* we *Phantom Figures* come and go.
                    (*first version, 1859 edition*)

b. We *are no other than a moving row*
  Of Magic Shadow-*shapes that* come and go
    Round *with* the Sun-*illumined Lantern held*
  In Midnight by the Master of the Show; . . .
                    (*fifth version, 1889 edition*)

5. T. S. Eliot, "A Lyric," originally written as an imitation of Ben Jonson when Eliot was sixteen, first stanza:

a. If Time and Space, as Sages say,
    Are things *which* cannot be,
  The *sun which does not feel decay*
    No greater is than we.
  So why, Love, should we *ever pray*
    To live a century?
  The *butterfly* that lives a day
    Has lived *eternity.*   (*1905 version*)

b. If space and time, as sages say,
    Are things *that* cannot be,
  The *fly* that lives a *single* day
    Has lived *as long as* we.
  But let us live while yet we *may,*
    While love and life are free,
  For time is time, and runs away,
    Though sages disagree.   (*1907 version*)

Donald Hall (b. 1928)
MY SON, MY EXECUTIONER

My son, my executioner,
  I take you in my arms,
Quiet and small and just astir,
  And whom my body warms.   4

Sweet death, small son, our instrument
  Of immortality,
Your cries and hungers document
  Our bodily decay.   8

We twenty-five and twenty-two,
  Who seemed to live forever,
Observe enduring life in you
  And start to die together.   12

1. The first line introduces a paradoxical truth, the basic theme of the poem. How would you sum up this truth in your own words?
2. Exactly what do these words denote: *instrument* (line 5), *document* (line 7)?
3. When first published, this poem had a fourth stanza:

I take into my arms the death
   Maturity exacts,
And name with my imperfect breath
   The mortal paradox.

Do you think the poet right or wrong to omit this stanza? Explain.

TRANSLATIONS

Poetry, said Robert Frost, is what gets lost in translation. If absolutely true, the comment is bad news for most of us, who have to depend on translations for our only knowledge of great poems in some other languages. However, some translators seem able to save a part of their originals and bring it across the language gap. At times they may even add more poetry of their own, as if to try to compensate for what is lost.

Unlike the writer of an original poem, the translator begins with a meaning that already exists. To convey it, he may decide to stick as closely as he can to the denotations of the original words or else to depart from them, more or less freely, after something he values more. The latter aim is evident in the *Imitations* of Robert Lowell, who said he had been "reckless with literal meaning" and instead had "labored hard to get the tone." Particularly defiant of translation are poems in dialect, uneducated speech, and slang: what can be used for English equivalents? Ezra Pound, in a bold move, translates the song of a Chinese peasant in *The Classic Anthology Defined by Confucius:*

Yaller bird, let my corn alone,
Yaller bird, let my crawps alone,
These folks here won't let me eat,
I wanna go back whaar I can meet
the folks I used to know at home,
      I got a home an' I wanna' git goin'.

Here, it is our purpose to judge a translation not by its fidelity to its original, but by the same standards we apply to any other poem written in English. To do so may be another way to see the difference between appropriate and inappropriate words.

Here are two versions of a famous poem by Callimachus from the Greek (or Palatine) Anthology, a collection of lyrics and epigrams written between 700 B.C. and A.D. 1000. Cory's translation reflects the era of Tennyson; that by Fitts is clearly from the era of Eliot and Pound. What are their differences? Which of these two modes in translation do you prefer? Why? One mode is not intrinsically superior to the other.

William Cory (1832–1892)

They told me, Heraclitus, they told me you were dead,
They brought me bitter news to hear and bitter tears to shed.
I wept as I remembered how often you and I
Had tired the sun with talking and sent him down the sky.   4

And now that thou art lying, my dear Old Carian guest,
A handful of grey ashes, long, long ago at rest,
Still are thy pleasant voices, thy nightingales, awake;
For Death, he taketh all away, but them he cannot take.   8

Dudley Fitts (1903–1968)
ELEGY ON HERAKLEITOS

One brought me the news of your death, O Herakleitos my friend,
And I wept for you, remembering
How often we had watched the sun set as we talked.

And you are ashes now, old friend from Halikarnassos,
Ashes now:
          but your nightingale songs live on,   5
And Death, the destroyer of every lovely thing,
Shall not touch them with his blind all-canceling fingers.

Federico García Lorca (1899–1936)

LA GUITARRA		GUITAR
Empieza el llanto		Begins the crying
de la guitarra.		of the guitar.
Se rompen las copas		From earliest dawn
de la madrugada.		the strokes are breaking.
Empieza el llanto	5	Begins the crying
de la guitarra.		of the guitar.
Es inútil		It is futile
callarla.		to stop its sound.
Es imposible		It is impossible
callarla.	10	to stop its sound.
Llora monótona		It is crying a monotone
como llora el agua,		like the crying of water,
como llora el viento		like the crying of wind
sobre la nevada.		over fallen snow.
Es imposible	15	It is impossible
callarla.		to stop its sound.
Llora por cosas		It is crying over things
lejanas.		far off.

Arena del Sur caliente	Burning sand of the South
que pide camelias blancas. 20	which covets white camelias.
Llora flecha sin blanco,	It is crying the arrow without aim,
la tarde sin mañana,	the evening without tomorrow,
y el primer pájaro muerto	and the first dead bird on the branch.
sobre la rama.	O guitar!
¡Oh, guitarra! 25	Heart heavily wounded
Corazón malherido	by five sharp swords.
por cinco espadas.	

— Translated by Keith Waldrop

QUESTIONS

1. Someone who knows Spanish should read aloud the original and the translation. Although it is impossible for any translation fully to capture the resonance of García Lorca's poem, in what places is the English version most nearly able to approximate it?
2. Another translation renders line 21: "It mourns for the targetless arrow." What is the difference between mourning for something and being the cry of it?
3. Throughout his translation, Waldrop closely follows the line divisions of the original, but in line 23 he combines García Lorca's lines 23 and 24. Can you see any point in his doing so? Would "on the branch" by itself be a strong line of English poetry?

Rainer Maria Rilke (1875–1926)

VORGEFÜHL

Ich bin wie eine Fahne von Fernen umgeben.
Ich ahne die Winde, die kommen, ich muss sie leben,
während die Dinge unten sich noch nicht rühren:
die Türen schliessen noch sanft, und in den Kaminen ist Stille;
die Fenster zittern noch nicht, und der Staub ist noch schwer. 5

Da weiss ich die Stürme schon und bin erregt wie das Meer.
Und breite mich aus und falle in mich hinein
und werfe mich ab und bin ganz allein
in dem grossen Sturm.

FOREBODING

I am a flag by distant space surrounded.
I feel winds coming, have to live through them,
while things below are not yet even stirring:
the doors still closing gently, the chimneys silent;
the windows not yet trembling, the dust heavy. 5

Then I feel storms and like the sea am shaken.
And spread myself out and fall back into me,
and hurl myself off, all alone
in the huge storm.

— Translated by Lori Weinstein

QUESTIONS

1. A less ominous title than "Foreboding" might be "Intimation" or "Presentiment." Which title do you prefer? Why?
2. What does this poem say that is true for all of us?

EXERCISE: *Comparing Translations*

Which English translation of each of the following poems is the best poetry? The originals may be of interest to some. For those who do not know the foreign language, the editor's line-by-line prose paraphrases may help indicate what the translator had to work with and how much of his translation is his own idea. In which do you find the diction most felicitous? In which do pattern and structure best move as one? What differences in tone are apparent? It is doubtful that any one translation will surpass the others in every detail.

Horace (65–8 B.C.)
ODES I (38)

Persicos odi, puer, apparatus,
Displicent nexae philyra coronae;
Mitte sectari, rosa quo locorum
   Sera moretur.   4
Simplici myrto nihil allabores
Sedulus curo: neque te ministrum
Dedecet myrtus neque me sub arta
   Vite bibentem.   8

ODES I (38). Prose translation: (1) Persian pomp, boy, I detest, (2) garlands woven of linden bark displease me; (3–4) give up searching for the place where the late-blooming rose is. (5–6) Put no laborious trimmings on simple myrtle: (6–7) for myrtle is unbecoming neither to you, a servant, nor to me, under the shade of this (8) vine, drinking.

1. SIMPLICITY

Boy, I hate their empty shows,
 Persian garlands I detest,
Bring me not the late-blown rose
 Lingering after all the rest: 4
Plainer myrtle pleases me
 Thus outstretched beneath my vine,
Myrtle more becoming thee,
 Waiting with thy master's wine.   8
   — William Cowper (1731–1800)

2. FIE ON EASTERN LUXURY!

Nay, nay, my boy — 'tis not for me,
 This studious pomp of Eastern luxury;
Give me no various garlands — fine
 With linden twine,
Nor seek, where latest lingering blows,
 The solitary rose.   6

Earnest I beg — add not with toilsome pain,
One far-sought blossom to the myrtle plain,
For sure, the fragrant myrtle bough
 Looks seemliest on thy brow;

Nor me mis-seems, while, underneath the vine,
Close interweaved, I quaff the rosy wine.   12
    — Hartley Coleridge (1796–1849)

3. FROM HORACE

Ah child, no Persian-perfect art!
Crowns composite and braided bast°   *linden bark*
They tease me. Never know the part
    Where roses linger last.   4

Bring natural myrtle, and have done:
Myrtle will suit your place and mine:
And set the glasses from the sun
    Beneath the tackled vine.   8
    — Gerard Manley Hopkins (1844–1889)

4. THE PREFERENCE DECLARED

Boy, I detest the Persian pomp;
    I hate those linden-bark devices;
And as for roses, holy Moses!
    They can't be got at living prices!   4
Myrtle is good enough for us, —
    For *you,* as bearer of my flagon;
For *me,* supine beneath this vine,
    Doing my best to get a jag on!   8
    — Eugene Field (1850–1895)

Charles Baudelaire (1821–1867)

RECUEILLEMENT

Sois sage, ô ma Douleur, et tiens-toi plus tranquille.
Tu réclamais le Soir; il descend; le voici:
Une atmosphère obscure enveloppe la ville,
Aux uns portant la paix, aux autres le souci.   4

Pendant que des mortels la multitude vile,
Sous le fouet du Plaisir, ce bourreau sans merci,
Va cueillir des remords dans la fête servile,
Ma Douleur, donne-moi la main; viens par ici,   8

Loin d'eux. Vois se pencher les défuntes Années,
Sur les balcons du ciel, en robes surannées;
Surgir du fond des eaux le Regret souriant;

Le Soleil moribond s'endormir sous une arche,
Et, comme un long linceul traînant à l'Orient,
Entends, ma chère, entends la douce Nuit qui marche.   14

"MEDITATION." Prose translation: (1) Behave yourself [as a mother would say to her child],
O my Sorrow, and keep calmer. (2) You called for Evening; it descends; here it is: (3) a
dim atmosphere envelops the city, (4) Bringing peace to some; to others anxiety. (5) While
the vile multitude of mortals (6) under the whip of Pleasure, that merciless executioner,
(7) go to gather remorse in the servile festival, (8) my Sorrow, give me your hand; come
this way, (9) far from them. See the dead years lean (10) on the balconies of the sky, in
old-fashioned dresses; (11) [See] Regret, smiling, emerge from the depths of the waters;
(12) [see] the dying Sun go to sleep under an arch; (13) and like a long shroud trailing in
the East, (14) hear, my darling, hear the soft Night who is walking.

1. PEACE, BE AT PEACE, O THOU MY HEAVINESS

Peace, be at peace, O thou my heaviness,
Thou callèdst for the evening, lo! 'tis here,
The City wears a somber atmosphere
That brings repose to some, to some distress.   4
Now while the heedless throng make haste to press
Where pleasure drives them, ruthless charioteer,
To pluck the fruits of sick remorse and fear,
Come thou with me, and leave their fretfulness.   8
See how they hang from heaven's high balconies,
The old lost years in faded garments dressed,
And see Regret with faintly smiling mouth;
And while the dying sun sinks in the west,
Hear how, far off, Night walks with velvet tread,
And her long robe trails all about the south.   14
                    — Lord Alfred Douglas (1870–1945)

2. INWARD CONVERSATION

Be reasonable, my pain, and think with more detachment.
You asked to see the dusk; it descends; it is here:
A sheath of dark light robes the city,
To some bringing peace, to some the end of peace.

Now while the rotten herds of mankind,   5
Flogged by pleasure, that lyncher without touch,
Go picking remorse in their filthy holidays,
Let us join hands, my pain; come this way,

Far from them. Look at the dead years that lean on
The balconies of the sky, in their clothes long out of date;   10
The sense of loss that climbs from the deep waters with a smile;

The sun, nearly dead, that drops asleep beneath an arch;
And listen to the night, like a long shroud being dragged
Toward the east, my love, listen, the soft night is moving.
                    — Robert Bly (b. 1926)

3. MEDITATION

Calm down, my Sorrow, we must move with care.
You called for evening; it descends; it's here.
The town is coffined in its atmosphere,
bringing relief to some, to others care.   4

Now while the common multitude strips bare,·
feels pleasure's cat o' nine tails on its back,
and fights off anguish at the great bazaar,
give me your hand, my Sorrow. Let's stand back;   8

back from these people! Look, the dead years dressed
in old clothes crowd the balconies of the sky.
Regret emerges smiling from the sea,

the sick sun slumbers underneath an arch,
and like a shroud strung out from east to west,
listen, my Dearest, hear the sweet night march!   14
                    — Robert Lowell (b. 1917)

17 Writing about Poems

Criticism, according to Ezra Pound, who wrote much of it, ought to consume itself and disappear. It is a safe guess that most writing about poetry will do so; but luckily, the student writing a paper about a poem need not have literary immortality as his goal. Such critical writing is a task he can undertake for his own immediate ends. Writing about a poem, he obliges himself to live with the poem, to examine it closely and intensively. By trying to communicate his understanding of the poem to others, then perhaps, if all goes well, he better reveals his understanding to himself.

The reader of this book has encountered brief discussions of poems, discussions the editor wrote to illustrate a particular point. A look at A. E. Housman's "Loveliest of Trees" (page 3) concentrated on seeing the poem in paraphrase. T. S. Eliot's "The *Boston Evening Transcript*" (page 204) was examined for its symbolism; W. B. Yeats's "Sailing to Byzantium" (page 254), for its elaborate development of metaphor.

It is time to offer a few model discussions by critics who not only read poetry with painstaking care but who also behold poems entire. Writing down the results of one's close reading of a poem may sound like a bore, but it doesn't need to be — as D. H. Lawrence demonstrates in the following remarks about a passage from Walt Whitman's "Song of Myself." Here, Lawrence's method is to work through Whitman line by line.

> I AM HE THAT ACHES WITH AMOROUS LOVE.
>
> What do you make of that? I AM HE THAT ACHES. First generalization. First uncomfortable universalization. WITH AMOROUS LOVE! Oh, God! Better a bellyache. A bellyache is at least specific. But the ACHE OF AMOROUS LOVE!
>
> Think of having that under your skin. All that!
>
> I AM HE THAT ACHES WITH AMOROUS LOVE.
>
> Walter, leave off. You are not HE. You are just a limited Walter. And your ache doesn't include all Amorous Love, by any means. If you ache you only ache with a small bit of amorous love, and there's so much more stays outside the cover of your ache, that you might be a bit milder about it.
>
> I AM HE THAT ACHES WITH AMOROUS LOVE.
>
> CHUFF! CHUFF! CHUFF!

CHU-CHU-CHU-CHU-CHUFF!

Reminds one of a steam-engine. A locomotive. They're the only things that seem to me to ache with amorous love. All that steam inside them. Forty million foot-pounds pressure. The ache of AMOROUS LOVE. Steam-pressure. CHUFF!

An ordinary man aches with love for Belinda, or his Native Land, or the Ocean, or the Stars, or the Oversoul: if he feels that an ache is in the fashion.

It takes a steam-engine to ache with AMOROUS LOVE. All of it.

Walt was really too superhuman. The danger of the superman is that he is mechanical.

They talk of his "splendid animality." Well, he'd got it on the brain, if that's the place for animality.

I AM HE THAT ACHES WITH AMOROUS LOVE:
DOES THE EARTH GRAVITATE, DOES NOT ALL MATTER, ACHING,
ATTRACT ALL MATTER?
SO THE BODY OF ME TO ALL I MEET OR KNOW.

What can be more mechanical? The difference between life and matter is that life, living things, living creatures, have the instinct of turning right away from *some* matter, and of blissfully ignoring the bulk of most matter, and of turning towards only some certain bits of specially selected matter. As for living creatures all helplessly hurtling together into one great snowball, why, most very living creatures spend the greater part of their time getting out of the sight, smell or sound of the rest of living creatures. Even bees only cluster on their own queen. And that is sickening enough. Fancy all white humanity clustering on one another like a lump of bees.

"And whoever walks a furlong without sympathy," declares Whitman, "walks to his own funeral dressed in his own shroud." Quoting this line gives Lawrence an excuse to retort: "Take off your hat then, my funeral procession of one is passing." Does it appear that Lawrence regards Whitman's faults, and sees nothing more? Read his essay, "Whitman," in its entirety in *Studies in Classic American Literature* (New York, 1923), and you will discover that Lawrence's final view of Whitman is admiring and affectionate.

Here are some examples of individual poems, each followed by a close reading by a perceptive critic. Notice that each critic, while minutely scrutinizing the poem, proceeds differently to tell his experience of it. Richard Wilbur, for a start, considers a poem by Poe in the light of two paraphrases.

Edgar Allan Poe (1809–1849)

SONNET — TO SCIENCE

Science! true daughter of Old Time thou art!
    Who alterest all things with thy peering eyes.
Why preyest thou thus upon the poet's heart,
    Vulture, whose wings are dull realities?

How should he love thee? or how deem thee wise,
  Who wouldst not leave him in his wandering
To seek for treasure in the jewelled skies,
  Albeit he soared with an undaunted wing?   8
Hast thou not dragged Diana from her car?
  And driven the Hamadryad from the wood
To seek a shelter in some happier star?
  Hast thou not torn the Naiad from her flood,   12
The Elfin from the green grass, and from me
  The summer dream beneath the tamarind tree?   14

SONNET — To SCIENCE. 9. *Diana:* Roman goddess of hunting and of chastity. The moon was her chariot. 10, 12: *Hamadryad, Naiad:* In Greek myth, feminine spirits who live in — and give life to — objects in nature. A Hamadryad inhabits a tree, a Naiad a lake or stream.

Richard Wilbur: COMMENTARY

This poem is unusual for Poe, because of its lucid logical progression and its air of being public speech. Most readers would assent to the following loose paraphrase: "The scientific spirit, now predominant, is like Time in that it destroys beauty: that is, Time destroys the objects in which we *find* beauty, while Science dispenses with the feelings and faculties through which we apprehend and create beauty. The poet, being committed to the praise and creation of beauty, has made a Promethean or Icarian resistance to the repressive spirit of the age, and like these heroes of myth has suffered for his presumption."

    If we take the poem this way — and I think the paraphrase is correct so far as it goes — it may be read as a standard romantic protest against Cartesian dualism, against the exclusion of value from the world of fact, against the idea that the astronomer's star and the botanist's grass-blade are the only *true* star and grass-blade. So understood, the poem may seem a hyperbolic warning that if the age does not grant poetry its own kind of truth, it will deprive itself of the highest and fullest means of ordering and enhancing human experience.

    But this is to accommodate Poe to our own prejudices. The poem is not hyperbolic; nor is the poet really asking that the subjective Elfin be restored to the objective grass. Poe means what he says, and what he says is this: that the scientific spirit and the universal prosaism which accompanies it have inherited the earth, outlawing the poetic imagination and exiling its subject-matter — the Beautiful — to "some happier star." In consequence, the poet is not concerned with the imaginative shaping of human life on the existing earth; his sole present recourse is to repudiate all human and mundane subject-matter, all "dull realities," and to pursue visions of those realms in which beauty was or is inviolate: the remote Earthly past, in which Naiad and Hamadryad went unchallenged, and the distant "happier star" to which they now have flown.

    We are at present inclined to think of poetic composition as an effort to

From the introduction to *Poe, Complete Poems, with an introduction and notes* (Laurel Poetry Series). Reprinted by permission of the author.

get our concerted faculties — our "whole souls" — to acknowledge and unify a maximum of diverse experience. Obviously Poe's outlaw poet cannot think of poetry in this way. He is allowed an absolute minimum of experience: his poetry is to consist of visionary gropings toward imaginary realms, and it will touch on the mundane only for the sake of negation. ("Oh! Nothing earthly . . ." are the opening words of "Al Aaraaf," the poem to which "Sonnet — To Science" is a prelude.) A poetry so exclusive in subject-matter is also obliged to exclude, in its composition, certain faculties of the poet. Poe distinguishes in his criticism three divisions of mind — Intellect, Taste, and the Moral Sense — and bars the first and last from the poetic act on the ground that poetry has nothing to do with Truth or Duty. If the poet's object is to get away from Earth and men, he is plainly bound to disregard the Moral Sense, which is involved with the conduct and passions of men; and he must also degrade the Intellect (which defers to fact and "dull realities"), restricting its function to rationalization.

Poe's poetry, then, is not a protest against the separation of mind and world but an extreme assertion of that separation. It does not issue from a harmony of the faculties and a reconciliation of their provinces, but aspires rather to that isolate freedom of the imagination which we enjoy in dreams. Its declared subject-matter is Beauty — which in poetry, as Yvor Winters has observed, is not properly a subject at all, but a consequence of the treatment of a subject.

In his review of the poems of Joseph Rodman Drake and Fitz-Greene Halleck, Poe showed himself entirely aware of the extent to which he had contracted the scope and nature of poetry. "If," he said, "there be any one circle of thought distinctly and palpably marked out from amid the jarring and tumultuous chaos of human intelligence, it is that evergreen and radiant Paradise which the true poet knows, and knows alone, as the limited realm of his authority — as the circumscribed Eden of his dreams."

Robert Frost (1874–1963)

DESIGN

I found a dimpled spider, fat and white,
On a white heal-all, holding up a moth
Like a white piece of rigid satin cloth —
Assorted characters of death and blight   4
Mixed ready to begin the morning right,
Like the ingredients of a witches' broth —
A snow-drop spider, a flower like a froth,
And dead wings carried like a paper kite.   8

What had that flower to do with being white,
The wayside blue and innocent heal-all?
What brought the kindred spider to that height,
Then steered the white moth thither in the night?
What but design of darkness to appall? —
If design govern in a thing so small.   14

Randall Jarrell: COMMENTARY

This is the Argument from Design with a vengeance; is the terrible negative from which the eighteenth century's Kodak picture (with its *Having wonderful time. Wish you were here* on the margin) had to be printed. If a watch, then a watch-maker; if a diabolical machine, then a diabolical mechanic — Frost uses exactly the logic that has always been used. And this little albino catastrophe is too whitely catastrophic to be accidental, too impossibly unlikely ever to be a coincidence: accident, chance, statistics, natural selection are helpless to account for such designed terror and heartbreak, such an awful symbolic per-version of the innocent being of the world. Frost's details are so diabolically good that it seems criminal to leave some unremarked; but notice how *dimpled, fat,* and *white* (all but one; all but one) come from our regular description of any baby; notice how the *heal-all,* because of its name, is the one flower in all the world picked to be the altar for this Devil's Mass; notice how *holding up* the moth brings something ritual and hieratic, a ghostly, ghastly formality, to this priest and its sacrificial victim; notice how terrible to the fingers, how full of the stilling rigor of death, that *white piece of rigid satin cloth* is. And *assorted characters of death and blight* is, like so many things in this poem, sharply am-biguous: *a mixed bunch of actors* or *diverse representative signs.* The tone of the phrase *assorted characters of death and blight* is beautifully developed in the ironic Breakfast-Club-calisthenics, Radio-Kitchen heartiness of *mixed ready to begin the morning right* (which assures us, so unreassuringly, that this isn't any sort of Strindberg *Spook Sonata,* but hard fact), and concludes in the *ingredients* of the witches' broth, giving the soup a sort of cuddly shimmer that the caul-dron in *Macbeth* never had; the *broth,* even, is brought to life — we realize that witches' broth *is* broth, to be supped with a long spoon. For sweet-sour, smil-ing awfulness *snow-drop spider* looks unsurpassable, until we come to the almost obscenely horrible (even the mouth-gestures are utilized) *a flower like froth;* this always used to seem to me the case of the absolutely inescapable effect, until a student of mine said that you could tell how beautiful the flower was because the poet compared it to froth; when I said to her, "But — but — but what does froth *remind* you of?" looking desperately into her blue eyes, she replied: "Fudge. It reminds me of making fudge."

And then, in the victim's own little line, how contradictory and awful everything is: *dead wings carried like a paper kite!* The *dead* and the *wings* work back and forth on each other heartbreakingly, and the contradictory pathos of the *carried* wings is exceeded by that of the matter-of-fact conversion into what has never lived, into a shouldered toy, of the ended life. *What had that flower to do with being white, / The wayside blue and innocent heal-all?* expresses as well as anything ever has the arbitrariness of our guilt, the fact that Original Sin is only Original Accident, so far as the creatures of this world are concerned. And *the wayside blue and innocent heal-all* is, down to the least sound, the last helpless, yearning, trailing-away sigh of too-precarious innocence, of a poten-tiality cancelled out almost before it began to exist. The *wayside* makes it uni-versal, commonplace, and somehow dearer to us; the *blue* brings in all the asso-ciations of the normal negated color (the poem is likely to remind the reader of

Melville's chapter on the Whiteness of the Whale, just as Frost may have been reminded); and the *innocent* is given a peculiar force and life by this context, just as the name *heal-all* here comes to sad, ironic, literal life: it healed all, itself it could not heal. The *kindred* is very moving in its half-forgiving ambiguity; and the Biblical *thither in the night* and the conclusive *steered* (with its careful echoes of "To a Water-Fowl" and a thousand sermons) are very moving and very serious in their condemnation, their awful mystery. The partly ambiguous, summing-up *What but design of darkness to appall* comes as something taken for granted, a relief almost, in its mere statement and generalization, after the almost unbearable actuality and particularity of what has come before. And then this whole appalling categorical machinery of reasoning-out, of conviction, of condemnation — it reminds one of the machine in *The Penal Colony* — is suddenly made merely hypothetical, a possible contradicted shadow, by one off-hand last-minute qualification: one that dismisses it, but that dismisses it only for a possibility still more terrifying, a whole new random, statistical, astronomical abyss underlying the diabolical machinery of the poem. "In large things, macroscopic phenomena of some real importance," the poem says, "the classical mechanics of design probably *does* operate — though in reverse, so far as the old Argument from Design is concerned; but these little things, things of no real importance, microscopic phenomena like a flower or moth or man or planet or solar system [we have so indissolubly identified ourselves with the moth and flower and spider that we cannot treat our own nature and importance, which theirs symbolize, as fundamentally different from theirs], are governed by the purely statistical laws of quantum mechanics, of random distribution, are they not?" I have given this statement of "what the poem says" — it says much more — an exaggeratedly physical, scientific form because both a metaphorically and literally astronomical view of things is so common, and so unremarked-on, in Frost. This poem, I think most people will admit, makes Pascal's "eternal silence of those infinite spaces" seem the hush between the movements of a cantata.

Gwendolyn Brooks (b. 1917)

First fight. Then fiddle. Ply the slipping string

First fight. Then fiddle. Ply the slipping string
With feathery sorcery; muzzle the note
With hurting love; the music that they wrote
Bewitch, bewilder. Qualify to sing   4
Threadwise. Devise no salt, no hempen thing
For the dear instrument to bear. Devote
The bow to silks and honey. Be remote
A while from malice and from murdering.   8
But first to arms, to armor. Carry hate
In front of you and harmony behind.
Be deaf to music and to beauty blind.
Win war. Rise bloody, maybe not too late   12
For having first to civilize a space
Wherein to play your violin with grace.   14

James A. Emanuel: COMMENTARY

One ought first to conclude what the poem is about — and remain, to borrow a phrase from Keats, "capable of being in uncertainties." A violinist, a professional soldier, a militant civil rights leader, and a mother protective of her disadvantaged children might each perceptively defend a different total interpretation. The largest theme of the sonnet, however, is the relationship between art and life, meaningfully comparable to themes in such diverse works as Langston Hughes' "The Blues I'm Playing," a short story; Robinson Jeffers' "The Bloody Sire," a poem; and E. M. Forster's "What I Believe," an essay. It suffices for our purpose to allow the final three lines to state the societal meaning, modified to individual dimensions most discernibly in the reference to "hurting love" in line 3.

The poet's mastery appears not so much in the meaning as in the style. The allusive imagery mounts richly around the basic image of a stringed instrument, ostensibly the violin of the final line, the "dear instrument" of line 6, plied with the "bow" of line 7. The "fiddle" of line 1, however, is but a disarming contrast to the violent image that swiftly magnifies the word "fight" in a historical context meaningful to racially oppressed people. The subsequent "slipping string," "sorcery," and "muzzle," even though they can refer to the actions of a virtuoso in the parlor or concert hall, also can refer to thuggee, the disciplined kind of murder offered to the goddess Kali by the courteous assassins of India finally suppressed by the British in the nineteenth century. The running noose of the Thugs, their unusual religious rites, and their silent three-on-one killing are thus brought subtly to the fore. The "hempen thing" of line 5, then, is the killer's strangling rope, unfavorably compared by the poet with the violin's "wise thread" (my inversion is as deliberate as hers), just as the "salt" of the same line is indirectly compared with rosin — and further contrasted with the "honey" of line 7, itself reminiscent of the raw sugar eaten by Thugs in rituals after slayings. And the Thugs were indeed "remote / A while . . . from murdering" (as in lines 7 and 8), often acting for long periods as delightful servants of their intended victims, awaiting thuggee.

One could discuss at length the poet's verbal skill: her crucial, compact, almost humorous imperatives; her deft consonance and soft assonance (as in lines 1 and 2, respectively); her other double images and oppositions ("feathery" versus "hurting" and "silks" versus hemp); her ironic near-comparisons ("sorcery" and bewilderment, "dear" and "honey"); her internal partial rhymes (as in lines 2, 5, 6, and 14); her pert, feminine sentientiousness (as in "Qualify to sing / Threadwise"). A similar command of form attaches to her transition in the sestet, for line 9 enhances both whole meaning and particular style; it enlarges the initial advice of line 1 through the figurative use of "armor" to define "hate" as a shield to protect a harmonizing purpose. Thus hate in this poem is to be battered; music and beauty, because they are to be temporarily ignored, are to be saved, are to be revitalized in that civilized "space" of time which always follows the cessation of hateful violence.

From "The Future of Negro Poetry: A Challenge for Critics," in *Black Expression: Essays By and About Black Americans in the Creative Arts,* edited by Addison Gayle, Jr. (New York, 1969). Reprinted by permission of David McKay, Inc.

A rigorous examination of this poem from Gwendolyn Brooks's Pulitzer prize-winning volume yields more to contemplate than has been suggested here; for example, the civil rights leader imagined as an explicator would not stop at this point. . . .

Matthew Arnold (1822–1888)

DOVER BEACH

The sea is calm tonight.
The tide is full, the moon lies fair
Upon the straits; — on the French coast the light
Gleams and is gone; the cliffs of England stand,
Glimmering and vast, out in the tranquil bay.   5
Come to the window, sweet is the night-air!
Only, from the long line of spray
Where the sea meets the moon-blanched land,
Listen! you hear the grating roar
Of pebbles which the waves draw back, and fling,   10
At their return, up the high strand,
Begin, and cease, and then again begin,
With tremulous cadence slow, and bring
The eternal note of sadness in.

Sophocles long ago   15
Heard it on the Aegean, and it brought
Into his mind the turbid ebb and flow
Of human misery; we
Find also in the sound a thought,
Hearing it by this distant northern sea.   20

The Sea of Faith
Was once, too, at the full, and round earth's shore
Lay like the folds of a bright girdle furled.
But now I only hear
Its melancholy, long, withdrawing roar,   25
Retreating, to the breath
Of the night-wind, down the vast edges drear
And naked shingles° of the world.   *gravel beaches*

Ah, love, let us be true
To one another! for the world, which seems   30
To lie before us like a land of dreams,
So various, so beautiful, so new,
Hath really neither joy, nor love, nor light,
Nor certitude, nor peace, nor help for pain;
And we are here as on a darkling° plain   *darkened or darkening* 35
Swept with confused alarms of struggle and flight,
Where ignorant armies clash by night.

James Dickey: COMMENTARY

"Dover Beach" has been called the first modern poem. If this is true, it is modern not so much in diction and technique — for its phrasing and its Miltonic inversions are obvious carryovers from a much older poetry — but in psychological orientation. Behind the troubled man standing at the lover's conventional moon-filled window looking on the sea, we sense — more powerfully because our hindsight confirms what Arnold only began to intuit — the shift in the human viewpoint from the Christian tradition to the impersonal world of Darwin and the nineteenth-century scientists. The way the world is seen, and thus the way men live, is conditioned by what men know about it, and they know more now than they ever have before. Things themselves — the sea, stars, darkness, wind — have not changed; it is the perplexed anxiety and helplessness of the newly dispossessed human being that now come forth from his mind and transmute the sea, the night air, the French coast, and charge them with the sinister implications of the entirely alien. What begins as a rather conventional — but very good — description of scenery turns slowly into quite another thing: a recognition of where the beholder stands in relation to these things; where he *really* stands. It is this new and comfortless knowledge as it overwhelms for all time the old and does away with the place where he thought he stood, where his tradition told him he stood, that creates the powerful and melancholy force of the poem.

In statement, "Dover Beach" goes very easily and gravely, near prose and yet not too near. It has something of the effect of overheard musing, though it is addressed, or half-addressed, to someone present. Its greatest technical virtue, to my mind, is its employment of sound-imagery, particularly in the deep, sustained vowels of lines like "Its melancholy, long, withdrawing roar." The lines also seem to me to *break* beautifully: ". . . on the French coast the light / Gleams, and is gone." I have tried many times to rearrange Arnold's lines, and have never succeeded in doing anything but diminish their subtlety, force, and conviction.

The one difficulty of the poem, it seems to me, is in the famous third strophe wherein the actual sea is compared to the Sea of Faith. If Arnold means that the Sea of Faith was formerly at high tide, and he hears now only the sound of the tide going out, one cannot help thinking also of the cyclic nature of tides, and the consequent coming of another high tide only a few hours after the present ebb. In other words, the figure of speech appears valid only on one level of the comparison; the symbolic half fails to sustain itself. Despite the magnificence of the writing in this section, I cannot help believing that it is the weakest part of the poem when it should be the strongest; the explicitness of the comparison seems too ready-made. Yet I have the poem as it is so deeply in memory that I cannot imagine it changed, and would not have it changed even if I knew it would be a better poem thereby.

In the sound of waves rolling pebbles, an eternal senseless motion, unignorable and meaningless, Arnold hears — as we ever afterwards must hear — human sadness, the tears of things. It links us to Sophocles and to all men at all times who have discovered in such a sound an expression of their own unrest,

From *Babel to Byzantium,* copyright © 1956, 1968 by James Dickey. Reprinted by permission of Farrar, Straus & Giroux, Inc.

and have therefore made of it "the eternal note of sadness." Yet our sadness has a depth that no other era has faced: a certainty of despair based upon our own examination of empirical evidence and the conclusions drawn by our rational faculty. These have revealed not God but the horror and emptiness of things, including those that we cannot help thinking beautiful: that *are* beautiful. By its direct, slow-speaking means, the poem builds toward its last nine lines, when the general resolves into the particular, divulging where *we* stand, what these things mean to *us*. The implication is that if love, morality, constancy, and the other traditional Western virtues are not maintained without supernatural sanction, there is nothing. The world that lies before us in such beauty that it seems to have come instantaneously from God's hand does not include, guarantee, or symbolize the qualities that men have assumed were also part of it. It is beautiful and impersonal, but we must experience it — and now suffer it — as persons. Human affection is revealed as a completely different thing than what we believed it to be; as different, in fact, as the world we were mistaken about. It is a different thing but also a new thing, with new possibilities of terror, choice, and meaning. The moment between the lovers thus takes on the qualities of a new expulsion from Eden: they tremble with fear but also with terrible freedom; they look eastward. The intense vulnerability of the emotional life takes place in an imperiled darkness among the sounds of the sea and against the imminence of violence, wars, armies blundering blindly into each other for no reason. Yet there is a new, fragile center to things: a man and a woman. In a word, it is love in what we have come to call the existential predicament. Nearly a hundred years ago, Arnold fixed unerringly and profoundly on the quality that more than any other was to characterize the emotion of love in our own century: desperation.

QUESTIONS

1. Do you think James Dickey is reading too much into Arnold's poem to find in it "the shift in the human viewpoint from the Christian tradition to the impersonal world of Darwin and the nineteenth-century scientists"? What statements in the poem support (or do not support) Dickey's contentions?
2. Read an article about Arnold and his ideas (such as the one in the *Encyclopedia Britannica*), then decide to what extent Dickey is using his knowledge of Arnold's writings and biography.
3. To what elements of "Dover Beach" does Dickey pay attention besides the poem's ideas? How well does he show these elements as contributing to what the poem is saying?
4. Discuss Dickey's objection to "the weakest part of the poem." How would you state his objection in your own words?
5. How does Dickey indicate that he has affection for the poem, and does not regard it merely as a mechanism to be dissected?

So far, all our examples of writing about poetry have dealt with single poems. Now, to show a writer engaged with a poet's work in its entirety, here is an essay, given in full, on the American poet Sylvia Plath (1932–1963). The writer, British critic A. Alvarez, has the advantage of having known Sylvia Plath personally and can draw from his own impressions. However, in writing about any well-known poet, the student at least can acquaint himself with the poet's biography. Besides the two poems that Alvarez quotes entire ("Ariel" and "Daddy"), five other poems of Sylvia Plath appear elsewhere in this book. Alvarez's probing essay may be still more meaningful if you read all of them.

A. Alvarez: SYLVIA PLATH

Prefatory Note

What follows was originally written as a memorial broadcast which went out on the B.B.C. Third Programme very shortly after Sylvia Plath's death in 1963. It was designed partly as a tribute and partly as an attempt to show how those strange last poems might be read. Clearly, their newness made some kind of explanation, or hints, seem necessary. The British Council had interviewed her and taped her reading some of the last poems not long before she died. I based my broadcast on these tapes, and planned it as little more than a running commentary. So inevitably it lacks the formal poise of a proper essay. And because it was written so close to her death — a time of great turmoil and confusion — it is far rougher than anything I would do today. But perhaps that roughness is a genuine part of the thing; it seems impossible now, without entirely recasting it, to polish it up much or amplify the many points that are made too briefly. I don't even believe that more elegance would be appropriate.

At the time, it seemed more important to try to define the extraordinary originality of her later poems — what they were doing and how they were doing it — than to dwell on the tragic circumstances of her death. I still believe that this is the right priority.

The broadcast was later published in *The Review* and seemed, as a result, to acquire some kind of underground critical currency. But in the process, some of the closing remarks have been misunderstood. So I have added a final note to try to get the emphasis right.

A. A., 1966

She was a tall, spindly girl with waist-length sandy hair, which she usually wore in a bun, and that curious, advertisement-trained, transatlantic air of anxious pleasantness. But this was merely a nervous social manner; under it, she was ruthless about her perceptions, wary and very individual.

She was born in 1932. Her parents were both teachers and both of German origin: her mother Austrian, her father pure Prussian; he died when she was nine. They lived in Boston, Massachusetts: "I went to public school," she wrote, "genuinely public. Everybody went."[1] Hers was Wellesley High School. From there she went to Smith College, remorselessly winning all the prizes. In 1955 she got a Fulbright Scholarship to Newnham College, Cambridge. Whilst there she met Ted Hughes, who at that point had published almost nothing; they were married in 1956, on Bloomsday. They went to America, where she taught at Smith for a year. In 1959 they returned to England and settled there for good — first in London, then in Devon. By this time she

[1] From "The All-Round Image," a talk prepared for the B.B.C. Third Programme.

had become a full-time exile and used to refer to herself as an English poet. In 1960 her first child, Frieda, was born and her first book, *The Colossus*, was published. Two years later she had a son, Nicholas. In the middle of January 1963 she published her first novel, *The Bell Jar*, using a pseudonym, Victoria Lukas, partly, she told me, because she didn't consider it a serious work — though it was more serious and achieved than she admitted, and got good reviews — and partly because she thought too many people would be hurt by it — which was probably true. She died one month later, on 11 February 1963.

Her first poem came out in *The Boston Traveller*, when she was eight-and-a-half. I have no idea what these earliest poems were like, though their subject-matter appears to have been conventional enough: "Birds, bees, spring, fall," she said in an interview,

> . . . all those subjects which are absolute gifts to the person who doesn't have any interior experience to write about.[2]

Clearly the poems were very precocious, like everything she did in her school and college days. She seemed effortlessly good at things: she was a prize scholar as well as a prize poet; and later, when she married, she was good at having children and keeping a house clean, cooking, making honey, even at riding horses. There was a ruthless efficiency in all she did which left no room for mistakes or uncertainties.

Poetry, however, is not made by efficiency — least of all Sylvia Plath's poetry. Instead, her extraordinary general competence was, I think, made necessary by what made her write: an underlying sense of violent unease. It took a great deal of efficiency to cope with that, to keep it in check. And when the efficiency finally failed, her world collapsed.

But she was disciplined in art, as in everything else. For a first volume, by someone still in her twenties, *The Colossus* is exceptionally accomplished. A poem like "The Ghost's Leave-taking" is fairly typical. It exhibits her broad and flexible range of language, in which the unexpected, right word comes so easily:

> . . . the waking head rubbishes out of the draggled lot
> Of sulphurous landscapes and obscure lunar conundrums

and her ability to make startling images out of humdrum objects:

> The oracular ghost who dwindles on pin-legs
> To a knot of laundry, with a classic bunch of sheets
> Upraised, as a hand, emblematic of farewell.

But that last line is also typical of the book's weakness: certainly, it's beautiful, but also peculiarly careful, held in check, a bit ornate and rhetorical. Throughout *The Colossus* she is using her art to keep the disturbance, out of which she made her verse, at a distance. It is as though she had not yet come to grips with her subject as an artist. She has Style, but not properly her own style. You can trace the influence of Ted Hughes, and there are also poems which sound like Theodore Roethke's — including the long "Poem for a Birthday," which stands

---

[2] From an interview and reading of poems made by her for the British Council.

last in the book and attempts, I think, to deal with a subject which later possessed her: her nervous breakdown and near suicide at the age of nineteen. It was this which also made the climax and main theme of her novel.

Most of the poems in *The Colossus* were written during the first three years of her marriage, from 1956 to 1959. The *real* poems began in 1960, after the birth of her daughter, Frieda. It is as though the child were a proof of her identity, as though it liberated her into her real self. I think this guess is borne out by the fact that her most creative period followed the birth of her son, two years later. This triggered off an extraordinary outburst: for two or three months, right up to her death, she was writing one, or two, sometimes three poems a day, seven days a week. She said, in a note written for the B.B.C.:

> These new poems of mine have one thing in common. They were all written at about four in the morning . . . that still blue, almost eternal hour before the baby's cry, before the glassy music of the milkman, settling his bottles.[3]

A poem like "Poppies in October" is simpler, much more direct, than those in *The Colossus*. The unexpectedness is still there, both in the language —

> a sky palely and flamily igniting its carbon monoxide

and the images —

> the woman in the ambulance whose red heart blooms
> through her coat so astoundingly.

But that leaping, arching imagination is no longer baroque, no longer a gesture on the surface of the poem. It is part of what she is actually saying. The poem is about the unexpectedness of the poppies, their gratuitous beauty in her own frozen life.

This change of tone and access of strength is partly, as she said herself, a technical development:

> May I say this: that the ones I've read are very recent, and I have found myself having to read them aloud to myself. Now this is something I didn't do. For example, my first book, *The Colossus* — I can't read any of the poems aloud now. I didn't write them to be read aloud. In fact, they quite privately bore me. Now these very recent ones — I've got to say them. I speak them to myself. Whatever lucidity they may have comes from the fact that I say them aloud.[4]

The difference, in short, is between finger-count and ear-count; one measures the rhythm by rules, the other catches the movement by the inner disturbance it creates. And she could only "write poems out loud" when she had discovered her own speaking voice; that is, her own identity.

The second main difference between this and her earlier verse is in the direct relevance of the experience. In "The Ghost's Leave-taking" the subject is nominally very personal — it's about the way dreams stay with you when

[3] From the introductory notes to "New Poems," a reading prepared for the B.B.C. Third Programme but never broadcast.
[4] From an interview and reading of poems made by her for the British Council.

you first wake up — but the effect is predominantly of very brilliant scene-setting. In "Poppies in October," on the other hand, what starts as a description finishes as a way of defining her own state of mind. This, I think, is the key to the later poems; the more vivid and imaginative the details are, the more resolutely she turns them inwards. The more objective they seem, the more subjective they, in fact, become. Take, for example, a poem about her favorite horse:

ARIEL

Stasis in darkness.
Then the substanceless blue
Pour of tor and distances.

God's lioness,
How one we grow,   5
Pivot of heels and knees! — The furrow

Splits and passes, sister to
The brown arc
Of the neck I cannot catch,

Nigger-eye   10
Berries cast dark
Hooks —

Black sweet blood mouthfuls,
Shadows.
Something else   15

Hauls me through air —
Thighs, hair;
Flakes from my heels.

White
Godiva, I unpeel —   20
Dead hands, dead stringencies.

And now I
Foam to wheat, a glitter of seas.
The child's cry

Melts in the wall.   25
And I
Am the arrow,

The dew that flies
Suicidal, at one with the drive
Into the red   30

Eye, the cauldron of morning.

The difficulty with this poem lies in separating one element from another. Yet that is also its theme; the rider is one with the horse, the horse is one with the furrowed earth, and the dew on the furrow is one with the rider. The movement of the imagery, like that of the perceptions, is circular. There is also another peculiarity: although the poem is nominally about riding a horse, it is curiously "substanceless" — to use her own word. You are made to *feel* the horse's physical presence, but not to see it. The detail is all inward. It is as though the horse itself were an emotional state. So the poem is not just about the stallion "Ariel," it is about what happens when the "stasis in darkness" ceases to be static, when the potential violence of the animal is unleashed. And also the violence of the rider.

In a way, most of her later poems are about just that: about the unleashing of power, about tapping the roots of her own inner violence. There is, of course, nothing so very extraordinary about that. I think that this, in general, is the direction all the best contemporary poetry is taking. She, certainly, did not claim to be original in the kind of writing she was doing:

> I've been very excited by what I feel is the new breakthrough that came with, say, Robert Lowell's *Life Studies.* This intense breakthrough into very serious, very personal emotional experience, which I feel has been partly taboo. Robert Lowell's poems about his experiences in a mental hospital, for example, interest me very much. These peculiar private and taboo subjects I feel have been explored in recent American poetry — I think particularly of the poetess Anne Sexton, who writes also about her experiences as a mother; as a mother who's had a nervous breakdown, as an extremely emotional and feeling young woman. And her poems are wonderfully craftsmanlike poems, and yet they have a kind of emotional and psychological depth which I think is something perhaps quite new and exciting.[5]

Robert Lowell and Anne Sexton make pretty distinguished company, but I think Sylvia Plath took further than either of them her analysis of the intolerable and the "taboo." And she did it in a wholly original way. For example, her poem "Fever 103°," which she described in this way:

> This poem is about two kinds of fire — the fires of hell, which merely agonize, and the fires of heaven, which purify. During the poem, the first sort of fire suffers itself into the second.[6]

Reading it for the first time, it sounds as though it were just free association on a theme: the theme that illness and pain are cumbersome and intolerable, but that if they go on long enough they cancel themselves out and the purity of death takes over. But the progress is not in fact haphazard. Death is there from the start: "dull, fat Cerberus . . . wheezes at the gate" right from the beginning. What the poem does is to work away at this idea of a heavy, mundane death until it is purified of all extraneous matter and only the essential bodilessness remains. At the same time this movement is also that of a personal catharsis. She is clarifying not only an abstract death but also her feelings about it, from the cluttered and insufferable to the pure and acceptable. Her method is to let

---

[5] From an interview and reading of poems made by her for the British Council.
[6] From the introductory notes to "New Poems," a reading prepared for the B.B.C. Third Programme but never broadcast.

image breed image until, in some curious way, they also breed statements, conclusions:

> They will not rise,
> But trundle round the globe
> Choking the aged and the meek,
> The weak
>
> Hothouse baby in its crib,
> The ghastly orchid
> Hanging its hanging garden in the air,
>
> Devilish leopard!
> Radiation turned it white
> And killed it in an hour.
>
> Greasing the bodies of adulterers
> Like Hiroshima ash and eating in.
> The sin. The sin.

The baby becomes the orchid, the spotted orchid the leopard, the beast of prey the adulteress; by which time the fever has become a kind of atomic radiation (perhaps she was remembering the film *Hiroshima mon amour,* where adultery, radiation and expiation were also joined inextricably together). The idea of the individual and the world purged of sin is established, and the poem is free to move on to the realm of purification.

Now, the movement is complicated. Often in these last poems it seems unnecessarily so. The images came so easily to her that sometimes they confuse each other until the poems choke in the obscurity of their own inventiveness. But they never suffer from the final insoluble obscurity of private references — as, say, Pound's do in the *Pisan Cantos.* The reasons for Sylvia Plath's images are always there, though sometimes you have to work hard to find them. She is, in short, always in intelligent control of her feelings. Her work bears out her theories:

> I think my poems come immediately out of the sensuous and emotional experiences I have, but I must say I cannot sympathize with these cries from the heart that are informed by nothing except a needle or a knife or whatever it is. I believe that one should be able to control and manipulate experiences, even the most terrifying — like madness, being tortured, this kind of experience — and one should be able to manipulate these experiences with an informed and intelligent mind. I think that personal experience shouldn't be a kind of shut box and mirror-looking narcissistic experience. I believe it should be generally relevant, to such things as Hiroshima and Dachau, and so on.[7]

It seems to me that it was only by her determination both to face her most inward and terrifying experiences and to use her intelligence in doing so — so as not to be overwhelmed by them — that she managed to write these extraor-

---

[7] From an interview and reading of poems made by her for the British Council.

dinary last poems, which are at once deeply autobiographical and yet detached, generally relevant.

"Lady Lazarus" is a stage further on from "Fever 103°;" its subject is the total purification of achieved death.[8] It is also far more intimately concerned with the drift of Sylvia Plath's life. The deaths of Lady Lazarus correspond to her own crises: the first just after her father died, the second when she had her nervous breakdown, the third perhaps a presentiment of the death that was shortly to come. Maybe this closeness of the subject helped make the poem so direct. The details don't clog each other: they are swept forward by the current of immediate feeling, marshalled by it and ordered. But what is remarkable about the poem is the objectivity with which she handles such personal material. She is not just talking about her own private suffering. Instead, it is the very closeness of her pain which gives it a general meaning; through it she assumes the suffering of all the modern victims. Above all, she becomes an imaginary Jew. I think this is a vitally important element in her work. For two reasons. First, because anyone whose subject is suffering has a ready-made modern example of hell on earth in the concentration camps. And what matters in them is not so much the physical torture — since sadism is general and perennial — but the way modern, as it were industrial, techniques can be used to destroy utterly the human identity. Individual suffering can be heroic provided it leaves the person who suffers a sense of his own individuality — provided, that is, there is an illusion of choice remaining to him. But when suffering is mass-produced, men and women become as equal and identityless as objects on an assembly-line, and nothing remains — certainly no values, no humanity. This anonymity of pain, which makes all dignity impossible, was Sylvia Plath's subject. Second, she seemed convinced, in these last poems, that the root of her suffering was the death of her father, whom she loved, who abandoned her and who dragged her after him into death. And in her fantasies her father was pure German, pure Aryan, pure anti-semite.

It all comes together in the most powerful of her last poems, "Daddy," about which she wrote the following bleak note:

> The poem is spoken by a girl with an Electra complex. Her father died while she thought he was God. Her case is complicated by the fact that her father was also a Nazi and her mother very possibly part Jewish. In the daughter the two strains marry and paralyse each other — she has to act out the awful little allegory before she is free of it.[9]

DADDY

You do not do, you do not do
Any more, black shoe
In which I have lived like a foot
For thirty years, poor and white,
Barely daring to breathe or Achoo.   5

---

[8] "Lady Lazarus": this complete poem will be found in the anthology at the back of this book. See page 412.
[9] From the introductory notes to "New Poems," a reading prepared for the B.B.C. Third Programme but never broadcast.

Daddy, I have had to kill you.
You died before I had time —
Marble-heavy, a bag full of God,
Ghastly statue with one grey toe
Big as a Frisco seal   10

And a head in the freakish Atlantic
Where it pours bean green over blue
In the waters off beautiful Nauset.
I used to pray to recover you.
Ach, du.   15

In the German tongue, in the Polish town
Scraped flat by the roller
Of wars, wars, wars.
But the name of the town is common.
My Polack friend   20

Says there are a dozen or two.
So I never could tell where you
Put your foot, your root,
I never could talk to you.
The tongue stuck in my jaw.   25

It stuck in a barb wire snare.
Ich, ich, ich, ich,
I could hardly speak.
I thought every German was you.
And the language obscene   30

An engine, an engine
Chuffing me off like a Jew.
A Jew to Dachau, Auschwitz, Belsen.
I began to talk like a Jew.
I think I may well be a Jew.   35

The snows of the Tyrol, the clear beer of Vienna
Are not very pure or true.
With my gypsy ancestress and my weird luck
And my Taroc pack and my Taroc pack
I may be a bit of a Jew.   40

I have always been scared of *you*,
With your Luftwaffe, your gobbledygoo.
And your neat moustache
And your Aryan eye, bright blue.
Panzer-man, panzer-man, O You —   45

Not God but a swastika
So black no sky could squeak through.
Every woman adores a Fascist,
The boot in the face, the brute
Brute heart of a brute like you.   50

You stand at the blackboard, daddy,
In the picture I have of you,
A cleft in your chin instead of your foot
But no less a devil for that, no not
Any less the black man who   55

Bit my pretty red heart in two.
I was ten when they buried you.
At twenty I tried to die
And get back, back, back at you.
I thought even the bones would do.   60

But they pulled me out of the sack,
And they stuck me together with glue.
And then I knew what to do.
I made a model of you,
A man in black with a Meinkampf look   65

And a love of the rack and the screw.
And I said I do, I do.
So daddy, I'm finally through.
The black telephone's off at the root,
The voices just can't worm through.   70

If I've killed one man, I've killed two —
The vampire who said he was you
And drank my blood for a year,
Seven years, if you want to know.
Daddy, you can lie back now.   75

There's a stake in your fat black heart
And the villagers never liked you.
They are dancing and stamping on you.
They always *knew* it was you.
Daddy, daddy, you bastard, I'm through.   80

"Lady Lazarus" ends with a final, defensive, desperate assertion of omnipotence:

> Out of the ash
> I rise with my red hair
> And I eat men like air.

Not even that defense is left her in "Daddy;" instead, she goes right down to the deep spring of her sickness and describes it purely. What comes through most powerfully, I think, is the terrible unforgivingness of her verse, the continual sense not so much of violence — although there is a good deal of that — as of violent resentment that this should have been done to *her*. What she does in the poem is, with a weird detachment, to turn the violence against herself so as to show that she can equal her oppressors with her self-inflicted oppression. And this is the strategy of the concentration camps. When suffering is there whatever you do, by inflicting it upon yourself you achieve your identity, you set yourself free.

Yet the tone of the poem, like its psychological mechanisms, is not single or simple, and she uses a great deal of skill to keep it complex. Basically, her trick is to tell this horror story in a verse form as insistently jaunty and ritualistic as a nursery rhyme. And this helps her to maintain towards all the protagonists — her father, her husband and herself — a note of hard and sardonic anger, as though she were almost amused that her own suffering should be so extreme, so grotesque. The technical psychoanalytic term for this kind of insistent gaiety to protect you from what, if faced nakedly, would be insufferable, is "manic defense." But what, in a neurotic, is a means of avoiding reality can become, for an artist, a source of creative strength, a way of handling the unhandleable, and presenting the situation in all its fullness. When she first read me the poem a few days after she wrote it, she called it a piece of "light verse." It obviously isn't, yet equally obviously it also isn't the racking personal confession that a mere description or précis of it might make it sound.

Yet neither is it unchangingly vindictive or angry. The whole poem works on one single, returning note and rhyme, echoing from start to finish:

> You do not do, you do not do . . .
> . . . I used to pray to recover you.
> Ach, du . . .

There is a kind of cooing tenderness in this which complicates the other, more savage note of resentment. It brings in an element of pity, less for herself and her own suffering than for the person who made her suffer. Despite everything, "Daddy" is a love poem.

When Sylvia Plath died I wrote an epitaph on her in *The Observer*, at the end of which I said "The loss to literature is inestimable." But someone pointed out to me that this wasn't quite true. The achievement of her final style is to make poetry and death inseparable. The one could not exist without the other. And this is right. In a curious way, the poems read as though they were written posthumously. It needed not only great intelligence and insight to handle the material of them, it also took a kind of bravery. Poetry of this order is a murderous art.

Postscript, 1966

These final remarks seem to have caused some confusion. I was *not* in any sense meaning to imply that breakdown or suicide is a validation of what I now call Extremist poetry. No amount of personal horror will make a good poet out of a bad one. Rather, the opposite: to know from evidence outside the poetry that a man has suffered a great deal will throw into high relief just how much he lacks as an artist.

I was also *not* in any sense meaning to imply that a breakdown or suicide is the necessary corollary or result of Extremist work. Obviously, the poet is not obliged to prove in his life that what he writes about is genuine. After all, he is a poet by virtue of his ability to create an imaginative world which has an objective existence apart from him. The poetry is its own proof. Indeed, the chances are that the more hip the art the squarer the life of the artist who creates it. A genuinely hip life leaves little time for art.

But I did mean to imply that this kind of writing involves an element of risk. The Extremist artist sets out deliberately to explore the roots of his emotions, the obscurest springs of his personality, maybe even the sickness he feels himself to be prey to, "giving himself over to it," as I have written elsewhere, "for the sake of the range and intensity of his art."[10] It is precisely here that the risk lies. I do not personally believe in the classical Freudian argument that art is therapeutic, that the artist is relieved of his fantasies by expressing them. On the contrary, the weird logic of art seems to be that the act of formal expression merely makes the dredged-up material more readily available to the artist. So the result of handling it in his art may well be that he finds himself living it out. Keats is the prime example of this devious mechanism: the poems of his great period — from the second *Hyperion* onwards — are all about death. Apparently, this great creative outburst was triggered off by nursing his brother Tom through his final illness. But if Tom's death were the cause, Keats's own may have been the ultimate effect. He had, that is, pushed death so much to the foreground of his consciousness that it became unavoidable; having written the poems there was nothing left for him to do except die.

I think much the same happened with Sylvia Plath. The very source of her creative energy was, it turned out, her self-destructiveness. But it was, precisely, a source of *living* energy, of her imaginative, creative power. So, though death itself may have been a side-issue, it was also an unavoidable risk in writing her kind of poem. My own impression of the circumstances surrounding her eventual death is that she gambled, not much caring whether she won or lost; and she lost. Had she won, the power of those last poems would have been in no way altered or falsified, and she would have been free to go on to other work. That she didn't is the real tragedy.

QUESTIONS

1. Quoting the poem "Fever 103°," Alvarez says, "The images came so easily to her that sometimes they confuse each other until the poems choke in the obscurity of their own inventiveness." Comment on the justice or injustice of this criticism. Refer to other Sylvia Plath poems.
2. If you didn't know the biographical details that Alvarez provides, what would you find obscure or puzzling in the poems "Daddy" and "Lady Lazarus"? Knowing these facts, what if anything still puzzles you?
3. Read other poems in this book by Sylvia Plath ("Cut," "Lady Lazarus," "Metaphors," "Morning Song," "Face Lift") and explain how in understanding them Alvarez's insights are useful to you.
4. How well do the poems of Sylvia Plath persuade you that, as she says in a statement quoted by Alvarez, her personal experiences are "generally relevant to such things as Hiroshima and Dachau"?
5. What changes does Alvarez find taking place between Plath's early poems and her late poems?
6. Discuss Alvarez's contention that "tapping the roots of her own inner violence" is "the direction all the best contemporary poetry is taking." What do you think he means?
7. In his final postscript, why does Alvarez take such care to distinguish between a poet's life and a poet's art? Discuss his contention that "the more hip the art the squarer the life of the artist who creates it." Can you think of any other artists besides Sylvia Plath of whom this contention might (or might not) be true?

[10] *Under Pressure* (Harmondsworth: Penguin, 1965), p. 185.

1. Choosing a poem from the anthology at the back of this book, or working on a poem assigned by your instructor, write an essay setting forth your understanding of it. Try to cope with any difficulties in the poem, explaining them for the benefit of anyone else. Pay attention not only to the poem's subject and theme, but also to whatever imagery, sound, metaphor, and symbolism you discover in it.

2. Write a comparison between two poems in the anthology in which you analyze each, reading closely (as Jarrell, Emanuel, and Alvarez do).

3. Write a Wilbur-like essay in which, using the method of paraphrase, you try coming up with better and better paraphrases of the poem until you find one that seems to fit.

4. Write a fresh essay on "Dover Beach" or on any poem of Sylvia Plath, stating your understanding of other elements of the poem that Dickey or Alvarez may have missed.

5. Leslie Fiedler, the critic and novelist, once wrote an essay in which he pretended to be a critic of the last century ("A Review of *Leaves of Grass* and *Hiawatha* as of 1855", in *American Poetry Review*, Vol. 2, No. 2, March/April 1973). Writing as if he subscribed to the tastes of the age, Fiedler declared Whitman's book shaggy and shocking, and awarded Professor Longfellow all the praise. If you can steep yourself in the literature of a former age (or recent past year) deeply enough to feel confident, such an essay might be fun to write (and to read). Write about some poem once fashionable, now forgotten; or about some poem once spurned, now esteemed. Your instructor might have some suggestions.

6. Write an essay examining two or more comparable poems from the anthology with special attention to their imagery, or to their use of myth, or to their use of irony.

7. Like James A. Emanuel in his discussion of Gwendolyn Brooks, write an analysis of a poem by a poet of a minority group, closely reading the poem, showing how the poet speaks for his or her people.

8. Write a D. H. Lawrence-style analysis of some poem in the anthology, going through the poem line by line and poking fun at its weaknesses. Then go through the same poem again and point out its strengths.

9. With Alvarez's essay on Sylvia Plath as your model, write an essay on the seven or more poems in this book by any one of the following poets: Shakespeare, Donne, Herrick, Blake, Wordsworth, Keats, Emily Dickinson, Whitman, Tennyson, Housman, Hopkins, Yeats, Hardy, Frost, Cummings, Williams, Wallace Stevens, and Roethke. As Alvarez does, freely incorporate any biographical information that seems pertinent to the close reading and understanding of the poems.

18 What Is Poetry?

Archibald MacLeish (b. 1892)

<small>ARS POETICA</small>

A poem should be palpable and mute
As a globed fruit,

Dumb
As old medallions to the thumb,   4

Silent as the sleeve-worn stone
Of casement ledges where the moss has grown —

A poem should be wordless
As the flight of birds.   8

A poem should be motionless in time
As the moon climbs,

Leaving, as the moon releases
Twig by twig the night-entangled trees,   12

Leaving, as the moon behind the winter leaves,
Memory by memory the mind —

A poem should be motionless in time
As the moon climbs.   16

A poem should be equal to:
Not true.

For all the history of grief
An empty doorway and a maple leaf.   20

For love
The leaning grasses and two lights above the sea —

A poem should not mean
But be.   24

What is poetry? By now, perhaps, you have formed your own idea, whether or not you feel able to define it. Just in case further efforts at definition can be useful, here are a few memorable ones (including, for a second look, some given earlier):

> the art of uniting pleasure with truth by calling imagination to the help of reason.
> — Samuel Johnson

> the imaginative expression of strong feeling, usually rhythmical . . . the spontaneous overflow of powerful feelings recollected in tranquillity.
> — William Wordsworth

> the best words in the best order.
> — Samuel Taylor Coleridge

> musical Thought.
> — Thomas Carlyle

> If I read a book and it makes my whole body so cold no fire can ever warm me, I know that it is poetry. If I feel physically as if the top of my head were taken off, I know that it is poetry. Is there any other way?
> — Emily Dickinson

> speech framed . . . to be heard for its own sake and interest even over and above its interest of meaning.
> — Gerard Manley Hopkins

> a revelation in words by means of the words.
> — Wallace Stevens

> not the assertion that something is true, but the making of that truth more fully real to us.
> — T. S. Eliot

> the clear expression of mixed feelings.
> — W. H. Auden

A poem differs from most prose in several ways. For one, both writer and reader tend to regard it differently. The poet's attitude is as if, sticking his neck out, he were to say: I offer this piece of writing to be read not as prose but as a poem — that is, more perceptively, thoughtfully, and considerately, with more attention to sounds and connotations. This is a great deal to expect, but in return, the reader has a right to his own expectations. He approaches the poem in the anticipation of out-of-the-ordinary knowledge and pleasure. He assumes that the poet may use certain enjoyable devices not available to prose: rime, alliteration, meter, and rhythms — definite, various, or emphatic. (The poet may not *always* choose to employ these things.) He expects the poet to make greater use, perhaps, of resources of meaning such as figurative language, allusion, symbol, and imagery. If he were reading prose, he might seek no more than meaning: no more than what could be paraphrased without serious loss. If he meets any figurative language or graceful turns of word order, he thinks them pleasant extras. But in poetry all these "extras" matter as much as the paraphraseable content, if not more. For, when we finish reading a good poem, we cannot explain precisely to ourselves what we have experienced — without repeating, word for word, the language of the poem itself.

It is doubtful that anyone can draw an immovable boundary between poetry and prose, nor does such an attempt seem necessary. Certain prose needs only to be arranged in lines to be seen as poetry — especially prose that conveys strong emotion in vivid, physical imagery and in terse, figurative, rhythmical language. Even in translation the words of Chief Joseph of the Nez Percé tribe, at the moment of his surrender to the U.S. Army in 1877, still move us and are memorable:

> Hear me, my warriors, my heart is sick and sad:
> Our chiefs are killed,
> The old men all are dead,
> It is cold and we have no blankets.
>
> The little children freeze to death.
>
> Hear me, my warriors, my heart is sick and sad:
> From where the sun now stands I will fight no more forever.

It may be that a poem can point beyond words to something still more essential. Language has its limits, and probably Edgar Allan Poe was the only poet ever to claim he could always find words for whatever he wished to express. For, of all a man can experience and all he can imagine, words say only part. "Human speech," said Flaubert, who strove after the best of it, "is like a cracked kettle on which we hammer out tunes to make bears dance, when what we long for is the compassion of the stars."

Like Yeats's chestnut-tree in "Among School Children" (which when asked whether it is leaf, blossom, or bole, has no answer), a poem is to be seen not as a confederation of form, rime, image, metaphor, tone, and theme, but as a whole. We study a poem one element at a time because the intellect best comprehends what it can separate. But only our total attention, involving the participation of our blood and marrow, can see all elements in a poem fused, all dancing together. Yeats knew how to make poems and how to read them:

> God guard me from those thoughts men think
> In the mind alone;
> He that sings a lasting song
> Thinks in a marrow-bone.

Throughout this book, we have been working on the assumption that the patient and conscious explication of poems will sharpen unconscious perceptions. We can only hope that it will; the final test lies in whether you care to go on by yourself, reading other poems, finding in them pleasure and enlightenment. Pedagogy must have a stop; so must the viewing of poems as if their elements fell into chapters. For the total experience of reading a poem surpasses the mind's categories. The wind in the grass, says a proverb, cannot be taken into the house.

Anthology

Sit a while dear son,
Here are biscuits to eat and here is milk to drink,
But as soon as you sleep and renew yourself in sweet clothes,
I kiss you with a good-by kiss and open the gates for your egress hence.

Long enough have you dream'd contemptible dreams,
Now I wash the gum from your eyes,
You must habit yourself to the dazzle of the light and of every moment of your
    life.

Long have you timidly waded holding a plank by the shore,
Now I will you to be a bold swimmer,
To jump off in the midst of the sea, rise again, nod to me, shout, and laugh-
    ingly dash with your hair.

                        — Walt Whitman, "Song of Myself"

Anonymous (English; sixteenth century)

WESTERN WIND

Western wind, when wilt thou blow,
The° small rain down can rain?   *(so that) the*
Christ, if my love were in my arms,
And I in my bed again!

Anonymous (traditional Scottish folk ballad)

EDWARD

"Why dois your brand° sae° drap wi' bluid,   *sword; so*
        Edward, Edward?
Why dois your brand sae drap wi' bluid?
    And why sae sad gang° yee, O?"   *go*
"O, I hae killed my hauke sae guid,
        Mither, mither,
O, I hae killed my hauke sae guid,
    And I had nae mair bot° hee, O."   *but*   8

"Your haukis bluid was nevir sae reid,
        Edward, Edward,
Your haukis bluid was nevir sae reid,
    My deir son I tell thee, O."
"O, I hae killed my reid-roan steid,
        Mither, mither,
O, I hae killed my reid-roan steid,
    That erst° was sa fair and frie°, O."   *once; free*   16

"Your steid was auld, and ye hae gat mair,
        Edward, Edward,
Your steid was auld, and ye hae gat mair,
    Sum other dule° ye drie°, O."   *sorrow; suffer*
"O, I hae killed my fadir deir,
        Mither, mither,
O, I hae killed my fadir deir,
    Alas, and wae° is mee, O!"   *woe*   24

"And whatten penance wul ye drie for that,
        Edward, Edward?
And whatten penance will ye drie for that?
    My deir son, now tell me, O."
"Ile set my feit in yonder boat,
        Mither, mither,
Ile set my feit in yonder boat,
    And Ile fare ovir the sea, O."   32

"And what wul ye doe wi' your towirs and your ha',
    Edward, Edward,
And what wul ye doe wi' your towirs and your ha',
    That were sae fair to see, O?"
"Ile let thame stand tul they doun fa',
    Mither, mither,
Ile let thame stand tul they doun fa',
    For here nevir mair maun° I bee, O."   *must* 40

"And what wul ye leive to your bairns° and your wife,   *children*
    Edward, Edward?
And what wul ye leive to your bairns and your wife,
    When ye gang ovir the sea, O?"
"The warldis° room, late° them beg thrae° life,   *world's; let; through*
    Mither, mither,
The warldis room, late them beg thrae life,
    For thame nevir mair wul I see, O."   48

"And what wul ye leive to your ain° mither deir,   *own*
    Edward, Edward?
And what wul ye leive to your ain mither deir?
    My deir son, now tell me, O."
"The curse of hell frae me sall ye beir,
    Mither, mither,
The curse of hell frae me sall ye beir,
    Sic° counseils° ye gave to me, O."   *such; counsel* 56

Anonymous (Scottish folk ballad)
SIR PATRICK SPENCE

The king sits in Dumferling toune,
    Drinking the blude-reid wine:
"O whar will I get guid sailor
    To sail this schip of mine?"   4

Up and spak an eldern knicht,
    Sat at the kings richt kne:
"Sir Patrick Spence is the best sailor
    That sails upon the se."   8

The king has written a braid letter,
    And signed it wi' his hand,
And sent it to Sir Patrick Spence,
    Was walking on the sand.   12

The first line that Sir Patrick red,
    A loud lauch lauchèd he;
The next line that Sir Patrick red,
    The teir blinded his ee.   16

"O wha° is this has don this deid,   *who*
   This ill deid don to me,
To send me out this time o' the yeir,
   To sail upon the se!   20

"Mak haste, mak haste, my mirry men all,
   Our guid schip sails the morne."
"O say na sae°, my master deir,   *so*
   For I feir a deadlie storme.   24

"Late late yestreen I saw the new moone,
   Wi' the auld moone in hir arme,
And I feir, I feir, my deir master,
   That we will cum to harme."   28

O our Scots nobles wer richt laith°   *loath*
   To weet° their cork-heild schoone°;   *wet; shoes*
Bot lang owre° a' the play wer playd,   *ere*
   Their hats they swam aboone°. *above (their heads)* 32

O lang, lang may their ladies sit,
   Wi' their fans into their hand,
Or ere° they se Sir Patrick Spence   *long before*
   Cum sailing to the land.   36

O lang, lang may the ladies stand,
   Wi' their gold kems° in their hair,   *combs*
Waiting for their ain° deir lords,   *own*
   For they'll se thame na mair.   40

Haf owre°, haf owre to Aberdour,   *halfway over*
   It's fiftie fadom deip,
And thair lies guid Sir Patrick Spence,
   Wi' the Scots lords at his feit.   44

Sir Patrick Spence. 9. *braid:* Broad, but broad in what sense? Among guesses are *plain-spoken, official,* and *on wide paper.*

Anonymous (traditional English folk ballad)
The Three Ravens

There were three ravens sat on a tree,
   Down a down, hay down, hay down,
There were three ravens sat on a tree,
   With a down,
There were three ravens sat on a tree,   5
They were as black as they might be.
   With a down derry, derry, derry, down, down.

The one of them said to his mate,
"Where shall we our breakfast take?"

"Down in yonder greene field,
There lies a knight slain under his shield.   10

"His hounds they lie down at his feet,
So well they can their master keep.

"His hawks they fly so eagerly,
There's no fowl dare him come nigh."   15

Down there comes a fallow doe,
As great with young as she might go.

She lift up his bloody head,
And kist his wounds that were so red.

She got him up upon her back,   20
And carried him to earthen lake°.   *the grave*

She buried him before the prime,
She was dead herself ere evensong time.

God send every gentleman
Such hawks, such hounds, and such a leman°.   *lover* 25

THE THREE RAVENS. The lines of refrain are repeated in each stanza. "Perhaps in the folk mind the doe is the form the soul of a human mistress, now dead, has taken," Albert B. Friedman has suggested (in *The Viking Book of Folk Ballads*). "Most probably the knight's beloved was understood to be an enchanted woman who was metamorphosed at certain times into an animal." 22–23. *prime, evensong:* Two of the canonical hours set aside for prayer and worship. Prime is at dawn, evensong at dusk.

Anonymous (Scottish ballad)
THE TWA CORBIES

As I was walking all alane,
I heard twa corbies° making a mane°;   *ravens; moan*
The tane° unto the t'other say,   *one*
"Where sall we gang° and dine today?"   *go* 4

"In behint yon auld fail dyke°,   *turf wall*
I wot° there lies a new slain knight;   *know*
And naebody kens° that he lies there,   *knows*
But his hawk, his hound, and lady fair.   8

"His hound is to the hunting gane,
His hawk to fetch the wild-fowl hame,
His lady's ta'en another mate,
So we may mak our dinner sweet.   12

"Ye'll sit on his white hause-bane°,   *neck bone*
And I'll pike out his bonny blue een;
Wi' ae° lock o' his gowden hair   *one*
We'll theek° our nest when it grows bare.   *thatch* 16

"Mony a one for him makes mane,
But nane sall ken where he is gane;
O'er his white banes, when they are bare,
The wind sall blaw for evermair." 20

THE TWA CORBIES. Sir Walter Scott, the first to print this ballad in his *Minstrelsy of the Scottish Border* (1802–1803), calls it "rather a counterpart than a copy" of "The Three Ravens." M. J. C. Hodgart and other scholars think he may have written most of it himself.

Geoffrey Chaucer (1340?–1400)

THE COMPLAINT OF CHAUCER TO HIS PURSE

To yow, my purse, and to noon other wight°   *person*
Complayne I, for ye be my lady dere!
I am so sory, now that ye been lyght;
For certes, but° ye make me hevy chere,   *unless*
Me were as leef be layd upon my bere;
For which unto your mercy thus I crye:
Beth hevy ageyn, or elles moote I dye!   7

Now voucheth sauf° this day, or° yt be nyght,   *vouchsafe; before*
That I of yow the blisful soun may here,
Or see your colour lyk the sonne bryght,
That of yelownesse hadde never pere.
Ye be my lyf, ye be myn hertes stere°,   *rudder*
Quene of comfort and of good companye:
Beth hevy ageyn, or elles moote I dye!   14

Now purse, that ben to me my lyves lyght
And saveour, as° doun in this world here,   *while*
Out of this toune helpe me thurgh your myght,
Syn that ye wole nat ben my tresorere;
For I am shave as nye as any frere.
But yet I pray unto your curtesye:
Beth hevy ageyn, or elles moote I dye!   21

Lenvoy de Chaucer:

O conquerour of Brutes Albyon,
Which that by lyne and free eleccion
Been verray° kyng, this song to yow I sende;   *true*
And ye, that mowen° alle oure harmes amende,   *can*
Have mynde upon my supplicacion!   26

THE COMPLAINT OF CHAUCER TO HIS PURSE. Chaucer appears to have sent this poem in 1399 to newly crowned Henry IV, who promptly added forty marks to the poet's annual salary. 19. *I am shave as nye as any frere:* I am as close-shaven (of money) as a friar's head. *Lenvoy de Chaucer:* In a *ballade,* the French form Chaucer imitates here, the *envoy* is usually the poet's parting address to his ruler or patron. 22. *Brutes Albyon:* Albion ("the white land") is another name for white-cliffed England. Old chroniclers thought Britain to have been founded by Brutus (a legendary hero, great-grandson of Aeneas) and named after him.

Sir Thomas Wyatt (1503?–1542)

WHOSO LIST TO HUNT, I KNOW WHERE IS AN HIND

Whoso list° to hunt, I know where is an hind,   *likes*
  But as for me, alas, I may no more;
  The vain travail hath wearied me so sore.
  I am of them that farthest come behind.   4
Yet may I by no means my wearied mind
  Draw from the deer, but as she fleeth afore,
  Fainting I follow. I leave off therefore,
  Since in a net I seek to hold the wind.   8
Who list her hunt, I put him out of doubt,
  As well as I, may spend his time in vain;
  And graven with diamonds in letters plain
There is written, her fair neck round about: 12
  Noli me tangere°, for Caesar's I am,   *Touch me not*
  And wild for to hold, though I seem tame.   14

WHOSO LIST TO HUNT. 13. *Caesar's:* Perhaps a reference to Henry VIII. Wyatt's sonnet (one theory goes) may be about Henry's second wife Anne Boleyn.

Sir Philip Sidney (1554–1586)

WITH HOW SAD STEPS, O MOON, THOU CLIMB'ST THE SKIES

With how sad steps, O Moon, thou climb'st the skies!
  How silently, and with how wan a face!
  What! may it be that even in heavenly place
  That busy archer his sharp arrows tries?   4
Sure, if that long-with-love-acquainted eyes
  Can judge of love, thou feel'st a lover's case.
  I read it in thy looks; thy languished grace
  To me, that feel the like, thy state descries.   8
Then, even of fellowship, O Moon, tell me:
  Is constant love deemed there but want of wit?
  Are beauties there as proud as here they be?
Do they above love to be loved, and yet   12
  Those lovers scorn whom that love doth possess?
  Do they call virtue there ungratefulness?   14

Christopher Marlowe (1564–1593)

THE PASSIONATE SHEPHERD TO HIS LOVE

Come live with me and be my love,
And we will all the pleasures prove
That valleys, groves, hills, and fields,
Woods, or steepy mountain yields.   4

And we will sit upon the rocks,
Seeing the shepherds feed their flocks
By shallow rivers, to whose falls
Melodious birds sing madrigals.   8

And I will make thee beds of roses
And a thousand fragrant posies,
A cap of flowers and a kirtle°   *skirt*
Embroidered all with leaves of myrtle;   12

A gown made of the finest wool
Which from our pretty lambs we pull;
Fair-linèd slippers for the cold,
With buckles of the purest gold;   16

A belt of straw and ivy buds,
With coral clasps and amber studs.
And if these pleasures may thee move,
Come live with me and be my love.   20

The shepherds' swains shall dance and sing
For thy delight each May morning.
If these delights thy mind may move,
Then live with me and be my love.   24

COMPARE:

"The Passionate Shepherd to His Love" with "The Bait" by John Donne (page
321) and "Live with Me" by Mick Jagger and Keith Richard (page 420).

William Shakespeare (1564–1616)

WHEN DAISIES PIED AND VIOLETS BLUE

When daisies pied and violets blue
    And lady-smocks all silver-white
And cuckoo-buds° of yellow hue   *buttercups*
    Do paint the meadows with delight,   4
The cuckoo then, on every tree,
Mocks married men; for thus sings he,   6
                "Cuckoo,
Cuckoo, cuckoo!" — O word of fear,
Unpleasing to a married ear!   9

When shepherds pipe on oaten straws,
    And merry larks are ploughmen's clocks,
When turtles tread°, and rooks, and daws,   *turtledoves mate*
    And maidens bleach their summer smocks,   13
The cuckoo then, on every tree,
Mocks married men; for thus sings he,   15

"Cuckoo,
Cuckoo, cuckoo!" — O word of fear,
Unpleasing to a married ear!   18

WHEN DAISIES PIED. This song and "When icicles hang by the wall" conclude the play
Love's Labor's Lost. 2. *lady-smocks:* Also named cuckoo-flowers. 8. *O word of fear:* Because
it sounds like the word *cuckold*.

William Shakespeare (1564–1616)
WHEN ICICLES HANG BY THE WALL

When icicles hang by the wall,
  And Dick the shepherd blows his nail,
And Tom bears logs into the hall,
  And milk comes frozen home in pail,   4
When blood is nipped and ways° be foul,   *roads*
  Then nightly sings the staring owl:
    "Tu-whit, tu-who!"
    A merry note,
While greasy Joan doth keel° the pot.   *cool (as by skimming*   9
                                                or stirring)

When all aloud the wind doth blow,
  And coughing drowns the parson's saw°,   *old saw, platitude*
And birds sit brooding in the snow,
  And Marian's nose looks red and raw,   13
When roasted crabs° hiss in the bowl,   *crab apples*
  Then nightly sings the staring owl:
    "Tu-whit, tu-who!"
    A merry note,
While greasy Joan doth keel the pot.   18

William Shakespeare (1564–1616)
LET ME NOT TO THE MARRIAGE OF TRUE MINDS

Let me not to the marriage of true minds
Admit impediments. Love is not love
Which alters when it alteration finds,
Or bends with the remover° to remove.   *the inconstant lover*   4
O, no! it is an ever-fixèd mark
That looks on tempests and is never shaken;
It is the star to every wand'ring bark,
Whose worth's unknown, although his height be taken.   8
Love's not Time's fool, though rosy lips and cheeks
Within his bending sickle's compass come;

Love alters not with his brief hours and weeks,
But bears it out even to the edge of doom.   12
    If this be error and upon me proved,
    I never writ, nor no man ever loved.   14

LET ME NOT TO THE MARRIAGE OF TRUE MINDS. 2. *impediments:* Any reasons not to seal the marriage contract. In the Church of England, among these might be *inconstancy* and *change of circumstance* (the sudden loss of one's fortune).

William Shakespeare (1564–1616)
FULL FATHOM FIVE THY FATHER LIES

Full fathom five thy father lies;
    Of his bones are coral made;
Those are pearls that were his eyes:
    Nothing of him that doth fade,   4
But doth suffer a sea change
Into something rich and strange.   6
Sea nymphs hourly ring his knell:
    Ding-dong.
Hark! now I hear them — Ding-dong, bell.   9

FULL FATHOM FIVE. The spirit Ariel sings this song in *The Tempest* to Ferdinand, prince of Naples, who mistakenly thinks his father drowned.

William Shakespeare (1564–1616)
POOR SOUL, THE CENTER OF MY SINFUL EARTH

Poor soul, the center of my sinful earth,
[. . .] these rebel powers that thee array,
Why dost thou pine within and suffer dearth,
Painting thy outward walls so costly gay?   4
Why so large cost, having so short a lease,
Dost thou upon thy fading mansion spend?
Shall worms, inheritors of this excess,
Eat up thy charge? Is this thy body's end?   8
Then, soul, live thou upon thy servant's loss,
And let that pine to aggravate° thy store;   *increase*
Buy terms divine in selling hours of dross;
Within be fed, without be rich no more: 12
    So shalt thou feed on Death, that feeds on men,
    And Death once dead, there's no more dying then.   14

POOR SOUL, THE CENTER OF MY SINFUL EARTH. The *Sonnets'* first printer made Shakespeare repeat himself in the second line: "My sinful earth these rebel powers that thee array." Subsequent editors have offered many guesses to fill in the missing two syllables: *Thrall to, Blind to, Fooled by, Starved by, Sieged by, Pressed by, Gilt with, Leagued with, Rebuke.*

William Shakespeare (1564–1616)

THAT TIME OF YEAR THOU MAYST IN ME BEHOLD

That time of year thou mayst in me behold
When yellow leaves, or none, or few, do hang
Upon those boughs which shake against the cold,
Bare ruined choirs where late the sweet birds sang.   4
In me thou see'st the twilight of such day
As after sunset fadeth in the west,
Which by-and-by black night doth take away,
Death's second self that seals up all in rest.   8
In me thou see'st the glowing of such fire
That on the ashes of his youth doth lie,
As the deathbed whereon it must expire,
Consumed with that which it was nourished by.   12
    This thou perceiv'st, which makes thy love more strong,
    To love that well which thou must leave ere long.   14

Thomas Campion (1567–1620)

THERE IS A GARDEN IN HER FACE

    There is a garden in her face
Where roses and white lilies grow;
    A heav'nly paradise is that place
Wherein all pleasant fruits do flow.   4
    There cherries grow which none may buy
    Till "Cherry-ripe" themselves do cry.   6

    Those cherries fairly do enclose
Of orient pearl a double row,
    Which when her lovely laughter shows,
They look like rose-buds filled with snow;   10
    Yet them nor° peer nor prince can buy,   *neither*
    Till "Cherry-ripe" themselves do cry.   12

    Her eyes like angels watch them still;
Her brows like bended bows do stand,
    Threat'ning with piercing frowns to kill
All that attempt, with eye or hand   16
    Those sacred cherries to come nigh
    Till "Cherry-ripe" themselves do cry.   18

THERE IS A GARDEN IN HER FACE. 6. *"Cherry-ripe"*: Cry of fruit-peddlers in London streets.

John Donne (1572–1631)
A Lecture upon the Shadow

Stand still, and I will read to thee
A lecture, love, in love's philosophy. 2
    These three hours that we have spent
    Walking here, two shadows went 4
Along with us, which we ourselves produced;
    But, now the sun is just above our head,
    We do those shadows tread,
And to brave clearness all things are reduced. 8
    So whilst our infant loves did grow,
    Disguises did, and shadows, flow
From us and our cares, but now 'tis not so. 11

That love hath not attained the high'st degree,
Which is still diligent lest others see. 13

Except our loves at this noon stay,
We shall new shadows make the other way. 15
    As the first were made to blind
    Others, these which come behind 17
Will work upon ourselves, and blind our eyes.
    If our loves faint, and westwardly decline,
    To me thou falsely thine,
And I to thee, mine actions shall disguise. 21
    The morning shadows wear away,
    But these grow longer all the day;
But oh, love's day is short, if love decay. 24

Love is a growing, or full constant light,
And his short minute after noon, is night. 26

John Donne (1572–1631)
A Valediction: Forbidding Mourning

As virtuous men pass mildly away,
    And whisper to their souls to go,
Whilst some of their sad friends do say
    The breath goes now, and some say no: 4

So let us melt, and make no noise,
    No tear-floods, nor sigh-tempests move;
'Twere profanation of our joys
    To tell the laity our love. 8

Moving of th' earth° brings harms and fears;   *earthquake*
    Men reckon what it did and meant;
But trepidation of the spheres,
    Though greater far, is innocent°.   *harmless* 12

Dull sublunary lovers' love
(Whose soul is sense) cannot admit
Absence, because it doth remove
    Those things which elemented° it.   *constituted*   16

But we, by a love so much refined
    That ourselves know not what it is,
Inter-assurèd of the mind,
    Care less, eyes, lips, and hands to miss.   20

Our two souls, therefore, which are one,
    Though I must go, endure not yet
A breach, but an expansiòn,
    Like gold to airy thinness beat.   24

If they be two, they are two so
    As stiff twin compasses are two:
Thy soul, the fixed foot, makes no show
    To move, but doth, if th' other do.   28

And though it in the center sit,
    Yet when the other far doth roam,
It leans and harkens after it,
    And grows erect as that comes home.   32

Such wilt thou be to me, who must,
    Like th' other foot, obliquely run;
Thy firmness makes my circle just°,   *perfect*
    And makes me end where I begun.   36

A VALEDICTION: FORBIDDING MOURNING. 11. *spheres:* In Ptolemaic astronomy, the concentric spheres surrounding the earth. The trepidation or motion of the ninth sphere was thought to change the date of the equinox.

John Donne (1572–1631)
BATTER MY HEART, THREE-PERSONED GOD, FOR YOU

Batter my heart, three-personed God, for You
As yet but knock, breathe, shine, and seek to mend.
That I may rise and stand, o'erthrow me, and bend
Your force to break, blow, burn, and make me new.   4
I, like an usurped town to another due,
Labor to admit You, but Oh! to no end.
Reason, Your viceroy in me, me should defend,
But is captived, and proves weak or untrue.   8
Yet dearly I love You, and would be lovèd fain,
But am betrothed unto Your enemy;
Divorce me, untie or break that knot again;
Take me to You, imprison me, for I,   12
Except You enthrall me, never shall be free,
Nor ever chaste, except You ravish me.   14

John Donne (1572–1631)

THE BAIT

Come live with me and be my love,
And we will some new pleasures prove,
Of golden sands and crystal brooks,
With silken lines and silver hooks.   4

There will the river whispering run,
Warmed by thy eyes more than the sun;
And there the enamored fish will stay,
Begging themselves they may betray.   8

When thou wilt swim in that live bath,
Each fish, which every channel hath,
Will amorously to thee swim,
Gladder to catch thee, than thou him.   12

If thou to be so seen be'st loath,
By sun or moon, thou dark'nest both;
And if myself have leave to see,
I need not their light, having thee.   16

Let others freeze with angling reeds°,   *rods*
And cut their legs with shells and weeds,
Or treacherously poor fish beset
With strangling snare or windowy net.   20

Let coarse bold hands from slimy nest
The bedded fish in banks out-wrest,
Or curious traitors, sleave-silk flies,
Bewitch poor fishes' wand'ring eyes.   24

For thee, thou need'st no such deceit,
For thou thyself art thine own bait;
That fish that is not catched thereby,
Alas, is wiser far than I.   28

COMPARE:

"The Bait" with "The Passionate Shepherd to His Love" by Christopher Marlowe (page 314) and "Live with Me" by Mick Jagger and Keith Richard (page 420).

Robert Herrick (1591–1674)

To the Virgins, to Make Much of Time

Gather ye rose-buds while ye may,
  Old Time is still a-flying;
And this same flower that smiles today,
  Tomorrow will be dying.   4

The glorious lamp of heaven, the sun,
  The higher he's a-getting,
The sooner will his race be run,
  And nearer he's to setting.   8

That age is best which is the first,
  When youth and blood are warmer;
But being spent, the worse, and worst
  Times still succeed the former.   12

Then be not coy, but use your time,
  And while ye may, go marry;
For having lost but once your prime,
  You may for ever tarry.   16

Compare:

"To the Virgins, to Make Much of Time" with "To His Coy Mistress" by Andrew Marvell (page 324).

George Herbert (1593–1633)

Love

Love bade me welcome; yet my soul drew back,
    Guilty of dust and sin.
But quick-eyed Love, observing me grow slack
    From my first entrance in,   4
Drew nearer to me, sweetly questioning
    If I lacked anything.   6

"A guest," I answered, "worthy to be here";
    Love said, "You shall be he."
"I, the unkind, ungrateful? Ah, my dear,
    I cannot look on Thee."   10
Love took my hand, and smiling did reply,
    "Who made the eyes but I?"   12

"Truth, Lord, but I have marred them; let my shame
    Go where it doth deserve."
"And know you not," says Love, "who bore the blame?"
    "My dear, then I will serve."   16
"You must sit down," says Love, "and taste My meat."
    So I did sit and eat.   18

Edmund Waller (1606–1687)

GO, LOVELY ROSE

Go, lovely rose,
Tell her that wastes her time and me
   That now she knows,
When I resemble her to thee,
How sweet and fair she seems to be.   5

Tell her that's young
And shuns to have her graces spied
   That hadst thou sprung
In deserts where no men abide,
Thou must have uncommended died.   10

Small is the worth
Of beauty from the light retired;
   Bid her come forth,
Suffer herself to be desired,
And not blush so to be admired.   15

Then die, that she
The common fate of all things rare
   May read in thee:
How small a part of time they share
That are so wondrous sweet and fair!   20

John Milton (1608–1674)

WHEN I CONSIDER HOW MY LIGHT IS SPENT

When I consider how my light is spent,
   Ere half my days in this dark world and wide,
   And that one talent which is death to hide
   Lodged with me useless, though my soul more bent   4
To serve therewith my Maker, and present
   My true account, lest He returning chide;
   "Doth God exact day-labor, light denied?"
   I fondly° ask. But Patience, to prevent   *foolishly* 8
That murmur, soon replies, "God doth not need
   Either man's work or His own gifts. Who best
   Bear His mild yoke, they serve Him best. His state
Is kingly: thousands at His bidding speed,
   And post o'er land and ocean without rest;
   They also serve who only stand and wait."   14

WHEN I CONSIDER HOW MY LIGHT IS SPENT. 1–2. *my light is spent / Ere half my days:* Milton had become blind before he was fifty (when half his life was spent out of a possible hundred years). 3. *that one talent:* For Christ's parable of the talents (measures of money), see Matthew 25:14–30.

Andrew Marvell (1621–1678)

To His Coy Mistress *on mortality*

Had we but world enough, and time,		
This coyness°, lady, were no crime.	modesty, reluctance	2
We would sit down and think which way		
To walk, and pass our long love's day.		4
Thou by the Indian Ganges' side		
Should'st rubies find; I by the tide		6
Of Humber would complain°. I would	sing sad songs	
Love you ten years before the Flood,		8
And you should, if you please, refuse		
Till the conversion of the Jews.		10
My vegetable° love should grow	vegetative, flourishing	
Vaster than empires, and more slow.		12
An hundred years should go to praise		
Thine eyes, and on thy forehead gaze,		14
Two hundred to adore each breast,		
But thirty thousand to the rest.		16
An age at least to every part,		
And the last age should show your heart.		18
For, lady, you deserve this state,		
Nor would I love at lower rate.		20
But at my back I always hear		
Time's winged chariot hurrying near;		22
And yonder all before us lie		
Deserts of vast eternity.		24
Thy beauty shall no more be found,		
Nor in thy marble vault shall sound		26
My echoing song; then worms shall try		
That long preserved virginity,		28
And your quaint honor turn to dust,		
And into ashes all my lust.		30
The grave's a fine and private place,		
But none, I think, do there embrace.		32
Now therefore, while the youthful hue		
Sits on thy skin like morning glew°,	glow	34
And while thy willing soul transpires		
At every pore with instant° fires,	eager	36
Now let us sport us while we may;		
And now, like am'rous birds of prey,		38
Rather at once our time devour,		
Than languish in his slow-chapped power,		40
Let us roll all our strength, and all		
Our sweetness, up into one ball;		42
And tear our pleasures with rough strife		
Thorough° the iron gates of life.	through	44
Thus, though we cannot make our sun		
Stand still, yet we will make him run.		46

[handwritten marginalia: "sing sad", "avoids sing-song jingle by punctuation", "pauses don't always fall at the end of the line", "sentence", "end line"]

To His Coy Mistress. 7. *Humber:* A river that flows by Marvell's town of Hull (on the side of the world opposite from the Ganges). 10. *conversion of the Jews:* An event that, according to St. John the Divine, is to take place just before the end of the world.

Compare:

"To His Coy Mistress" with "To the Virgins, to Make Much of Time" by Robert Herrick (page 322).

John Dryden (1631–1700)
To the Memory of Mr. Oldham

Farewell, too little and too lately known,
Whom I began to think and call my own;   2
For sure our souls were near allied, and thine
Cast in the same poetic mold with mine.   4
One common note on either lyre did strike,
And knaves and fools we both abhorred alike.   6
To the same goal did both our studies drive:
The last set out the soonest did arrive.   8
Thus Nisus fell upon the slippery place,
While his young friend performed and won the race.   10
O early ripe! to thy abundant store
What could advancing age have added more?   12
It might (what Nature never gives the young)
Have taught the numbers° of thy native tongue.   *meters*   14
But satire needs not those, and wit will shine
Through the harsh cadence of a rugged line.   16
A noble error, and but seldom made,
When poets are by too much force betrayed.   18
Thy gen'rous fruits, though gathered ere their prime,
Still showed a quickness; and maturing time
But mellows what we write to the dull sweets of rhyme.   21
Once more, hail, and farewell! farewell, thou young
But ah! too short, Marcellus of our tongue!   23
Thy brows with ivy and with laurels bound;
But fate and gloomy night encompass thee around.   25

To the Memory of Mr. Oldham. John Oldham, poet best remembered for his *Satires upon the Jesuits,* had died at thirty. 9–10. *Nisus, his young friend:* These two close friends, as Virgil tells us in the *Aeneid,* ran a race for the prize of an olive crown. 23. *Marcellus:* Had he not died in his twentieth year, he would have succeeded the Roman emperor Augustus. 25. This line echoes the *Aeneid* (VI, 886), in which Marcellus is seen walking under the black cloud of his impending doom.

Compare:

"To the Memory of Mr. Oldham" with "To an Athlete Dying Young" by A. E. Housman (page 354).

Jonathan Swift (1667–1745)

The Day of Judgment

Once, with a whirl of thought oppressed,
I sunk from reverie to rest.   2
An horrid vision seized my head,
I saw the graves give up their dead!   4
Jove, armed with terrors, burst the skies,
And thunder roars, and lightning flies!   6
Confused, amazed, its fate unknown,
The world stands trembling at his throne!   8
While each pale sinner hangs his head,
Jove, nodding, shook the heavens, and said: 10
"Offending race of human kind,
By nature, custom, learning, blind;   12
You who, through frailty, slipped aside;
And you who never fell — through pride;   14
And you by differing churches shammed,
Who come to see each other damned   16
(So some folks told you, but they knew
No more of Jove's designs than you);   18
The world's mad business now is o'er,
And I resent these pranks no more.   20
I to such blockheads set my wit!
I damn such fools! — Go, go, you're *bit*°."   *outwitted, defeated (slang)*   22

Compare:

"The Day of Judgment" with "Channel Firing" by Thomas Hardy (page 346).

Alexander Pope (1688–1744)

Epigram Engraved on the Collar of a Dog Which I Gave to His Royal Highness

I am his Highness' dog at Kew;
Pray tell me, sir, whose dog are you?

Thomas Gray (1716–1771)

Elegy Written in a Country Churchyard

The curfew tolls the knell of parting day,
  The lowing herd wind slowly o'er the lea,
The plowman homeward plods his weary way,
  And leaves the world to darkness and to me.   4

Now fades the glimmering landscape on the sight,
    And all the air a solemn stillness holds,
Save where the beetle wheels his droning flight,
    And drowsy tinklings lull the distant folds;   8

Save that from yonder ivy-mantled tow'r
    The moping owl does to the moon complain
Of such, as wand'ring near her secret bow'r,
    Molest her ancient solitary reign.   12

Beneath those rugged elms, that yew tree's shade,
    Where heaves the turf in many a mold'ring heap,
Each in his narrow cell forever laid,
    The rude forefathers of the hamlet sleep.   16

The breezy call of incense-breathing morn,
    The swallow twitt'ring from the straw-built shed,
The cock's shrill clarion, or the echoing horn°,   *fox-hunters' horn*
    No more shall rouse them from their lowly bed.   20

For them no more the blazing hearth shall burn,
    Or busy housewife ply her evening care;
No children run to lisp their sire's return,
    Or climb his knees the envied kiss to share.   24

Oft did the harvest to their sickle yield,
    Their furrow oft the stubborn glebe° has broke;   *turf*
How jocund did they drive their team afield!
    How bowed the woods beneath their sturdy stroke!   28

Let not Ambition mock their useful toil,
    Their homely joys, and destiny obscure;
Nor Grandeur hear with a disdainful smile
    The short and simple annals of the poor.   32

The boast of heraldry, the pomp of pow'r,
    And all that beauty, all that wealth e'er gave,
Awaits alike th' inevitable hour.
    The paths of glory lead but to the grave.   36

Nor you, ye proud, impute to these the fault,
    If Mem'ry o'er their tomb no trophies raise,
Where through the long-drawn aisle and fretted° vault   *decorated*
    The pealing anthem swells the note of praise.   40

Can storied° urn or animated bust   *inscribed*
    Back to its mansion call the fleeting breath?
Can Honor's voice provoke the silent dust,
    Or Flatt'ry soothe the dull cold ear of Death?   44

Perhaps in this neglected spot is laid
    Some heart once pregnant with celestial fire;
Hands that the rod of empire might have swayed,
    Or waked to ecstasy the living lyre.   48

But knowledge to their eyes her ample page
    Rich with the spoils of time did ne'er unroll;
Chill Penury repressed their noble rage,
    And froze the genial current of the soul.   52

Full many a gem of purest ray serene,
    The dark unfathomed caves of ocean bear:
Full many a flower is born to blush unseen,
    And waste its sweetness on the desert air.   56

Some village Hampden, that with dauntless breast
    The little tyrant of his field withstood;
Some mute inglorious Milton here may rest,
    Some Cromwell guiltless of his country's blood.   60

Th' applause of list'ning senates to command,
    The threats of pain and ruin to despise,
To scatter plenty o'er a smiling land,
    And read their hist'ry in a nation's eyes,   64

Their lot forbade: nor circumscribed alone
    Their growing virtues, but their crimes confined;
Forbade to wade through slaughter to a throne,
    And shut the gates of mercy on mankind,   68

The struggling pangs of conscious truth to hide,
    To quench the blushes of ingenuous shame,
Or heap the shrine of Luxury and Pride
    With incense kindled at the Muse's flame.   72

Far from the madding° crowd's ignoble strife,   *frenzied*
    Their sober wishes never learned to stray;
Along the cool sequestered vale of life
    They kept the noiseless tenor of their way.   76

Yet ev'n these bones from insult to protect
    Some frail memorial still erected nigh,
With uncouth rhymes and shapeless sculpture decked,
    Implores the passing tribute of a sigh.   80

Their name, their years, spelt by th' unlettered Muse,
    The place of fame and elegy supply:
And many a holy text around she strews,
    That teach the rustic moralist to die.   84

For who to dumb Forgetfulness a prey,
    This pleasing anxious being e'er resigned,
Left the warm precincts of the cheerful day,
    Nor cast one longing ling'ring look behind?   88

On some fond breast the parting soul relies,
    Some pious drops the closing eye requires;
Ev'n from the tomb the voice of Nature cries,
    Ev'n in our ashes live their wonted° fires.   *customary* 92

For thee, who mindful of th' unhonored dead
  Dost in these lines their artless tale relate;
If chance, by lonely contemplation led,
  Some kindred spirit shall inquire thy fate,   96

Haply some hoary-headed swain° may say,   *shepherd*
  "Oft have we seen him at the peep of dawn
Brushing with hasty steps the dews away
  To meet the sun upon the upland lawn.   100

"There at the foot of yonder nodding beech
  That wreathes its old fantastic roots so high,
His listless length at noontide would he stretch,
  And pore upon the brook that babbles by.   104

"Hard by yon wood, now smiling as in scorn,
  Mutt'ring his wayward fancies he would rove,
Now drooping, woeful wan, like one forlorn,
  Or crazed with care, or crossed in hopeless love.   108

"One morn I missed him on the customed hill,
  Along the heath and near his fav'rite tree;
Another came; not yet beside the rill,
  Nor up the lawn, nor at the wood was he;   112

"The next with dirges due in sad array
  Slow through the churchway path we saw him borne.
Approach and read (for thou canst read) the lay,
  Graved on the stone beneath yon aged thorn."   116

The Epitaph

Here rests his head upon the lap of Earth
  A youth to Fortune and to Fame unknown.
Fair Science° frowned not on his humble birth,   *Knowledge*
  And Melancholy marked him for her own.   120

Large was his bounty, and his soul sincere,
  Heav'n did a recompense as largely send:
He gave to Mis'ry all he had, a tear,
  He gained from Heav'n ('twas all he wished) a friend.   124

No farther seek his merits to disclose,
  Or draw his frailties from their dread abode,
(There they alike in trembling hope repose),
  The bosom of his Father and his God.   128

ELEGY WRITTEN IN A COUNTRY CHURCHYARD. 57. *Hampden:* John Hampden, who had resisted illegal taxes imposed by Charles I. 98. *him:* Sometimes taken to mean Gray himself, but more probably his best friend Richard West.

COMPARE:

"Elegy Written in a Country Churchyard" with "Church Going" by Philip Larkin (page 397).

Christopher Smart (1722–1771)

FOR I WILL CONSIDER MY CAT JEOFFRY

For I will consider my Cat Jeoffry.
For he is the servant of the Living God, duly and daily serving him.
For at the first glance of the glory of God in the East he worships in his
    way.
For is this done by wreathing his body seven times round with elegant
    quickness.
For then he leaps up to catch the musk°, which is the   *catnip*
    blessing of God upon his prayer.   5
For he rolls upon prank to work it in.
For having done duty and received blessing he begins to consider himself.
For this he performs in ten degrees.
For first he looks upon his fore-paws to see if they are clean.
For secondly he kicks up behind to clear away there.   10
For thirdly he works it upon stretch° with the fore-paws   *he works his*
    extended.   *muscles, stretching*
For fourthly he sharpens his paws by wood.
For fifthly he washes himself.
For sixthly he rolls upon wash.
For seventhly he fleas himself, that he may not be interrupted upon the
    beat°.   *his patrol*   15
For eighthly he rubs himself against a post.
For ninthly he looks up for his instructions.
For tenthly he goes in quest of food.
For having considered God and himself he will consider his neighbor.
For if he meets another cat he will kiss her in kindness.   20
For when he takes his prey he plays with it to give it a chance.
For one mouse in seven escapes by his dallying.
For when his day's work is done his business more properly begins.
For he keeps the Lord's watch in the night against the Adversary.
For he counteracts the powers of darkness by his electrical skin and glar-
    ing eyes.   25
For he counteracts the Devil, who is death, by brisking about the life.
For in his morning orisons he loves the sun and the sun loves him.
For he is of the tribe of Tiger.
For the Cherub Cat is a term of the Angel Tiger.
For he has the subtlety and hissing of a serpent, which in goodness he
    suppresses.   30
For he will not do destruction if he is well-fed, neither will he spit with-
    out provocation.
For he purrs in thankfulness when God tells him he's a good Cat.
For he is an instrument for the children to learn benevolence upon.
For every house is incomplete without him, and a blessing is lacking in
    the spirit.
For the Lord commanded Moses concerning the cats at the departure of
    the Children of Israel from Egypt.   35
For every family had one cat at least in the bag.

For the English Cats are the best in Europe.

For he is the cleanest in the use of his fore-paws of any quadruped.

For the dexterity of his defense is an instance of the love of God to him
exceedingly.

For he is the quickest to his mark of any creature. 40

For he is tenacious of his point.

For he is a mixture of gravity and waggery.

For he knows that God is his Savior.

For there is nothing sweeter than his peace when at rest.

For there is nothing brisker than his life when in motion. 45

For he is of the Lord's poor, and so indeed is he called by benevolence
perpetually — Poor Jeoffry! poor Jeoffrey! the rat has bit thy throat.

For I bless the name of the Lord Jesus that Jeoffrey is better.

For the divine spirit comes about his body to sustain it in complete cat.

For his tongue is exceeding pure so that it has in purity what it wants in
music.

For he is docile and can learn certain things. 50

For he can sit up with gravity which is patience upon approbation.

For he can fetch and carry, which is patience in employment.

For he can jump over a stick which is patience upon proof positive.

For he can spraggle upon waggle at the word of command.

For he can jump from an eminence into his master's bosom. 55

For he can catch the cork and toss it again.

For he is hated by the hypocrite and miser.

For the former is afraid of detection.

For the latter refuses the charge.

For he camels his back to bear the first notion of business. 60

For he is good to think on, if a man would express himself neatly.

For he made a great figure in Egypt for his signal services.

For he killed the Icneumon-rat, very pernicious by land.

For his ears are so acute that they sting again.

For from this proceeds the passing quickness of his attention. 65

For by stroking of him I have found out electricity.

For I perceived God's light about him both wax and fire.

For the electrical fire is the spiritual substance which God sends from
heaven to sustain the bodies both of man and beast.

For God has blessed him in the variety of his movements.

For, though he cannot fly, he is an excellent clamberer. 70

For his motions upon the face of the earth are more than any other quadruped.

For he can tread to all the measures upon the music.

For he can swim for life.

For he can creep.

For I will consider my Cat Jeoffry. This is a self-contained extract from Smart's long
poem *Jubilate Agno* ("Rejoice in the Lamb"), written during his confinement for insanity.
35. *For the Lord commanded Moses concerning the cats:* No such command is mentioned in
Scripture. 54. *spraggle upon waggle:* W. F. Stead, in his edition of Smart's poem, suggests
that this means Jeoffry will sprawl when his master waggles a finger or a stick. 59. *the
charge:* Perhaps the cost of feeding a cat.

William Blake (1757–1827)
LONG JOHN BROWN AND LITTLE MARY BELL

Little Mary Bell had a fairy in a nut,
Long John Brown had the Devil in his gut;
Long John Brown loved Little Mary Bell,
And the fairy drew the Devil into the nut-shell.   4

Her fairy skipped out and her fairy skipped in;
He laughed at the Devil saying "Love is a sin."
The Devil he raged and Devil he was wroth,
And the Devil entered into the young man's broth.   8

He was soon in the gut of the loving young swain,
For John eat and drank to drive away love's pain;
But all he could do he grew thinner and thinner,
Though he eat and drank as much as ten men for his dinner.   12

Some said he had a wolf in his stomach day and night,
Some said he had the Devil and they guessed right;
The fairy skipped about in his glory, joy and pride,
And he laughed at the Devil till poor John Brown died.   16

Then the fairy skipped out of the old nut-shell,
And woe and alack for pretty Mary Bell!
For the Devil crept in when the fairy skipped out,
And there goes Miss Bell with her fusty old nut.   20

William Blake (1757–1827)
THE SICK ROSE

O Rose, thou art sick!
The invisible worm
That flies in the night,
In the howling storm,   4

Has found out thy bed
Of crimson joy,
And his dark secret love
Does thy life destroy.   8

William Blake (1757–1827)
THE TYGER

Tyger! Tyger! burning bright
In the forests of the night,
What immortal hand or eye
Could frame thy fearful symmetry?   4

In what distant deeps or skies
Burnt the fire of thine eyes?
On what wings dare he aspire?
What the hand dare seize the fire? 8

And what shoulder, and what art,
Could twist the sinews of thy heart?
And when thy heart began to beat,
What dread hand? and what dread feet? 12

What the hammer? what the chain?
In what furnace was thy brain?
What the anvil? what dread grasp
Dare its deadly terrors clasp? 16

When the stars threw down their spears,
And watered heaven with their tears,
Did he smile his work to see?
Did he who made the Lamb make thee? 20

Tyger! Tyger! burning bright
In the forests of the night,
What immortal hand or eye
Dare frame thy fearful symmetry? 24

William Wordsworth (1770–1850)
Composed upon Westminster Bridge

Earth has not anything to show more fair:
Dull would he be of soul who could pass by
A sight so touching in its majesty:
This City now doth, like a garment, wear 4
The beauty of the morning; silent, bare,
Ships, towers, domes, theatres, and temples lie
Open unto the fields, and to the sky;
All bright and glittering in the smokeless air. 8
Never did sun more beautifully steep
In his first splendor, valley, rock, or hill;
Ne'er saw I, never felt, a calm so deep!
The river glideth at his own sweet will:
Dear God! the very houses seem asleep;
And all that mighty heart is lying still! 14

William Wordsworth (1770–1850)
To Toussaint L'Ouverture

Toussaint, the most unhappy man of men!
Whether the whistling rustic tend his plough
Within thy hearing, or thy head be now
Pillowed in some deep dungeon's earless den; — 4

O miserable Chieftain! where and when
Wilt thou find patience! Yet die not; do thou
Wear rather in thy bonds a cheerful brow:
Though fallen thyself, never to rise again,   8
Live, and take comfort. Thou hast left behind
Powers that will work for thee; air, earth, and skies:
There's not a breathing of the common wind
That will forget thee; thou hast great allies;
Thy friends are exultations, agonies,
And love, and man's unconquerable mind.   14

To Toussaint L'Ouverture. Pierre Dominique Toussaint L'Ouverture (1743–1803),
Haitian black soldier and statesman, had led his fellow slaves in a successful revolution
against Haiti's French colonial government. But in 1802, when Wordsworth wrote these
lines, Napoleon had imprisoned Toussaint in France, where he later died.

Samuel Taylor Coleridge (1772–1834)

Kubla Khan

Or, a Vision in a Dream. A Fragment.

In Xanadu did Kubla Khan
A stately pleasure-dome decree:
Where Alph, the sacred river, ran
Through caverns measureless to man
   Down to a sunless sea.   5
So twice five miles of fertile ground
With walls and towers were girdled round;
And there were gardens bright with sinuous rills,
Where blossomed many an incense-bearing tree;
And here were forests ancient as the hills,   10
Enfolding sunny spots of greenery.

But oh! that deep romantic chasm which slanted
Down the green hill athwart a cedarn cover!
A savage place! as holy and enchanted
As e'er beneath a waning moon was haunted   15
By woman wailing for her demon-lover!
And from this chasm, with ceaseless turmoil seething,
As if this earth in fast thick pants were breathing,
A mighty fountain momently was forced:
Amid whose swift half-intermitted burst   20
Huge fragments vaulted like rebounding hail,
Or chaffy grain beneath the thresher's flail:
And 'mid these dancing rocks at once and ever
It flung up momently the sacred river.
Five miles meandering with a mazy motion   25
Through wood and dale the sacred river ran,
Then reached the caverns measureless to man,
And sank in tumult to a lifeless ocean:

And 'mid this tumult Kubla heard from far
Ancestral voices prophesying war!   30

    The shadow of the dome of pleasure
    Floated midway on the waves;
    Where was heard the mingled measure
    From the fountain and the caves.
It was a miracle of rare device,   35
A sunny pleasure-dome with caves of ice!

    A damsel with a dulcimer
    In a vision once I saw:
    It was an Abyssinian maid,
    And on her dulcimer she played,   40
    Singing of Mount Abora.
    Could I revive within me
    Her symphony and song,
    To such a deep delight 'twould win me,
That with music loud and long,   45
I would build that dome in air,
That sunny dome! those caves of ice!
And all who heard should see them there,
And all should cry, Beware! Beware!
His flashing eyes, his floating hair!   50
Weave a circle round him thrice,
And close your eyes with holy dread,
For he on honey-dew hath fed,
And drunk the milk of Paradise.

KUBLA KHAN. There was an actual Kublai Khan, a thirteenth-century Mongol emperor,
and a Chinese city of Xamdu; but Coleridge's dream vision also borrows from travelers'
descriptions of such other exotic places as Abyssinia and America. 51. *circle:* A magic
circle drawn to keep away evil spirits.

George Gordon, Lord Byron (1788–1824)
LINES INSCRIBED UPON A CUP FORMED FROM A SKULL

Start not — or deem my spirit fled;
    In me behold the only skull,
From which, unlike a living head,
    Whatever flows is never dull.   4

I lived, I loved, I quaffed, like thee:
    I died: let earth my bones resign;
Fill up — thou canst not injure me;
    The worm hath fouler lips than thine.   8

Better to hold the sparkling grape,
    Than nurse the earth-worm's slimy brood;
And circle in the goblet's shape
    The drink of gods, than reptile's food.   12

Where once my wit, perchance, hath shone,
  In aid of others' let me shine;
And when, alas! our brains are gone,
  What nobler substitute than wine?   16

Quaff while thou canst: another race,
  When thou and thine, like me, are sped,
May rescue thee from earth's embrace,
  And rhyme and revel with the dead.   20

Why not? since through life's little day
  Our heads such sad effects produce;
Redeemed from worms and wasting clay,
  This chance is theirs, to be of use.   24

John Keats (1795–1821)

ODE ON A GRECIAN URN

Thou still unravished bride of quietness,
  Thou foster-child of silence and slow time,
Sylvan historian, who canst thus express
  A flowery tale more sweetly than our rhyme: 4
What leaf-fringed legend haunts about thy shape
  Of deities or mortals, or of both,
    In Tempe or the dales of Arcady?
  What men or gods are these? What maidens loth?
What mad pursuit? What struggle to escape?
    What pipes and timbrels? What wild ecstasy?   10

Heard melodies are sweet, but those unheard
  Are sweeter; therefore, ye soft pipes, play on;
Not to the sensual° ear, but, more endeared,   *physical*
  Pipe to the spirit ditties of no tone: 14
Fair youth, beneath the trees, thou canst not leave
  Thy song, nor ever can those trees be bare;
    Bold Lover, never, never canst thou kiss,
Though winning near the goal — yet, do not grieve;
    She cannot fade, though thou hast not thy bliss,
  For ever wilt thou love, and she be fair!   20

Ah, happy, happy boughs! that cannot shed
  Your leaves, nor ever bid the Spring adieu;
And, happy melodist, unwearièd,
  For ever piping songs for ever new;   24
More happy love! more happy, happy love!
  For ever warm and still to be enjoyed,
    For ever panting, and for ever young;
All breathing human passion far above,
  That leaves a heart high-sorrowful and cloyed,
    A burning forehead, and a parching tongue.   30

Who are these coming to the sacrifice?
  To what green altar, O mysterious priest,
Lead'st thou that heifer lowing at the skies,
  And all her silken flanks with garlands drest?   34
What little town by river or sea shore,
  Or mountain-built with peaceful citadel,
    Is emptied of this folk, this pious morn?
And, little town, thy streets for evermore
  Will silent be; and not a soul to tell
    Why thou art desolate, can e'er return.   40

O Attic shape! Fair attitude! with brede°   *design*
  Of marble men and maidens overwrought,
With forest branches and the trodden weed;
  Thou, silent form, dost tease us out of thought   44
As doth Eternity: Cold Pastoral!
  When old age shall this generation waste,
    Thou shalt remain, in midst of other woe
Than ours, a friend to man, to whom thou say'st,
Beauty is truth, truth beauty, — that is all
  Ye know on earth, and all ye need to know.   50

ODE ON A GRECIAN URN. 7. *Tempe, dales of Arcady:* Valleys in Greece. 41. *Attic:* Athenian,
possessing a classical simplicity and grace. 49–50: If Keats had put the urn's words in
quotation marks, critics might have been spared much ink. Does the urn say just "beauty
is truth, truth beauty," or does its statement take in the whole of the last two lines?

COMPARE:

"Ode on a Grecian Urn" with "Lapis Lazuli" by William Butler Yeats (page 356)
and "Anecdote of the Jar" by Wallace Stevens (page 212).

John Keats (1795–1821)

WHEN I HAVE FEARS THAT I MAY CEASE TO BE

When I have fears that I may cease to be
  Before my pen has gleaned my teeming brain,
Before high-piled books, in charact'ry°,   *printed words*
  Hold like rich garners the full-ripened grain;   4
When I behold, upon the night's starred face,
  Huge cloudy symbols of a high romance,
And think that I may never live to trace
  Their shadows, with the magic hand of chance;   8
And when I feel — fair creature of an hour! —
  That I shall never look upon thee more,
Never have relish in the faery power
  Of unreflecting love! — then on the shore   12
Of the wide world I stand alone, and think
Till Love and Fame to nothingness do sink.   14

Alfred, Lord Tennyson (1809–1892)

CROSSING THE BAR

Sunset and evening star,
   And one clear call for me!
And may there be no moaning of the bar,
   When I put out to sea,   4

But such a tide as moving seems asleep,
   Too full for sound and foam,
When that which drew from out the boundless deep
   Turns again home.   8

Twilight and evening bell,
   And after that the dark!
And may there be no sadness of farewell,
   When I embark;   12

For though from out our bourne of Time and Place
   The flood may bear me far,
I hope to see my Pilot face to face
   When I have crossed the bar.   16

Alfred, Lord Tennyson (1809–1892)

ULYSSES

It little profits that an idle king,
By this still hearth, among these barren crags,
Matched with an agèd wife, I mete and dole
Unequal laws unto a savage race
That hoard, and sleep, and feed, and know not me.   5
I cannot rest from travel; I will drink
Life to the lees. All times I have enjoyed
Greatly, have suffered greatly, both with those
That loved me, and alone; on shore, and when
Through scudding drifts the rainy Hyades   10
Vexed the dim sea. I am become a name;
For always roaming with a hungry heart
Much have I seen and known — cities of men
And manners, climates, councils, governments,
Myself not least, but honored of them all —   15
And drunk delight of battle with my peers,
Far on the ringing plains of windy Troy.
I am a part of all that I have met;
Yet all experience is an arch wherethrough
Gleams that untraveled world whose margin fades   20
Forever and forever when I move.
How dull it is to pause, to make an end,
To rust unburnished, not to shine in use!

As though to breathe were life! Life piled on life
Were all too little, and of one to me   25
Little remains; but every hour is saved
From that eternal silence, something more,
A bringer of new things; and vile it were
For some three suns to store and hoard myself,
And this grey spirit yearning in desire   30
To follow knowledge like a sinking star,
Beyond the utmost bound of human thought.
    This is my son, mine own Telemachus,
To whom I leave the scepter and the isle —
Well-loved of me, discerning to fulfill   35
This labor, by slow prudence to make mild
A rugged people, and through soft degrees
Subdue them to the useful and the good.
Most blameless is he, centered in the sphere
Of common duties, decent not to fail   40
In offices of tenderness, and pay
Meet adoration to my household gods,
When I am gone. He works his work, I mine.
    There lies the port; the vessel puffs her sail;
There gloom the dark, broad seas. My mariners,   45
Souls that have toiled, and wrought, and thought with me —
That ever with a frolic welcome took
The thunder and the sunshine, and opposed
Free hearts, free foreheads — you and I are old;
Old age hath yet his honor and his toil.   50
Death closes all; but something ere the end,
Some work of noble note, may yet be done,
Not unbecoming men that strove with Gods.
The lights begin to twinkle from the rocks;
The long day wanes; the slow moon climbs; the deep   55
Moans round with many voices. Come, my friends,
'Tis not too late to seek a newer world.
Push off, and sitting well in order smite
The sounding furrows; for my purpose holds
To sail beyond the sunset, and the baths   60
Of all the western stars, until I die.
It may be that the gulfs will wash us down;
It may be we shall touch the Happy Isles,
And see the great Achilles, whom we knew.
Though much is taken, much abides; and though   65
We are not now that strength which in old days
Moved earth and heaven, that which we are, we are —
One equal temper of heroic hearts,
Made weak by time and fate, but strong in will
To strive, to seek, to find, and not to yield.   70

ULYSSES. 10. *Hyades:* Daughters of Atlas, who were transformed into a group of stars.
Their rising with the sun was thought to be a sign of rain. 63. *Happy Isles:* Elysium, a
paradise believed to be attainable by sailing west.

Robert Browning (1812–1889)

SOLILOQUY OF THE SPANISH CLOISTER

Gr-r-r — there go, my heart's abhorrence!
  Water your damned flower-pots, do!
If hate killed men, Brother Lawrence,
  God's blood, would not mine kill you!   4
What? your myrtle-bush wants trimming?
  Oh, that rose has prior claims —
Needs its leaden vase filled brimming?
  Hell dry you up with its flames!   8

At the meal we sit together;
  Salve tibi° I must hear   *Hail to thee!*
Wise talk of the kind of weather,
  Sort of season, time of year: 12
Not a plenteous cork-crop: scarcely
  Dare we hope oak-galls, I doubt;
What's the Latin name for "parsley"?
  What's the Greek name for "swine's snout"?   16

Whew! We'll have our platter burnished,
  Laid with care on our own shelf!
With a fire-new spoon we're furnished,
  And a goblet for ourself,   20
Rinsed like something sacrificial
  Ere 'tis fit to touch our chaps —
Marked with L. for our initial!
  (He-he! There his lily snaps!)   24

Saint, forsooth! While brown Dolores
  Squats outside the Convent bank
With Sanchicha, telling stories,
  Steeping tresses in the tank,   28
Blue-black, lustrous, thick like horsehairs,
  — Can't I see his dead eye glow,
Bright as 'twere a Barbary corsair's?
  (That is, if he'd let it show!)   32

When he finishes refection,
  Knife and fork he never lays
Cross-wise, to my recollection,
  As do I, in Jesu's praise.   36
I, the Trinity illustrate,
  Drinking watered orange-pulp —
In three sips the Arian frustrate;
  While he drains his at one gulp!   40

Oh, those melons! if he's able
  We're to have a feast; so nice!
One goes to the Abbot's table,
  All of us get each a slice.   44

How go on your flowers? None double?
  Not one fruit-sort can you spy?
Strange! — And I, too, at such trouble,
  Keep them close-nipped on the sly!   48

There's a great text in Galatians,
  Once you trip on it, entails
Twenty-nine distinct damnations,
  One sure, if another fails;   52
If I trip him just a-dying,
  Sure of heaven as sure can be,
Spin him round and send him flying
  Off to hell, a Manichee?   56

Or, my scrofulous French novel
  On grey paper with blunt type!
Simply glance at it, you grovel
  Hand and foot in Belial's gripe;   60
If I double down its pages
  At the woeful sixteenth print,
When he gathers his greengages,
  Ope a sieve and slip it in't?   64

Or, there's Satan! — one might venture
  Pledge one's soul to him, yet leave
Such a flaw in the indenture
  As he'd miss till, past retrieve,   68
Blasted lay that rose-acacia
  We're so proud of! Hy, Zy, Hine. . . .
'St, there's Vespers! Plena gratia
  Ave, Virgo!° Gr-r-r — you swine!   Hail, Virgin, full of grace!

SOLILOQUY OF THE SPANISH CLOISTER. 3. *Brother Lawrence:* One of the speaker's fellow
monks. 31. *Barbary corsair:* A pirate operating off the Barbary coast of Africa. 39. *Arian:*
A follower of Arius, heretic who denied the doctrine of the Trinity. 49. *a great text in
Galatians:* A difficult verse in this book of the Bible. Brother Lawrence will be damned as
a heretic if he wrongly interprets it. 56. *Manichee:* Another kind of heretic, one who (after
the Persian philosopher Mani) sees in the world a constant struggle between good and
evil, neither able to win. 60. *Belial:* Here, not specifically Satan but (as used in the Old
Testament) a name for wickedness. 70. *Hy, Zy, Hine:* Possibly the sound of a bell to announce evening devotions, possibly the beginning of a formula to summon the Devil.

Herman Melville (1819–1891)

THE BERG

A Dream

I saw a ship of martial build
(Her standards set, her brave apparel on)
Directed as by madness mere
Against a stolid iceberg steer,
Nor budge it, though the infatuate ship went down.   5

The impact made huge ice-cubes fall
Sullen, in tons that crashed the deck;
But that one avalanche was all —
No other movement save the foundering wreck.

Along the spurs of ridges pale,   10
Not any slenderest shaft and frail,
A prism over glass-green gorges lone,
Toppled; or lace of traceries fine,
Nor pendant drops in grot or mine
Were jarred, when the stunned ship went down.   15
Nor sole the gulls in cloud that wheeled
Circling one snow-flanked peak afar,
But nearer fowl the floes that skimmed
And crystal beaches, felt no jar.

No thrill transmitted stirred the lock   20
Or jack-straw needle-ice at base;
Towers undermined by waves — the block
Atilt impending — kept their place.
Seals, dozing sleek on sliddery ledges
Slipped never, when by loftier edges   25
Through very inertia overthrown,
The impetuous ship in bafflement went down.

Hard Berg (methought), so cold, so vast,
With mortal damps self-overcast;
Exhaling still thy dankish breath —   30
Adrift dissolving, bound for death;
Though lumpish thou, a lumbering one —
A lumbering lubbard loitering slow,
Impingers rue thee and go down,
Sounding thy precipice below,   35
Nor stir the slimy slug that sprawls
Along thy dead indifference of walls.

THE BERG. 21. *jack-straw needle-ice:* In the children's game of jack-straws, players try to extricate one wire or straw from a heap without knocking down the rest. 24. *sliddery:* A word Melville apparently coined.

COMPARE:

"The Berg" with "The Convergence of the Twain" by Thomas Hardy (page 347).

Walt Whitman (1819–1892)
I Saw in Louisiana a Live-Oak Growing

I saw in Louisiana a live-oak growing,
All alone stood it and the moss hung down from the branches,
Without any companion it grew there uttering joyous leaves of dark
    green,
And its look, rude, unbending, lusty, made me think of myself,
But I wonder'd how it could utter joyous leaves standing alone there
    without its friend near, for I knew I could not,   5
And I broke off a twig with a certain number of leaves upon it, and twined
    around it a little moss,
And brought it away, and I have placed it in sight in my room,
It is not needed to remind me as of my own dear friends,
(For I believe lately I think of little else than of them,)
Yet it remains to me a curious token, it makes me think of manly love;   10
For all that, and though the live-oak glistens there in Louisiana solitary
    in a wide flat space,
Uttering joyous leaves all its life without a friend a lover near,
I know very well I could not.

Walt Whitman (1819–1892)
The City Dead-House

By the city dead-house by the gate,
As idly sauntering wending my way from the clangor,
I curious pause, for lo, an outcast form, a poor dead prostitute brought,
Her corpse they deposit unclaim'd, it lies on the damp brick pavement,
The divine woman, her body, I see the body, I look on it alone,   5
That house once full of passion and beauty, all else I notice not,
Nor stillness so cold, nor running water from faucet, nor odors morbific
    impress me,
But the house alone — that wondrous house — that delicate fair house —
    that ruin!
That immortal house more than all the rows of dwellings ever built!
Or white-domed capitol with majestic figure surmounted, or all the old
    high-spired cathedrals,   10
That little house alone more than them all — poor, desperate house!
Fair, fearful wreck — tenement of a soul — itself a soul,
Unclaim'd, avoided house — take one breath from my tremulous lips,
Take one tear dropt aside as I go for thought of you,
Dead house of love — house of madness and sin, crumbled, crush'd,   15
House of life, erewhile talking and laughing — but ah, poor house, dead
    even then,
Months, years, an echoing, garnish'd house — but dead, dead, dead.

COMPARE:

"The City Dead-House" with "The Harlot's House" by Oscar Wilde (page 351).

George Meredith (1828–1909)

Lucifer in Starlight

On a starred night Prince Lucifer uprose,
   Tired of his dark dominion, swung the fiend
   Above the rolling ball in cloud part screened,
Where sinners hugged their specter of repose.   4
Poor prey to his hot fit of pride were those.
   And now upon his western wing he leaned,
   Now his huge bulk o'er Afric's sands careened,
Now the black planet shadowed Arctic snows.   8
Soaring through wider zones that pricked his scars
   With memory of the old revolt from Awe,
He reached a middle height, and at the stars,
Which are the brain of heaven, he looked, and sank.
Around the ancient track marched, rank on rank,
   The army of unalterable law.   14

Dante Gabriel Rossetti (1828–1882)

The Woodspurge

The wind flapped loose, the wind was still,
Shaken out dead from tree and hill;
I had walked on at the wind's will —
I sat now, for the wind was still.   4

Between my knees my forehead was —
My lips, drawn in, said not Alas!
My hair was over in the grass,
My naked ears heard the day pass.   8

My eyes, wide open, had the run
Of some ten weeds to fix upon;
Among those few out of the sun,
The woodspurge flowered, three cups in one.   12

From perfect grief there need not be
Wisdom or even memory;
One thing then learnt remains to me —
The woodspurge has a cup of three.   16

Emily Dickinson (1830–1886)

Because I could not stop for Death

Because I could not stop for Death –
He kindly stopped for me –
The Carriage held but just Ourselves –
And Immortality.   4

We slowly drove – He knew no haste
And I had put away
My labor and my leisure too,
For His Civility –   8

We passed the School, where Children strove
At Recess – in the Ring –
We passed the Fields of Gazing Grain –
We passed the Setting Sun –   12

Or rather – He passed Us –
The Dews drew quivering and chill –
For only Gossamer, my Gown –
My Tippet° – only Tulle –   *cape*   16

We paused before a House that seemed
A Swelling of the Ground –
The Roof was scarcely visible –
The Cornice – in the Ground –   20

Since then – 'tis Centuries – and yet
Feels shorter than the Day
I first surmised the Horses' Heads
Were toward Eternity –   24

BECAUSE I COULD NOT STOP FOR DEATH. In the version of this poem printed by Emily
Dickinson's first editors in 1890, stanza four was left out. In line 9 *strove* was replaced by
played; line 10 was made to read "Their lessons scarcely done"; line 20, "The cornice but
a mound"; line 21, "Since then 'tis centuries, but each"; and capitalization and punctuation were made conventional.

Emily Dickinson (1830–1886)

I STARTED EARLY – TOOK MY DOG

I started Early – Took my Dog –
And visited the Sea –
The Mermaids in the Basement
Came out to look at me –   4

And Frigates – in the Upper Floor
Extended Hempen Hands –
Presuming Me to be a Mouse –
Aground – upon the Sands –   8

But no Man moved Me – till the Tide
Went past my simple Shoe –
And past my Apron – and my Belt
And past my Bodice – too –   12

And made as He would eat me up –
As wholly as a Dew
Upon a Dandelion's Sleeve –
And then – I started – too –   16

And He – He followed – close behind –
I felt His Silver Heel
Upon my Ankle – Then my Shoes
Would overflow with Pearl –   .   20

Until We met the Solid Town –
No One He seemed to know –
And bowing – with a Mighty look –
At me – The Sea withdrew –   24

Emily Dickinson (1830–1886)
THE SOUL SELECTS HER OWN SOCIETY

The Soul selects her own Society –
Then – shuts the Door –
To her divine Majority –
Present no more –   4

Unmoved – she notes the Chariots – pausing –
At her low Gate –
Unmoved – an Emperor be kneeling
Upon her Mat –   8

I've known her – from an ample nation –
Choose One –
Then – close the Valves of her attention –
Like Stone –
                                                          12

Thomas Hardy (1840–1928)
CHANNEL FIRING

That night your great guns, unawares,
Shook all our coffins as we lay,
And broke the chancel window-squares,
We thought it was the Judgment-day   4

And sat upright. While drearisome
Arose the howl of wakened hounds:
The mouse let fall the altar-crumb,
The worms drew back into the mounds,   8

The glebe cow drooled. Till God called, "No;
It's gunnery practice out at sea
Just as before you went below;
The world is as it used to be: 12

"All nations striving strong to make
Red war yet redder. Mad as hatters
They do no more for Christés sake
Than you who are helpless in such matters.   16

"That this is not the judgment-hour
For some of them's a blessed thing,
For if it were they'd have to scour
Hell's floor for so much threatening . . .   20

"Ha, ha. It will be warmer when
I blow the trumpet (if indeed
I ever do; for you are men,
And rest eternal sorely need)."   24

So down we lay again. "I wonder,
Will the world ever saner be,"
Said one, "than when He sent us under
In our indifferent century!"   28

And many a skeleton shook his head.
"Instead of preaching forty year,"
My neighbor Parson Thirdly said,
"I wish I had stuck to pipes and beer."   32

Again the guns disturbed the hour,
Roaring their readiness to avenge,
As far inland as Stourton Tower,
And Camelot, and starlit Stonehenge.   36

CHANNEL FIRING. 9. *glebe:* Land belonging to the church, used for grazing. 35. *Stourton Tower:* A fictional medieval landmark, Hardy's invention. 36. *Camelot:* Where King Arthur held court; *Stonehenge:* Circle of huge stones thought to be the ruins of a prehistoric place of worship.

COMPARE:

"Channel Firing" with "The Day of Judgment" by Jonathan Swift (page 326) and "The Fury of Aeriel Bombardment" by Richard Eberhart (page 45).

Thomas Hardy (1840–1928)

THE CONVERGENCE OF THE TWAIN

Lines on the Loss of the "Titanic"

I

      In a solitude of the sea
      Deep from human vanity,
And the Pride of Life that planned her, stilly couches she.   3

II

      Steel chambers, late the pyres
      Of her salamandrine fires,
Cold currents thrid°, and turn to rhythmic tidal lyres.   *thread*   6

III

Over the mirrors meant
To glass the opulent
The sea-worm crawls — grotesque, slimed, dumb, indifferent.   9

IV

Jewels in joy designed
To ravish the sensuous mind
Lie lightless, all their sparkles bleared and black and blind.   12

V

Dim moon-eyed fishes near
Gaze at the gilded gear
And query: "What does this vaingloriousness down here?"   15

VI

Well: while was fashioning
This creature of cleaving wing,
The Immanent Will that stirs and urges everything   18

VII

Prepared a sinister mate
For her — so gaily great —
A Shape of Ice, for the time far and dissociate.   21

VIII

And as the smart ship grew
In stature, grace, and hue,
In shadowy silent distance grew the Iceberg too.   24

IX

Alien they seemed to be:
No mortal eye could see
The intimate welding of their later history,   27

X

Or sign that they were bent
By paths coincident
On being anon twin halves of one august event.   30

XI

Till the Spinner of the Years
Said "Now!" And each one hears,
And consummation comes, and jars two hemispheres.   33

THE CONVERGENCE OF THE TWAIN. The luxury liner *Titanic*, supposedly unsinkable, went down in 1912 when she struck an iceberg on her first Atlantic voyage. 5. *salamandrine*: Like the salamander, a lizard that supposedly thrives in fires, or like a spirit of the same name that inhabits fire (according to alchemists).

COMPARE:

"The Convergence of the Twain" with "The Berg" by Herman Melville (page 341).

Thomas Hardy (1840–1928)

During Wind and Rain

They sing their dearest songs —
He, she, all of them — yea,
Treble and tenor and bass,
   And one to play;
With the candles mooning each face. . . .
   Ah, no; the years O!
How the sick leaves reel down in throngs!   7

They clear the creeping moss —
Elders and juniors — aye,
Making the pathways neat
   And the garden gay;
And they build a shady seat. . . .
   Ah, no; the years, the years;
See, the white storm-birds wing across!   14

They are blithely breakfasting all —
Men and maidens — yea,
Under the summer tree,
   With a glimpse of the bay,
While pet fowl come to the knee. . . .
   Ah, no! the years O!
And the rotten rose is ript from the wall.   21

They change to a high new house,
He, she, all of them — aye,
Clocks and carpets and chairs
   On the lawn all day,
And brightest things that are theirs. . . .
   Ah, no; the years, the years;
Down their carved names the rain-drop plows.   28

Gerard Manley Hopkins (1844–1889)

The Windhover

To Christ Our Lord

I caught this morning morning's minion, king-
   dom of daylight's dauphin, dapple-dawn-drawn Falcon, in his riding
   Of the rolling level underneath him steady air, and striding
High there, how he rung upon the rein of a wimpling wing   4
In his ecstasy! then off, off forth on swing,
   As a skate's heel sweeps smooth on a bow-bend: the hurl and gliding
   Rebuffed the big wind. My heart in hiding
Stirred for a bird, — the achieve of, the mastery of the thing!   8

Brute beauty and valor and act, oh, air, pride, plume, here
   Buckle! and the fire that breaks from thee then, a billion
Times told lovelier, more dangerous, O my chevalier!

   No wonder of it: shéer plód makes plow down sillion°   *furrow*
Shine, and blue-bleak embers, ah my dear,
   Fall, gall themselves, and gash gold-vermilion.   14

THE WINDHOVER. A windhover is a kestrel, or small falcon, so called because it can hover
upon the wind. 3. *rung . . . wing:* A horse is "rung upon the rein" when its trainer holds
the end of a long rein and has the horse circle him. The possible meanings of *wimpling*
include (1) curving; (2) pleated, arranged in many little folds one on top of another; (3)
rippling or undulating like the surface of a flowing stream.

Katie V. Hall (1855?–1940?)

THE OLD, FILTHY BEER PAIL

How dark to my mind are the scenes of my childhood,
   As sad recollections recall them to me;
Instead of the pure, running brook and the wildwood
   Were rivers of sin flowing steady and free.   4
The theaters, shows and saloons that were handy,
   The staggering men who went in them by scores,
I ne'er shall be able to blot from my mem'ry
   While toiling down here upon life's weary shores.   8

How oft did my father and mother then send me
   With pitcher or pail for the light, foaming beer;
Or else, some near neighbors would offer me pennies
   To bring them a pint their low spirits to cheer(?).   12
Ah! thus did the devil lay traps for my footsteps,
   To blight my young life ere I knew his dark plan;
And as I returned with the dirty old beer pail,
   He whispered, "Now taste it, and be like a man."   16

How well I remember the boys on the corners,
   Their cigarets rolling and lighting by turn;
Then gazing in wonder upon the vile pictures
   Where more of the devil's black arts they might learn.   20
Then think of the swearing and lewd conversation
   That blighted and poisoned my young, tender heart.
Ah! can you but weep at such awful temptations
   That come to a boy or a girl in these parts?   24

The wide-open doors of saloons and low houses
   Were waiting to greet me wherever I turned;
I saw at the bars, and at wine tables sitting,
   The fallen of earth who fair purity spurned.   28
Ah, sad! yes, so sad is the dark recollection
   Of days of my youth in this "Sodom" of sin.
Oh, blest is the child who is reared in the country,
   Away from Chicago's defilement and din!   32

Oh! can you not help them — these sinned-against children?
　　Oh! should they be left to drift on with the tide?
Those innocent, angel-faced, dear little rosebuds,
　　'Twere better they had in their babyhood died.　　　　36
Arouse ye, arouse ye, brave men of this nation!
　　Vote down the vile places which ruin the young!
Remove from their pathway these glaring temptations,
　　And then a glad victory song may be sung.　　　　40

THE OLD, FILTHY BEER PAIL. These lines are modeled after Samuel Woodworth's "The
Old Oaken Bucket" (see p. 243) and may be sung to the same tune.

Oscar Wilde (1856–1900)

THE HARLOT'S HOUSE

We caught the tread of dancing feet,
We loitered down the moonlit street,
And stopped beneath the harlot's house.

Inside, above the din and fray,
We heard the loud musicians play
The "Treues Liebes Herz" of Strauss.　　　　6

Like strange mechanical grotesques,
Making fantastic arabesques,
The shadows raced across the blind.

We watched the ghostly dancers spin
To sound of horn and violin,
Like black leaves wheeling in the wind.　　　　12

Like wire-pulled automatons,
Slim silhouetted skeletons
Went sidling through the slow quadrille.

They took each other by the hand,
And danced a stately saraband;
Their laughter echoed thin and shrill.　　　　18

Sometimes a clockwork puppet pressed
A phantom lover to her breast,
Sometimes they seemed to try to sing.

Sometimes a horrible marionette
Came out, and smoked its cigarette
Upon the steps like a live thing.　　　　24

Then, turning to my love, I said,
"The dead are dancing with the dead,
The dust is whirling with the dust."

But she — she heard the violin,
And left my side, and entered in:
Love passed into the house of lust.　　　　30

Then suddenly the tune went false,
The dancers wearied of the waltz,
The shadows ceased to wheel and whirl.

And down the long and silent street,
The dawn, with silver-sandaled feet,
Crept like a frightened girl.   36

THE HARLOT'S HOUSE. 6. *"Treues Liebes Herz"*: "True Love's Heart," a waltz.

COMPARE:

"The Harlot's House" with "The City Dead-House" by Walt Whitman (page 343).

A. E. Housman (1859–1936)

TERENCE, THIS IS STUPID STUFF

"Terence, this is stupid stuff:
You eat your victuals fast enough;
There can't be much amiss, 'tis clear,
To see the rate you drink your beer.   4
But oh, good Lord, the verse you make,
It gives a chap the belly-ache.
The cow, the old cow, she is dead;
It sleeps well, the horned head: 8
We poor lads, 'tis our turn now
To hear such tunes as killed the cow.
Pretty friendship 'tis to rhyme
Your friends to death before their time   12
Moping melancholy mad:
Come, pipe a tune to dance to, lad."

Why, if 'tis dancing you would be,
There's brisker pipes than poetry.   16
Say, for what were hop-yards meant,
Or why was Burton built on Trent?
Oh many a peer of England brews
Livelier liquor than the Muse,   20
And malt does more than Milton can
To justify God's ways to man.
Ale, man, ale's the stuff to drink
For fellows whom it hurts to think: 24
Look into the pewter pot
To see the world as the world's not.
And faith, 'tis pleasant till 'tis past:
The mischief is that 'twill not last.   28
Oh I have been to Ludlow fair
And left my necktie God knows where,

And carried half-way home, or near,
Pints and quarts of Ludlow beer: 32
Then the world seemed none so bad,
And I myself a sterling lad;
And down in lovely muck I've lain,
Happy till I woke again.   36
Then I saw the morning sky:
Heigho, the tale was all a lie;
The world, it was the old world yet,
I was I, my things were wet,   40
And nothing now remained to do
But begin the game anew.

  Therefore, since the world has still
Much good, but much less good than ill,   44
And while the sun and moon endure
Luck's a chance, but trouble's sure,
I'd face it as a wise man would,
And train for ill and not for good.   48
'Tis true, the stuff I bring for sale
Is not so brisk a brew as ale:
Out of a stem that scored the hand
I wrung it in a weary land.   52
But take it: if the smack is sour,
The better for the embittered hour;
It should do good to heart and head
When your soul is in my soul's stead;   56
And I will friend you, if I may,
In the dark and cloudy day.

  There was a king reigned in the East:
There, when kings will sit to feast,   60
They get their fill before they think
With poisoned meat and poisoned drink.
He gathered all that springs to birth
From the many-venomed earth;   64
First a little, thence to more,
He sampled all her killing store;
And easy, smiling, seasoned sound,
Sate the king when healths went round.   68
They put arsenic in his meat
And stared aghast to watch him eat;
They poured strychnine in his cup
And shook to see him drink it up: 72
They shook, they stared as white's their shirt:
Them it was their poison hurt.
— I tell the tale that I heard told.
Mithridates, he died old.   76

TERENCE, THIS IS STUPID STUFF. 1. *Terence:* As a name for himself, Housman takes that of a
Roman poet, author of satiric comedies. 18. *why was Burton built on Trent?* The answer is:
to use the river's water in the town's brewing industry.

A. E. Housman (1859–1936)

To an Athlete Dying Young

The time you won your town the race
We chaired you through the market-place;
Man and boy stood cheering by,
And home we brought you shoulder-high.   4

Today, the road all runners come,
Shoulder-high we bring you home,
And set you at your threshold down,
Townsman of a stiller town.   8

Smart lad, to slip betimes away
From fields where glory does not stay,
And early though the laurel grows
It withers quicker than the rose.   12

Eyes the shady night has shut
Cannot see the record cut,
And silence sounds no worse than cheers
After earth has stopped the ears.   16

Now you will not swell the rout
Of lads that wore their honors out,
Runners whom renown outran
And the name died before the man.   20

So set, before its echoes fade,
The fleet foot on the sill of shade,
And hold to the low lintel up
The still-defended challenge-cup.   24

And round that early-laureled head
Will flock to gaze the strengthless dead,
And find unwithered on its curls
The garland briefer than a girl's.   28

COMPARE:

"To an Athlete Dying Young" with "To the Memory of Mr. Oldham" by John
Dryden (page 325).

William Butler Yeats (1865–1939)

Crazy Jane Talks with the Bishop

I met the Bishop on the road
And much said he and I.
"Those breasts are flat and fallen now,
Those veins must soon be dry;
Live in a heavenly mansion,
Not in some foul sty."   6

"Fair and foul are near of kin,
And fair needs foul," I cried.
"My friends are gone, but that's a truth
Nor° grave nor bed denied,   *neither*
Learned in bodily lowliness
And in the heart's pride.   12

"A woman can be proud and stiff
When on love intent;
But Love has pitched his mansion in
The place of excrement;
For nothing can be sole or whole
That has not been rent."   18

William Butler Yeats (1865–1939)

For Anne Gregory

"Never shall a young man,
Thrown into despair
By those great honey-colored
Ramparts at your ear,
Love you for yourself alone
And not your yellow hair."   6

"But I can get a hair-dye
And set such color there,
Brown, or black, or carrot,
That young men in despair
May love me for myself alone
And not my yellow hair."   12

"I heard an old religious man
But yesternight declare
That he had found a text to prove
That only God, my dear,
Could love you for yourself alone
And not your yellow hair."   18

William Butler Yeats (1865–1939)

LAPIS LAZULI

For Harry Clifton

I have heard that hysterical women say
They are sick of the palette and fiddle-bow,
Of poets that are always gay,
For everybody knows or else should know   4
That if nothing drastic is done
Aeroplane and Zeppelin will come out,
Pitch like King Billy bomb-balls in
Until the town lie beaten flat.   8

All perform their tragic play,
There struts Hamlet, there is Lear,
That's Ophelia, that Cordelia;
Yet they, should the last scene be there,   12
The great stage curtain about to drop,
If worthy their prominent part in the play,
Do not break up their lines to weep.
They know that Hamlet and Lear are gay;   16
Gaiety transfiguring all that dread.
All men have aimed at, found and lost;
Black out; Heaven blazing into the head:
Tragedy wrought to its uttermost.   20
Though Hamlet rambles and Lear rages,
And all the drop-scenes drop at once
Upon a hundred thousand stages,
It cannot grow by an inch or an ounce.   24

On their own feet they came, or on shipboard,
Camel-back, horse-back, ass-back, mule-back,
Old civilizations put to the sword.
Then they and their wisdom went to rack: 28
No handiwork of Callimachus,
Who handled marble as if it were bronze,
Made draperies that seemed to rise
When sea-wind swept the corner, stands;   32
His long lamp-chimney shaped like the stem
Of a slender palm, stood but a day;
All things fall and are built again,
And those that build them again are gay.   36

Two Chinamen, behind them a third,
Are carved in lapis lazuli,
Over them flies a long-legged bird,
A symbol of longevity;   40
The third, doubtless a serving-man,
Carries a musical instrument.

Every discoloration of the stone,
Every accidental crack or dent,   44
Seems a water-course or an avalanche,
Or lofty slope where it still snows
Though doubtless plum or cherry-branch
Sweetens the little half-way house   48
Those Chinamen climb towards, and I
Delight to imagine them seated there;
There, on the mountain and the sky,
On all the tragic scene they stare.   52
One asks for mournful melodies;
Accomplished fingers begin to play.
Their eyes mid many wrinkles, their eyes,
Their ancient, glittering eyes, are gay.   56

LAPIS LAZULI. Lapis lazuli is a deep blue semi-precious stone. A friend had given Yeats the carving made from it, which he describes in lines 37–56. 7. *King Billy:* William of Orange, king of England who used cannon against the Irish in the Battle of the Boyne, 1690. Yeats also may have in mind Kaiser Wilhelm II of Germany, who sent zeppelins to bomb London in World War I. 29. *Callimachus:* Athenian sculptor, fifth century B.C.

COMPARE:

"Lapis Lazuli" with "Ode on a Grecian Urn" by John Keats (page 336) and "Anecdote of the Jar" by Wallace Stevens (page 212).

William Butler Yeats (1865–1939)

LONG-LEGGED FLY

That civilization may not sink,
Its great battle lost,
Quiet the dog, tether the pony
To a distant post;   4
Our master Caesar is in the tent
Where the maps are spread,
His eyes fixed upon nothing,
A hand under his head.   8
Like a long-legged fly upon the stream
His mind moves upon silence.   10

That the topless towers be burnt
And men recall that face,
Move most gently if move you must
In this lonely place.   14
She thinks, part woman, three parts a child,
That nobody looks; her feet
Practice a tinker shuffle
Picked up on a street.   18
Like a long-legged fly upon the stream
Her mind moves upon silence.   20

That girls at puberty may find
The first Adam in their thought,
Shut the door of the Pope's chapel,
Keep those children out. 24
There on that scaffolding reclines
Michael Angelo.
With no more sound than the mice make
His hand moves to and fro. 28
Like a long-legged fly upon the stream
His mind moves upon silence. 30

LONG-LEGGED FLY. This "fly" is the fresh-water insect also known as the water strider. 11. *topless towers:* Of Troy, burned by the Greeks. Yeats echoes the description of Helen of Troy (whose abduction started the war) given in Christopher Marlowe's play *The Tragical History of Dr. Faustus:* "Was this the face that launched a thousand ships, / And burnt the topless towers of Ilium?" 23. *the Pope's chapel:* Michelangelo had to lie on his back while painting in the Sistine Chapel his frescoes showing the creation, fall, and final judgment of man.

William Butler Yeats (1865–1939)

THE MAGI

Now as at all times I can see in the mind's eye,
In their stiff, painted clothes, the pale unsatisfied ones
Appear and disappear in the blue depth of the sky
With all their ancient faces like rain-beaten stones, 4
And all their helms of silver hovering side by side,
And all their eyes still fixed, hoping to find once more,
Being by Calvary's turbulence unsatisfied,
The uncontrollable mystery on the bestial floor. 8

Edwin Arlington Robinson (1869–1935)

MR. FLOOD'S PARTY

Old Eben Flood, climbing alone one night
Over the hill between the town below
And the forsaken upland hermitage
That held as much as he should ever know 4
On earth again of home, paused warily.
The road was his with not a native near;
And Eben, having leisure, said aloud,
For no man else in Tilbury Town to hear: 8

"Well, Mr. Flood, we have the harvest moon
Again, and we may not have many more;
The bird is on the wing, the poet says,
And you and I have said it here before. 12

Drink to the bird." He raised up to the light
The jug that he had gone so far to fill,
And answered huskily: "Well, Mr. Flood,
Since you propose it, I believe I will."   16

Alone, as if enduring to the end
A valiant armor of scarred hopes outworn,
He stood there in the middle of the road
Like Roland's ghost winding° a silent horn.   *blowing*   20
Below him, in the town among the trees,
Where friends of other days had honored him,
A phantom salutation of the dead
Rang thinly till old Eben's eyes were dim.   24

Then, as a mother lays her sleeping child
Down tenderly, fearing it may awake,
He set the jug down slowly at his feet
With trembling care, knowing that most things break;   28
And only when assured that on firm earth
It stood, as the uncertain lives of men
Assuredly did not, he paced away,
And with his hand extended paused again: 32

"Well, Mr. Flood, we have not met like this
In a long time; and many a change has come
To both of us, I fear, since last it was
We had a drop together. Welcome home!"   36
Convivially returning with himself,
Again he raised the jug up to the light;
And with an acquiescent quaver said:
"Well, Mr. Flood, if you insist, I might.   40

"Only a very little, Mr. Flood —
For auld lang syne. No more, sir; that will do."
So, for the time, apparently it did,
And Eben evidently thought so too;   44
For soon amid the silver loneliness
Of night he lifted up his voice and sang,
Secure, with only two moons listening,
Until the whole harmonious landscape rang —   48

"For auld lang syne." The weary throat gave out,
The last word wavered; and the song being done,
He raised again the jug regretfully
And shook his head, and was again alone.   52
There was not much that was ahead of him,
And there was nothing in the town below —
Where strangers would have shut the many doors
That many friends had opened long ago.   56

MR. FLOOD'S PARTY. 11. *the poet:* Omar Khayyám, Persian poet, a praiser of wine, whose
Rubáiyát, translated by Edward FitzGerald, included the lines:

Come, fill the Cup, and in the fire of Spring
Your Winter-garment of Repentance fling:
   The Bird of Time has but a little way
To flutter and the Bird is on the Wing.

20. *Roland's ghost . . . horn:* In the battle of Roncesvalles (eighth century), Roland fought to his death, refusing to sound his horn for help until all hope was gone.

COMPARE:

"Mr. Flood's Party" with "Provide, Provide" by Robert Frost (page 361).

Walter de la Mare (1873–1956)

THE LISTENERS

"Is there anybody there?" said the Traveller,
   Knocking on the moonlit door;
And his horse in the silence champed the grasses
   Of the forest's ferny floor: 4
And a bird flew up out of the turret,
   Above the Traveller's head:
And he smote upon the door again a second time;
   "Is there anybody there?" he said.   8
But no one descended to the Traveller;
   No head from the leaf-fringed sill
Leaned over and looked into his grey eyes,
   Where he stood perplexed and still.   12
But only a host of phantom listeners
   That dwelt in the lone house then
Stood listening in the quiet of the moonlight
   To that voice from the world of men: 16
Stood thronging the faint moonbeams on the dark stair,
   That goes down to the empty hall,
Hearkening in an air stirred and shaken
   By the lonely Traveller's call.   20
And he felt in his heart their strangeness,
   Their stillness answering his cry,
While his horse moved, cropping the dark turf,
   'Neath the starred and leafy sky;   24
For he suddenly smote on the door, even
   Louder, and lifted his head: —
"Tell them I came, and no one answered,
   That I kept my word," he said.   28
Never the least stir made the listeners,
   Though every word he spake
Fell echoing through the shadowiness of the still house
   From the one man left awake: 32
Ay, they heard his foot upon the stirrup,
   And the sound of iron on stone,
And how the silence surged softly backward,
   When the plunging hoofs were gone.   36

Robert Frost (1874–1963)

PROVIDE, PROVIDE

The witch that came (the withered hag)
To wash the steps with pail and rag,
Was once the beauty Abishag,　　　　　　　　　　　3

The picture pride of Hollywood.
Too many fall from great and good
For you to doubt the likelihood.　　　　　　　　　6

Die early and avoid the fate,
Or if predestined to die late,
Make up your mind to die in state.　　　　　　　9

Make the whole stock exchange your own!
If need be occupy a throne,
Where nobody can call *you* crone.　　　　　　　12

Some have relied on what they knew;
Others on simply being true.
What worked for them might work for you.　　　15

No memory of having starred
Atones for later disregard,
Or keeps the end from being hard.　　　　　　18

Better to go down dignified
With boughten friendship at your side
Than none at all. Provide, provide!　　　　　　21

COMPARE:

"Provide, Provide" with "Mr. Flood's Party" by Edwin Arlington Robinson (page 358).

Robert Frost (1874–1963)

STOPPING BY WOODS ON A SNOWY EVENING

Whose woods these are I think I know.
His house is in the village though;
He will not see me stopping here
To watch his woods fill up with snow.　　　　4

My little horse must think it queer
To stop without a farmhouse near
Between the woods and frozen lake
The darkest evening of the year.　　　　　　8

He gives his harness bells a shake
To ask if there is some mistake.
The only other sound's the sweep
Of easy wind and downy flake.　　　　　　　12

The woods are lovely, dark and deep,
But I have promises to keep,
And miles to go before I sleep,
And miles to go before I sleep.   16

COMPARE:

"Stopping by Woods on a Snowy Evening" with "The Snow Man" by Wallace
Stevens (page 364).

Wallace Stevens (1879–1955)
THE EMPEROR OF ICE-CREAM

Call the roller of big cigars,
The muscular one, and bid him whip
In kitchen cups concupiscent curds.
Let the wenches dawdle in such dress
As they are used to wear, and let the boys
Bring flowers in last month's newspapers.   6
Let be be finale of seem.
The only emperor is the emperor of ice-cream.   8

Take from the dresser of deal,
Lacking the three glass knobs, that sheet
On which she embroidered fantails once
And spread it so as to cover her face.
If her horny feet protrude, they come
To show how cold she is, and dumb.   14
Let the lamp affix its beam.
The only emperor is the emperor of ice-cream.   16

THE EMPEROR OF ICE-CREAM. 9. *deal:* Fir or pine wood used to make cheap furniture.

Wallace Stevens (1879–1955)
PETER QUINCE AT THE CLAVIER

I

Just as my fingers on these keys
Make music, so the selfsame sounds
On my spirit make a music, too.

Music is feeling, then, not sound;
And thus it is that what I feel,   5
Here in this room, desiring you,

Thinking of your blue-shadowed silk,
Is music. It is like the strain
Waked in the elders by Susanna.

Of a green evening, clear and warm, 10
She bathed in her still garden, while
The red-eyed elders watching, felt

The basses of their beings throb
In witching chords, and their thin blood
Pulse pizzicati of Hosanna. 15

II

In the green water, clear and warm,
Susanna lay.
She searched
The touch of springs,
And found 20
Concealed imaginings.
She sighed,
For so much melody.

Upon the bank, she stood
In the cool 25
Of spent emotions.
She felt, among the leaves,
The dew
Of old devotions.

She walked upon the grass, 30
Still quavering.
The winds were like her maids,
On timid feet,
Fetching her woven scarves,
Yet wavering. 35

A breath upon her hand
Muted the night.
She turned —
A cymbal crashed,
And roaring horns. 40

III

Soon, with a noise like tambourines,
Came her attendant Byzantines.

They wondered why Suzanna cried
Against the elders by her side;

And as they whispered, the refrain 45
Was like a willow swept by rain.

Anon, their lamps' uplifted flame
Revealed Susanna and her shame.

And then, the simpering Byzantines
Fled, with a noise like tambourines. 50

IV

Beauty is momentary in the mind —
The fitful tracing of a portal;
But in the flesh it is immortal.

The body dies; the body's beauty lives.
So evenings die, in their green going,   55
A wave, interminably flowing.
So gardens die, their meek breath scenting
The cowl of winter, done repenting.
So maidens die, to the auroral
Celebration of a maiden's choral.   60

Susanna's music touched the bawdy strings
Of those white elders; but, escaping,
Left only Death's ironic scraping.
Now, in its immortality, it plays
On the clear viol of her memory,   65
And makes a constant sacrament of praise.

PETER QUINCE AT THE CLAVIER. In Shakespeare's *Midsummer Night's Dream*, Peter Quince is a clownish carpenter who stages a mock-tragic play. In The Book of Susanna in the Apocrypha, two lustful elders who covet Susanna, a virtuous married woman, hide in her garden, spy on her as she bathes, then threaten to make false accusations against her unless she submits to them. When she refuses, they cry out, and her servants come running. All ends well when the prophet Daniel cross-examines the elders and proves them liars. 15. *pizzicati*: Thin notes made by plucking a stringed instrument. 42. *Byzantines*: Susanna's maidservants.

Wallace Stevens (1879–1955)

THE SNOW MAN

One must have a mind of winter
To regard the frost and the boughs
Of the pinetrees crusted with snow;

And have been cold a long time
To behold the junipers shagged with ice,   5
The spruces rough in the distant glitter

Of the January sun; and not to think
Of any misery in the sound of the wind,
In the sound of a few leaves,

Which is the sound of the land   10
Full of the same wind
That is blowing in the same bare place

For the listener, who listens in the snow,
And, nothing himself, beholds
Nothing that is not there and the nothing that is.   15

COMPARE:

"The Snow Man" with "Stopping by Woods on a Snowy Evening" by Robert
Frost (page 361).

James Joyce (1882–1941)
I HEAR AN ARMY CHARGING UPON THE LAND

I hear an army charging upon the land,
    And the thunder of horses plunging, foam about their knees:
Arrogant, in black armor, behind them stand,
    Disdaining the reins, with fluttering whips, the charioteers.   4

They cry unto the night their battle-name:
    I moan in sleep when I hear afar their whirling laughter.
They cleave the gloom of dreams, a blinding flame,
    Clanging, clanging upon the heart as upon an anvil.   8

They come shaking in triumph their long, green hair:
    They come out of the sea and run shouting by the shore.
My heart, have you no wisdom thus to despair?
    My love, my love, my love, why have you left me alone?   12

William Carlos Williams (1883–1963)
DANSE RUSSE

If when my wife is sleeping
and the baby and Kathleen
are sleeping
and the sun is a flame-white disc
in silken mists   5
above shining trees, —
if I in my north room
dance naked, grotesquely
before my mirror
waving my shirt round my head   10
and singing softly to myself:
"I am lonely, lonely.
I was born to be lonely,
I am best so!"
If I admire my arms, my face,   15
my shoulders, flanks, buttocks
against the yellow drawn shades, —

Who shall say I am not
the happy genius° of my household?   *guardian spirit*

DANSE RUSSE. The title means "Russian ballet."

William Carlos Williams (1883–1963)
To Waken an Old Lady

Old age is
a flight of small
cheeping birds
skimming
bare trees   5
above a snow glaze.
Gaining and failing
they are buffetted
by a dark wind —
But what?   10
On harsh weedstalks
the flock has rested,
the snow
is covered with broken
seedhusks   15
and the wind tempered
by a shrill
piping of plenty.

Ezra Pound (1885–1972)
The River-Merchant's Wife: a Letter

While my hair was still cut straight across my forehead
I played about the front gate, pulling flowers.
You came by on bamboo stilts, playing horse,
You walked about my seat, playing with blue plums.
And we went on living in the village of Chokan: 5
Two small people, without dislike or suspicion.
At fourteen I married My Lord you.
I never laughed, being bashful.
Lowering my head, I looked at the wall.
Called to, a thousand times, I never looked back.   10

At fifteen I stopped scowling,
I desired my dust to be mingled with yours
Forever and forever and forever.
Why should I climb the lookout?

At sixteen you departed,   15
You went into far Ku-to-yen, by the river of swirling eddies,
And you have been gone five months.
The monkeys make sorrowful noise overhead.

You dragged your feet when you went out.
By the gate now, the moss is grown, the different mosses,   20
Too deep to clear them away!
The leaves fall early this autumn, in wind.
The paired butterflies are already yellow with August
Over the grass in the West garden;
They hurt me. I grow older.   25
If you are coming down through the narrows of the river Kiang,
Please let me know beforehand,
And I will come out to meet you
       As far as Cho-fu-sa.

THE RIVER-MERCHANT'S WIFE: A LETTER. A free translation from the Chinese poet Li Po (eighth century).

D. H. Lawrence (1885–1930)
THE ELEPHANT IS SLOW TO MATE —

The elephant, the huge old beast,
      is slow to mate;
he finds a female, they show no haste,
      they wait   4

for the sympathy in their vast shy hearts
      slowly, slowly to rouse
as they loiter along the river-beds
      and drink and browse   8

and dash in panic through the brake
      of forest with the herd,
and sleep in massive silence, and wake
      together, without a word.   12

So slowly the great hot elephant hearts
      grow full of desire,
and the great beasts mate in secret at last,
      hiding their fire.   16

Oldest they are and the wisest of beasts
      so they know at last
how to wait for the loneliest of feasts
      for the full repast.   20

They do not snatch, they do not tear;
      their massive blood
moves as the moon-tides, near, more near,
      till they touch in flood.   24

Marianne Moore (1887–1972)

A Grave

Man looking into the sea,
taking the view from those who have as much right to it as you have to
     yourself,
it is human nature to stand in the middle of a thing,
but you cannot stand in the middle of this;
the sea has nothing to give but a well excavated grave.   5
The firs stand in a procession, each with an emerald turkey-foot at the top,
reserved as their contours, saying nothing;
repression, however, is not the most obvious characteristic of the sea;
the sea is a collector, quick to return a rapacious look.
There are others besides you who have worn that look —   10
whose expression is no longer a protest; the fish no longer investigate
     them
for their bones have not lasted:
men lower nets, unconscious of the fact that they are desecrating a grave,
and row quickly away — the blades of the oars
moving together like the feet of water-spiders as if there were no such
     thing as death.   15
The wrinkles progress among themselves in a phalanx — beautiful under
     networks of foam,
and fade breathlessly while the sea rustles in and out of the seaweed;
the birds swim through the air at top speed, emitting catcalls as hereto-
     fore —
the tortoise-shell scourges about the feet of the cliffs, in motion beneath
     them;
and the ocean, under the pulsation of lighthouses and noise of bell-buoys,   20
advances as usual, looking as if it were not that ocean in which dropped
     things are bound to sink —
in which if they turn and twist, it is neither with volition nor con-
     sciousness.

T. S. Eliot (1888–1965)

The Love Song of J. Alfred Prufrock

S'io credessi che mia risposta fosse
A persona che mai tornasse al mondo,
Questa fiamma staria senza piu scosse.
Ma perciocche giammai di questo fondo
Non torno vivo alcun, s'i'odo il vero,
Senza tema d'infamia ti rispondo.

Let us go then, you and I,
When the evening is spread out against the sky
Like a patient etherized upon a table; powerless, at the
Let us go, through certain half-deserted streets, mercy of others

The muttering retreats   5
Of restless nights in one-night cheap hotels
And sawdust restaurants with oyster-shells:
Streets that follow like a tedious argument
Of insidious intent
To lead you to an overwhelming question . . .   10
Oh, do not ask, "What is it?"
Let us go and make our visit.

In the room the women come and go   *Cutting down society*
Talking of Michelangelo.
                          passivity
The yellow fog that rubs its back upon the window-panes,   15
The yellow smoke that rubs its muzzle on the window-panes
Licked its tongue into the corners of the evening,
Lingered upon the pools that stand in drains,
Let fall upon its back the soot that falls from chimneys,
Slipped by the terrace, made a sudden leap,   20
And seeing that it was a soft October night,
Curled once about the house, and fell asleep.

And indeed there will be time
For the yellow smoke that slides along the street, *from the*
Rubbing its back upon the window-panes;   *bible*   25
There will be time, there will be time
To prepare a face to meet the faces that you meet;
There will be time to murder and create,
And time for all the works and days of hands
That lift and drop a question on your plate;   30
Time for you and time for me,
And time yet for a hundred indecisions,
And for a hundred visions and revisions,
Before the taking of a toast and tea.

In the room the women come and go   35
Talking of Michelangelo.

And indeed there will be time
To wonder, "Do I dare?" and, "Do I dare?" *—passive*
Time to turn back and descend the stair,
With a bald spot in the middle of my hair —   *aging - he talks*   40
[They will say: "How his hair is growing thin!"] *about this through*
My morning coat, my collar mounting firmly to the chin, *out the poem.*
My necktie rich and modest, but asserted by a simple pin —
[They will say: "But how his arms and legs are thin!"]
Do I dare   45
Disturb the universe?
In a minute there is time
For decisions and revisions which a minute will reverse.

For I have known them all already, known them all: —
Have known the evenings, mornings, afternoons,   50

I have measured out my life with coffee spoons;
I know the voices dying with a dying fall
Beneath the music from a farther room.
   So how should I presume?

And I have known the eyes already, known them all —   55
The eyes that fix you in a formulated phrase,
And when I am formulated, sprawling on a pin,
When I am pinned and wriggling on the wall,
Then how should I begin
To spit out all the butt-ends of my days and ways?   60
   And how should I presume?

And I have known the arms already, known them all —
Arms that are braceleted and white and bare
[But in the lamplight, downed with light brown hair!]
Is it perfume from a dress   65
That makes me so digress?
Arms that lie along a table, or wrap about a shawl.
  And should I then presume?
  And how should I begin?

      . . . . .

Shall I say, I have gone at dusk through narrow streets   70
And watched the smoke that rises from the pipes
Of lonely men in shirt-sleeves, leaning out of windows? . . .

I should have been a pair of ragged claws
Scuttling across the floors of silent seas.

      . . . . .

And the afternoon, the evening, sleeps so peacefully!   75
Smoothed by long fingers,
Asleep . . . tired . . . or it malingers,
Stretched on the floor, here beside you and me.
Should I, after tea and cakes and ices,
Have the strength to force the moment to its crisis?   80
But though I have wept and fasted, wept and prayed,
Though I have seen my head [grown slightly bald] brought in upon a
    platter,
I am no prophet — and here's no great matter;
I have seen the moment of my greatness flicker,
And I have seen the eternal Footman hold my coat, and snicker,   85
And in short, I was afraid.

And would it have been worth it, after all,
After the cups, the marmalade, the tea,
Among the porcelain, among some talk of you and me,
Would it have been worth while,   90
To have bitten off the matter with a smile,
To have squeezed the universe into a ball
To roll it toward some overwhelming question,
To say: "I am Lazarus, come from the dead,

Come back to tell you all, I shall tell you all" —   95
If one, settling a pillow by her head,
    Should say: "That is not what I meant at all.
    That is not it, at all."

And would it have been worth it, after all,
Would it have been worth while,   100
After the sunsets and the dooryards and the sprinkled streets,
After the novels, after the teacups, after the skirts that trail along the
        floor —
And this, and so much more? —
It is impossible to say just what I mean!
But as if a magic lantern threw the nerves in patterns on a screen: 105
Would it have been worth while
If one, settling a pillow or throwing off a shawl,
And turning toward the window, should say:
    "That is not it at all,
    That is not what I meant, at all."

undecisive character . . *(he is not the heroic*   110
stature even of an
indecisive character)

No! I am not Prince Hamlet, nor was meant to be;
Am an attendant lord, one that will do
To swell a progress, start a scene or two,
Advise the prince; no doubt, an easy tool,
Deferential, glad to be of use,   115
Politic, cautious, and meticulous;
Full of high sentence, but a bit obtuse;

concerned with growing old.

At times, indeed, almost ridiculous —
Almost, at times, the Fool. *(He may really be bright)*

I grow old . . . I grow old . . .   120
I shall wear the bottoms of my trousers rolled.   *— going to affect a sporty look. That*

Shall I part my hair behind? Do I dare to eat a peach?   *was the in*
I shall wear white flannel trousers, and walk upon the beach.   *thing, a symbol of youth.*
I have heard the mermaids singing, each to each.   *Ulysees*   125

I do not think that they will sing to me.   *they sang to him but will*
                                                         not sing to Prufrock.

I have seen them riding seaward on the waves
Combing the white hair of the waves blown back
When the wind blows the water white and black.

We have lingered in the chambers of the sea
By sea-girls wreathed with seaweed red and brown
Till human voices wake us, and we drown.   130

THE LOVE SONG OF J. ALFRED PRUFROCK. The epigraph, from Dante's *Inferno,* is the speech
of one dead and damned, who thinks that his hearer also is going to remain in Hell. Count
Guido da Montefeltro, whose sin has been to give false counsel after a corrupt prelate had
offered him prior absolution and whose punishment is to be wrapped in a constantly
burning flame, offers to tell Dante his story: "If I thought my reply were to someone who
could ever return to the world, this flame would waver no more. But since, I'm told, nobody ever escapes from this pit, I'll tell you without fear of ill fame." 29. *works and days:*

Title of a poem by Hesiod (eighth century B.C.), depicting his life as a hard-working Greek farmer and exhorting his brother to be like him. 82. *head . . . platter:* Like that of John the Baptist, prophet and praiser of chastity, whom King Herod beheaded at the demand of Herodias, his unlawfully wedded wife (see Mark 6:17–28). 92–93. *squeezed . . . To roll it:* An echo from Marvell's "To His Coy Mistress," lines 41–42 (see p. 324). 94. *Lazarus:* Probably the Lazarus whom Christ called forth from the tomb (John 11:1–44), but possibly the beggar seen in Heaven by the rich man in Hell (Luke 16:19–25).

T. S. Eliot (1888–1965)

Sweeney among the Nightingales

ὤμοι, πέπληγμαι καιρίαν πληγὴν ἔσω.

Apeneck Sweeney spreads his knees
Letting his arms hang down to laugh,
The zebra stripes along his jaw
Swelling to maculate° giraffe.   *opposite of immaculate*   4

The circles of the stormy moon
Slide westward toward the River Plate,
Death and the Raven drift above
And Sweeney guards the hornèd gate.   8

Gloomy Orion and the Dog
Are veiled; and hushed the shrunken seas;
The person in the Spanish cape
Tries to sit on Sweeney's knees   12

Slips and pulls the table cloth
Overturns a coffee-cup,
Reorganized upon the floor
She yawns and draws a stocking up;   16

The silent man in mocha brown
Sprawls at the window-sill and gapes;
The waiter brings in oranges
Bananas figs and hothouse grapes;   20

The silent vertebrate in brown
Contracts and concentrates, withdraws;
Rachel *née*° Rabinovitch   *born*
Tears at the grapes with murderous paws;   24

She and the lady in the cape
Are suspect, thought to be in league;
Therefore the man with heavy eyes
Declines the gambit, shows fatigue,   28

Leaves the room and reappears
Outside the window, leaning in,
Branches of wistaria
Circumscribe a golden grin;   32

The host with someone indistinct
Converses at the door apart,
The nightingales are singing near
The Convent of the Sacred Heart,   36

And sang within the bloody wood
When Agamemnon cried aloud,
And let their liquid siftings fall
To stain the stiff dishonored shroud.   40

SWEENEY AMONG THE NIGHTINGALES. *"Nightingale:* a harlot . . . Because most active at
night" (Eric Partridge, *Dictionary of Slang and Unconventional English*). The Greek epigraph ("Aagh, I am struck a deep death-blow!"), from Aeschylus' tragedy of *Agamemnon*
is the king's cry when he is stabbed by his wife, Clytemnestra. 6. *River Plate:* Rio de la
Plata, dividing Uruguay from Argentina, "the shallowest of rivers" (Elizabeth Drew,
T. S. Eliot: The Design of His Poetry). 7, 9. *Raven; Orion and the Dog:* Two constellations and
a star, visible in the Southern Hemisphere. To ancient Egyptians the Dog meant fertility;
Nile waters rise when it appears. 8. *hornèd gate:* According to Homer and Virgil, pleasant
lying dreams come from the underworld through gates of ivory, ominous truth-telling
dreams through gates of horn. 37. *bloody wood:* Wood of Nemi (Greece), where an old
king, to be succeeded, had to be ritually slain. (Eliot is merging myths: Agamemnon died
in his bath.)

John Crowe Ransom (b. 1888)

BELLS FOR JOHN WHITESIDE'S DAUGHTER

There was such speed in her little body,
And such lightness in her footfall,
It is no wonder her brown study
Astonishes us all.   4

Her wars were bruited in our high window.
We looked among orchard trees and beyond,
Where she took arms against her shadow,
Or harried unto the pond   8

The lazy geese, like a snow cloud
Dripping their snow on the green grass,
Tricking and stopping, sleepy and proud,
Who cried in goose, Alas,   12

For the tireless heart within the little
Lady with rod that made them rise
From their noon apple-dreams, and scuttle
Goose-fashion under the skies!   16

But now go the bells, and we are ready;
In one house we are sternly stopped
To say we are vexed at her brown study,
Lying so primly propped.   20

COMPARE:

"Bells for John Whiteside's Daughter" with "Elegy for Jane" by Theodore
Roethke (page 383).

E. E. Cummings (1894–1962)

ALL IN GREEN WENT MY LOVE RIDING

All in green went my love riding
on a great horse of gold
into the silver dawn.

four lean hounds crouched low and smiling
the merry deer ran before.   5

Fleeter be they than dappled dreams
the swift sweet deer
the red rare deer.

Four red roebuck at a white water
the cruel bugle sang before.   10

Horn at hip went my love riding
riding the echo down
into the silver dawn.

four lean hounds crouched low and smiling
the level meadows ran before.   15

Softer be they than slippered sleep
the lean lithe deer
the fleet flown deer.

Four fleet does at a gold valley
the famished arrow sang before.   20

Bow at belt went my love riding
riding the mountain down
into the silver dawn.

four lean hounds crouched low and smiling
the sheer peaks ran before.   25

Paler be they than daunting death
the sleek slim deer
the tall tense deer.

Four tall stags at a green mountain
the lucky hunter sang before.   30

All in green went my love riding
on a great horse of gold
into the silver dawn.

four lean hounds crouched low and smiling
my heart fell dead before.   35

COMPARE:

"All in green went my love riding" with the ballads "The Three Ravens" and
"The Twa Corbies" (pages 311–312).

E. E. Cummings (1894–1962)
WHEN SERPENTS BARGAIN FOR THE RIGHT TO SQUIRM

when serpents bargain for the right to squirm
and the sun strikes to gain a living wage —
when thorns regard their roses with alarm
and rainbows are insured against old age   4

when every thrush may sing no new moon in
if all screech-owls have not okayed his voice
— and any wave signs on the dotted line
or else an ocean is compelled to close   8

when the oak begs permission of the birch
to make an acorn — valleys accuse their
mountains of having altitude — and march
denounces april as a saboteur   12

then we'll believe in that incredible
unanimal mankind(and not until)   14

E. E. Cummings (1894–1962)
NEXT TO OF COURSE GOD AMERICA I

"next to of course god america i
love you land of the pilgrims' and so forth oh
say can you see by the dawn's early my
country 'tis of centuries come and go   4
and are no more what of it we should worry
in every language even deafanddumb
thy sons acclaim your glorious name by gorry
by jingo by gee by gosh by gum   8
why talk of beauty what could be more beaut-
iful than these heroic happy dead
who rushed like lions to the roaring slaughter
they did not stop to think they died instead
then shall the voice of liberty be mute?"

He spoke. And drank rapidly a glass of water   14

Hart Crane (1899–1932)
BLACK TAMBOURINE

The interests of a black man in a cellar
Mark tardy judgment on the world's closed door.
Gnats toss in the shadow of a bottle,
And a roach spans a crevice in the floor.   4

Æsop, driven to pondering, found
Heaven with the tortoise and the hare;
Fox brush and sow ear top his grave
And mingling incantations on the air.   8

The black man, forlorn in the cellar,
Wanders in some mid-kingdom, dark, that lies,
Between his tambourine, stuck on the wall,
And, in Africa, a carcass quick with flies.   12

COMPARE:

"Black Tambourine" with "The Weary Blues" by Langston Hughes (page 378).

Yvor Winters (1900–1968)
AT THE SAN FRANCISCO AIRPORT

To My Daughter, 1954

This is the terminal: the light
Gives perfect vision, false and hard;
The metal glitters, deep and bright.
Great planes are waiting in the yard —
They are already in the night.   5

And you are here beside me, small,
Contained and fragile, and intent
On things that I but half recall —
Yet going whither you are bent.
I am the past, and that is all.   10

But you and I in part are one:
The frightened brain, the nervous will,
The knowledge of what must be done,
The passion to acquire the skill
To face that which you dare not shun.   15

The rain of matter upon sense
Destroys me momently. The score:
There comes what will come. The expense
Is what one thought, and something more —
One's being and intelligence.   20

This is the terminal, the break.
Beyond this point, on lines of air,
You take the way that you must take;
And I remain in light and stare —
In light, and nothing else, awake.   25

Kenneth Fearing (1902–1961)

DIRGE

1-2-3 was the number he played but today the number came 3-2-1;
Bought his Carbide at 30 and it went to 29; had the favorite at Bowie but
    the track was slow —

O executive type, would you like to drive a floating-power, knee-action,
    silk-upholstered six? Wed a Hollywood star? Shoot the course in 58?
    Draw to the ace, king, jack?
O fellow with a will who won't take no, watch out for three cigarettes on
    the same, single match; O democratic voter born in August under
    Mars, beware of liquidated rails —

Denouement to denouement, he took a personal pride in the certain,
    certain way he lived his own, private life,   5
But nevertheless, they shut off his gas; nevertheless, the bank foreclosed;
    nevertheless, the landlord called; nevertheless, the radio broke,
And twelve o'clock arrived just once too often,
Just the same he wore one gray tweed suit, bought one straw hat, drank
    one straight Scotch, walked one short step, took one long look,
    drew one deep breath,
Just one too many,

And wow he died as wow he lived,   10
Going whop to the office and blooie home to sleep and biff got married
    and bam had children and oof got fired,
Zowie did he live and zowie did he die,

With who the hell are you at the corner of his casket, and where the hell're
    we going on the right-hand silver knob, and who the hell cares
    walking second from the end with an American Beauty wreath
    from why the hell not,

Very much missed by the circulation staff of the New York Evening Post;
    deeply mourned by the B.M.T.
Wham, Mr. Roosevelt; pow, Sears Roebuck; awk, big dipper; bop,
    summer rain;   15
Bong, Mr., bong, Mr., bong, Mr., bong.

DIRGE. 2. *Carbide:* The Union Carbon & Carbide Co. 14. *B.M.T.:* Brooklyn-Manhattan
Transit, a New York subway line.

COMPARE:

"Dirge" with "The Unknown Citizen" by W. H. Auden (page 12).

Langston Hughes (1902–1967)

THE WEARY BLUES

Droning a drowsy syncopated tune,
Rocking back and forth to a mellow croon,
    I heard a Negro play.
Down on Lenox Avenue the other night
By the pale dull pallor of an old gas light   5
    He did a lazy sway . . . .
    He did a lazy sway . . . .
To the tune o' those Weary Blues.
With his ebony hands on each ivory key
He made that poor piano moan with melody.   10
    O Blues!
Swaying to and fro on his rickety stool
He played that sad raggy tune like a musical fool
    Sweet Blues!
Coming from a black man's soul.   15
    O Blues!
In a deep song voice with a melancholy tone
I heard that Negro sing, that old piano moan —
    "Ain't got nobody in all this world,
    Ain't got nobody but ma self.   20
    I's gwine to quit ma frownin'
    And put ma troubles on the shelf."
Thump, thump, thump, went his foot on the floor.
He played a few chords then he sang some more —
    "I got the Weary Blues   25
    And I can't be satisfied.
    Got the Weary Blues
    And can't be satisfied —
    I ain't happy no mo'
    And I wish that I had died."   30
And far into the night he crooned that tune.
The stars went out and so did the moon.
The singer stopped playing and went to bed
While the Weary Blues echoed through his head.
He slept like a rock or a man that's dead.   35

COMPARE:

"The Weary Blues" with "Black Tambourine" by Hart Crane (page 375) and the anonymous "Good Mornin', Blues" (page 121).

Countee Cullen (1903–1946)

SATURDAY'S CHILD

Some are teethed on a silver spoon,
With the stars strung for a rattle;
I cut my teeth as the black racoon —
For implements of battle.   4

Some are swaddled in silk and down,
And heralded by a star;
They swathed my limbs in a sackcloth gown
On a night that was black as tar.   8

For some, godfather and goddame
The opulent fairies be;
Dame Poverty gave me my name,
And Pain godfathered me.   12

For I was born on Saturday —
"Bad time for planting a seed,"
Was all my father had to say,
And, "One mouth more to feed."   16

Death cut the strings that gave me life,
And handed me to Sorrow,
The only kind of middle wife
My folks could beg or borrow.   20

William Empson (b. 1906)

LEGAL FICTION

Law makes long spokes of the short stakes of men.
Your well fenced out real estate of mind
No high flat of the nomad citizen
Looks over, or train leaves behind.   4

Your rights extend under and above your claim
Without bound; you own land in Heaven and Hell;
Your part of earth's surface and mass the same,
Of all cosmos' volume, and all stars as well. 8

Your rights reach down where all owners meet, in Hell's
Pointed exclusive conclave, at earth's center
(Your spun farm's root still on that axis dwells);
And up, through galaxies, a growing sector.   12

You are nomad yet; the lighthouse beam you own
Flashes, like Lucifer, through the firmament.
Earth's axis varies; your dark central cone
Wavers, a candle's shadow, at the end.   16

COMPARE:

"Legal Fiction" with "The Definition of Love" by Andrew Marvell (page 95).

W. H. Auden (1907–1973)

As I Walked Out One Evening

As I walked out one evening,
　Walking down Bristol Street,
The crowds upon the pavement
　Were fields of harvest wheat.

And down by the brimming river
　I heard a lover sing
Under an arch of the railway:
　"Love has no ending.

"I'll love you, dear, I'll love you
　Till China and Africa meet,
And the river jumps over the mountain
　And the salmon sing in the street,

"I'll love you till the ocean
　Is folded and hung up to dry
And the seven stars go squawking
　Like geese about the sky.

"The years shall run like rabbits,
　For in my arms I hold
The Flower of the Ages,
　And the first love of the world."

But all the clocks in the city
　Began to whirr and chime:
"O let not Time deceive you,
　You cannot conquer Time.

"In the burrows of the Nightmare
　Where Justice naked is,
Time watches from the shadow
　And coughs when you would kiss.

"In headaches and in worry
　Vaguely life leaks away,
And Time will have his fancy
　Tomorrow or today.

"Into many a green valley
　Drifts the appalling snow;
Time breaks the threaded dances
　And the diver's brilliant bow.

"O plunge your hands in water,
　Plunge them in up to the wrist;
Stare, stare in the basin
　And wonder what you've missed.

4

8

12

16

20

24

28

32

36

40

"The glacier knocks in the cupboard,
    The desert sighs in the bed,
And the crack in the teacup opens
    A lane to the land of the dead.   44

"Where the beggars raffle the banknotes
    And the Giant is enchanting to Jack,
And the Lily-white Boy is a Roarer,
    And Jill goes down on her back.   48

"O look, look in the mirror,
    O look in your distress;
Life remains a blessing
    Although you cannot bless.   52

"O stand, stand at the window
    As the tears scald and start;
You shall love your crooked neighbor
    With your crooked heart."   56

It was late, late in the evening,
    The lovers they were gone;
The clocks had ceased their chiming,
    And the deep river ran on.   60

W. H. Auden (1907–1973)

Musée des Beaux Arts

About suffering they were never wrong,
The Old Masters: how well they understood
Its human position; how it takes place
While someone else is eating or opening a window or just walking
        dully along;
How, when the aged are reverently, passionately waiting   5
For the miraculous birth, there always must be
Children who did not specially want it to happen, skating
On a pond at the edge of the wood:
They never forgot
That even the dreadful martyrdom must run its course   10
Anyhow in a corner, some untidy spot
Where the dogs go on with their doggy life and the torturer's
        horse
Scratches its innocent behind on a tree.

In Brueghel's *Icarus*, for instance: how everything turns away
Quite leisurely from the disaster; the ploughman may   15
Have heard the splash, the forsaken cry,

But for him it was not an important failure; the sun shone
As it had to on the white legs disappearing into the green
Water; and the expensive delicate ship that must have seen
Something amazing, a boy falling out of the sky,   20
Had somewhere to get to and sailed calmly on.

COMPARE:

"Musée des Beaux Arts" with "The Old and the New Masters" by Randall
Jarrell (page 388).

A. D. Hope (b. 1907)
THE BRIDES

Down the assembly line they roll and pass
Complete at last, a miracle of design;
Their chromium fenders, the unbreakable glass,
The fashionable curve, the air-flow line.   4

Grease to the elbows Mum and Dad enthuse,
Pocket their spanners° and survey the bride;   *wrenches*
Murmur: 'A sweet job! All she needs is juice!
Built for a life-time — sleek as a fish. Inside   8

'He will find every comfort: the full set
Of gadgets; knobs that answer to the touch
For light or music; a place for his cigarette;
Room for his knees; a honey of a clutch.'   12

Now slowly through the show-room's flattering glare
See her wheeled in to love, console, obey,
Shining and silent! Parson with a prayer
Blesses the number-plate, she rolls away   16

To write her numerals in his book of life;
And now, at last, stands on the open road,
Triumphant, perfect, every inch a wife,
While the corks pop, the flash-light bulbs explode.   20

Her heavenly bowser-boy assumes his seat;
She prints the soft dust with her brand-new treads,
Swings towards the future, purring with a sweet
Concatenation of the poppet heads.   24

THE BRIDES. 21. *bowser-boy:* Gasoline-pump attendant (British and Australian slang).
24. *Concatenation:* Coupling, linking together. *poppet heads:* Valve heads. *Poppet* can also
mean puppet or little person.

COMPARE:

"The Brides" with "Before Bed" by Keith Waldrop (page 415).

Theodore Roethke (1908–1963)
Dolor

I have known the inexorable sadness of pencils,
Neat in their boxes, dolor of pad and paper-weight,
All the misery of manilla folders and mucilage,
Desolation in immaculate public places,
Lonely reception room, lavatory, switchboard,   5
The unalterable pathos of basin and pitcher,
Ritual of multigraph, paper-clip, comma,
Endless duplication of lives and objects.
And I have seen dust from the walls of institutions,
Finer than flour, alive, more dangerous than silica,   10
Sift, almost invisible, through long afternoons of tedium,
Dropping a fine film on nails and delicate eyebrows,
Glazing the pale hair, the duplicate gray standard faces.

Theodore Roethke (1908–1963)
Elegy for Jane

My Student, Thrown by a Horse

I remember the neckcurls, limp and damp as tendrils;
And her quick look, a sidelong pickerel smile;
And how, once startled into talk, the light syllables leaped for her,
And she balanced in the delight of her thought,
A wren, happy, tail into the wind,   5
Her song trembling the twigs and small branches.
The shade sang with her;
The leaves, their whispers turned to kissing;
And the mold sang in the bleached valleys under the rose.

Oh, when she was sad, she cast herself down into such a pure depth,   10
Even a father could not find her:
Scraping her cheek against straw;
Stirring the clearest water.

My sparrow, you are not here,
Waiting like a fern, making a spiny shadow.   15
The sides of wet stones cannot console me,
Nor the moss, wound with the last light.

If only I could nudge you from this sleep,
My maimed darling, my skittery pigeon.
Over this damp grave I speak the words of my love: 20
I, with no rights in this matter,
Neither father nor lover.

Compare:

"Elegy for Jane" with "Bells for John Whiteside's Daughter" by John Crowe Ransom (page 373).

Theodore Roethke (1908–1963)

Frau Bauman, Frau Schmidt, and Frau Schwartze

Gone the three ancient ladies
Who creaked on the greenhouse ladders,
Reaching up white strings
To wind, to wind
The sweet-pea tendrils, the smilax,   5
Nasturtiums, the climbing
Roses, to straighten
Carnations, red
Chrysanthemums; the stiff
Stems, jointed like corn,   10
They tied and tucked, —
These nurses of nobody else.
Quicker than birds, they dipped
Up and sifted the dirt;
They sprinkled and shook;   15
They stood astride pipes,
Their skirts billowing out wide into tents,
Their hands twinkling with wet;
Like witches they flew along rows
Keeping creation at ease;   20
With a tendril for needle
They sewed up the air with a stem;
They teased out the seed that the cold kept asleep, —
All the coils, loops, and whorls.
They trellised the sun; they plotted for more than themselves.   25

I remember how they picked me up, a spindly kid,
Pinching and poking my thin ribs
Till I lay in their laps, laughing,
Weak as a whiffet,
Now, when I'm alone and cold in my bed,   30
They still hover over me,
These ancient leathery crones,
With their bandannas stiffened with sweat,
And their thorn-bitten wrists,
And their snuff-laden breath blowing lightly over me in my first sleep. 35

Frau Bauman, Frau Schmidt, and Frau Schwartze. Roethke's father ran a commercial
greenhouse in Saginaw, Michigan. 29. *whiffet:* A little puff of air; also, a small dog.

Theodore Roethke (1908–1963)

The Meadow Mouse

1

In a shoe box stuffed in an old nylon stocking
Sleeps the baby mouse I found in the meadow,
Where he trembled and shook beneath a stick
Till I caught him up by the tail and brought him in,
Cradled in my hand,   5
A little quaker, the whole body of him trembling,
His absurd whiskers sticking out like a cartoon-mouse,
His feet like small leaves,
Little lizard-feet,
Whitish and spread wide when he tried to struggle away,   10
Wriggling like a miniscule puppy.

Now he's eaten his three kinds of cheese and drunk from his bottle-cap
        watering-trough —
So much he just lies in one corner,
His tail curled under him, his belly big
As his head; his bat-like ears   15
Twitching, tilting toward the least sound.

Do I imagine he no longer trembles
When I come close to him?
He seems no longer to tremble.

2

But this morning the shoe-box house on the back porch is empty.   20
Where has he gone, my meadow mouse,
My thumb of a child that nuzzled in my palm? —
To run under the hawk's wing,
Under the eye of the great owl watching from the elm-tree,
To live by courtesy of the shrike, the snake, the tom-cat.   25

I think of the nestling fallen into the deep grass,
The turtle gasping in the dusty rubble of the highway,
The paralytic stunned in the tub, and the water rising, —
All things innocent, hapless, forsaken.

Muriel Rukeyser (b. 1913)

Boy with His Hair Cut Short

Sunday shuts down on this twentieth-century evening.
The L passes. Twilight and bulb define
the brown room, the overstuffed plum sofa,
the boy, and the girl's thin hands above his head.
A neighbor radio sings stocks, news serenade.   5

He sits at the table, head down, the young clear neck exposed,
watching the drugstore sign from the tail of his eye;
tattoo, neon, until the eye blears, while his
solicitous tall sister, simple in blue, bending
behind him, cuts his hair with her cheap shears. 10

The arrow's electric red always reaches its mark,
successful neon! He coughs, impressed by that precision.
His child's forehead, forever protected by his cap,
is bleached against the lamplight as he turns head
and steadies to let the snippets drop. 15

Erasing the failure of weeks with level fingers,
she sleeks the fine hair, combing: "You'll look fine tomorrow!
You'll surely find something, they can't keep turning you down;
the finest gentleman's not so trim as you!" Smiling, he raises
the adolescent forehead wrinkling ironic now. 20

He sees his decent suit laid out, new-pressed,
his carfare on the shelf. He lets his head fall, meeting
her earnest hopeless look, seeing the sharp blades splitting,
the darkened room, the impersonal sign, her motion,
the blue vein, bright on her temple, pitifully beating. 25

Karl Shapiro (b. 1913)

THE DIRTY WORD

The dirty word hops in the cage of the mind like the Pondicherry
vulture, stomping with its heavy left claw on the sweet meat of the brain
and tearing it with its vicious beak, ripping and chopping the flesh.
Terrified, the small boy bears the big bird of the dirty word into the house,
and grunting, puffing, carries it up the stairs to his own room in the skull. 5
Bits of black feather cling to his clothes and his hair as he locks the staring
creature in the dark closet.

All day the small boy returns to the closet to examine and feed the
bird, to caress and kick the bird, that now snaps and flaps its wings
savagely whenever the door is opened. How the boy trembles and delights 10
at the sight of the white excrement of the bird! How the bird leaps and
rushes against the walls of the skull, trying to escape from the zoo of the
vocabulary! How wildly snaps the sweet meat of the brain in its rage.

And the bird outlives the man, being freed at the man's death-
funeral by a word from the rabbi. 15

(But I one morning went upstairs and opened the door and entered
the closet and found in the cage of my mind the great bird dead. Softly
I wept it and softly removed it and softly buried the body of the bird in
the hollyhock garden of the house I lived in twenty years before. And out
of the worn black feathers of the wing have I made these pens to write 20
these elegies, for I have outlived the bird, and I have murdered it in my
early manhood.)

David Ignatow (b. 1914)
GET THE GASWORKS

Get the gasworks into a poem,
and you've got the smoke and smokestacks,
the mottled red and yellow tenements,
and grimy kids who curse with the pungency
of the odor of gas. You've got America, boy.   5

Sketch in the river and barges,
all dirty and slimy.
How do the seagulls stay so white?
And always cawing like little mad geniuses?
You've got the kind of living   10
that makes the kind of thinking we do:
gaswork smokestack whistle tooting wisecracks.
They don't come because we like it that way,
but because we find it outside our window each morning,
in soot on the furniture,   15
and trucks carrying coal for gas,
the kid hot after the ball under the wheel.
He gets it over the belly, all right.
He dies there.

So the kids keep tossing the ball around   20
after the funeral.
So the cops keep chasing them,
so the mamas keep hollering,
and papa flings his newspaper outward,
in disgust with discipline.   25

Randall Jarrell (1914–1965)
THE DEATH OF THE BALL TURRET GUNNER

From my mother's sleep I fell into the State
And I hunched in its belly till my wet fur froze.
Six miles from earth, loosed from its dream of life,
I woke to black flack and the nightmare fighters.
When I died they washed me out of the turret with a hose.

THE DEATH OF THE BALL TURRET GUNNER. This poem is from a collection published in
1945. Mr. Jarrell has written: "A ball turret was a plexiglass sphere set into the belly of a
B-17 or B-24, and inhabited by two .50 caliber machine-guns and one man, a short small
man. When this gunner tracked with his machine-guns a fighter attacking his bomber
from below, he revolved with the turret; hunched upside-down in his little sphere, he
looked like the fetus in the womb. The fighters which attacked him were armed with
cannon firing explosive shells. The hose was a steam hose."

Randall Jarrell (1914–1965)

THE OLD AND THE NEW MASTERS

About suffering, about adoration, the old masters
Disagree. When someone suffers, no one else eats
Or walks or opens the window — no one breathes
As the sufferers watch the sufferer.
In *St. Sebastian Mourned by St. Irene*   5
The flame of one torch is the only light.
All the eyes except the maidservant's (she weeps
And covers them with a cloth) are fixed on the shaft
Set in his chest like a column; St. Irene's
Hands are spread in the gesture of the Madonna,   10
Revealing, accepting, what she does not understand.
Her hands say: "Lo! Behold!"
Beside her a monk's hooded head is bowed, his hands
Are put together in the work of mourning.
It is as if they were still looking at the lance   15
Piercing the side of Christ, nailed on his cross.
The same nails pierce all their hands and feet, the same
Thin blood, mixed with water, trickles from their sides.
The taste of vinegar is on every tongue
That gasps, "My God, my God, why hast Thou forsaken me?"   20
They watch, they are, the one thing in the world.

So, earlier, everything is pointed
In van der Goes' *Nativity*, toward the naked
Shining baby, like the needle of a compass.
The different orders and sizes of the world: 25
The angels like Little People, perched in the rafters
Or hovering in mid-air like hummingbirds;
The shepherds, so big and crude, so plainly adoring;
The medium-sized donor, his little family,
And their big patron saints; the Virgin who kneels   30
Before her child in worship; the Magi out in the hills
With their camels — they ask directions, and have pointed out
By a man kneeling, the true way; the ox
And the donkey, two heads in the manger
So much greater than a human head, who also adore;   35
Even the offerings, a sheaf of wheat,
A jar and a glass of flowers, are absolutely still
In natural concentration, as they take their part
In the salvation of the natural world.
The time of the world concentrates   40
On this one instant: far off in the rocks
You can see Mary and Joseph and their donkey
Coming to Bethlehem; on the grassy hillside
Where their flocks are grazing, the shepherds gesticulate
In wonder at the star; and so many hundreds   45

Of years in the future, the donor, his wife,
And their children are kneeling, looking: everything
That was or will be in the world is fixed
On its small, helpless, human center.

After a while the masters show the crucifixion   50
In one corner of the canvas: the men come to see
What is important, see that it is not important.
The new masters paint a subject as they please,
And Veronese is prosecuted by the Inquisition
For the dogs playing at the feet of Christ,   55
The earth is a planet among galaxies.
Later Christ disappears, the dogs disappear: in abstract
Understanding, without adoration, the last master puts
Colors on canvas, a picture of the universe
In which a bright spot somewhere in the corner   60
Is the small radioactive planet men called Earth.

COMPARE:

"The Old and the New Masters" with "Musée des Beaux Arts" by W. H. Auden
(page 381).

John Frederick Nims (b. 1914)
LOVE POEM

My clumsiest dear, whose hands shipwreck vases,
At whose quick touch all glasses chip and ring,
Whose palms are bulls in china, burs in linen,
And have no cunning with any soft thing   4

Except all ill-at-ease fidgeting people:
The refugee uncertain at the door
You make at home; deftly you steady
The drunk clambering on his undulant floor.   8

Unpredictable dear, the taxi drivers' terror,
Shrinking from far headlights pale as a dime
Yet leaping before red apoplectic streetcars —
Misfit in any space. And never on time.   12

A wrench in clocks and the solar system. Only
With words and people and love you move at ease.
In traffic of wit expertly manoeuvre
And keep us, all devotion, at your knees.   16

Forgetting your coffee spreading on our flannel,
Your lipstick grinning on our coat,
So gayly in love's unbreakable heaven
Our souls on glory of spilt bourbon float.   20

Be with me, darling, early and late. Smash glasses —
I will study wry music for your sake.
For should your hands drop white and empty
All the toys of the world would break.   24

COMPARE:

"Love Poem" with "Love Song: I and Thou" by Alan Dugan (page 402).

Henry Reed (b. 1914)
NAMING OF PARTS

Today we have naming of parts. Yesterday,
We had daily cleaning. And tomorrow morning,
We shall have what to do after firing. But today,
Today we have naming of parts. Japonica
Glistens like coral in all of the neighboring gardens,
      And today we have naming of parts.   6

This is the lower sling swivel. And this
Is the upper sling swivel, whose use you will see,
When you are given your slings. And this is the piling swivel,
Which in your case you have not got. The branches
Hold in the gardens their silent, eloquent gestures,
      Which in our case we have not got.   12

This is the safety-catch, which is always released
With an easy flick of the thumb. And please do not let me
See anyone using his finger. You can do it quite easy
If you have any strength in your thumb. The blossoms
Are fragile and motionless, never letting anyone see
      Any of them using their finger.   18

And this you can see is the bolt. The purpose of this
Is to open the breech, as you see. We can slide it
Rapidly backwards and forwards: we call this
Easing the spring. And rapidly backwards and forwards
The early bees are assaulting and fumbling the flowers:
      They call it easing the Spring.   24

They call it easing the Spring: it is perfectly easy
If you have any strength in your thumb: like the bolt,
And the breech, and the cocking-piece, and the point of balance,
Which in our case we have not got; and the almond-blossom
Silent in all of the gardens and the bees going backwards and forwards,
      For today we have naming of parts.   30

COMPARE:

"Naming of Parts" with "The Fury of Aerial Bombardment" by Richard
Eberhart (page 45).

William Stafford (b. 1914)

Gasoline makes game scarce.
In Elko, Nevada, I remember a stuffed wildcat
someone had shot on Bing Crosby's ranch.
I stood in the filling station
breathing fumes and reading the snarl of a map. 5

There were peaks to the left so high
they almost got away in the heat;
Reno and Las Vegas were ahead.
I had promise of the California job,
and three kids with me. 10

It takes a lot of miles to equal one wildcat
today. We moved into a housing tract.
Every dodging animal carries my hope in Nevada.
It has been a long day, Bing.
Wherever I go is your ranch. 15

Dylan Thomas (1914–1953)

AFTER THE FUNERAL

In Memory of Ann Jones

After the funeral, mule praises, brays,
Windshake of sailshaped ears, muffle-toed tap
Tap happily of one peg in the thick
Grave's foot, blinds down the lids, the teeth in black,
The spittled eyes, the salt ponds in the sleeves, 5
Morning smack of the spade that wakes up sleep,
Shakes a desolate boy who slits his throat
In the dark of the coffin and sheds dry leaves,
That breaks one bone to light with a judgment clout,
After the feast of tear-stuffed time and thistles 10
In a room with a stuffed fox and a stale fern,
I stand, for this memorial's sake, alone
In the snivelling hours with dead, humped Ann
Whose hooded, fountain heart once fell in puddles
Round the parched worlds of Wales and drowned each sun 15
(Though this for her is a monstrous image blindly
Magnified out of praise; her death was a still drop;
She would not have me sinking in the holy
Flood of her heart's fame; she would lie dumb and deep
And need no druid of her broken body). 20
But I, Ann's bard on a raised hearth, call all
The seas to service that her wood-tongued virtue

Babble like a bellbuoy over the hymning heads,
Bow down the walls of the ferned and foxy woods
That her love sing and swing through a brown chapel,   25
Bless her bent spirit with four, crossing birds.
Her flesh was meek as milk, but this skyward statue
With the wild breast and blessed and giant skull
Is carved from her in a room with a wet window
In a fiercely mourning house in a crooked year.   30
I know her scrubbed and sour humble hands
Lie with religion in their cramp, her threadbare
Whisper in a damp word, her wits drilled hollow,
Her fist of a face died clenched on a round pain;
And sculptured Ann is seventy years of stone.   35
These cloud-sopped, marble hands, this monumental
Argument of the hewn voice, gesture and psalm
Storm me forever over her grave until
The stuffed lung of the fox twitch and cry Love
And the strutting fern lay seeds on the black sill.   40

Dudley Randall (b. 1914)

BALLAD OF BIRMINGHAM

*(On the Bombing of a Church in
Birmingham, Alabama, 1963)*

"Mother dear, may I go downtown
Instead of out to play,
And march the streets of Birmingham
In a Freedom March today?"   4

"No, baby, no, you may not go,
For the dogs are fierce and wild,
And clubs and hoses, guns and jail
Aren't good for a little child."   8

"But, mother, I won't be alone.
Other children will go with me,
And march the streets of Birmingham
To make our country free."   12

"No, baby, no, you may not go,
For I fear those guns will fire.
But you may go to church instead
And sing in the children's choir."   16

She has combed and brushed her night-dark hair,
And bathed rose petal sweet,
And drawn white gloves on her small brown hands,
And white shoes on her feet.   20

The mother smiled to know her child
Was in the sacred place,
But that smile was the last smile
To come upon her face.   24

For when she heard the explosion,
Her eyes grew wet and wild.
She raced through the streets of Birmingham
Calling for her child.   28

She clawed through bits of glass and brick,
Then lifted out a shoe.
"O here's the shoe my baby wore,
But, baby, where are you?"   32

COMPARE:

"Ballad of Birmingham" with the folk ballads "Edward" (page 309) and "The
Cruel Mother" (page 102).

Robert Lowell (b. 1917)

SKUNK HOUR

For Elizabeth Bishop

Nautilus Island's hermit
heiress still lives through winters in her Spartan cottage;
her sheep still graze above the sea.
Her son's a bishop. Her farmer
is first selectman in our village;
she's in her dotage.   6

Thirsting for
the hierarchic privacy
of Queen Victoria's century,
she buys up all
the eyesores facing her shore,
and lets them fall.   12

The season's ill —
we've lost our summer millionaire,
who seemed to leap from an L. L. Bean
catalogue. His nine-knot yawl
was auctioned off to lobstermen.
A red fox stain covers Blue Hill.   18

And now our fairy
decorator brightens his shop for fall;
his fishnet's filled with orange cork,
orange, his cobbler's bench and awl;
there is no money in his work,
he'd rather marry.   24

One dark night,
my Tudor Ford climbed the hill's skull;
I watched for love-cars. Lights turned down,
they lay together, hull to hull,
where the graveyard shelves on the town. . . .
My mind's not right.   30

A car radio bleats,
"Love, O careless Love. . . ." I hear
my ill-spirit sob in each blood cell,
as if my hand were at its throat. . . .
I myself am hell;
nobody's here —   36

only skunks, that search
in the moonlight for a bite to eat.
They march on their soles up Main Street:
white stripes, moonstruck eyes' red fire
under the chalk-dry and spar spire
of the Trinitarian Church.   42

I stand on top
of our back steps and breathe the rich air —
a mother skunk with her column of kittens swills the garbage pail.
She jabs her wedge-head in a cup
of sour cream, drops her ostrich tail,
and will not scare.   48

William Jay Smith (b. 1918)

AMERICAN PRIMITIVE

Look at him there in his stovepipe hat,
His high-top shoes, and his handsome collar;
Only my Daddy could look like that,
And I love my Daddy like he loves his Dollar.   4

The screen door bangs, and it sounds so funny —
There he is in a shower of gold;
His pockets are stuffed with folding money,
His lips are blue, and his hands feel cold.   8

He hangs in the hall by his black cravat,
The ladies faint, and the children holler:
Only my Daddy could look like that,
And I love my Daddy like he loves his Dollar.   12

Howard Nemerov (b. 1920)

THE GOOSE FISH

On the long shore, lit by the moon
To show them properly alone,
Two lovers suddenly embraced
So that their shadows were as one.
The ordinary night was graced   5
For them by the swift tide of blood
That silently they took at flood,   7
And for a little time they prized
        Themselves emparadised.   9

Then, as if shaken by stage-fright
Beneath the hard moon's bony light,
They stood together on the sand
Embarrassed in each other's sight
But still conspiring hand in hand,   14
Until they saw, there underfoot,
As though the world had found them out,   16
The goose fish turning up, though dead,
        His hugely grinning head.   18

There in the china light he lay,
Most ancient and corrupt and grey.
They hesitated at his smile,
Wondering what it seemed to say
To lovers who a little while   23
Before had thought to understand,
By violence upon the sand,   25
The only way that could be known
        To make a world their own.   27

It was a wide and moony grin
Together peaceful and obscene;
They knew not what he would express,
So finished a comedian
He might mean failure or success,   32
But took it for an emblem of
Their sudden, new and guilty love   34
To be observed by, when they kissed,
        That rigid optimist.   36

So he became their patriarch,
Dreadfully mild in the half-dark.
His throat that the sand seemed to choke,
His picket teeth, these left their mark
But never did explain the joke   41
That so amused him, lying there
While the moon went down to disappear   43
Along the still and tilted track
        That bears the zodiac.   45

Richard Wilbur (b. 1921)

JUNK

Huru Welandes
                    worc ne geswiced
monna ænigum
                    ðara ðe Mimming can
heardne gehealdan.
                    Waldere

An axe angles
                    from my neighbor's ashcan;
It is hell's handiwork,
                              the wood not hickory,
The flow of the grain
                              not faithfully followed.
The shivered shaft
                    rises from a shellheap
Of plastic playthings,
                              paper plates,   5
And the sheer shards
                    of shattered tumblers
That were not annealed
                              for the time needful.
At the same curbside,
                    a cast-off cabinet
Of wavily-warped
                    unseasoned wood
Waits to be trundled
                              in the trash-man's truck.   10
Haul them off! Hide them!
                              The heart winces
For junk and gimcrack,
                              for jerrybuilt things
And the men who make them
                              for a little money,
Bartering pride
                    like the bought boxer
Who pulls his punches,
                              or the paid-off jockey   15
Who in the home stretch
                    holds in his horse.
Yet the things themselves
                              in thoughtless honor
Have kept composure,
                              like captives who would not
Talk under torture.
                    Tossed from a tailgate
Where the dump displays
                              its random dolmens°,   *prehistoric*   20
                                                                    gravestones

396   Anthology

Its black barrows
                    and blazing valleys,
They shall waste in the weather
                            toward what they were.
The sun shall glory
                    in the glitter of glass-chips,
Foreseeing the salvage
                        of the prisoned sand,
And the blistering paint
                        peel off in patches,   25
That the good grain
                    be discovered again.
Then burnt, bulldozed,
                        they shall all be buried
To the depth of diamonds,
                            in the making dark
Where halt Hephaestus
                        keeps his hammer
And Wayland's work
                    is worn away.   30

JUNK. Richard Wilbur notes: "The epigraph, taken from a fragmentary Anglo-Saxon
poem, concerns the legendary smith Wayland, and may roughly be translated: 'Truly,
Wayland's handiwork — the sword Mimming which he made — will never fail any man
who knows how to use it bravely.'" 29. *Hephaestus:* Another smith and artisan, the Greek
god of fire, said to have forged armor for Achilles.

Philip Larkin (b. 1922)

CHURCH GOING

Once I am sure there's nothing going on
I step inside, letting the door thud shut.
Another church: matting, seats, and stone,
And little books; sprawlings of flowers, cut
For Sunday, brownish now; some brass and stuff
Up at the holy end; the small neat organ;
And a tense, musty, unignorable silence,
Brewed God knows how long. Hatless, I take off
My cycle-clips in awkward reverence,   9

Move forward, run my hand around the font.
From where I stand, the roof looks almost new —
Cleaned, or restored? Someone would know: I don't.
Mounting the lectern, I peruse a few
Hectoring large-scale verses, and pronounce
"Here endeth" much more loudly than I'd meant.
The echoes snigger briefly. Back at the door
I sign the book, donate an Irish sixpence,
Reflect the place was not worth stopping for.   18

Yet stop I did: in fact I often do,
And always end much at a loss like this,
Wondering what to look for; wondering, too,
When churches fall completely out of use
What we shall turn them into, if we shall keep
A few cathedrals chronically on show,
Their parchment, plate, and pyx in locked cases,
And let the rest rent-free to rain and sheep.
Shall we avoid them as unlucky places?   27

Or, after dark, will dubious women come
To make their children touch a particular stone;
Pick simples° for a cancer; or on some   *medicinal plants*
Advised night see walking a dead one?
Power of some sort or other will go on
In games, in riddles, seemingly at random;
But superstition, like belief, must die,
And what remains when disbelief has gone?
Grass, weedy pavement, brambles, buttress, sky,   36

A shape less recognizable each week,
A purpose more obscure. I wonder who
Will be the last, the very last, to seek
This place for what it was; one of the crew
That tap and jot and know what rood-lofts were?
Some ruin-bibber, randy for antique,
Or Christmas-addict, counting on a whiff
Of gown-and-bands and organ-pipes and myrrh?
Or will he be my representative,   45

Bored, uninformed, knowing the ghostly silt
Dispersed, yet tending to this cross of ground
Through suburb scrub because it held unsplit
So long and equably what since is found
Only in separation — marriage, and birth,
And death, and thoughts of these — for which was built
This special shell? For, though I've no idea
What this accoutred frowsty° barn is worth,   *musty*
It pleases me to stand in silence here;   54

A serious house on serious earth it is,
In whose blent air all our compulsions meet,
Are recognized, and robed as destinies.
And that much never can be obsolete,
Since someone will forever be surprising
A hunger in himself to be more serious,
And gravitating with it to this ground,
Which, he once heard, was proper to grow wise in,
If only that so many dead lie round.   63

COMPARE:

"Church Going" with "Elegy Written in a Country Churchyard" by Thomas Gray (page 326).

James Dickey (b. 1923)

CHERRYLOG ROAD

Off Highway 106
At Cherrylog Road I entered
The '34 Ford without wheels,
Smothered in kudzu,
With a seat pulled out to run
Corn whiskey down from the hills,   6

And then from the other side
Crept into an Essex
With a rumble seat of red leather
And then out again, aboard
A blue Chevrolet, releasing
The rust from its other color,   12

Reared up on three building blocks.
None had the same body heat;
I changed with them inward, toward
The weedy heart of the junkyard,
For I knew that Doris Holbrook
Would escape from her father at noon   18

And would come from the farm
To seek parts owned by the sun
Among the abandoned chassis,
Sitting in each in turn
As I did, leaning forward
As in a wild stock-car race   24

In the parking lot of the dead.
Time after time, I climbed in
And out the other side, like
An envoy or movie star
Met at the station by crickets.
A radiator cap raised its head,   30

Become a real toad or a kingsnake
As I neared the hub of the yard,
Passing through many states,
Many lives, to reach
Some grandmother's long Pierce-Arrow
Sending platters of blindness forth   36

From its nickel hubcaps
And spilling its tender upholstery
On sleepy roaches,
The glass panel in between
Lady and colored driver
Not all the way broken out, 42

The back-seat phone
Still on its hook.
I got in as though to exclaim,
"Let us go to the orphan asylum,
John; I have some old toys
For children who say their prayers." 48

I popped with sweat as I thought
I heard Doris Holbrook scrape
Like a mouse in the southern-state sun
That was eating the paint in blisters
From a hundred car tops and hoods.
She was tapping like code, 54

Loosening the screws,
Carrying off headlights,
Sparkplugs, bumpers,
Cracked mirrors and gear-knobs,
Getting ready, already,
To go back with something to show 60

Other than her lips' new trembling
I would hold to me soon, soon,
Where I sat in the ripped back seat
Talking over the interphone,
Praying for Doris Holbrook
To come from her father's farm 66

And to get back there
With no trace of me on her face
To be seen by her red-haired father
Who would change, in the squalling barn,
Her back's pale skin with a strop,
Then lay for me 72

In a bootlegger's roasting car
With a string-triggered 12-gauge shotgun
To blast the breath from the air.
Not cut by the jagged windshields,
Through the acres of wrecks she came
With a wrench in her hand, 78

Through dust where the blacksnake dies
Of boredom, and the beetle knows
The compost has no more life.

Someone outside would have seen
The oldest car's door inexplicably
Close from within: 84

I held her and held her and held her,
Convoyed at terrific speed
By the stalled, dreaming traffic around us,
So the blacksnake, stiff
With inaction, curved back
Into life, and hunted the mouse   90

With deadly overexcitement,
The beetles reclaimed their field
As we clung, glued together,
With the hooks of the seat springs
Working through to catch us red-handed
Amidst the gray breathless batting   96

That burst from the seat at our backs.
We left by separate doors
Into the changed, other bodies
Of cars, she down Cherrylog Road
And I to my motorcycle
Parked like the soul of the junkyard   102

Restored, a bicycle fleshed
With power, and tore off
Up Highway 106, continually
Drunk on the wind in my mouth,
Wringing the handlebar for speed,
Wild to the wreckage forever.   108

Denise Levertov (b. 1923)
COME INTO ANIMAL PRESENCE

Come into animal presence.
No man is so guileless as
the serpent. The lonely white
rabbit on the roof is a star
twitching its ears at the rain.   5
The llama intricately
folding its hind legs to be seated
not disdains but mildly
disregards human approval.
What joy when the insouciant   10
armadillo glances at us and doesn't
quicken its trotting
across the track into the palm brush.

What is this joy? That no animal
falters, but knows what it must do?   15

That the snake has no blemish,
that the rabbit inspects his strange surroundings
in white star-silence? The llama
rests in dignity, the armadillo
has some intention to pursue in the palm-forest.   20
Those who were sacred have remained so,
holiness does not dissolve, it is a presence
of bronze, only the sight that saw it
faltered and turned from it.
An old joy returns in holy presence.   25

Alan Dugan (b. 1923)

LOVE SONG: I AND THOU

Existential love poem.

Nothing is plumb, level or square:
  the studs are bowed, the joists
are shaky by nature, no piece fits
  any other piece without a gap
or pinch, and bent nails   5
  dance all over the surfacing
like maggots. By Christ
  I am no carpenter. I built
the roof for myself, the walls
  for myself, the floors   10
for myself, and got
  hung up in it myself. I
danced with a purple thumb
  at this house-warming, drunk
with my prime whiskey: rage.   15
  Oh I spat rage's nails
into the frame-up of my work:
  it held. It settled plumb,
level, solid, square and true
  for that great moment. Then   20
it screamed and went on through,
  skewing as wrong the other way.
God damned it. This is hell,
  but I planned it, I sawed it,
I nailed it, and I   25
  will live in it until it kills me.
I can nail my left palm
  to the left-hand cross-piece but
I can't do everything myself.
  I need a hand to nail the right,   30
a help, a love, a you, a wife.

COMPARE:

"Love Song: I and Thou" with "Love Poem" by John Frederick Nims (page 389).

402   Anthology

[Handwritten annotations:]
That's why 'THOU' instead of an object. We live in a world that is absurd. All meaning is in meeting other people.

Using metaphor to represent nothing is plumb, nothing is level like be but all meaning is square.

Donald Justice (b. 1925)

In Bertram's Garden

Jane looks down at her organdy skirt
As if *it* somehow were the thing disgraced,
For being there, on the floor, in the dirt,
And she catches it up about her waist,   4
Smooths it out along one hip,
And pulls it over the crumpled slip.   6

On the porch, green-shuttered, cool,
Asleep is Bertram, that bronze boy,
Who, having wound her around a spool,
Sends her spinning like a toy   10
Out to the garden, all alone,
To sit and weep on a bench of stone.   12

Soon the purple dark will bruise
Lily and bleeding-heart and rose,
And the little Cupid lose
Eyes and ears and chin and nose,   16
And Jane lie down with others soon
Naked to the naked moon.   18

Robert Creeley (b. 1926)

Kore

As I was walking
   I came upon
chance walking
   the same road upon.   4

As I sat down
   by chance to move
later
   if and as I might,   8

light the wood was,
   light and green,
and what I saw
   before I had not seen.   12

It was a lady
   accompanied
by goat men
   leading her.   16

Her hair held earth.
   Her eyes were dark.
A double flute
   made her move.   20

"O love,
   where are you
leading
   me now?"   24

Kore. In Greek mythology, Kore is the maiden name of Persephone.

Compare:

"Kore" with "Bavarian Gentians" by D. H. Lawrence (page 217).

Robert Creeley (b. 1926)
I Know a Man

As I sd to my
friend, because I am
always talking, — John, I

sd, which was not his
name, the darkness sur-   5
rounds us, what

can we do against
it, or else, shall we &
why not, buy a goddamn big car,

drive, he sd, for   10
christ's sake, look
out where yr going.

Allen Ginsberg (b. 1926)
In back of the real

railroad yard in San Jose
   I wandered desolate
in front of a tank factory
   and sat on a bench
near the switchman's shack.   5

A flower lay on the hay on
   the asphalt highway
— the dread hay flower
   I thought — It had a
brittle black stem and   10
   corolla of yellowish dirty
spikes like Jesus' inchlong
   crown, and a soiled
dry center cotton tuft
   like a used shaving brush   15
that's been lying under
   the garage for a year.

Yellow, yellow flower, and
   flower of industry,
tough spikey ugly flower,   20
   flower nonetheless,
with the form of the great yellow
   Rose in your brain!
This is the flower of the World.

COMPARE:

"In back of the real" with "Flower in the Crannied Wall" by Alfred, Lord
Tennyson (page 82) and "To see a world in a grain of sand" by William Blake
(page 83).

James Merrill (b. 1926)
LABORATORY POEM

Charles used to watch Naomi, taking heart
And a steel saw, open up turtles, live.
While she swore they felt nothing, he would gag
At blood, at the blind twitching, even after
The murky dawn of entrails cleared, revealing
Contours he knew, egg-yellows like lamps paling.   6

Well then. She carried off the beating heart
To the kymograph and rigged it there, a rag
In fitful wind, now made to strain, now stopped
By her solutions tonic or malign
Alternately in which it would be steeped.
What the heart bore, she noted on a chart,   12

For work did not stop only with the heart.
He thought of certain human hearts, their climb
Through violence into exquisite disciplines
Of which, as it now appeared, they all expired.
Soon she would fetch another and start over,
Easy in the presence of her lover.   18

W. D. Snodgrass (b. 1926)
THE OPERATION

From stainless steel basins of water
They brought warm cloths and they washed me,
From spun aluminum bowls, cold Zephiran sponges, fuming;
Gripped in the dead yellow glove, a bright straight razor
Inched on my stomach, down my groin,   5
Paring the brown hair off. They left me
White as a child, not frightened. I was not
Ashamed. They clothed me, then,

In the thin, loose, light, white garments,
The delicate sandals of poor Pierrot,   10
A schoolgirl first offering her sacrament.

I was drifting, inexorably, on toward sleep.
In skullcaps, masked, in blue-green gowns, attendants
Towed my cart, afloat in its white cloths,
The body with its tributary poisons borne   15
Down corridors of the diseased, thronging:
The scrofulous faces, contagious grim boys,
The huddled families, weeping, a staring woman
Arched to her gnarled stick, — a child was somewhere
Screaming, screaming — then, blind silence, the elevator rising   20
To the arena, humming, vast with lights; blank hero,
Shackled and spellbound, to enact my deed.

Into flowers, into women, I have awakened.
Too weak to think of strength, I have thought all day,
Or dozed among standing friends. I lie in night, now,   25
A small mound under linen like the drifted snow.
Only by nurses visited, in radiance, saying, Rest.
Opposite, ranked office windows glare; headlamps, below,
Trace out our highways; their cargoes under dark tarpaulins,
Trucks climb, thundering, and sirens may   30
Wail for the fugitive. It is very still. In my brandy bowl
Of sweet peas at the window, the crystal world
Is inverted, slow and gay.

THE OPERATION. 3. *Zephiran:* Like Zephirus, Greek personification of the west wind: gentle, cool and soothing. 10. *Pierrot:* Traditional clown in French pantomime, white-faced, wearing loose pantaloons.

COMPARE:

"The Operation" with "Face Lift" by Sylvia Plath (page 412).

Galway Kinnell (b. 1927)
TO CHRIST OUR LORD

The legs of the elk punctured the snow's crust
And wolves floated lightfooted on the land
Hunting Christmas elk living and frozen;
Inside snow melted in a basin, and a woman basted
A bird spread over coals by its wings and head.   5

Snow had sealed the windows; candles lit
The Christmas meal. The Christmas grace chilled
The cooked bird, being long-winded and the room cold.
During the words a boy thought, is it fitting
To eat this creature killed on the wing?   10

He had killed it himself, climbing out
Alone on snowshoes in the Christmas dawn,
The fallen snow swirling and the snowfall gone,
Heard its throat scream as the rifle shouted,
Watched it drop, and fished from the snow the dead.   15

He had not wanted to shoot. The sound
Of wings beating into the hushed air
Had stirred his love, and his fingers
Froze in his gloves, and he wondered,
Famishing, could he fire? Then he fired.   20

Now the grace praised his wicked act. At its end
The bird on the plate
Stared at his stricken appetite.
There had been nothing to do but surrender,
To kill and to eat; he ate as he had killed, with wonder.   25

At night on snowshoes on the drifting field
He wondered again, for whom had love stirred?
The stars glittered on the snow and nothing answered.
Then the Swan spread her wings, cross of the cold north,
The pattern and mirror of the acts of earth.   30

W. S. Merwin (b. 1927)
FOR THE ANNIVERSARY OF MY DEATH

Every year without knowing it I have passed the day
When the last fires will wave to me
And the silence will set out
Tireless traveller
Like the beam of a lightless star   5

Then I will no longer
Find myself in life as in a strange garment
Surprised at the earth
And the love of one woman
And the shamelessness of men   10
As today writing after three days of rain
Hearing the wren sing and the falling cease
And bowing not knowing to what

James Wright (b. 1927)
A BLESSING

Just off the highway to Rochester, Minnesota,
Twilight bounds softly forth on the grass.
And the eyes of those two Indian ponies
Darken with kindness.

They have come gladly out of the willows 5
To welcome my friend and me.
We step over the barbed wire into the pasture
Where they have been grazing all day, alone.
They ripple tensely, they can hardly contain their happiness
That we have come. 10
They bow shyly as wet swans. They love each other.
There is no loneliness like theirs.
At home once more,
They begin munching the young tufts of spring in the darkness.
I would like to hold the slenderer one in my arms, 15
For she has walked over to me
And nuzzled my left hand.
She is black and white,
Her mane falls wild on her forehead,
And the light breeze moves me to caress her long ear 20
That is delicate as the skin over a girl's wrist.
Suddenly I realize
That if I stepped out of my body I would break
Into blossom.

James Wright (b. 1927)

TROUBLE

Well, look, honey, where I come from,
when a girl says she's in trouble, she's in trouble.
                (Judy Holliday)

Leering across Pearl Street,
Crum Anderson yipped:
"Hey Pugh!
I see your sister
Been rid bareback. 5
She swallow a watermelon?
Fred Gordon! Fred Gordon! Fred Gordon!"

"Wayya mean? She can get fat, can't she?"

Fat? Willow and lonesome Roberta, running
Alone down Pearl Street in the rain the last time 10
I ever saw her, smiling a smile
Crum Anderson will never know,
Wondering at her body.

Sixteen years, and
All that time she thought she was nothing 15
But skin and bones.

Philip Levine (b. 1928)

To a Child Trapped in a Barber Shop

You've gotten in through the transom
    and you can't get out
till Monday morning or, worse,
    till the cops come.   4

That six-year-old red face
    calling for mama
is yours; it won't help you
    because your case   8

is closed forever, hopeless.
    So don't drink
the Lucky Tiger, don't
    fill up on grease   12

because that makes it a lot worse,
    that makes it a crime
against property and the state
    and that costs time.   16

We've all been here before,
    we took our turn
under the electric storm
    of the vibrator   20

and stiffened our wills to meet
    the close clippers
and heard the true blade mowing
    back and forth   24

on a strip of dead skin,
    and we stopped crying.
You think your life is over?
    It's just begun.   28

Anne Sexton (b. 1928)

FOR ELEANOR BOYLAN TALKING WITH GOD

God has a brown voice,
as soft and full as beer.
Eleanor, who is more beautiful than my mother,
is standing in her kitchen talking
and I am breathing in my cigarettes like poison.   5
She stands in her lemon-colored sun dress
motioning to God with her wet hands
glossy from the washing of egg plates.
She tells him! She tells him like a drunk
who doesn't need to see to talk.   10
It's casual but friendly.
God is as close as the ceiling.

Though no one can ever know,
I don't think he has a face.
He had a face when I was six and a half.   15
Now he is large, covering up the sky
like a great resting jellyfish.
When I was eight I thought the dead people
stayed up there like blimps.
Now my chair is as hard as a scarecrow   20
and outside the summer flies sing like a choir.
Eleanor, before he leaves tell him . . .
Oh Eleanor, Eleanor,
tell him before death uses you up.

Adrienne Rich (b. 1929)

THE INSUSCEPTIBLES

Then the long sunlight lying on the sea
Fell, folded gold on gold; and slowly we   2
Took up our decks of cards, our parasols,
The picnic hamper and the sandblown shawls   4
And climbed the dunes in silence. There were two
Who lagged behind as lovers sometimes do,   6
And took a different road. For us the night
Was final, and by artificial light   8
We came indoors to sleep. No envy there
Of those who might be watching anywhere   10
The lustres of the summer dark, to trace
Some vagrant splinter blazing out of space.   12
No thought of them, save in a lower room
To leave a light for them when they should come.   14

COMPARE:

"The Insusceptibles" with "Different persuasions" by Marge Piercy (page 416).

Gary Snyder (b. 1930)

MILTON BY FIRELIGHT

Piute Creek, August 1955

"O hell, what do mine eyes
  with grief behold?"
Working with an old
Singlejack miner, who can sense
The vein and cleavage   5
In the very guts of rock, can
Blast granite, build
Switchbacks that last for years
Under the beat of snow, thaw, mule-hooves.
What use, Milton, a silly story   10
Of our lost general parents,
  eaters of fruit?

The Indian, the chainsaw boy,
And a string of six mules
Came riding down to camp   15
Hungry for tomatoes and green apples.
Sleeping in saddle-blankets
Under a bright night-sky
Han River slantwise by morning.
Jays squall   20
Coffee boils

In ten thousand years the Sierras
Will be dry and dead, home of the scorpion.
Ice-scratched slabs and bent trees.
No paradise, no fall,   25
Only the weathering land
The wheeling sky,
Man, with his Satan
Scouring the chaos of the mind.
Oh Hell!   30

Fire down
Too dark to read, miles from a road
The bell-mare clangs in the meadow
That packed dirt for a fill-in
Scrambling through loose rocks   35
On an old trail
All of a summer's day.

MILTON BY FIRELIGHT. 1–2. *"Oh hell, what do mine eyes with grief behold?"* Satan's envious
words as he looks upon Adam and Eve in the Garden of Eden (Book IV, line 358 in
Milton's *Paradise Lost*).

Sylvia Plath (1932–1963)

FACE LIFT

You bring me good news from the clinic,
Whipping off your silk scarf, exhibiting the tight white
Mummy-cloths, smiling: I'm all right.
When I was nine, a lime-green anesthetist
Fed me banana gas through a frog-mask. The nauseous vault
Boomed with bad dreams and the Jovian voices of surgeons.
Then mother swam up, holding a tin basin.
O I was sick.   8

They've changed all that. Traveling
Nude as Cleopatra in my well-boiled hospital shift,
Fizzy with sedatives and unusually humorous,
I roll to an anteroom where a kind man
Fists my fingers for me. He makes me feel something precious
Is leaking from the finger-vents. At the count of two
Darkness wipes me out like chalk on a blackboard . . .
I don't know a thing.   16

For five days I lie in secret,
Tapped like a cask, the years draining into my pillow.
Even my best friend thinks I'm in the country.
Skin doesn't have roots, it peels away easy as paper.
When I grin, the stitches tauten. I grow backward. I'm twenty,
Broody and in long skirts on my first husband's sofa, my fingers
Buried in the lambswool of the dead poodle;
I hadn't a cat yet.   24

Now she's done for, the dewlapped lady
I watched settle, line by line, in my mirror —
Old sock-face, sagged on a darning egg.
They've trapped her in some laboratory jar.
Let her die there, or wither incessantly for the next fifty years,
Nodding and rocking and fingering her thin hair.
Mother to myself, I wake swaddled in gauze,
Pink and smooth as a baby.   32

COMPARE:
"Face Lift" with "The Operation" by W. D. Snodgrass (page 405).

Sylvia Plath (1932–1963)

LADY LAZARUS

I have done it again.
One year in every ten
I manage it —

A sort of walking miracle, my skin
Bright as a Nazi lampshade,   5
My right foot

A paperweight,
My face a featureless, fine
Jew linen.

Peel off the napkin   10
O my enemy.
Do I terrify? —

The nose, the eye pits, the full set of teeth?
The sour breath
Will vanish in a day.   15

Soon, soon the flesh
The grave cave ate will be
At home on me

And I a smiling woman.
I am only thirty.   20
And like the cat I have nine times to die.

This is Number Three.
What a trash
To annihilate each decade.

What a million filaments.   25
The peanut-crunching crowd
Shoves in to see

Them unwrap me hand and foot —
The big strip tease.
Gentleman, ladies,   30

These are my hands,
My knees.
I may be skin and bone,

Nevertheless, I am the same, identical woman.
The first time it happened I was ten.   35
It was an accident.

The second time I meant
To last it out and not come back at all.
I rocked shut

As a seashell.   40
They had to call and call
And pick the worms off me like sticky pearls.

Dying
Is an art, like everything else.
I do it exceptionally well.   45

I do it so it feels like hell.
I do it so it feels real.
I guess you could say I've a call.

It's easy enough to do it in a cell.
It's easy enough to do it and stay put.   50
It's the theatrical

Comeback in broad day
To the same place, the same face, the same brute
Amused shout:

"A miracle!"   55
That knocks me out.
There is a charge

For the eyeing of my scars, there is a charge
For the hearing of my heart —
It really goes.   60

And there is a charge, a very large charge
For a word or a touch
Or a bit of blood

Or a piece of my hair or my clothes.
So, so, Herr Doktor.   65
So, Herr Enemy.

I am your opus,
I am your valuable,
The pure gold baby

That melts to a shriek.   70
I turn and burn.
Do not think I underestimate your great concern.

Ash, ash —
You poke and stir.
Flesh, bone, there is nothing there —   75

A cake of soap,
A wedding ring,
A gold filling.

Herr God, Herr Lucifer,
Beware   80
Beware.

Out of the ash
I rise with my red hair
And I eat men like air.

Sylvia Plath (1932–1963)

MORNING SONG

Love set you going like a fat gold watch. *Imagery*
The midwife slapped your footsoles, and your bald cry   *Birth of the baby*
Took its place among the elements.

Our voices echo, magnifying your arrival. New statue. *the baby*
In a drafty museum, your nakedness *her image* *of the world*
Shadows our safety. We stand round blankly as walls. *mortality*

I'm no more your mother *separation between*
Than the cloud that distils a mirror to reflect its own slow *her & the baby*
Effacement at the wind's hand.

All night your moth-breath *wallpaper*   10
Flickers among the flat pink roses. I wake to listen:
A far sea moves in my ear.

One cry, and I stumble from bed, cow-heavy and floral
In my Victorian nightgown.
Your mouth opens clean as a cat's. The window square   *dawn — the light breaks the*   15
Whitens and swallows its dull stars. And now you try   *stars.*
Your handful of notes;
The clear vowels rise like balloons. *the baby crying*

COMPARE:

"Morning Song" with "My Son, My Executioner" by Donald Hall (page 273),
and "Preface to a Twenty Volume Suicide Note" by Imamu Amiri Baraka
(page 416).

Keith Waldrop (b. 1932)

BEFORE BED

"what shall we do for our sister?" — Cant. 8:8

Girls with fat thighs and no breasts
stare at the daughters of television.
All they know bound into that bright box,
they cannot tell bay leaves from
savory. They are learning what they will   5
never understand. Their mothers
packed every little hope into a cedar chest,
more than a man could carry. They watch,
uncomprehending, diaphanous movements in snow.
If they hope, they hope for a ring of   10
cheap music and boobies like mountains,
no other dream worth sleeping for.

BEFORE BED. The epigraph refers to the Song of Solomon: "We have a little sister, and she hath no breasts: what shall we do for our sister in the day when she shall be spoken for? If she be a wall, we will build upon her a palace of silver: and if she be a door, we will inclose her with boards of cedar." 4. *bay leaves:* Laurels, into which (in Greek mythology) the nymph Daphne was changed and which (in Roman times) were used for crowns. 5. *savory:* Herb used in cooking.

COMPARE:

"Before Bed" with "The Brides" by A. D. Hope (page 382).

Imamu Amiri Baraka [LeRoi Jones] (b. 1934)
PREFACE TO A TWENTY VOLUME SUICIDE NOTE

For Kellie Jones, Born 16 May 1959

Lately, I've become accustomed to the way
The ground opens up and envelopes me
Each time I go out to walk the dog.
Or the broad edged silly music the wind
Makes when I run for a bus . . .   5

Things have come to that.

And now, each night I count the stars,
And each night I get the same number.
And when they will not come to be counted,
I count the holes they leave.   10

Nobody sings anymore.

And then last night I tiptoed up
To my daughter's room and heard her
Talking to someone, and when I opened
The door, there was no one there . . .   15
Only she on her knees, peeking into

Her own clasped hands.

COMPARE:

"Preface to a Twenty Volume Suicide Note" with "Morning Song" by Sylvia Plath (page 415) and "My Son, My Executioner" by Donald Hall (page 273).

Marge Piercy (b. 1936)
DIFFERENT PERSUASIONS

You are rumpled like a sweater
smelling of burnt leaves and dried sea grasses.
Your smile belongs to an archaic boy of wasting stone on Delos.
You change shape like spilled mercury.

There is no part of you that touches me,   5
not even your laugh catching like fur in your nose.
I am with you on a glacier,
white snowfield gouged with bluegreen crevasses
deep and the color of your eyes.
There is no place to go,   10
we cannot lie down.
In the distance your people wait.
We blaze like a refinery on the ice.
A dry snow begins to descend.
Your hands fall clasped to your sides.   15
Your eyes freeze to the rim of the sky.
Already I cannot see you for the snow.
The heavy iron gates
are closing in my breasts.

COMPARE:

"Different persuasions" with "The Insusceptibles" by Adrienne Rich (page
410).

Lucille Clifton (b. 1936)

THE LOST BABY POEM

the time i dropped your almost body down
down to meet the waters under the city
and run one with the sewage to the sea
what did i know about waters rushing back
what did i know about drowning   5
or being drowned

you would have been born into winter
in the year of the disconnected gas
and no car   we would have made the thin
walk over Genesee hill into the Canada wind   10
to watch you slip like ice into strangers' hands
you would have fallen naked as snow into winter
if you were here i could tell you these
and some other things

if i am ever less than a mountain   15
for your definite brothers and sisters
let the rivers pour over my head
let the sea take me for a spiller
of seas   let black men call me stranger
always   for your never named sake   20

C. K. Williams (b. 1936)
Hood

Remember me? I was the one
in high school you were always afraid of.
I kept cigarettes in my sleeve, wore
engineer's boots, long hair, my collar
up in back and there were always   5
girls with me in the hallways.

You were nothing. I had it in for you —
when I peeled rubber at the lights
you cringed like a teacher.
And when I crashed and broke both lungs   10
on the wheel, you were so relieved
that you stroked the hard Ford paint
like a breast and your hands shook.

Bob Dylan (b. 1941)
Subterranean Homesick Blues

Johnny's in the basement
Mixing up the medicine
I'm on the pavement
Thinking about the government
The man in the trenchcoat   5
Badge out, laid off
Says he's got a bad cough
Wants to get paid off
Look out kid
It's something you did   10
God knows when
But you're doin' it again
You better duck down the alley way
Lookin' for a new friend
The man in the coonskin cap   15
By the pig pen
Wants eleven dollar bills
You only got ten.

Maggie comes fleet foot
Face full of black soot   20
Talkin' that the heat put
Plants in the bed but
The phone's tapped anyway
Maggie says that many say
They must bust in early May   25
Orders from the D.A.

Look out kid
Don't matter what you did
Walk on your tip toes
Don't try No-Doz   30
Better stay away from those
That carry around a fire hose
Keep a clean nose
Watch the plain clothes
You don't need a weather man   35
To tell which way the wind blows.

Get sick get well
Hang around an ink well
Ring bell, hard to tell
If anything is goin' to sell   40
Try hard, get barred
Get back, write braille
Get jailed, jump bail
Join the army, if you fail
Look out kid, you're gonna get hit   45
But users, cheaters
Six time losers
Hang around the theatres
Girl by the whirl pool's
Lookin' for a new fool   50
Don't follow leaders
Watch the parkin' meters.

Ah, get born, keep warm
Short pants, romance, learn to dance
Get dressed, get blessed   55
Try to be a success
Please her, please him, buy gifts
Don't steal, don't lift
Twenty years of schoolin'
And they put you on the day shift   60
Look out kid, they keep it all hid
Better jump down a manhole
Light yourself a candle, don't wear sandals
Try to avoid the scandals
Don't wanna be a bum   65
You better chew gum
The pump don't work
'Cause the vandals took the handles.

Nikki Giovanni (b. 1943)

KIDNAP POEM

ever been kidnapped
by a poet
if i were a poet
i'd kidnap you

put you in my phrases   5
and meter you to jones beach
or maybe coney island
or maybe just to my house

lyric you in lilacs
dash you in the rain   10
alliterate the beach
to complement my see

play the lyre for you
ode you with my love song
anything to win you   15
wrap you in the red Black green
show you off to mama

yeah if i were
a poet i'd kid
nap you   .   20

Mick Jagger (b. 1943) and Keith Richard (b. 1943)

LIVE WITH ME

I've got nasty habits,
I take tea at three —
Yes, and the meat I eat for dinner
It must be hung up for a week —
My best friend he shoots water rats   5
And a-feeds them to his geese —
Don'cha think there's a place for you —
In between the sheets?

Come now, honey, we can build a place for three —
Come now, honey, don'cha wanna live with me?   10

There's a score of hare-brained children,
They are locked in the nursery —
They got earphone heads,
They got dirty necks —

They're so twentieth century.   15
Well, they queue up for the bathroom
Round about seven thirty-five —
Don'cha think we need a woman's touch
To make it come alive?

You'd look good pram-pushin' down the High Street —   20
Come now, honey, don'cha wanna live with me?

Oh, the servants they're so helpful, dear!
The cook she is a whore —
Yes, the butler has a place for her
Behind the pantry door —   25
The maid, she's French, she got no sense,
She's from the Crazy Horse,
And when she strips the chauffeur flips,
The footman's eyes are crossed —

Oh, don'cha think there's a place for us   30
Right across the street?
Don'cha think there's a place for you
In between the sheets?

COMPARE:

"Live with Me" with "The Passionate Shepherd to His Love" by Christopher
Marlowe (page 314) and "The Bait" by John Donne (page 321).

James Tate (b. 1943)

FLIGHT

For K.

Like a glum cricket
the refrigerator is singing
and just as I am convinced

that it is the only noise
in the building, a pot falls   5
in 2 B. The neighbors on

both sides of me suddenly
realize that they have not
made love to their wives

since 1947. The racket   10
multiplies. The man downhall
is teaching his dog to fly.

The fish are disgusted
and beat their heads blue
against a cold aquarium. I too   15

lose control and consider
the dust huddled in the corner
a threat to my endurance.

Were you here, we would not
tolerate mongrels in the air,   20
nor the conspiracies of dust.

We would drive all night,
your head tilted on my shoulder.
At dawn, I would nudge you

with my anxious fingers and say,   25
Already we are in Idaho.

Greg Kuzma (b. 1944)

PEACE, SO THAT

every stinking son of a bitch
can come home
to his lawn mower and rice paddy,
every punished son of a bitch
can return to his father's bedside,   5
every child of every bastard
every child of every hero of peace
of war
can talk it over with the man he blames,
every woman, mother, wife, daughter,   10
will rise in our arms like the tide,
every bomb be water
every bullet be smashed into frying pans,
every knife sharpened again
to cut fruit in thin slices   15
every word flung out like a bullet
in anger
come back to putrefy the tongue,
every man who has sat silent
beware of his silence,   20
every rising of the blood
make love to a woman, a man,
every killer have only mirrors
to shoot at,
every child a thumb to suck,   25
every house its chance
to sink to the earth's calling,
every dead shall have no good reasons.

And we be a long time at this.

INDEX OF FIRST LINES

About suffering, about adoration, the old masters, 388

About suffering they were never wrong, 381

After the doctor checked to see, 185

After the funeral, mule praises, brays, 391

A garden is a lovesome thing, 247

A garden is a *lovesome* thing? 247

Ah, look at all tne lonely people! 122

Ah child, no Persian-perfect art! 278

A line in long array where they wind betwixt green islands, 184

All in green went my love riding, 374

Although I shelter from the rain, 270

Always to want to, 63

Among twenty snowy mountains, 186

An ant on the tablecloth, 211

An axe angles, 396

A noiseless patient spider, 214

anyone lived in a pretty how town, 48

Apeneck Sweeney spreads his knees, 372

A piece of green pepper, 75

A poem should be palpable and mute, 302

a politician is an arse upon, 175

As I sd to my, 404

As I walked out one evening, 380

As I was laying on the green, 53

As I was walking, 403

As I was walking all alane, 312

A slumber did my spirit seal, 129

As the cat, 74

A sudden blow: the great wings beating still, 223

As virtuous men pass mildly away, 319

A sweet disorder in the dress, 140

Avenge, O Lord, thy slaughtered saints, whose bones, 32

A white horse came to our farm once, 61

Batter my heart, three-personed God, for You, 320

Beat! beat! drums! — blow! bugles! blow! 159

Beautifully Janet slept, 251

Because I could not stop for Death, 344

Begins the crying, 275

Bent double, like old beggars under sacks, 19

Be reasonable, my pain, and think with more detachment, 279

Black reapers with the sound of steel on stones, 77

Borgia, thou once wert almost too august, 155

Boy, I detest the Persian pomp, 278

Boy, I hate their empty shows, 277

Bright star! would I were steadfast as thou art, 262

Buffalo Bill's, 181

By the city dead-house by the gate, 343

Call the roller of big cigars, 362

Calm down, my Sorrow, we must move with care, 279

Charles used to watch Naomi, taking heart, 405

Christmas Eve, and twelve of the clock, 218

Come into animal presence, 401

Come live with me and be my love (Donne), 321

Come live with me and be my love (Marlowe), 314

Dark house, by which once more I stand, 158

Death, though I see him not, is near, 50

Do not go gentle into that good night, 176

Down the assembly line they roll and pass, 382

Drink to me only with thine eyes, 101

Driving down the concrete vein, 99

Droning a drowsy syncopated tune, 378

Dylan Thomas, 176

Earth has not anything to show more fair, 333

Empieza el llanto, 275
Etienne de Silhouette, 176
ever been kidnapped, 420
Every man in the world thinks his banner the best, 265
every stinking son of a bitch, 422
Every year without knowing it I have passed the day, 407

Fa, mi, fa, re, la, mi, 120
Farewell, too little and too lately known, 325
Fear no more the heat o' th' sun, 115
First fight. Then fiddle. Ply the slipping string, 285
Flower in the crannied wall, 82
For I will consider my Cat Jeoffry, 330
For the bumps bangs & scratches of, 97
Fra bank to bank, fra wood to wood I rin, 264
Frankie she was a good woman, Johnny he was her man, 118
Friend, on this scaffold Thomas More lies dead, 64
From low to high doth dissolution climb, 54
From my mother's sleep I fell into the State, 387
From stainless steel basins of water, 405
From the wash the laundress sends, 98
Full fathom five thy father lies, 317

Gasoline makes game scarce, 391
Gather ye rose-buds while ye may, 322
Get the gasworks into a poem, 387
"Get up!" the caller calls, "Get up!" 263
Girls with fat thighs and no breasts, 415
Glory be to God for dappled things, 129
Go, lovely rose, 323
Go and catch a falling star, 166
God bless our good and gracious King, 174
God has a brown voice, 410
Gone the three ancient ladies, 384
Gr-r-r — there go, my heart's abhorrence! 340

Had we but world enough, and time, 324
Have you ever had a witch bloom like a highway, 7
Haze, char, and the weather of All Souls', 38
He clasps the crag with crooked hands, 80
Here a little child I stand, 23
Here lies Sir Tact, a diplomatic fellow, 65
Here she lies, a pretty bud, 183
Her whole life is an epigram: smack smooth, and neatly penned, 175

He stood, and heard the steeple, 132
He was found by the Bureau of Statistics to be, 12
He would declare and could himself believe, 147
"Hiram, I think the sump is backing up, 248
How dark to my mind are the scenes of my childhood, 350
How did they fume, and stamp, and roar, and chafe! 188
How shall we mourn you who are killed and wasted, 141

I am a cowboy in the boat of Ra, 235
I am a flag by distant space surrounded, 276
I am his Highness' dog at Kew, 326
I caught a tremendous fish, 72
I caught this morning morning's minion, king-, 349
Ich bin wie eine Fahne von Fernen umgeben, 276
If i had a nickel, 98
If in his study he hath so much care, 174
If I should touch her she would shriek and weeping, 30
If I were only dafter, 137
I found a ball of grass among the hay, 38
I found a dimpled spider, fat and white, 283
If when my wife is sleeping, 365
If you wander far enough, 24
I had a chair at every hearth, 270
I have done it again, 412
I have eaten, 67
I have heard that hysterical women say, 356
I have known the inexorable sadness of pencils, 383
I hear an army charging upon the land, 365
I heard a Fly buzz – when I died, 207
I knew a woman, lovely in her bones, 97
I like to see it lap the Miles, 17
I love it, I love it! and who shall dare, 245
I'm a riddle in nine syllables, 83
I met a traveler from an antique land, 257
I met the Bishop on the road, 355
In a shoe box stuffed in an old nylon stocking, 385
In a solitude of the sea, 347
In Breughel's great picture, The Kermess, 183
in Just-, 190
In Stamford, at the edge of town, a giant statue stands, 222
In the desert, 184
In the morning, in the morning, 5
In this little urn is laid, 198
In Xanadu did Kubla Khan, 334

I placed a jar in Tennessee, 212
I remember the neckcurls, limp and damp as tendrils, 383
I saw a ship of martial build, 341
I saw in Louisiana a live-oak growing, 343
I shoot the Hippopotamus, 136
I shudder thinking, 39
I sing of a maiden that is makeless, 99
I sit at a gold table with my girl, 148
I sometimes sleep with other girls, 20
I started Early – Took my Dog, 345
"Is there anybody there?" said the Traveller, 360
It did not last: the Devil, howling *Ho!* 132
It dropped so low – in my Regard, 84
I tell you, hopeless grief is passionless, 173
It is a cold and snowy night. The main street is deserted, 76
It little profits that an idle king, 338
It's a little Walden, 94
It's of a rich squire in Bristol I'll tell, 111
It was a big boxy wreck of a house, 18
It was a lover and his lass, 139
It was a miniature country once, 266
It was in and about the Martinmas time, 107
It was my bridal night I remember, 163
It was not Death, for I stood up, 6
I've got nasty habits, 420
I wakened on my hot, hard bed, 128
I wandered lonely as a cloud, 10
I wander through each chartered street, 57
I wanted to be a cauliflower, 191
I weep when the gay are around me, 251
I who by day am function of the light, 61
I woke up this mornin' with the blues all round my bed, 121

James Watt, 176
Jane looks down at her organdy skirt, 403
Jenny kissed me when we met, 141
John Anderson my jo, John, 244
Johnny's in the basement, 418
Julius Caesar, 133
Just as my fingers on these keys, 362
Just off the highway to Rochester, Minnesota, 407

Lady, when I behold the roses sprouting, 103
Lately, I've become accustomed to the way, 416
Law makes long spokes of the short stakes of men, 379
Leering across Pearl Street, 408
Let me not to the marriage of true minds, 316
Let me take this other glove off, 27

Let us go then, you and I, 368
Life, friends, is boring. We must not say so, 30
Life is like a jagged tooth, 240
Like a drummer's brush, 141
Like a glum cricket, 421
Little Mary Bell had a fairy in a nut, 332
Lo, as a careful housewife runs to catch, 212
"London: JOHN LANE, *The Bodley Head,* 151
Long-expected one and twenty, 59
Look at him there in his stovepipe hat, 394
Lord, who createdst man in wealth and store, 193
Love bade me welcome; yet my soul drew back, 322
Loveliest of trees, the cherry now, 3
Love set you going like a fat gold watch, 415

Madam Life's a piece in bloom, 240
Man looking into the sea, 368
Many-maned scud-thumper, tub, 128
Márgarét, are you grieving, 252
Mother, I cannot mind my wheel, 35
"Mother dear, may I go downtown, 392
Much have I traveled in the realms of gold, 63
My arm sweeps down, 191
My clumsiest dear, whose hands shipwreck vases, 389
my drum, hollowed out thru the thin slit, 192
My heart aches, and a drowsy numbness pains, 70
My heart leaps up when I behold, 54
My love is of a birth as rare, 95
My mistress' eyes are nothing like the sun, 171
My mother bore me in the southern wild, 261
My prime of youth is but a frost of cares, 90
My son, my executioner, 273
My wife is my shirt, 241

Nature and Nature's laws lay hid in night, 132
Nautilus Island's hermit, 393
Nay, nay, my boy — 'tis not for me, 277
"Never shall a young man, 355
"next to of course god america i, 375
Not, I'll not, carrion comfort, Despair, not feast on thee, 49
Not every man has gentians in his house, 217
Nothing is plumb, level or square, 402
Not marble nor the gilded monuments, 7
Now as at all times I can see in the mind's eye, 358

Now as I was young and easy under the apple boughs, 167

O Captain! my Captain! our fearful trip is done, 260
Off Highway 106, 399
"O hell, what do mine eyes, 411
Old age is, 366
Old Eben Flood, climbing alone one night, 358
Old houses were scaffolding once, 75
"O 'Melia, my dear, this does everything crown! 44
O Moon, when I gaze on thy beautiful face, 240
On a starred night Prince Lucifer uprose, 344
Once, with a whirl of thought oppressed, 326
Once I am sure there's nothing going on, 397
Once upon a time I spent a summer, 189
One brought me the news of your death, O Herakleitos my friend, 275
One day a wag — what would the wretch be at? 22
One must have a mind of winter, 364
One thing that literature would be greatly the better for, 86
1-2-3 was the number he played but today the number came 3-2-1, 377
On the long shore, lit by the moon, 395
On top of old Smoky, all covered with snow, 106
Opusculum paedagogum, 69
O Rose, thou art sick! 332
Out of a fired ship which by no way, 213
O what can ail thee, knight-at-arms, 228
O wind, rend open the heat, 78
O with what key, 195

Paper come out — done strewed de news, 54
Peace, be at peace, O thou my heaviness, 279
Persicos odi, puer, apparatus, 277
Poor soul, the center of my sinful earth, 317
Proud Maisie is in the wood, 169

Quite unexpectedly as Vasserot, 8

railroad yard in San Jose, 404
Razors pain you, 150
Remember me? I was the one, 418
Rivers arise; whether thou be the son, 140
Rose-cheeked Laura, come, 120

Rough wind, that moanest loud, 156
r-p-o-p-h-e-s-s-a-g-r, 196

Said, Pull her up a bit will you, Mac, I want to unload there, 43
Science! true daughter of Old Time thou art! 281
"See, here's the workbox, little wife, 26
Seeds in a dry pod, tick, tick, tick, 177
Shall I compare thee to a summer's day? 99
She even thinks that up in heaven, 22
She is as in a field a silken tent, 213
She lay in her girlish sleep at ninety-six, 85
She sat down below a thorn, 102
Shlup, shlup, the dog, 178
Shut not so soon; the dull-eyed night, 65
Since there's no help, come let us kiss and part, 172
Sir, say no more, 9
Sir Christopher Wren, 176
Skirting the river road, (my forenoon walk, my rest,), 77
Slow, slow, fresh fount, keep time with my salt tears, 148
Softly, in the dusk, a woman is singing to me, 246
Sois sage, ô ma Douleur, et tiens-toi plus tranquille, 278
Some are teethed on a silver spoon, 379
Some say the world will end in fire, 65
so much depends, 13
So smooth, so sweet, so silv'ry is thy voice, 61
s sz sz SZ sz SZ sz ZS zs ZS zs zs z, 201
Stand still, and I will read to thee, 319
Start not — or deem my spirit fled, 335
Stasis in darkness, 293
Stella this day is thirty-four, 33
Stone gullets among, 197
Sunday shuts down on this twentieth-century evening, 385
Sunset and evening star, 338
Suzanne takes you down, 123
Swinging chick, 121

Tears, idle tears, I know not what they mean, 246
Tell me not, Sweet, I am unkind, 19
Temptations still nest in it like basilisks, 62
"Terence, this is stupid stuff, 352
That civilization may not sink, 357
That is no country for old men. The young, 254
That night your great guns, unawares, 346
That time of year thou mayst in me behold, 318
That which her slender waist confined, 93
The Angel that presided o'er my birth, 134

The apparition of these faces in the crowd, 67

the Cambridge ladies who live in furnished souls, 66

The caryophyllaceae, 53

The crops are all in and the peaches are rotting, 113

The curfew tolls the knell of parting day, 326

The dirty word hops in the cage of the mind like the Pondicherry, 386

Thee for my recitative, 17

The elephant, the huge old beast, 367

"The famous bard, he comes! The vision nears!" 175

The fog comes, 263

The fortunes of war, I tell you plain, 96

the horizon of holland, 200

The houses are haunted, 60

The interests of a black man in a cellar, 375

The jeweled steps are already quite white with dew, 62

The kingdom of heaven is likened unto a man which sowed good seed in his field, 209

The king sits in Dumferling toune, 310

The legs of the elk punctured the snow's crust, 406

The Lightning is a yellow Fork, 205

Then the long sunlight lying on the sea, 410

The only response, 184

The piercing chill I feel, 68

The radiance of that star that leans on me, 95

The readers of the *Boston Evening Transcript*, 204

There is a garden in her face, 318

There ought to be capital punishment for cars, 249

There was a man of double deed, 84

There was such speed in her little body, 373

There were three ravens sat on a tree, 311

The sea is calm tonight, 287

The silver swan, who living had no note, 120

The Soul selects her own Society, 346

The splendor falls on castle walls, 131

The thing could barely stand. Yet taken, 244

the time i dropped your almost body down, 417

The time you won your town the race, 354

The trees they do grow high, and the leaves they do grow green, 110

The tusks tnat clashed in mighty brawls, 256

The whiskey on your breath, 14

"The wind doth blow today, my love, 116

The wind flapped loose, the wind was still, 344

The wind stood up and gave a shout, 88

The witch that came (the withered hag), 361

The world is charged with the grandeur of God, 137

The world is too much with us; late and soon, 219

They didn't hire him, 75

The year's at the spring, 116

They flee from me that sometime did me seke, 157

They say that Richard Cory owns, 105

They sing their dearest songs, 349

They told me, Heraclitus, they told me you were dead, 275

This darksome burn, horseback brown, 158

This is the terminal: the light, 376

This living hand, now warm and capable, 164

Thou ill-formed offspring of my feeble brain, 16

Thou still unravished bride of quietness, 336

Thread the nerves through the right holes, 13

Three poets, in three distant ages born, 64

Today we have naming of parts. Yesterday, 390

To freight cars in the air, 159

To see a world in a grain of sand, 83

Toussaint, the most unhappy man of men! 333

To yow, my purse, and to noon other wight, 313

Traveling through the dark I found a deer, 250

Treason doth never prosper; what's the reason? 174

Tree at my window, window tree, 92

True Thomas lay on Huntlie bank, 225

Turning and turning in the widening gyre, 220

'Twas brillig, and the slithy toves, 50

Two boys uncoached are tossing a poem together, 5

Tyger! Tyger! burning bright, 332

Venerable Mother Toothache, 221

Victory comes late, 182

Watching the shied core, 64

We caught the tread of dancing feet, 351

We dance round in a ring and suppose, xxx

We real cool. We, 147

Western wind, when wilt thou blow, 309
We stood by a pond that winter day, 208
What, still alive at twenty-two, 248
What a thrill, 76
What happens to a dream deferred? 87
What is our life? A play of passion, 209
Wheesht, wheesht, my foolish hert, 44
When daisies pied and violets blue, 315
Whenever Richard Cory went down town, 105
When God at first made man, 91
When icicles hang by the wall, 316
When I consider how my light is spent, 323
When I have fears that I may cease to be, 337
When I saw that clumsy crow, 213
When I saw your head bow, I knew I had beaten you, 39
When I shall be without regret, 264
When my mother died I was very young, 32
when serpents bargain for the right to squirm, 375
While going the road to sweet Athy, 28
While in this cavernous place employed, 85
While my hair was still cut straight across my forehead, 366
Who could believe an ant in theory? 98
Whose woods these are I think I know, 361
Whoso list to hunt, I know where is an hind, 314

Who will go drive with Fergus now, 127
"Why dois your brand sae drap wi' bluid, 309
Wilt Thou forgive that sin where I begun, 93
With how sad steps, O Moon, thou climb'st the skies! 314
With rue my heart is laden, 141
With serving still, 149
Women in uniform, 213

Yet once more, O ye laurels, and once more, 229
Yield, 169
Yillow, yillow, yillow, 51
You are rumpled like a sweater, 416
You bring me good news from the clinic, 412
You do not do, you do not do, 296
You praise the firm restraint with which they write, 164
Your smiling, or the hope, the thought of it, 82
You serve the best wines always, my dear sir, 174
You that with allegory's curious frame, 210
You've gotten in through the transom, 409
You who dump the beer cans in the lake, 29
You would think the fury of aerial bombardment, 45

INDEX OF AUTHORS AND TITLES

After the Funeral, 391
Age, 50
ALLEN, EDWARD
Best Line Yet, The, 222
All in green went my love riding, 374
ALPAUGH, ERN, AND DEWEY G. PELL
Swinging Chick, 121
ALVAREZ, A.
Sylvia Plath (Commentary), 290
American Primitive, 394
AMMONS, A. R.
Auto Mobile, 97
Spring Coming, 53
Anecdote of the Jar, 212
Angel that presided o'er my birth, The, 134
ANONYMOUS
As I was laying on the green, 53
Bonny Barbara Allan, 107
Cruel Mother, The, 102
Edward, 309
Fa, mi, fa, re, la, mi, 120
fortunes of war, I tell you plain, The, 96
Frankie and Johnny, 117
Good Mornin', Blues, 121
I sing of a maiden that is makeless, 99
Johnny, I Hardly Knew Ye, 28
Julius Caesar, 133
Lady, when I behold the roses sprouting, 103
O Moon, when I gaze on thy beautiful face, 240
On Top of Old Smoky, 106
Scottsboro, 54
silver swan, who living had no note, The, 120
Sir Patrick Spence, 310
Squire and Milkmaid, or, Blackberry Fold, 111
Still Growing, 110
There was a man of double deed, 84
Thomas the Rimer, 225
Three Ravens, The, 311
Twa Corbies, The, 312

Unquiet Grave, The, 116
Western Wind, 309
Another Grace for a Child, 23
Antiquary, 174
anyone lived in a pretty how town, 48
Ariel, 293
ARNOLD, MATTHEW
Dover Beach, 287
Ars Poetica, 302
Art, 22
As Bad as a Mile, 64
As I Walked Out One Evening, 380
As I was laying on the green, 53
At the Altar, 148
At the San Francisco Airport, 376
Atticus, 188
AUDEN, W. H.
As I Walked Out One Evening, 380
James Watt, 176
Musée des Beaux Arts, 381
Unknown Citizen, The, 12
Author to Her Book, The, 16
Auto Mobile, 97

Bait, The, 321
Ballad of Birmingham, 392
BARAKA, IMAMU AMIRI (LeRoi Jones)
Preface to a Twenty Volume Suicide Note, 416
Batter my heart, three-personed God, for You, 320
BAUDELAIRE, CHARLES
Recueillement, 278
Bavarian Gentians, 217
Beat! Beat! Drums! 159
Because I could not stop for Death, 344
BEDDOES, THOMAS LOVELL
Resurrection Song, 13
BEERBOHM, MAX
On the imprint of the first English edition of "The Works of Max Beerbohm," 151
Before Bed, 415

BELLOC, HILAIRE
Hippopotamus, The, 136
Bells for John Whiteside's Daughter, 373
BENTLEY, EDMUND CLERIHEW
Sir Christopher Wren, 176
Berg, The, 341
BERRYMAN, JOHN
Life, friends, is boring. We must not say
so, 30
Best Line Yet, The, 222
BETJEMAN, JOHN
In Westminster Abbey, 27
BIERCE, AMBROSE
Art, 22
Bird-Singing Stream, 198
BISHOP, ELIZABETH
Fish, The, 72
Black Tambourine, 375
BLAKE, WILLIAM
Angel that presided o'er my birth, The,
134
Chimney Sweeper, The, 32
Her whole life is an epigram, 175
Little Black Boy, The, 261
London, 57
Long John Brown and Little Mary Bell,
332
Sick Rose, The, 332
To see a world in a grain of sand, 83
Tyger, The, 332
Blessing, A, 407
BLY, ROBERT
Driving to Town Late to Mail a Letter, 76
Inward Conversation (translation), 279
Bonny Barbara Allan, 107
"Boston Evening Transcript," The, 204
BOYD, MARK ALEXANDER
Fra bank to bank, fra wood to wood I
rin, 264
Boy with His Hair Cut Short, 385
BRADSTREET, ANNE
Author to Her Book, The, 16
BRAUTIGAN, RICHARD
Haiku Ambulance, 75
Have You Ever Had a Witch Bloom like
a Highway, 7
Brides, The, 382
Bright star! would I were steadfast as thou
art, 262
BROOKS, FRED EMERSON
Pat's Opinion of Flags, 265
BROOKS, GWENDOLYN
First fight. Then fiddle. Ply the slipping
string, 285
We Real Cool, 147
BROWN, T. E.
My Garden, 247
BROWNING, ELIZABETH BARRETT
Grief, 173
BROWNING, ROBERT
Soliloquy of the Spanish Cloister, 340

year's at the spring, The, 116
Buffalo Bill's, 181
Bull Calf, The, 244
BURNS, ROBERT
John Anderson my jo, John, 244
Burnt Ship, A, 213
BUSON, TANIGUCHI
piercing chill I feel, The, 68
BYNNER, WITTER. See Morgan, Emanuel
BYRON, GEORGE GORDON, LORD
Lines Inscribed upon a Cup Formed
from a Skull, 335

Cambridge ladies who live in furnished
souls, the, 66
CAMPBELL, ROY
On Some South African Novelists, 164
CAMPION, THOMAS
Rose-cheeked Laura, come, 120
There is a garden in her face, 318
Carrion Comfort, 49
CARROLL, LEWIS
Jabberwocky, 50
Castoff Skin, 85
Catch, 5
Cauliflower, The, 191
Cavalier Lyric, 20
Cavalry Crossing a Ford, 184
Channel Firing, 346
CHARLES, DORTHI
Concrete Cat, 201
Charm Against the Toothache, A, 221
CHAUCER, GEOFFREY
Complaint of Chaucer to His Purse, The,
313
Cherrylog Road, 399
Chimney Sweeper, The, 32
Church Going, 397
CIARDI, JOHN
Credibility, 98
City Dead-House, The, 343
Civil Servant, A, 85
CLARE, JOHN
Mouse's Nest, 38
CLIFTON, LUCILLE
lost baby poem, the, 417
COHEN, LEONARD
Suzanne, 123
Cold Irish Earth, The, 39
COLERIDGE, HARTLEY
Fie on Eastern Luxury! (translation), 277
COLERIDGE, SAMUEL TAYLOR
Kubla Khan, 334
Come into Animal Presence, 401
Complaint of Chaucer to His Purse, The,
313
Composed upon Westminster Bridge, 333
Concrete Cat, 201
Convergence of the Twain, The, 347

COOK, ELIZA
 Old Arm-Chair, The, 245
CORMAN, CID
 Tortoise, The, 63
CORNFORD, FRANCES
 Watch, The, 128
CORY, WILLIAM
 Heraclitus (translation), 275
COWPER, WILLIAM
 Simplicity (translation), 277
CRANE, HART
 Black Tambourine, 375
CRANE, STEPHEN
 Heart, The, 184
Crazy Jane Talks with the Bishop, 355
Credibility, 98
CREELEY, ROBERT
 I Know a Man, 404
 Kore, 403
 Oh No, 24
Crossing the Bar, 338
Cruel Mother, The, 102
CULLEN, COUNTEE
 For a Lady I Know, 22
 Saturday's Child, 379
CUMMINGS, E. E.
 All in green went my love riding, 374
 anyone lived in a pretty how town, 48
 Buffalo Bill's, 181
 Cambridge ladies who live in furnished
  souls, the, 66
 in Just-, 190
 next to of course god america i, 375
 politician, a, 175
 r-p-o-p-h-e-s-s-a-g-r, 196
 when serpents bargain for the right to
  squirm, 375
CUNNINGHAM, J. V.
 Epitaph, 264
 Friend, on this scaffold Thomas More
  lies dead, 64
 Motto for a Sun Dial, 61
 You serve the best wines always, my
  dear sir (translation), 174
Cut, 76

Dalliance of the Eagles, The, 77
Dance, The, 183
Danse Russe, 365
Dark house, by which once more I stand,
 158
DAVISON, PETER
 Last Word, The, 39
Day of Judgment, The, 326
Dead Hand, 62
Death of the Ball Turret Gunner, The, 387
Definition of Love, The, 95
DE LA MARE, WALTER
 Listeners, The, 360

Delay, 95
Delight in Disorder, 140
Departmental, 211
Descent of Winter, The (section 10/30),
 159
Design, 283
DICKEY, JAMES
 Cherrylog Road, 399
 Commentary (to Arnold's "Dover
  Beach"), 288
DICKINSON, EMILY
 Because I could not stop for Death, 344
 I heard a Fly buzz – when I died, 207
 I like to see it lap the Miles, 17
 I started Early – Took my Dog, 345
 It dropped so low – in my Regard, 84
 It was not Death, for I stood up, 6
 Lightning is a yellow Fork, The, 205
 Soul selects her own Society, The, 346
 Victory comes late, 182
Different persuasions, 416
diPASQUALE, EMANUEL
 Rain, 141
Dirge, 377
Dirge, A, 156
Dirty Word, The, 386
Disillusionment of Ten O'Clock, 60
DODGSON, CHARLES LUTWIDGE. See Car-
 roll, Lewis
Dolor, 383
DONNE, JOHN
 Antiquary, 174
 Bait, The, 321
 Batter my heart, three-personed God,
  for You, 320
 Burnt Ship, A, 213
 Hymn to God the Father, A, 93
 Lecture upon the Shadow, A, 319
 Song ("Go and catch a falling star"), 166
 Valediction: Forbidding Mourning, A,
  319
Do Not Go Gentle into That Good Night,
 176
DOOLITTLE, HILDA. See H. D.
DOUGLAS, LORD ALFRED
 Peace, be at peace, O thou my heaviness
  (translation), 279
Dover Beach, 287
DRAYTON, MICHAEL
 Since there's no help, come let us kiss
  and part, 172
Dream Deferred, 87
Driving to Town Late to Mail a Letter, 76
DRYDEN, JOHN
 Lines Printed Under the Engraved Por-
  trait of Milton, 64
 To the Memory of Mr. Oldham, 325
DUGAN, ALAN
 Love Song: I and Thou, 402
Dulce et Decorum Est, 19
During Wind and Rain, 349

Dylan, Bob
    Subterranean Homesick Blues, 418
Dylan Thomas, 176

Eagle, The, 80
Easter Wings, 193
Eberhart, Richard
    Fury of Aerial Bombardment, The, 45
Edward, 309
Eight O'Clock, 132
Eleanor Rigby, 122
Elegy, Written with His Own Hand in the
    Tower Before His Execution, 90
Elegy for Jane, 383
Elegy on Herakleitos, 275
Elegy Written in a Country Churchyard,
    326
Elephant Is Slow to Mate, The, 367
Eliot, T. S.
    "Boston Evening Transcript," The, 204
    Love Song of J. Alfred Prufrock, The, 368
    Sweeney among the Nightingales, 372
Emanuel, James A.
    Commentary (to G. Brooks's "First
    fight. . . ."), 286
Emperor of Ice-Cream, The, 362
Empson, William
    Legal Fiction, 379
End of the World, The, 8
Epigram Engraved on the Collar of a Dog
    Which I Gave to His Royal Highness,
    326
Epitaph (Cunningham), 264
Epitaph (Steele), 65
Etienne de Silhouette, 176

Fa, mi, fa, re, la, mi, 120
Face Lift, 412
Fall of the House of Usher, The, 18
Fearing, Kenneth
    Dirge, 377
Fear no more the heat o' th' sun, 115
Fern Hill, 167
Field, Eugene
    Preference Declared, The (translation),
    278
Fie on Eastern Luxury! 277
Finkel, Donald
    Gesture, 191
Finlay, Ian Hamilton
    Horizon of Holland, The, 200
Fire and Ice, 65
First fight. Then fiddle. Ply the slipping
    string, 285
First Practice, 185
Fish, The, 72
Fitts, Dudley
    Elegy on Herakleitos (translation), 275

.05, 98
Flight, 421
Flower in the Crannied Wall, 82
Fog, 263
For a Lady I Know, 22
For Anne Gregory, 355
Foreboding, 276
For Eleanor Boylan Talking with God, 410
For I will consider my Cat Jeoffry, 330
For the Anniversary of My Death, 407
fortunes of war, I tell you plain, The, 96
Fra bank to bank, fra wood to wood I rin,
    264
Francis, Robert
    Catch, 5
Frankie and Johnny, 117
Frau Bauman, Frau Schmidt, and Frau
    Schwartze, 384
Friend, on this scaffold Thomas More lies
    dead, 64
From "Hitch Haiku," 75
From Horace, 278
Frost, Robert
    Departmental, 211
    Design, 283
    Fire and Ice, 65
    Never Again Would Birds' Song Be the
    Same, 147
    Provide, Provide, 361
    Secret Sits, The, xxx
    Silken Tent, The, 213
    Stopping by Woods on a Snowy Eve-
    ning, 361
    Tree at My Window, 92
Full fathom five thy father lies, 317
Fury of Aerial Bombardment, The, 45

García Lorca, Federico
    La guitarra (The Guitar), 275
Gesture, 191
Get the Gasworks, 387
Get Up! 263
Gildner, Gary
    First Practice, 185
Ginsberg, Allen
    In back of the real, 404
Giovanni, Nikki
    Kidnap Poem, 420
Go, lovely rose, 323
God's Grandeur, 137
Good Mornin', Blues, 121
Goose Fish, The, 395
Grave, A, 368
Graves, Robert
    Civil Servant, A, 85
Gray, Thomas
    Elegy Written in a Country Churchyard,
    326
Grief, 173

GRIEVE, CHRISTOPHER MURRAY. *See* Mac-
  Diarmid, Hugh
GROSS, RONALD
  Yield, 169
Guitar, 275
GUITERMAN, ARTHUR
  On the Vanity of Earthly Greatness, 256
GUTHRIE, WOODY
  Plane Wreck at Los Gatos (Deportee), 113

H. D.
  Heat, 78
Haiku Ambulance, 75
HAINES, JOHN
  Cauliflower, The, 191
HALL, DONALD
  My Son, My Executioner, 273
HALL, KATIE V.
  Old, Filthy Beer Pail, The, 350
HARDY, THOMAS
  Channel Firing, 346
  Convergence of the Twain, The, 347
  During Wind and Rain, 349
  Neutral Tones, 208
  Oxen, The, 218
  Ruined Maid, The, 44
  Workbox, The, 26
Harlot's House, The, 351
HARRINGTON, SIR JOHN
  Of Treason, 174
Have You Ever Had a Witch Bloom like
  a Highway, 7
Heart, The, 184
Heat, 78
HEATH-STUBBS, JOHN
  Charm Against the Toothache, A, 221
HECHT, ANTHONY
  Japan, 266
HENLEY, WILLIAM ERNEST
  Madam Life's a piece in bloom, 240
Heraclitus, 275
HERBERT, GEORGE
  Easter Wings, 193
  Love, 322
  Pulley, The, 91
HERRICK, ROBERT
  Another Grace for a Child, 23
  Delight in Disorder, 140
  To Daisies, Not to Shut So Soon, 65
  To the Virgins, to Make Much of Time,
    322
  Upon a Child That Died, 183
  Upon Julia's Voice, 61
  Upon Prew His Maid, 198
Her whole life is an epigram, 175
Hippopotamus, The, 136
"Hitch Haiku," From, 75
HOLLANDER, JOHN
  Skeleton key, 195

Hood, 418
HOPE, A. D.
  Brides, The, 382
HOPKINS, GERARD MANLEY
  Carrion Comfort, 49
  From Horace (translation), 278
  God's Grandeur, 137
  Inversnaid, 158
  Pied Beauty, 129
  Spring and Fall, 252
  Windhover, The, 349
HORACE
  Odes I (38), 277
Horizon of Holland, The, 200
HOUSMAN, A. E.
  Eight O'Clock, 132
  From the wash the laundress sends, 98
  In the morning, in the morning, 5
  Loveliest of trees, the cherry now, 3
  Terence, this is stupid stuff, 352
  To an Athlete Dying Young, 354
  With rue my heart is laden, 141
How shall we mourn you who are killed
  and wasted, 141
HUGHES, LANGSTON
  Dream Deferred, 87
  Weary Blues, The, 378
HUGHES, TED
  Secretary, 30
HULME, T. E.
  Image, 75
HUNT, LEIGH
  Rondeau ("Jenny kissed me"), 141
Hymn to God the Father, A, 93

I Am a Cowboy in the Boat of Ra, 235
IGNATOW, DAVID
  Get the Gasworks, 387
I hear an army charging upon the land, 365
I heard a Fly buzz – when I died, 207
I Knew a Woman, 97
I Know a Man, 404
I like to see it lap the Miles, 17
Image, 75
Impromptu on Charles II, 174
In a Station of the Metro, 67
In back of the real, 404
In Bertram's Garden, 403
in Just-, 190
Insusceptibles, The, 410
Intended for Sir Isaac Newton in West-
  minster Abbey, 132
In the Elegy Season, 38
In the morning, in the morning, 5
Inversnaid, 158
Inward Conversation, 279
In Westminster Abbey, 27
I Remember, 163

I Saw in Louisiana a Live-Oak Growing, 343
I sing of a maiden that is makeless, 99
I started Early – Took my Dog, 345
It did not last, 132
It dropped so low – in my Regard, 84
It was a lover and his lass, 139
It was not Death, for I stood up, 6
I Wandered Lonely as a Cloud, 10

Jabberwocky, 50
JAGGER, MICK, AND KEITH RICHARD
  Live with Me, 420
James Watt, 176
Janet Waking, 251
Japan, 266
JARRELL, RANDALL
  Commentary (to Frost's "Design"), 284
  Death of the Ball Turret Gunner, The, 387
  Old and the New Masters, The, 388
JENNINGS, ELIZABETH
  Delay, 95
Jewel Stairs' Grievance, The, 62
John Anderson my jo, John, 244
Johnny, I Hardly Knew Ye, 28
JOHNSON, SAMUEL
  Short Song of Congratulation, A, 59
JONES, LEROI. See Baraka, Imamu Amiri
JONSON, BEN
  Slow, slow, fresh fount, keep time with my salt tears, 148
  To Celia, 101
JOYCE, JAMES
  I hear an army charging upon the land, 365
Julius Caesar, 133
Junk, 396
JUSTICE, DONALD
  In Bertram's Garden, 403

KEATS, JOHN
  Bright star! would I were steadfast as thou art, 262
  La Belle Dame sans Merci, 228
  Ode on a Grecian Urn, 336
  Ode to a Nightingale, 70
  On First Looking into Chapman's Homer, 63
  This living hand, now warm and capable, 164
  When I have fears that I may cease to be, 337
KERR, ALEXANDER, LITT. D.
  Mary and Her Dead Canary, 251
Kidnap Poem, 420
KILGORE, JAMES C.
  White Man Pressed the Locks, The, 99
KINGSMILL, HUGH

What, still alive at twenty-two, 248
KINNELL, GALWAY
  To Christ Our Lord, 406
KNOTT, BILL. See Saint Geraud
KOCH, KENNETH
  Mending Sump, 248
Kore, 403
Kubla Khan, 334
KUZMA, GREG
  Peace, so that, 422

La Belle Dame sans Merci, 228
Laboratory Poem, 405
La Chute, 192
Lady, when I behold the roses sprouting, 103
Lady Lazarus, 412
La guitarra (Guitar), 275
Lamentation of the Old Pensioner, The, 270
LANDOR, WALTER SAVAGE
  Age, 50
  Mother, I Cannot Mind My Wheel, 35
  On Seeing a Hair of Lucretia Borgia, 155
Lapis Lazuli, 356
LARKIN, PHILIP
  As Bad as a Mile, 64
  Church Going, 397
Last Word, The, 39
LAWRENCE, D. H.
  Bavarian Gentians, 217
  Elephant Is Slow to Mate, The, 367
  Piano, 246
LAYTON, IRVING
  Bull Calf, The, 244
Lecture upon the Shadow, A, 319
Leda and the Swan, 223
Legal Fiction, 379
LENNON, JOHN, AND PAUL MCCARTNEY
  Eleanor Rigby, 122
Let me not to the marriage of true minds, 316
LEVERTOV, DENISE
  Come into Animal Presence, 401
  Six Variations (part iii), 178
LEVINE, PHILIP
  To a Child Trapped in a Barber Shop, 409
Life, 240
Life, friends, is boring. We must not say so, 30
Lightning is a yellow Fork, The, 205
LINDON, J. A.
  My Garden, 247
Lines Inscribed upon a Cup Formed from a Skull, 335
Lines Printed Under the Engraved Portrait of Milton, 64
Listeners, The, 360
Little Black Boy, The, 261
Live with Me, 420

Lo, as a careful housewife runs to catch, 212
London, 57
Long John Brown and Little Mary Bell, 332
Long-Legged Fly, 357
lost baby poem, the, 417
Love, 322
LOVELACE, RICHARD
  To Lucasta, 19
Loveliest of trees, the cherry now, 3
Love Poem, 389
Love Song: I and Thou, 402
Love Song of J. Alfred Prufrock, The, 368
LOWELL, ROBERT
  At the Altar, 148
  Meditation (translation), 279
  Skunk Hour, 393
LOY, MINA
  Omen of Victory, 213
Lucifer in Starlight, 344
LUNN, HUGH KINGSMILL. See Kingsmill,
  Hugh
Lycidas, 229

McCARTNEY, PAUL, AND JOHN LENNON
  Eleanor Rigby, 122
MACDIARMID, HUGH
  Wheesht, Wheesht, 44
McKUEN, ROD
  Thoughts on Capital Punishment, 249
MACLEISH, ARCHIBALD
  Ars Poetica, 302
  End of the World, The, 8
Madam Life's a piece in bloom, 240
Magi, The, 358
MAGLOW, T. O.
  Dylan Thomas, 176
Malediction, 29
MARLOWE, CHRISTOPHER
  Passionate Shepherd to His Love, The,
    314
MARTIAL
  You serve the best wines always, my
    dear sir, 174
MARVELL, ANDREW
  Definition of Love, The, 95
  To His Coy Mistress, 324
Mary and Her Dead Canary, 251
MASTERS, EDGAR LEE
  Petit, the Poet, 177
MATTHEW
  Parable of the Good Seed, The, 209
Meadow Mouse, The, 385
Meditation, 279
MELVILLE, HERMAN
  Berg, The, 341
Mending Sump, 248
MEREDITH, GEORGE
  Lucifer in Starlight, 344
MERRILL, JAMES

Laboratory Poem, 405
MERWIN, W. S.
  Dead Hand, 62
  For the Anniversary of My Death, 407
Metamorphosis, 51
Metaphors, 83
MILES, JOSEPHINE
  Reason, 43
MILTON, JOHN
  Lycidas, 229
  On the Late Massacre in Piemont, 32
  Rivers arise; whether thou be the son,
    140
  When I consider how my light is spent,
    323
Milton by Firelight, 411
MOORE, MARIANNE
  Grave, A, 368
MORGAN, EDWIN
  Siesta of a Hungarian Snake, 201
MORGAN, EMANUEL
  Opus 6, 137
Morning Song, 415
Mother, I Cannot Mind My Wheel, 35
Motto for a Sun Dial, 61
Mouse's Nest, 38
Mr. Flood's Party, 358
Musée des Beaux Arts, 381
Mutability, 54
My Garden, 247
My Garden, 247
My heart leaps up when I behold, 54
My mistress' eyes are nothing like the
  sun, 171
My Papa's Waltz, 14
My Son, My Executioner, 273
My Wife Is My Shirt, 241

Naming of Parts, 390
NASH, OGDEN
  Very Like a Whale, 86
NEMEROV, HOWARD
  Goose Fish, The, 395
Neutral Tones, 208
Never Again Would Birds' Song Be the
  Same, 147
next to of course god america i, 375
Night Crow, 213
NIMS, JOHN FREDERICK
  Love Poem, 389
  Visiting Poet, 175
Noiseless Patient Spider, A, 214
Not marble nor the gilded monuments, 7

O Captain! My Captain! 260
Ode on a Grecian Urn, 336
Odes I (38), 277
Ode to a Nightingale, 70

Of Treason, 174
Oh No, 24
Old, Filthy Beer Pail, The, 350
Old and the New Masters, The, 388
Old Arm-Chair, The, 245
Old Pensioner, The, 270
OLSON, CHARLES
   La Chute, 192
Omen of Victory, 213
O Moon, when I gaze on thy beautiful
   face, 240
On a Girdle, 93
On First Looking into Chapman's Homer,
   63
On Seeing a Hair of Lucretia Borgia, 155
On Some South African Novelists, 164
On Stella's Birthday, 33
On the imprint of the first English edition
   of "The Works of Max Beerbohm," 151
On the Late Massacre in Piemont, 32
On the Vanity of Earthly Greatness, 256
On Top of Old Smoky, 106
Operation, The, 405
Opus 6, 137
OWEN, GUY
   White Stallion, The, 61
OWEN, WILFRED
   Dulce et Decorum Est, 19
Oxen, The, 218
Ozymandias, 257

Parable of the Good Seed, The, 209
PARKER, DOROTHY
   Résumé, 150
Passionate Shepherd to His Love, The, 314
Pat's Opinion of Flags, 265
Peace, be at peace, O thou my heaviness,
   279
Peace, so that, 422
PELL, DEWEY G., AND ERN ALPAUGH
   Swinging Chick, 121
Peter Quince at the Clavier, 362
Petit, the Poet, 177
Piano, 246
Pied Beauty, 129
piercing chill I feel, The, 68
PIERCY, MARGE
   Different persuasions, 416
Plane Wreck at Los Gatos (Deportee), 113
PLATH, SYLVIA
   Ariel, 293
   Cut, 76
   Daddy, 296
   Face Lift, 412
   Lady Lazarus, 412
   Metaphors, 83
   Morning Song, 415
POE, EDGAR ALLAN
   Sonnet — To Science, 281

Poem (Saint Geraud), 184
Poem (Williams), 74
politician, a, 175
Poor soul, the center of my sinful earth, 317
POPE, ALEXANDER
   Atticus, 188
   Epigram Engraved on the Collar of a
      Dog Which I Gave to His Royal High-
      ness, 326
   Intended for Sir Isaac Newton in West-
      minster Abbey, 132
POUND, EZRA
   In a Station of the Metro, 67
   Jewel Stairs' Grievance, The, 62
   River-Merchant's Wife: a Letter, The, 366
Preface to a Twenty Volume Suicide Note,
   416
Preference Declared, The, 278
Proud Maisie, 169
Provide, Provide, 361
Pulley, The, 91

Rain, 141
RALEIGH, SIR WALTER
   What is our life? A play of passion, 209
RANDALL, DUDLEY
   Ballad of Birmingham, 392
RANSOM, JOHN CROWE
   Bells for John Whiteside's Daughter, 373
   Janet Waking, 251
Reapers, 77
Reason, 43
Recueillement, 278
Red Wheelbarrow, The, 13
Reed, Henry
   Naming of Parts, 390
REED, ISHMAEL
   .05, 98
   I Am a Cowboy in the Boat of Ra, 235
Remembering Kevan MacKenzie, 189
Résumé, 150
Resurrection Song, 13
REZNIKOFF, CHARLES
   How shall we mourn you who are killed
      and wasted, 141
RICH, ADRIENNE
   Insusceptibles, The, 410
RICHARD, KEITH, AND MICK JAGGER
   Live with Me, 420
Richard Cory (Robinson), 105
Richard Cory (Simon), 105
RILKE, RAINER MARIA
   Vorgefühl (Foreboding), 276
River-Merchant's Wife: a Letter, The, 366
Rivers arise; whether thou be the son,
   140
ROBINSON, EDWIN ARLINGTON
   Mr. Flood's Party, 358
   Richard Cory, 105

ROCHESTER, JOHN WILMOT, EARL OF
  Impromptu on Charles II, 174
ROETHKE, THEODORE
  Dolor, 383
  Elegy for Jane, 383
  Frau Bauman, Frau Schmidt, and Frau
    Schwartze, 384
  I Knew a Woman, 97
  Meadow Mouse, The, 385
  My Papa's Waltz, 14
  Night Crow, 213
Rondeau ("Jenny kissed me"), 141
Rose-cheeked Laura, come, 120
ROSSETTI, DANTE GABRIEL
  Woodspurge, The, 344
r-p-o-p-h-e-s-s-a-g-r, 196
Ruined Maid, The, 44
RUKEYSER, MURIEL
  Boy with His Hair Cut Short, 385

Sailing to Byzantium, 254
SAINT GERAUD
  Poem ("The only response"), 184
SANDBURG, CARL
  Fog, 263
Saturday's Child, 379
SCOTT, SIR WALTER
  Proud Maisie, 169
Scottsboro, 54
Second Coming, The, 220
Secretary, 30
Secret Sits, The, xxx
SEXTON, ANNE
  For Eleanor Boylan Talking with God,
    410
  You All Know the Story of the Other
    Woman, 94
SHAKESPEARE, WILLIAM
  Fear no more the heat o' th' sun, 115
  Full fathom five thy father lies, 317
  It was a lover and his lass, 139
  Let me not to the marriage of true minds,
    316
  Lo, as a careful housewife runs to catch,
    212
  My mistress' eyes are nothing like the
    sun, 171
  Not marble nor the gilded monuments, 7
  Poor soul, the center of my sinful earth,
    317
  Shall I compare thee to a summer's day?
    99
  That time of year thou mayst in me be-
    hold, 318
  When daisies pied and violets blue, 315
  When icicles hang by the wall, 316
Shall I compare thee to a summer's day? 99
SHAPIRO, KARL
  Dirty Word, The, 386

SHELLEY, PERCY BYSSHE
  Dirge, A, 156
  Ozymandias, 257
Short Song of Congratulation, A, 59
Sick Rose, The, 332
SIDNEY, SIR PHILIP
  With how sad steps, O Moon, thou
    climb'st the skies, 314
  You that with allegory's curious frame,
    210
Siesta of a Hungarian Snake, 201
Silken Tent, The, 213
silver swan, who living had no note, The,
    120
Simile for Her Smile, A, 82
SIMMONS, JAMES
  Cavalier Lyric, 20
SIMON, PAUL
  Richard Cory, 105
Simplicity, 277
Since there's no help, come let us kiss and
    part, 172
Sir, say no more, 9
Sir Christopher Wren, 176
Sir Patrick Spence, 310
Six Variations (part iii), 178
Skeleton key, 195
SKINNER, KNUTE
  Cold Irish Earth, The, 39
SKIPSEY, JOSEPH
  Get Up! 263
Skunk Hour, 393
Slow, slow, fresh fount, keep time with my
    salt tears, 148
Slumber Did My Spirit Seal, A, 129
SMART, CHRISTOPHER
  For I will consider my Cat Jeoffrey, 330
SMITH, STEVIE
  I Remember, 163
SMITH, WILLIAM JAY
  American Primitive, 394
SNODGRASS, W. D.
  Operation, The, 405
Snow Man, The, 364
SNYDER, GARY
  From "Hitch Haiku," 75
  Milton by Firelight, 411
Soliloquy of the Spanish Cloister, 340
Song ("Go and catch a falling star"), 166
Sonnet — To Science, 281
Soul selects her own Society, The, 346
SPACKS, BARRY
  Malediction, 29
splendor falls on castle walls, The, 131
Spring and Fall, 252
Spring Coming, 53
SQUIRE, J. C.
  It did not last, 132
Squire and Milkmaid, or, Blackberry Fold,
    111

Stafford, William
  Traveling Through the Dark, 250
  Written on the Stub of the First Pay-
    check, 391
Steele, Timothy
  Epitaph, 65
Stephens, James
  Wind, The, 88
Stevens, Wallace
  Anecdote of the Jar, 212
  Disillusionment of Ten O'Clock, 60
  Emperor of Ice-Cream, The, 362
  Metamorphosis, 51
  Peter Quince at the Clavier, 362
  Snow Man, The, 364
  Study of Two Pears, 69
  Thirteen Ways of Looking at a Black-
    bird, 186
Stickney, Trumbull
  Sir, say no more, 9
Still Growing, 110
Stone Gullets, 197
Stopping by Woods on a Snowy Evening,
  361
Study of Two Pears, 69
Subterranean Homesick Blues, 418
Suzanne, 123
Sweeney among the Nightingales, 372
Swenson, May
  Stone Gullets, 197
Swift, Jonathan
  Day of Judgment, The, 326
  On Stella's Birthday, 33
Swinging Chick, 121

Tate, James
  Flight, 421
Taylor, Henry
  Remembering Kevan MacKenzie, 189
Tears, idle tears, I know not what they
  mean, 246
Tennyson, Alfred, Lord
  Crossing the Bar, 338
  Dark house, by which once more I
    stand, 158
  Eagle, The, 80
  Flower in the Crannied Wall, 82
  splendor falls on castle walls, The, 131
  Tears, idle tears, I know not what they
    mean, 246
  Ulysses, 338
Terence, this is stupid stuff, 352
Ter Maat, Cornelius J.
  Etienne de Silhouette, 176
That time of year thou mayst in me be-
  hold, 318
There is a garden in her face, 318
There was a man of double deed, 84

They flee from me that sometime did me
  sekë, 157
Thirteen Ways of Looking at a Blackbird,
  186
This Is Just to Say, 67
This living hand, now warm and capable,
  164
Thomas, Dylan
  After the Funeral, 391
  Do Not Go Gentle into That Good Night,
    176
  Fern Hill, 167
Thomas the Rimer, 225
Thoughts on Capital Punishment, 249
Three Ravens, The, 311
Tichborne, Chidiock
  Elegy, Written with His Own Hand in
    the Tower Before His Execution, 90
To a Child Trapped in a Barber Shop, 409
To a Locomotive in Winter, 17
To an Athlete Dying Young, 354
To Celia, 101
To Christ Our Lord, 406
To Daisies, Not to Shut So Soon, 65
To freight cars in the air, 159
To His Coy Mistress, 324
To Lucasta, 19
Toomer, Jean
  Reapers, 77
Tortoise, The, 63
To see a world in a grain of sand, 83
To the Memory of Mr. Oldham, 325
To the Virgins, to Make Much of Time,
  322
To Toussaint L'Ouverture, 333
To Waken an Old Lady, 366
Traveling Through the Dark, 250
Treasone, Grace
  Life, 240
Tree at My Window, 92
Tropp, Stephen
  My Wife Is My Shirt, 241
Trouble, 408
Twa Corbies, The, 312
Tyger, The, 332

Ulysses, 338
Unknown Citizen, The, 12
Unquiet Grave, The, 116
Updike, John
  Winter Ocean, 128
Upon a Child That Died, 183
Upon Julia's Voice, 61
Upon Prew His Maid, 198

Valediction: Forbidding Mourning, A, 319
Very Like a Whale, 86
Victory comes late, 182

Visiting Poet, 175
Vorgefühl (Foreboding), 276

WALDROP, KEITH
  Before Bed, 415
  Guitar (translation), 275
WALLER, EDMUND
  Go, lovely rose, 323
  On a Girdle, 93
WANG WEI
  Bird-Singing Stream, 198
Watch, The, 128
Weary Blues, The, 378
WEINSTEIN, LORI
  Foreboding (translation), 276
We Real Cool, 147
Western Wind, 309
What, still alive at twenty-two, 248
What is our life? A play of passion, 209
Wheesht, Wheesht, 44
When daisies pied and violets blue, 315
When icicles hang by the wall, 316
When I consider how my light is spent, 323
When I have fears that I may cease to be, 337
when serpents bargain for the right to squirm, 375
White Man Pressed the Locks, The, 99
White Stallion, The, 61
WHITMAN, RUTH
  Castoff Skin, 85
WHITMAN, WALT
  Beat! Beat! Drums! 159
  Cavalry Crossing a Ford, 184
  City Dead-House, The, 343
  Dalliance of the Eagles, The, 77
  I Saw in Louisiana a Live-Oak Growing, 343
  Noiseless Patient Spider, A, 214
  O Captain! My Captain! 260
  To a Locomotive in Winter, 17
WHITTEMORE, REED
  Fall of the House of Usher, The, 18
Who Goes with Fergus? 127
Whoso list to hunt, I know where is an hind, 314
WILBUR, RICHARD
  Commentary (to Poe's "Sonnet — To Science"), 282
  In the Elegy Season, 38
  Junk, 396
  Simile for Her Smile, A, 82
WILDE, OSCAR
  Harlot's House, The, 351
WILLIAMS, C. K.
  Hood, 418
WILLIAMS, WILLIAM CARLOS
  Dance, The, 183
  Danse Russe, 365

Descent of Winter, The (section 10/30), 159
Poem ("As the cat"), 74
Red Wheelbarrow, The, 13
This Is Just to Say, 67
To Waken an Old Lady, 366
Wind, The, 88
Windhover, The, 349
Winter Ocean, 128
WINTERS, YVOR
  At the San Francisco Airport, 376
With how sad steps, O Moon, thou climb'st the skies, 314
With rue my heart is laden, 141
With serving still, 149
Woodspurge, The, 344
WORDSWORTH, WILLIAM
  Composed upon Westminster Bridge, 333
  I Wandered Lonely as a Cloud, 10
  Mutability, 54
  My heart leaps up when I behold, 54
  Slumber Did My Spirit Seal, A, 129
  To Toussaint L'Ouverture, 333
  World Is Too Much with Us, The, 219
Workbox, The, 26
World Is Too Much with Us, The, 219
WRIGHT, JAMES
  Blessing, A, 407
  Trouble, 408
Written on the Stub of the First Paycheck, 391
WYATT, SIR THOMAS
  They flee from me that sometime did me sekë, 157
  Whoso list to hunt, I know where is an hind, 314
  With serving still, 149

year's at the spring, The, 116
YEATS, WILLIAM BUTLER
  Crazy Jane Talks with the Bishop, 355
  For Anne Gregory, 355
  Lamentation of the Old Pensioner, The, 270
  Lapis Lazuli, 356
  Leda and the Swan, 223
  Long-Legged Fly, 357
  Magi, The, 358
  Old Pensioner, The, 270
  Sailing to Byzantium, 254
  Second Coming, The, 220
  Who Goes with Fergus? 127
Yield, 169
You All Know the Story of the Other Woman, 94
You serve the best wines always, my dear sir, 174
You that with allegory's curious frame, 210

To the Student

As publishers, we realize that one way to improve education is to improve textbooks. We also realize that you, the student, largely determine the success or failure of textbooks. Although the instructor assigns them, the student buys and uses them. If enough of you don't like a book and make your feelings known, the chances are your instructor will not assign it again.

Usually only instructors are asked about the quality of a text; their opinion alone is considered as revisions are planned or as new books are developed. Now, Little, Brown would like to ask you about X. J. Kennedy's *An Introduction to Poetry, 3rd Edition:* how you liked or disliked it; why it was interesting or dull; if it taught you anything. Please fill in this form and return it to us at: Little, Brown and Co., College Division, 34 Beacon Street, Boston, Mass. 02106. It is your chance to affect directly the publication of future textbooks.

_____

School: _____

Course title: _____

Other texts required: _____

1. Did you like the book? _____

2. Was it too easy? _____

    Was it too difficult? _____

3. Which poems did you like most? _____

    _____

    Which poems did you like least? _____

    _____

4. Which chapters did you like most? _____

    _____

Which chapters did you like least? _____

_____

5. Did you like the cover design? _____

6. Were the excercises useful? _____

  How might they be changed? _____

_____

_____

7. Do you feel that you have a greater appreciation of poetry from

  using this book? _____

_____

8. Do you feel that the professor should continue to assign this book

  next year? _____

9. Will you keep this book for your library? _____

10. Please add any comments or suggestions. _____

_____

_____

_____

_____

11. May we quote you in our promotion efforts for this book?

  _____ Yes _____ No

_____   _____
Date   Signature

_____
Address